THE DREAM
IN CLINICAL
PRACTICE

THE DREAM
IN CLINICAL
PRACTICE

edited by

Joseph M. Natterson, M.D.

NEW YORK   •   JASON ARONSON   •   LONDON

for Samuel and Anna N.

Man struggles
and God chuckles.
—*old German and Yiddish saying*

CLASSICAL PSYCHOANALYSIS AND ITS APPLICATIONS

A Series of Books
Edited by Robert Langs, M.D.

SERIES INTRODUCTION

Dreams remain today the royal road to the unconscions and hence to dynamic psychotherapy. It is no coincidence that Freud's monumental insights into unconscious processes and mental ills were achieved initially through the analysis of dreams. And it is no less true now than in the Vienna of 1900 that whoever strives to master the art and science of psychotherapy must have a sound knowledge of dream processes and formation, including their relation to psychopathological syndromes and the therapeutic situation. Joseph Natterson has rendered a great service, to both psychoanalysis and the broader field of psychotherapy, in bringing together this excellent collection. Here are many of the newer clinical perspectives on dreams and the patients who dream them, as well as detailed accounts of how dreams are currently serving therapists in virtually every type of therapeutic setting. Dr. Natterson has through his editorial dedication and skill provided a broad audience a comprehensive volume that testifies once again to the continuing vitality and relevance of psychoanalytically founded thinking.

Robert Langs, M.D.

CONTENTS

PART II
THE DREAM IN THE
VARIOUS PSYCHOPATHOLOGICAL STATES

Contents

Dreams and the "bridging" therapeutic approach □
Evacuation function of dreams in schizophrenics
□ Trauma in the life and dreams of schizophrenics
□ Repair of psychosis through dreams □ "Intellectual"
approach to dreams □ Primary process, dreams, and
psychotic phenomena □ Concreteness versus abstractness
in dreams and thoughts of schizophrenics □ "Dreamlike"
dreams as a sign of improvement □ Pharmacological
interventions and dreams in schizophrenics

Chapter 7. The Dream in Manic-Depressive Psychosis   111
Ping-nie Pao, M.D.

The diagnostic term "manic-depressive" □ Clinical
examples of dreams in manic-depressives □ Mania and
depression as parallel states □ Dreams in the four phases
of the manic-depressive psychosis □ The blank dream
during mania □ Manifest content in the dreams of
depressives □ Conclusion

Chapter 8. The Dream in the Depressive Personality   131
Walter Bonime, M.D. with Florence Bonime
Dreams reflecting depressive anger □ Dreams of self-
rescue from depression □ Dreams and five features of
depressives □ Dreams combining depression and
restitution □ Dreams and manipulation in depressives
□ Anxiety with depression □ Dreams and contact with
feelings □ Dream metaphors of angry unwillingness
□ Dreams as reflections of depressive traits

Chapter 9. The Dream in Obsessive States   149
Arnold Namrow, M.D.
Therapeutic movement through dream-work □ Dream
production as resistance □ Circumstantiality and
indirectness in dreams and associations □ Conclusion

Chapter 10. The Dream in Dissociative States   163
Stephen S. Marmer, M.D.
Concepts of multiple personality and
dreams □ Dissociation, splitting, and multiple
personality □ Clinical example □ Dreams of a multiple

formed unconscious affect □ Clinical examples □ Dreams
as substitutes for grief in waking life □ Role of the dream
in illness formation

PART III
THE DREAM IN SPECIAL THERAPEUTIC SITUATIONS

PART IV
THE DREAM IN THE
VARIOUS PSYCHOTHERAPEUTIC MODALITIES

prognostic importance of the initial dream □ Archetypal
themes and reintegration □ Compensatory role of dreams
□ Noncompensatory or complementary dreams □ Fairy
tale archetypes in children's dreams □ Mythological
archetypes in adult dreams □ Dreams and the cultural
unconscious □ Mattoon's paradigm for correct dream
interpretation □ The flexibility of Jungian dream
interpretation

PREFACE

In my more than twenty years as a psychoanalyst, I have consistently valued the use of dreams in psychotherapy, and have often regretted the incompleteness of readily accessible contemporary work on dreams. *The Dream in Clinical Practice* was developed as a resource to meet this very real need.

I cannot recall how or when the idea for this project first occurred. Bernard Gordon and I had completed a book on dreams and had often discussed the insufficiencies noted above. My decision to develop a carefully selected set of essays for students, clinicians, and other interested readers arose in this context. Early in 1976 I discussed this project with Bernard Gordon, and he responded with perceptive criticism and strong encouragement. My original concept spanned a much wider range than the present book. Anthropological aspects of dreaming, dreams in literature and films, dreams in relation to painting and sculpture were some of the other topics that I had planned to include in the project.

At this point, in the autumn of 1977, my friend Robert Langs arranged a meeting with Jason Aronson. Dr. Aronson was immediately enthusiastic about the project. However, he was equally adamant that the book be limited to clinical subjects. Happily, I heeded his advice. I believe that the title, *The Dream in Clinical Practice,* was suggested by him as well.

Subsequently, I contacted many colleagues and practitioners in related fields, exploring possibilities for participation in the project. Many agreed to participate, and many declined. Almost all, however, were encouraging about the importance of the project.

Dr. Alvin Goldfarb had agreed to contribute a chapter on dreams in geriatric patients. His tragic death occurred before he had written his chapter. I regret that the book does not include a chapter on this important subject.

As the work progressed, I was fortunate to enjoy the help of a number of people whose contributions I wish to acknowledge. Dorothy Israel has diligently and capably handled the correspondence and many of the tedious but crucial details of the project. For many months Helen Meek was my editorial assistant. She reviewed all available chapters for problems of internal structure, style and grammar, and also made some valuable creative contributions. Norma Glickman also assisted me in the numerous editorial tasks. She participated in the work of chapter revision, systematizing of references and footnotes, and manuscript preparation. Her efforts and accomplishments have been enormous. Amy Natterson's library research was indispensable for one important portion of the book. She did this work during the summer of 1978.

Marquis Wallace, Stephen Marmer, and Robert Shain not only contributed chapters but also rendered invaluable editorial service at various times. They finally became an editorial committee, working with me on the copy-edited manuscript.

Louis Breger made numerous valuable suggestions throughout the course of the project. Arnold Wilson provided timely assistance with one portion of the book. My wife, Idell Natterson, who is a psychotherapist, maintained a constructive interest throughout. I discussed many problems and possibilities pertinent to the book with her. It is with deep gratitude that I acknowledge her assistance.

All these people gave their knowledge and their friendship unstintingly. I do not know how I can offer my thanks in sufficient measure.

Joan Langs, Michael Farrin, and John Simmons provided crucial editorial guidance during the final stages of production. Other persons provided help at various times. These are: Robert Butler, Martin Grotjahn, Roy Whitman, Harold Searles, Rosalyn Benitez, Jona Perlmutter, Martin Berezin, Walter Bonime, Joseph Wheelwright, Lena Pincus, and Claire Oksner. It is possible that I have overlooked the constructive role of some others. I have tried to acknowledge all those who, in addition to contributing chapters, helped in the creation of this volume. If some oversight has occurred, I offer my sincere apology.

INTRODUCTION

It was my intention, in planning and bringing together this volume of original essays, to enhance and further the use of dreams in the various psychotherapies. Although the importance of working with dreams is increasingly appreciated in virtually all quarters, the full potential of such work has yet to be realized. In correlating the multiple dimensions of dream utilization in modern psychotherapy, it has been my hope to effect a cross-fertilization of these diverse but interrelated points of view. The goal is to be comprehensive but not encyclopedic. I have allowed my psychoanalytic orientation and experience to influence the organization of the book and the selection of specific topics and authors. I did not wish to attempt, let alone simulate, a neutrality that could only vitiate the effort: an orientation is both necessary and desirable for any serious worker. This should not be taken to imply any implacable hostility on my part toward schools of thought other than my own. Quite to the contrary, it is my confirmed opinion that competing approaches can only enrich the entire field.

Historically, as a result of Freud's epochal work, clinical theory and practice regarding dreams is hardly to be distinguished from psychoanalysis generally. Today, although psychoanalytic practice and investigation continue to produce the more substantial contributions in this sphere, our knowledge now extends far beyond the borders of psychoanalysis into other psychotherapeutic territories. Psychiatrists, psychologists, social

workers, marriage and family counselors, and other mental health professionals of various disciplines currently work with dreams in their efforts
to help people with their social, interpersonal, and intrapsychic difficulties. Despite what might be characterized as a nonintrospective trend
within some of these approaches to emotional and behavioral problems,
there has occurred at the same time, I believe, a countervailing prolifera-
tion of depth psychology, once the province of psychoanalysis and its
closer relatives, into many of the newer modalities. They have thereby
achieved for themselves the psychodynamic insights once proper to
psychoanalysis alone, and have as a result incorporated work with dreams
into their treatment models.

These nonanalytic areas of dream utilization are of great variety and
clinical importance, and stand in significant and complex interrelation
with psychoanalysis. A psychiatrist who is managing a chronic schizophrenic is very likely to find important diagnostic, therapeutic, and
prognostic clues in his patient's dreams. Similarly, a social worker who is
attempting to counsel a family through a crisis involving a delinquent son
or daughter may perceive that the dreams of the father or mother portray
the family dynamics and thereby contribute a crucial component of the
social work approach to the family and its problems.

The essays in this volume are intended for a wide range of readers,
from the undergraduate psychology student to the seasoned clinician.
Almost any chapter could provide the inexperienced but interested reader
a challenging introduction to the meaning and use of dreams in therapy.
Medical students learning the fundamentals of psychotherapy might find
the book of similar value. Psychiatric residents, graduate students in
clinical psychology, and social work students might use it as an axis around
which to structure and systematize their developing knowledge and skills.
Those training in psychoanalysis, or in other advanced areas of clinical
theory and practice, will find between these covers much to deepen their
understanding and to broaden their perspectives. The experienced practitioner might use the book in a variety of ways. He may wish to obtain an
up-to-date survey of current views on dreams or to satisfy his curiosity
about the manifold ways that dreams are employed by professionals of
different theoretical orientation. Or perhaps the clinician not particularly
experienced in working with dreams may wish to enhance his skills in this
area.

Although the volume was developed with a professional audience in
mind, and with a decidedly clinical emphasis, it is hoped that nonprofes-
sionals with some background in dynamic psychology—whether attained

through academic work, private reading, or personal experience in psychotherapy—might also find the book rewarding. A casual stroll through these pages will afford a vivid impression of the similarities and differences among the Freudian, Jungian, and existential analytic approaches, to mention only a few. At some points the differences will appear mainly semantic and the similarities more significant; elsewhere quite fundamental differences will surface and, I think, be illuminating. Nothing should preclude reading the book piecemeal, if that is the reader's desire, as each chapter possesses a certain degree of autonomy.

Finally, it has occurred to me, upon perusing once again the various sections and chapters that make up this volume, that they constitute as well their own subtext; the book could, in all conscience I think, be subtitled "A Manual of Dynamic Psychotherapy." For by virtue of its arrangement and comprehensiveness, and of the fact that the process of understanding the unconscious factors involved in the dream work epitomizes the method of psychodynamic treatment generally, this collection becomes by implication a veritable handbook of psychotherapy and clinical management. With dreams as the central focus, an exposition of modern psychotherapy has been achieved in a nondidactic and informal manner. The unconscious fantasies we call dreams are presented in a variety of therapeutic situations and clinical states, and are shown to reflect psychic structural variations based on and expressive of intrapsychic conflicts and specific developmental vicissitudes. As these are elucidated, the defensive modes become comprehensible; as these defenses are seen to operate in the therapeutic situation, transference and resistance are revealed in their manifold forms and expressions.

Thus the reader is presented the entire repertoire of therapeutic interventions in a manner both lucid and open to contextual examination. Responses to interventions, whether positive or negative, can be studied, and progressive and regresssive therapeutic developments can then be related to preceding events. In each instance the entire series of events is spun out around a continuous core of dreams, a fact that returns us, quite ineluctably it would seem, to that one remarkable fact with which we started: the unique centrality of dreams to virtually every psychotherapeutic endeavor.

Part I

CLINICAL THEORY OF DREAMS

CHAPTER 1

THE MANIFEST DREAM AND ITS LATENT MEANING

Louis Breger, Ph.D.

The distinction between manifest and latent content lies at the heart of dream interpretation, as central to work with dreams in psychoanalysis today as when Freud first proposed it in 1900. We listen to a patient report a dream, note the nuances, tone, and points of feeling in the report, hear the associations, all within the context of a given hour and state of the transference—and the still larger context provided by the patient's history, character, and previous hours—and, from all this, offer an interpretation. What is this interpretation? What does it communicate to the patient that he is not aware of? In a general way, an interpretation illuminates the manifest dream—and some portion of the surrounding information or context of associations, history, transference—by drawing attention to the latent content, latent dream thoughts, or latent meaning. memories? An affective quality missing from the original dream report? Links of meaning between the dream and aspects of the patient's life? The disguised significance of the symbolism? Or the connection of the dream to the process of analysis that the patient does not see? I think that "latent content" can refer to all of these, and probably other things, and this multiplicity of referants should alert us to the fact that we are dealing with a broad and difficult idea, a concept that will require some exploration. Let me begin by going back to Freud's original definitions.

Freud develops the concepts of manifest and latent dream content in

The Interpretation of Dreams (1900) in a way that closely overlaps the broader concepts of conscious and unconscious. He points out that he arrived at an understanding of dreams from earlier work with neurotic symptoms; he came to view the seemingly meaningless dream as the equally inexplicable symptom: the mystery in both cases was a disguise for impulses and conflicts that were resistant to awareness, that existed in the unconscious. The manifest dream is, thus, one of a series of phenomena that give disguised, symbolic expression to unconscious conflict; others in the series include neurotic symptoms, parapraxes, typical styles of thought and relationship—character structure—and, of special usefulness in the psychoanalytic process, the transference. The manifest dream arises from the latent content just as a slip of the tongue, a symptom, or a transference manifestation does from the unconscious. And it follows that interpreting a dream in terms of its latent meaning is one instance of making the unconscious conscious, of working toward insight—the goal of psychoanalysis as therapy.

Yet the same sort of questions can be raised about the unconscious as I raised earlier about latent content. What do we mean by this concept? What does it mean to become conscious of something that was formerly unconscious? Obviously we are dealing with broad and complex issues central to the theoretical structure of psychoanalysis. These are processes that have been extensively discussed by Freud and many later psychoanalysts and it may be presumptuous for me to think that I can add very much to our understanding of the manifest-latent and, behind it, the conscious-unconscious distinction. Nevertheless, if I am able to provoke the reader to consider these well-known ideas in a slightly new way, I will have achieved my purpose.

Freud's principal definitions of manifest-latent and conscious-unconscious were set forth during his early work, prior to the introduction of a systematic theory of ego, superego, identification, and internalized relationships. As late as 1915, in "The Unconscious," the definitions of conscious and unconscious are given in terms of processes and regions in psychological space, though at the end of that essay "the ego" and "object cathexis" make their appearance. The centrality of the ego and the internal representations of relationships—most clearly the superego in Freud's own work—are set forth in *The Ego and the Id* in 1923. They become increasingly important aspects of the unconscious, although, as was typical of Freud, he did not revise his earlier work, such as the theory of dreams, to align it with these later developments. In the present exploration of manifest and latent dream content, we must be alert to the central role of representations of the self (ego) and others (objects) as components of the unconscious. We can be guided in this regard by Freud's later work as well as by that large group of psychoanalysts who, with a variety of terms (the ego, self, identity, object relations, internal objects, introjection) call attention to the fact that a central portion of the unconscious consists of the residue of conflictual (painful, traumatic, anxiety-ridden) relationships. In addition, our exploration will be guided by what seems to me a converging modern view of psychoanalytic theory as centrally concerned with meaning and the interpretation of human experience. I have in mind the work of the late George Klein (1976); Robert Jay Lifton (1976); Jane Loevinger (1976); Paul Ricoeur (1970); Roy Schafer (1976, 1978); Yankelovich and Barrett (1970); and my own forthcoming book (Breger, in press).

THE DREAM AS A CONSTRUCTION

Let us begin with a closer consideration of what is meant, in the clinical context, by manifest and latent dream content. As should be obvious, there is only one actual dream: the private, largely visual drama that occurs during sleep. No one can see this—can know it firsthand—but the dreamer. And even he, most of the time, cannot recall it the next day. But some dreams are recalled, more or less well and with more or less revision, omission, and elaboration, and are put into words. That is, certain private, visual dramas are made over into public, linguistic communications from patient to analyst. It is this verbal, or written, dream report that is called the "manifest dream." I stress these distinctions to emphasize that even at the level of the manifest dream we are dealing with processes of translation (from visual to verbal), of communication (from private to public), and of construction and reconstruction (by the dreamer in making his report and by the analyst in attempting to picture it). The manifest dream or dream report is thus a psychological *construction* whose form is shaped by all the factors that affect such constructions: availability of certain self and object schemes, attention and interest in recall, anticipation of how the listener will react, skill at describing a subjective experience, anxiety, guilt, and so forth. Since much of what goes into constructing a manifest dream report occurs relatively automatically—the dream is either recalled in the morning or it is not, reported in the course of an analytic hour however it comes along, and certain associations occur and others do not—we may not feel we are "constructing" anything. But "psychological construction" has a much wider meaning than this; in a general sense, all transactions between the person and the world involve constructions in which the perceiver, thinker, speaker, actor, or dreamer brings to bear his perceptual-cognitive schemas, linguistic structures or grammar, self and object models, and memory and dream schemas, in an interactive process. This is what Piaget means when he speaks of "the child's construction of reality"; reality does not exist "out there" as an unchanging substance, independent of our action; it is only known via interaction with a perceiver-thinker-actor who constructs it in terms of his existing models, thought patterns, schemas, or mental structures. Because schemas change with development and are different in different individuals, the reality of a one-year-old is far different from that of a six-year-old or, again, a sixty-year-old. Dream reality is different from that of an awake, problem-solving state and we may distinguish the reality of a "neurotic," "psychotic," or relatively "normal" person. In all these examples we infer a difference in psychological structure or schema on the basis of differences in behavior or reported experience.

These definitions of construction and schema, sketchily presented here, will prove central to the coming discussion which will, I hope, clarify their meaning further. We will see that latent content is not "content" at all but a particular form of construction or interpretation. Interpreting a manifest dream by delineating its latent content can then be seen as a process of reconstruction: in therapy it is a way of redefining personal (self and other) schemas.

WHAT IS "LATENT" IN A DREAM?

There is obviously no latent *content* of a dream; if there is content we have a manifest dream of some type; if there is no content there is no dream. What, then, is "latent"? Is it the dream itself, dreamt and now forgotten? This is one possible meaning of the "latent dream"; it accords with the definition of latent as that which is potential or dormant. Instances of this are common enough: we awake "knowing" we had a dream that we cannot recapture. Later, it all "comes back," stimulated by some event of the day. Sometimes, in the course of an analytic session, a patient will spontaneously recall a dream that he had forgotten, the trigger being some related association, thought, or feeling during the hour. The dream was dreamt, perhaps recalled on awakening and then forgotten; it exists in a latent or potential state from which it can sometimes be retrieved, as these examples illustrate. Is this what is usually meant by the "latent dream" or "latent dream content"? I think not. Forgotten dreams can be remembered, say, during an analytic hour, yet we still speak of them as manifest dreams whose latent content remains to be analyzed or discovered. And other dreams may be clearly recalled, yet their meaning is unknown to the dreamer, in which case we likewise speak of a manifest dream with a disguised or latent meaning. Attempting to equate the latent content with the forgotten dream puts one in the same constricted position as did the early psychoanalytic theory that defined the unconscious as a repository of forgotten traumatic memories. This amnesia model proved of quite limited value, both as a theory of neurotic symptom formation and as the basis for the cathartic treatment method. It captured a part of the processes of repression and the unconscious, but only a small part. Looking back from the vantage point of additional psychoanalytic experience, we now know that one can recover a forgotten or repressed memory yet still be plagued with unconscious conflicts. Repression involves more than forgetting or amnesia and there are many "mechanisms of defense," in addition to repression, which function to keep aspects of experience unconscious. And there is more to the unconscious than these mechanisms. The forgotten dream, like the forgotten traumatic event, is not what is latent in any but the most minor sense of the term.

Knowing one has had a dream but not being able to recall or report it may be viewed in another way that gets closer to the central meaning of latent content. For this inability to remember is a communication to oneself and one's analyst, a communication that may be part of an *active disavowal* that the dream—with its particular feelings, fears, and fantastic images—has anything to do with oneself. Like the hysteric who cannot recall the traumatic events associated with the onset of symptoms, and thus attempts to affirm that the events did not happen to her, the unreportable dream may be an attempt to separate the dream experience from the public, conscious version of oneself. And it is essentially such unconscious processes of disavowal, of dissociation from self, that one constantly encounters with remembered and reported dreams. Thus, in a psychoanalytic session a dream may be reported—we have a clearly remembered manifest dream—yet we still speak of the latent content or the latent meaning. What is "latent" is not some forgotten part of the dream, not even additional associations and the memories that they might lead to, but a different *construction* of the material at hand, a construction or interpretation which connects the dream—along with associations, affects and other aspects of the patient—to the conscious ego or sense of self. *Pointing to the latent content of a dream is almost always a case of finding the person of the dreamer in the dream.* Some examples of commonly occurring instances may help to clarify this point.

A patient describes a dream as an interesting spectacle that he witnessed, almost as if it were a movie or TV program written and acted by others. "Isn't that fascinating," such a style of reporting implies, "you don't think it has anything to do with me?" While one step up from the unremembered dream, such a mode of experiencing and reporting serves to disconnect the dream from the person. If the analyst is to do anything, he must help this patient feel that the dream was written, produced, directed, and acted by himself.

Another patient may have the clear sense that the dream is his own; indeed, he may feel frightened, troubled, guilty, or angry in relation to it. Yet much of it may remain a mystery. "I recognize myself but where did those other people come from?" "I can't figure out why *that* happened." People, locations, emotions, actions, may all be mysterious, not understood or confused. Again, a principal function of such symbolic "disguise" is to keep from awareness the role of the person's own impulses, actions, wishes, and conflicts. As the analyst works at clarifying such confusions, mysteries, and blocks to understanding, he helps the patient find himself in the dream, helps him to see the impulses and wishes he was too frightened or guilty to consciously acknowledge.

Another patient may report a dream filled with blood, gore, and murderous violence, yet say, "Maybe I was upset when I dreamt that, but it all seems bland now, like a corny old movie." The dream is recalled and potentially connected to oneself but the affective impact is blunted and denied. The communication is of the form, "I had this dream, but my anger is not to be taken seriously." In this instance, the analyst's interpretive task is to point out the minimization of threatening affect, with the goal of connecting such feelings to the conscious self.

The process of working with reported dream material, even in patients well along in psychoanalysis, lends itself to a great variety of defensive or resistive operations which keep the meaning of the dream hidden or latent. The patient may connect the people, scenes, and actions in the dream to various day residues: "Joe was in the dream because I talked to him yesterday and I guess there was an argument because I saw that TV program last night where everyone was arguing." While associations to day residues may often prove useful, when the patient stops with them he is communicating, "This is all the dream means, it has nothing to do with my feelings about Joe or what he represents, nothing to do with my wish to argue." Again, the analyst's task is to point out the constriction of meaning involved in the patient's exclusive focus on day residues.

Now, as all these examples have illustrated, when we make interpretations of this sort we are not, strictly speaking, uncovering latent or hidden content. The interpretive task is, rather, to suggest alternative ways of viewing the dream report. *The therapist points to what the patient does not see, or denies, or claims not to feel, or is confused or mystified by.* If a good working relationship is present, at least a part of the patient's communication is, "I don't understand this, it is unintelligible to me, I need your help in making sense out of it." And the analyst, with his interpretations and constructions, suggests ways that the dream may be understood by linking aspects of it to the patient's experience of self.

LATENT CONTENT, LATENT MEANING, ALTERNATIVE CONSTRUCTIONS

The opening sentence of *The Interpretation of Dreams* reads:

> In the pages that follow I shall bring forward proof that there is a psychological technique which makes it possible to interpret dreams, and that, if that procedure is employed, every dream reveals itself as a psychical structure which has a meaning and which can be inserted at an assignable point in the mental activities of waking life [Freud, 1900, p. 1].

Freud is saying, in a very clear way, that to interpret a dream is to make a relatively meaningless psychological event more meaningful, to take an unconnected phenomenon and give it a place in the "mental activities of waking life." What is latent is not content, but meaning: the analyst, with his interpretation, provides a construction—a model or mini-theory—that suggests a more complete, coherent—and hence more meaningful—explanation for the dream in the surrounding context of the patient's associations, relationships, and life history.

But Freud also uses the terms "latent content" and, perhaps even more misleading, "latent dream thoughts"—implying that what is latent is a repository of specific content: thoughts, repressed ideas, traumatic memories, and forbidden impulses. Indeed, when an insightful dream interpretation is made, it can release new material—new associations, forgotten memories, withheld emotions—which is how we, as analysts, often judge the correctness of our interpretations. Doesn't this release of fresh material "from the unconscious" indicate that it is *content* that is latent? Let me attempt to further clarify this question.

When a patient reports a dream, the report is surrounded by other sorts of communications. He may lead up to the dream by describing events of the day that preceded it, and the report itself is then followed by more communications. As every analyst knows, the forms of these surrounding communications are as varied as are people. One patient may meticulously associate to each element in the dream while another may take off into fantasies stimulated by the general theme or feeling tone. Another may block: "I can't think of anything, I don't know what that dream means," or the report may be followed by silence, itself a communication. Still another may "change the subject": go directly from the dream to seemingly unrelated matters. And some patients, experienced in analysis, may attempt to relate the dream to the analyst or aspects of the process, while others may fearfully avoid doing so. It is a good analytic or therapeutic rule to treat everything that surrounds the reported dream as an association, as material potentially related to it. This includes silence, the seemingly unrelated material, casual remarks on entering the office, and so on. All are potential clues that may be used in understanding the meaning of a particular dream. Using as much of this information as seems important, the analyst arrives at his interpretation, his way of drawing together the dream, the surrounding communications, and his knowledge of the patient, into a meaningful whole. When such an interpretation works—when it releases a flow of rich confirmatory feelings, ideas, and memories—we speak of having penetrated to the unconscious or of the release of the latent thoughts or content. Yet, while this is the way we talk about and experience the effects of a successfully interpreted dream, a further clarification is required. There is always *content* surrounding a dream. A "wrong" interpretation is followed by content. Even with no interpretation, this patient surrounds his version of the dream with comments, qualifications, and feelings. So it is not the case that a correct interpretation produces new content that rushes in to fill a void of no content; rather, it is a matter of the contrast of one kind of content with another. The content that follows a successful interpretation is of a special *quality*, and it is this quality that we have in mind when we speak of the release of unconscious material or latent dream content. What is this quality? Essentially it comes from a feeling of intelligibility, meaningfulness, and coherence. That is to say, the patient had a version of what his dream meant—however fragmentary, incomplete, and unspoken—but it was a version that could only be maintained by ignoring large chunks of evidence. The version suggested by the analyst's interpretation encompasses more of the evidence and, when the timing and relationship are right—the patient not too anxious or resistant—he can hear and use the new version suggested by the analyst's interpretation. The "release" of unconscious material is the patient putting the new, more intelligible version to work on previously unconnected pieces of information. So what feels like new content—and it often feels that way to both patient and analyst—is, more accurately, a realignment, a bringing together of warded off or defended thoughts, feelings, fantasies, impulses, views of oneself and important others.

It is not hidden *content* that is latent in a dream, but hidden *meaning*. This is easier to see in some patients than in others. For instance, the person who relies heavily on repression may feel blank and unknowing in relation to a dream, and the analyst's interpretation may release "forgotten" material that seems to fill in the blank. By contrast, an obsessive-compulsive patient may provide the ingredients for a "correct" interpretation, but bury them in such a profusion of competing explanations and qualifications that their significance is obscured. In such a case, the correct interpretation consists of cutting through the extraneous material and highlighting the core issue. With both kinds of patients, the overall goal is to provide a more intelligible version of their personal experience.

In sum, "latent content," or even "latent meaning," are somewhat misleading concepts; we should, more accurately, speak of *alternative constructions*. The patient has a construction of his symptoms and neurosis; that is, he has a version that is highly defended or with key feelings and thoughts dissociated from his conscious self. The analyst suggests a construction—a way of viewing the dream and the related thoughts, and emotions—in a more coherent form that ties together much more of the "data" of personal experience.

The recognition that we are dealing with *alternative constructions* should alert us to the fact that there is, indeed, more than one interpretation to a dream, just as there is to a symptom or neurotic pattern more generally. Since the patient's version is so often inadequate—by virtue of all that goes into making him a patient—it is easy for us as therapists to believe that there is *a* hidden (latent, unconscious) meaning that we know and the patient does not. There are two kinds of dangers here, two kinds of misuse of interpretation that are ever present in psychoanalytic work. The first is the danger associated with certainty, with the feeling that we, as analysts, know the "real" content of the unconscious and must force (however slowly and carefully) the patient to accept it. This approach tends to go along with a concrete view of "latent content" and, at its worst, leads to those Procrustean interpretive stands where all patients are fit within some narrow mold. The awareness that interpretations are alternative constructions can help guard against this sort of psychoanalytic egocentrism.

The second danger lies at the other extreme; it is the danger of forgetting all the important truths that Freud discovered about infantile sexuality, human aggression, and the ubiquity of anxiety and guilt. To put it another way, while a variety of alternative constructions of a dream, symptom, or neurosis are possible, not all alternatives are equal: psychoanalytic experience consistently points to certain central configurations of impulse, anxiety, and defense of early experience and later character that we rely on as general guidelines in formulating our interpretations. I do not think that our use of this sort of psychoanalytic experience contradicts the idea that interpretations are alternative constructions; it simply indicates that the process of formulating such interpretations occurs in a context where much experience has accumulated. We would be foolish to ignore such experience, yet we can use it without falling prey to the first danger: that of taking the guidelines and clinical rules-of-thumb for established laws.

Throughout the foregoing discussion, certain connections between the latent meaning of a dream and the unconscious meaning of neurotic symptoms and character problems have been noted. Similarly, it is clear that the model of interpreting a dream is the same, or very close to, the model of other types of psychoanalytic interpretation. A neurosis (and I am using the term broadly and loosely) is like a dream; it embodies a set of rules, largely unconscious, that govern the patient's view of himself and others. Psychoanalytic interpretations, of both dreams and neurotic phenomena, involve the exposure of such "rules"—schemas of personal action, persistent fantasies, modes in which characteristic relationships with key others are structured—to conscious view. Thus, the interpretation of the latent meaning of a dream is one instance of the kind of interpretations that constitute psychoanalytic work more generally, interpretive work whose aim is insight, "making the unconscious conscious," or, as I have been describing it, shifting from constricted "theories," schemas, or sets of rules about oneself and others to more comprehensive, meaningful, and coherent ones. This account of psychoanalytic interpretation may seem a bit abstract and unemotional, so let me turn, now, to an actual case which will bring together examples of dreams and dream interpretations with other kinds of interpretive work over the course of an analysis.

A WAY OUT OF SADOMASOCHISM: THE CASE OF EMILY FOX

The patient, whom I will call Emily Fox, was an attractive, charming, outgoing woman in her late twenties. She sought analysis because she was unable to live with her husband in their newly-purchased home, found herself having an affair with another man (and was soon involved in a second affair), and felt guilty, frightened, and uncertain about why she was doing these things. She was anxious, though not overwhelmingly so, depressed at times, but mostly unable to feel deeply; she spoke of being a chameleon, of going through the motions of life.

She described her husband, Henry, as intelligent, kind, and considerate, with many interests and values that coincided with her own; she saw him as an ideal partner in many ways. During the preceding four years he had been completing his work in a professional school while she, despite a teaching credential, worked as a secretary to support them. He had now graduated, taken a well-paying position where it was apparent he would be successful, and they had moved from a small apartment near the university to their new home. It was at this time, and in this setting, that she found herself unable to remain in the marriage—but also unable to give it up. She kept her affairs secret, and could neither live with him nor effect a complete separation. There were no children, though the graduation and move had raised this possibility.

The one complaint she did voice against her husband concerned her unsatisfactory sex life. He was too nice, too square, too inexperienced; she felt guilty because she had some premarital sexual experience and he did not; he didn't turn her on or excite her, she never had orgasms, though she always faked it. The men she became sexually involved with outside the marriage—and there were a series of them over the next few years—tended to be the opposite: in fact, the first was a handsome Don Juan, an athlete and "stud" who she more or less deliberately chose for these qualities. He was her "coach," taught her new techniques, they "fucked their brains out," though it later came to light that she usually didn't have orgasms with him, either. Over the next few years a pattern emerged in her relations with men: they were tall and attractive, yet only available to her for sex; in some cases she almost prostituted herself. She was very jealous of possible rivals, and she took men away from other women, as well as unconsciously arranging to lose them. If the men were unattached or simply interested in her, she would not become involved. Finally, the men tended to be "bad" in some minor way which she elaborated in her fantasies: one had a history of fighting and delinquency as an adolescent, another drank too much and got fired from his job, and so on.

Several things emerged about her need to maintain this series of ultimately unsatisfying relationships. First, they were the enactment of a masochistic fantasy: she continually felt like the abused sexual victim of these big, bad men. And second, her neurosis—or perversion (see Stoller 1975, for one of the best theoretical accounts of this kind of disturbance)— consisted of acting out or living out this pattern of relationships in which she divided herself between two or more men as a protection against a complete emotional commitment. It was not only orgasms that she did not feel; we came to see how she was blocked from commitment, and could not feel in a variety of other ways as well.

A central task of the analysis, persistently worked at over a period of years, was the interpretation of this living out, its diminution, and her concomitant increased emotional commitment to the analytic relationship. As this shift in the balance occurred, she was able to bring into the analysis the fantasies and emotions that she had warded off with the living out of her masochistic pattern. We were eventually able to penetrate to the unconscious core of her neurosis—to reveal the innermost "latent content"—and it is the unravelling of this material that I wish to illustrate with several key dreams. But first a sketch of her history and background.

Emily was the first of three children; a brother, Bob, was born when she was three, and a sister, Barbara, a little over a year later. Her mother's mother had died when the mother was young and the maternal grandfather—a large, gruff German immigrant—lived with the family in their house in a large eastern city until Emily was eight. "Granpop" was an important figure in her early life. There were memories of being his favorite little girl, of a sexualized closeness and, antecedent to her masochism, of performing for his friends—what we came to call "being Granpop's little slave girl"—as well as outbursts of violent discipline from him that caused her great pain. When she was eight the family moved to the suburbs, but Granpop didn't come; he remarried at that time and Emily was more or less conscious of her anger and jealousy at the new wife, whom she refused to call "Grandma." This woman died a year later.

Father worked all his life as a middle-level civil servant and her feelings toward him were quite mixed. At times she felt close and loving, at other times enraged at his inadequacies and his inhibitions which kept him from showing her affection. Mother was clearly the emotional hub of the family. She was simultaneously warm, loving, generous and devoted to her children and also, in Emily's eyes, stupid, uneducated, erratic, and disturbed. Sexually provocative with men and repressive with her daughter, she was "hung up" on her father (Granpop) and unable to provide a consistent or acceptable model of femininity. Emily grew up an outwardly "good" and dutiful child, did well in school, went off to a small local college where unsatisfactory relations with boyfriends foreshadowed the problems to come. She married her husband, a "nice guy" from the neighborhood (she imagined herself more sophisticated and sexually experienced) whom she had known slightly in high school, and they moved across the country as he pursued his professional education.

This sketch of her family and history is largely in the terms that it emerged in the early phase of the analysis and, aside from the involvement with Granpop, connects only superficially with what were later to prove the central experiences that formed her neurotic character. I will save this material until later and present it as it emerged from the analysis of her dreams.

The First Dream

About four months into the analysis she reported a dream, not the first of the analysis, but one of special importance.

"I was living with my family in a farming village or pueblo and some Arab marauders came and bargained with the farmers for twenty young women that they wanted to take away to their oasis in the desert. I'm one of the women: we are bathed, oiled, and prepared for the trip across the desert on camelback. I enjoy this trek, I feel strong, tough, and able to withstand the hardship. We get to the oasis and we [all the women] are taken into an underground cavern or dungeon where we are placed in compartments around the side of a sort of cave. It feels cold and there is water dripping. The other women all seem complacent and happy, but I feel more and more suspicious. I don't trust them, it seems like there is going to be some kind of sacrifice—like the Aztecs used to do—of one or all of us. I also feel threatened in a sexual way."

Her associations were mainly to the untrustworthy men and connected to anger at the various men she was currently involved with. She associated being carried off to her husband's taking her across the country and to anger at him for being a weak man like her father. An interpretive comment that she was feeling less depressed and guilty as her anger was more openly expressed led to further associations concerning Granpop, his loss, and her fear that her anger can drive men away, leaving her alone.

The reader, no doubt, can see much more in this rich and complicated dream than we dealt with at this early phase of the analysis. A major theme at this time concerned her anger at men and its roots in her disappointment with her father and grandfather. While expressing these feelings gave her relief from the immediate guilt and depression, the anger and complaints were centered on issues close to consciousness— complaints about her husband's "nice guy" qualities or her father's inadequacy and stinginess which forced her to work to buy her own clothes—which hardly explained the degree of her fearfulness, her inability to live with her husband or the masochistic relationships. Let us approach some "deeper" explanations as these are suggested by the dream—dimensions that only emerged much later in the analysis.

First, the dream is almost a classic representation of sexual-masochistic surrender. She is the victim who draws strength from her ability to endure pain and hardship. And it is others who possess all the sadism. She experiences herself in the dream as she does in life, the victim of other people's mistreatment and brutality. Second, the dream may be taken in its transference aspect: analysis is a journey away from her past and family into the underground cavern of her unconscious. And, like all the other relationships of intimacy in her life, she is prepared and expects to experience it as a masochistic victim. Indeed, this was a difficult resistance for a long time: she outwardly complied with the analysis in almost every particular, yet did not achieve major improvements (she continued to live out the pattern with men) and, with fantasy and the displacing of emotion (she would cry in her car after the session, feel sexually excited or hurt with a boyfriend and nothing with me), kept herself protected from a full emotional involvement. Finally, there is a point—just hinted at in the dream—of the emergence of intense anxiety: the Aztec sacrifice. The wet underground cave with women in compartments suggests the inside of a woman's body, especially a pregnant woman. And the Aztec sacrifice suggests the image of that body being cut open and some living thing being ripped out. We will see, later, where these images came from and how they related to her sadomasochism.

The Second Dream

The following dream was reported ten months later, about fourteen months into the analysis.

"Dorothy and I are students at some kind of dental hygiene college or school [in reality, Dorothy was a young woman who had replaced Emily as secretary when she left to take another job]. There is a man who is the head of the school, he looks like a middle-aged banker in a suit, he has a very polished outward manner, but he seems sinister to me, as if he is some kind of devil disguised as a banker. We [Dorothy and she] are walking around the halls of the school and I realize that a girl, one of the other students, has been killed. I open one of the doors—it's a bathroom and it looks like the bathtub is filled with blood and guts, so I quickly close the door. Then I'm scared, we have to act like nothing happened and sneak out of the building—not let on that we know a crime has been committed. We meet the schoolmaster-banker guy on the stairs and he's smiling and acting like everything is all right. But when he shakes hands I see blood under his fingernail, so I know he murdered the other girl. We escape—we run across the street—now it's this street [where she comes for analysis]. In the end I'm down at the airport and it feels like we are waiting for my father to come and pick us up."

Her associations, as well as material in adjacent hours, all concerned the theme of her abivalence toward men: her anger at them, the feeling that they exploit her and can't be trusted, and her extreme dependency and fear of being alone. She was, at this point, more able to explore this ambivalence in the analytic relationship, for I seem clearly represented in the dream. Still, as with the first dream, we had not penetrated to the "deeper" levels. What was the meaning of the blood and guts she can only briefly sneak a look at? Who does Dorothy—her "replacement"—stand for? Whose murderous wishes are depicted and who is the real victim? From the material so far presented there are obvious connections with masculinity-femininity. Does the murdered young girl symbolize Emily's "castration" and resulting penis envy—her wish to retaliate by castrating men in revenge? She was certainly angry at them and this was a construction of some usefulness though, in the end, it turned out not as central as others. The deeper meaning of this dream, like the first one, was not reconstructed until much later.

The Infantile Neurosis

I will just comment briefly on certain key issues that emerged over the next three years of the analysis. A good deal of work was done on the connection of her early role as "Granpop's little slave girl" and the way in which this served as a prototype for her current masochistic relations with tall, "bad" men. (Having two men, father and Granpop, had an obvious connection with her current penchant for always having at least two men "in her life.") Of particular importance was her jealous rage when he left her for his new wife. The fact that the woman died a year later gave support to the guilt Emily already felt concerning her anger at rivals and her wish that they would be removed. As we worked through this Granpop transference—she revealed that she sometimes cringed on the couch, half expecting I would whack her in the head as Granpop used to—it became clear that the Granpop pattern had developed as both a displacement and repetition of a still earlier traumatic relationship with her mother. This brought us finally to the origins of that nucleus of fear of being alone, rage, jealousy and the specific images of blood, guts, and a particular kind of murder.

From a variety of converging dreams, associations, and fantasies it became clear that she was terrified of pregnancy, childbirth, and infants. (In a secondary sense this was why she couldn't stay in her marriage: having children was the natural next step.) There was a dream in which she was a pioneer woman, crossing the West in a wagon train, who begins to bleed from a pregnancy and knows she will die since there are no doctors available. As these fears were expressed, a crucial early event was reexperienced. When she was two (nineteen months, as she later found out by checking with her mother), her mother, five months pregnant, began to bleed. Granpop, who had lost his first wife to uterine cancer, was panicked. There was a vivid image of mother in bed with her legs raised, of blood all over, of Granpop and an aunt scurrying around while she, Emily, sat in a chair, her feet dangling far above the floor, frightened and forgotten. Mother had the miscarriage at home and was then taken to the hospital where she remained for some time. Emily was cared for by Granpop, father, and the aunt who lived nearby.

This experience was traumatic in at least two major ways: there was the obvious fear connected with the blood and possible death, communicated in a contagious way by the adults who, with their own background and fears, were insensitive to the special reactions of the nineteen-month-old Emily and unable to give her the needed support. And there was the loss of the very special closeness with mother. As she knows from seeing her mother with other babies, including her grandchildren, she is a real "earth mother" with infants, she holds them on her hip as she goes about her housework and is very warm and physically affectionate. The trauma of the miscarriage was the first instance of Emily's loss of this close, loving relationship with mother, a loss that was repeated two more times before she was five, with the births of her brother and sister. In each instance she saw mother's belly swell, raising the possibility of blood, death, and loss, and both times she lost mother to the hospital and, more importantly, to her replacement, the new baby.

Beginning in those early years, she evolved a "solution" to her dilemma, a solution played out in private doll games and lived out in the real-fantasy relations with her father and, especially, with Granpop who had no wife. In this fantasy solution she turned her rejection and abandonment by mother around; she imagined/played at being the favorite, Granpop's special love; in a sense she replaced his other daughter, her mother, just as her brother and sister had replaced her. Later she came to emphasize her coolness and emotional control as qualities that made her superior to her volatile and expressive mother. The games and fantasies also expressed her rage and wish to destroy her rivals. But, even during these early years, it felt much too dangerous to express this anger openly, for, in contrast to her fantasied superiority, she was really just a little girl completely dependent on the love and care of her mother. Her parents, and Granpop with his German background, would not tolerate anger or defiance toward authority; outwardly she was rewarded for being a "good girl," "Mommy's helper" with the new baby, and a "big girl" (one who didn't cry, show temper or act like a baby). So the desire to be a baby, along with jealousy, rage, and the wish to remove her rivals, went underground into games and fantasies when it was turned on herself. Dolls were killed and she was tied up by evil-doers, awaiting her rescue by some man: Granpop as mother-substitute. In other words, the sadism was disconnected from herself while she became consciously identified with the victim.

This "solution"—the infantile neurosis that was the prototype for her adult sadomasochistic life pattern—was necessary at age five but, of course, it left her frustrated, anxious, and guilty as an adult. One of the most basic sources of her rage at men, experienced most vividly in the transference and in relation to her husband, was that we were not her mother! She wanted to be held and cuddled like an infant and was always, at base, frustrated and angry over demands for other, more mature forms of relationships, especially sex. The uncovering of the infantile neurosis also explained her intensely jealous reactions to rivals. It suggests that the murder in the second dream, coupled with the presence of Dorothy—her replacement—symbolized her wish to murder her baby sister. Several other related issues were clarified: her almost phobic reaction to menstrual blood and a similar fearful response to the shape of pregnant women.

There was a clear mother transference during this period and, in this context, she was finally able to reexperience her murderous jealousy of her mother and sister, with its attendant guilt and turning of sadism to masochism.

The Third Dream

This dream and the one to follow were reported on adjacent days, in the late phase of the analysis.

"Henry [her husband, from whom she remained separated at this time] is going to marry someone else and my mother is going back to protest the marriage. I fly home to stop her—we have a big argument where she says she'll stand up in the church and protest and I say, 'What could you say about it?' Then I go to talk with Henry; he's at a summer beach house like in the movie *Julia,* with screened-in porches. He goes in by lifting an edge of the screen and oozing under, and I get frantic that I can't get through and yell for him to help me, but he just calmly points to a chair next to where he is sitting, so I have to go all around halls and rooms to finally get there. There are some cheese and crackers and a big knife on a table; he sits in the 'Papa bear's chair' and I sit in a smaller one. I'm telling him about mother going to break up the wedding and he says, 'It doesn't matter.' I get more and more upset and tell him, 'Please don't marry her, you don't know her.' He's very nice but he doesn't change. I get hysterical and start slugging him in the face—wham, wham—the phone rings and he picks it up, 'Sure you can borrow the garden hose'—[he talks calmly to a neighbor]. He is so imperturbable it just makes me angrier. I reach over to the little table [as she says this, she gestures with her arm, touches a small table next to the couch and laughs as if in recognition of a connection] and grab the knife and stab him. I'm worried, but he's not even bleeding— nothing I do can change him. I melt, crumble to the floor, and then wake up crying, with my heart pounding."

There were a variety of associations to the dream, including many of the insights we had worked on in recent months: (1) Henry did have a new girlfriend, and Emily was jealous; he was "helping her" now but in the dream wouldn't help Emily; (2) being held and cuddled by her current boyfriend didn't work anymore; (3) it wasn't really Henry—she was angry with her mother for leaving her, and took it out on him; (4) she was angry because he was a man who didn't bleed out of a "slit" the way she did; (5) she can't get to her mother anymore because Barbara (her sister) is there, nor to Granpop because of his new wife; (6) she has to do things on her own now, not with some fantasy of being little. All these associations and insights were useful to her and she felt much less anxious and guilty as the hour proceeded. Yet something was missing: the obvious transference connection depicted in the dream (the impassive man, unresponsive to her pleas and feelings, the connection of the table). My focus on this led to a rush of feeling and additional association: that she is more and more committed to me and the analysis and, as she feels herself getting better, fears the impending loss. And then she began to be aware of her anger at me for "taking away her fantasy," for the way in which analytic insight is making it impossible for her to continue her pattern of sadomasochistic, divided relationships. So in the throes of this mother transference—that is, when she is giving up the fantasy solution of other men as mother-substitutes and feels herself most completely committed to the analyst-as-mother—she experiences, in this dream and its associations, intense rage at a rival who will replace her and has the specific wish to stab the mother-husband-analyst.

The Fourth Dream

"It's like scenes in a movie to show time going by: I'm with a man, warm and cuddly in bed; then I'm pregnant; then I'm holding a baby; then the baby is two and the police come to the door. I know my husband has been killed. Then I'm at the funeral. The baby is there, I go and look in the casket and it's you! [the analyst]. I hate you for leaving me and have this terrible sad feeling."

Her associations touched on the reality of the feeling in the dream: "I'll never get married again, or have a baby—it's too vulnerable." Then she spoke of the reality of her involvement with the analysis, how she caught herself on the way to the hour "plotting to gather men around me again," as a protection against feeling left and alone but then realized that she must continue to work it out. This was followed by an "achy-clawing" feeling, like a baby reaching out to be held. She then reported a dreamlike series of associations: the baby reaching out to be held, fantasies of stabbing someone, she saw scissors—very sharp—babies crawling around on the floor. She is sewing, a baby is crawling toward the sharp scissors, she has to get there so it doesn't cut itself; no, she is pregnant—like in the dream—it's so the baby won't stab her in the belly, to kill the other baby! She came out of this reverie with "It doesn't take Sigmund Freud to figure that out; I want to stab my mother and kill the next baby—it wasn't Bob [her brother, the first sibling replacement], it was Barbara—that time I knew what was going to happen." She then went on with a variety of confirmatory associations, including her rage at "having to be Barbara's little slave girl, helping Mommy with the diapers, because I needed her love so much." At the heart of it all was the powerful realization that she feels and acts like an abandoned infant who wants to kill her mother and sister and that her whole life is run by jealousy.

It is interesting to note the multiple identifications in this dream and its associations; they are much like her play as a young child in which she took different roles and acted out the various feelings. She is the baby in danger who must be saved (as she felt when abandoned or left alone); she is the mother who must protect the baby (her identification with her "good mother," being "Mommy's helper," a "big girl"); she is the pregnant mother with her rival inside (the masochism, she attacks herself); and finally, she is the enraged and jealous baby who wants to stab her "bad mother" and kill her rival (the most unconscious of her early wishes and fantasies). We assume she was aware of her jealous rage and wish to stab mother at the time her mother was pregnant with Barbara. But even then, an open expression of these feelings and wishes was extremely dangerous; they quickly became hidden in the private world of symbolic play and fantasy. Thus, the reconstruction of them in the analysis brings out material from the "deepest" level of the unconscious. In her unconscious version, the different rival figures became blended and time-distorted. Thus, her wish to kill her sister *in utero,* the actual bloody miscarriage that occurred earlier, and the later death of Granpop's second wife were all felt to be the same: her murderous wish toward rivals was responsible; she was both powerful and guilty.

There is much material in these two dreams that could be further explored but I will leave that aside and focus on the core issue: the reversal of masochism back into sadism. In the third dream and her associations to the fourth we see a striking contrast to the earlier dreams and to her conscious feelings of victimization. She can now dream and think of herself as the aggressor. In reconstructing these early memories, images, feelings, and fantasies associated with the creation of her neurosis, we reached the point of the original rage and jealousy which this time—in the analytic relationship—could be openly expressed, rather than turned on herself. In this sense, we undid the symbolic complexities of the fantasy solution to her original infantile dilemma, where she turned to the masochistic fantasy solution because she could not express her rage openly.

DISCUSSION

Let us return now to the consideration of latent content, latent meaning, and alternative constructions, and the more general issue of becoming conscious of the unconscious, and see what the case of Emily Fox illustrates about the version of these concepts I presented earlier. One reason I chose this particular case is that the dramatic memory of her mother's miscarriage, along with the reexperiencing of the murderous fantasies, are as clear instances of the "recovery" of unconscious material as we see in psychoanalysis. This certainly *seems* like an uncovering of "latent content"—of actual unconscious memories, fantasies, and feelings—so it should prove a good test of the claims that what is latent is not "content" but meaning; that becoming conscious of what was previously unconscious is a matter of developing an *alternative construction* of the self.

What was unconscious in Emily that became conscious in the course of her analysis? Here is a list, not necessarily in the order they occurred:

1. *Specific memories from early childhood.* The trauma of mother's miscarriage and subsequent absence and the rage during the later pregnancies were the most striking. There were also important memories of grandfather's abandonment of her for his second wife and her jealousy at that time. These memories were most like the "recovery" of deep unconscious material—and so I described them in the report—yet even in these instances she probably did not reproduce duplicates of the original experiences in the analysis. It was more a case of allowing herself to get into an approximation of the original emotional state—to regress in the analysis—and then producing memory-fantasies with the schemas active in that state.

2. *Consciousness of her unconscious.* As happens in most successful analyses, she came to see that a great deal of what she did and felt in her adult life was dictated by sources she was not aware of. She did not know this at first, but later came to speak of her "whole life being a fantasy," of "playing out games," "macho sex trips," and of "my gathering men around me."

3. *Her masochism.* First, she became aware of how masochistic she was. She saw that there was a meaningful pattern to her never having orgasms despite wild sexual adventures, not letting herself feel openly in the analysis, not being able to stay with her husband, working beneath her level of skill and education as a secretary, and putting herself in a position to be abused by "big, bad men." She became aware of the consistency and

force of this pattern of self-denial and victimization, and of its gratifications as well, of her fear and guilt, and then of the prototype for the pattern in her childhood.

4. *The infantile neurosis.* Eventually, we reconstructed the specific play-fantasy solution to the dilemma posed by her abandonment, anxiety, and rage at her mother and saw how she play-lived it out, first with her grandfather and then with the men in her adult life.

5. *Her rage, jealousy and sadistic fantasies.* She came to see how, for her, the world was filled with rivals for her primary love object; how she was driven to replace them—kill them—and how angry she was, and how frightened and guilty at the degree and extent of her rage. She sought revenge on men for what her mother had done to her; there was a great deal of hostility behind her compliant facade, especially with me and her husband.

6. *The transference.* While I have not emphasized it in this account, the major work in the analysis revolved around transference interpretations. She came to see how she related to me as a compliant slave-girl, divided herself between me and other men, felt rage at her rivals (other patients) and, eventually, felt like killing me because I was not her exclusive mother, even as she felt close and appreciative of my help.

In these examples of how Emily became conscious of her unconscious we can see a variety of operations at work. In some cases, events were forgotten—for example, the childhood traumas—while in others they were remembered, but without much emotion. Sometimes she experienced the event and the feeling, but to the wrong person, for instance when she was frightened and angry because of what men did to her. And sometimes she turned things around, did to others what she felt had been done to her. In all these instances we achieved various levels or degrees of awareness as the analysis progressed. There were a variety of constructions—for instance, early work dealing with anger at her father for his stinginess during her adolescence or the whole Granpop pattern—that were not wrong so much as they were incomplete. Such constructions brought more of her feelings and actions into consciousness but they did not tell the entire story of her fear and rage toward men—a story that could only be completed with the reconstruction of the earlier material regarding her mother.

This work of construction and reconstruction, of bringing to light forgotten events and feelings, of experiencing new ways (or long repressed old ways) of acting in an intimate relationship, first in the analytic situation and then with others, proceeded gradually over more than four years of analysis. Each part of this process involved insight, a change from unconscious to conscious, the making manifest of what was latent. No single recovered or reconstructed memory, no single shift from sub-missiveness to assertion, no single insight into her masochistic pattern, in and of itself, was crucial. It was, rather, the gradual development along all these lines that constituted the overall change in her character structure.

With this change completed, it is possible to look back and summarize the overall shift from a life dominated by unconscious motivation to her reconstructed, more insightful, self. When she began the analysis she had a conscious version—or several related versions—of herself. She was a nice, compliant, somewhat subservient, young woman, afraid to talk back to her boss or to work up to her level of skill, and angry at men for taking advantage of her. This version was maintained by a variety of operations which kept from consciousness—displaced, rationalized, reversed, mini-mized—the whole set of feelings and wishes which, as we have seen, came to light in the course of the analysis. This was a very unstable situation; she could not really keep this defended version of herself going. Too many inexplicable feelings kept breaking through. Most of her sex life, with all its feelings of power, dominance and submission, was lived in secret. She kept "doing" things—leaving her husband, seducing different men—that did not fit her conscious image or version of herself. It was like an inadequate scientific theory or an outmoded religion that is constantly challenged by observations it cannot explain. The instability, along with the painful feelings and lack of real satisfaction in relationships, is what drove her to analysis. The gradual accumulation of insight in the analysis involved more and more open expression of the warded off experiences, feelings, and actions. What was before expressed in secret fantasy or played-lived out in relationships, where it was felt to happen to others—dolls, dream figures, men, herself going through the motions or "faking it"—was gradually felt to be *her* in a living-feeling, committed relation-ship. Along with this shift in the mode of experiencing, there was insight of the more intellectual variety. She came to understand how and why she did what she did. These changes in both experience and understanding constituted the change in her character structure. She ceased to feel every woman as a rival, and made close women friends for the first time in years; she was no longer subject to severe anxiety when "left" or threatened with being alone; she stopped dividing herself between two or more men, stopped taking her revenge on them; and she could be openly angry with me, her husband, and her mother, as well as more emotionally committed. All these changes were part of a new structure of the self (or expanded self and object schemas), a structure which, like a new and better scientific theory, could encompass more of the data of her life. With this new, expanded version of herself, she could tolerate her rage. It did not mean she would kill her love objects, or be left by them, and she was not a horribly guilty child for feeling it. She could understand where it came from and, eventually, stop directing it at substitute figures.

This change in character structure—in one's basic "theory" about how one is—is like a personal Copernican revolution, like a powerful religious conversion experience. One clings to the old, neurotic version just as the committed believer does to his belief system. In Emily's case there was a protracted and difficult struggle—the familiar resistance—in modifying the version of herself that had developed in early childhood to deal with her painful and threatening situation. Part of the difficulty of changing came from exchanging the security of the known for the unknown, as it does in any shift in a major belief system. But the main source of the resistance involved painful emotions, as it usually does. Her old version of herself protected her from directly feeling like a helpless and abandoned child and like a guilty, jealous killer. To give up the old, unconscious, defended version was to reexperience herself in those painful, humiliating, and guilty ways, as a necessary prelude to the reconstruction of herself in a broader, more coherent form. In this new form—this new theory or model of herself—there was a place for jealousy, rage, and sadistic fantasies, for fear, guilt, and revenge, as well as for adult commitment and, perhaps even someday, for pregnancy and motherhood.

To say that this new version of herself was "latent," or existed in her unconscious, is to say that she and I had the capability of working together to achieve the reorganization of her life experience that we finally did achieve. It was latent in the sense that the form of a statue is latent in a piece of marble: such a potential is only brought into existence by the activity of the sculptor, just as the patient and analyst create a new consciousness, from the materials of the patient's life, with their activity over the course of the analysis.

References

Breger, L. (in press). *Freud's Unfinished Journey: Conventional and Critical Perspectives in Psychoanalytic Theory.* London: Routledge and Kegan Paul.
Freud, S. (1900). The interpretation of dreams. *Standard Edition* 4:1–338 and 5:339–627.
——— (1915). The unconscious. *Standard Edition* 14:159–215.
——— (1923). The ego and the id. *Standard Edition* 19:1–66.

Klein, G. S. (1976). *Psychoanalytic Theory: An Exploration of Essentials.* New York: International Universities Press.

Lifton, R. J. (1976). *The Life of the Self.* New York: Simon and Schuster.

Loevinger, J. (1976). *Ego Development.* San Francisco: Jossey-Bass.

Ricoeur, P. (1970). *Freud and Philosophy: An Essay on Interpretation.* New Haven: Yale University Press.

Schafer, R. (1976). *A New Language for Psychoanalysis.* New Haven: Yale University Press.

——— (1978). *Language and Insight.* New Haven: Yale University Press.

Stoller, R. J. (1975). *Perversion: The Erotic Form of Hatred.* New York: Pantheon.

Yankelovich, D., and Barrett, W. (1970). *Ego and Instinct.* New York: Random House.

CHAPTER 2

DREAMS IN WHICH THE ANALYST APPEARS AS HIMSELF

Robert D. Gillman, M.D.

Dreams in which the analyst appears as part of the manifest content occur in more than eighty percent of clinical psychoanalyses. The analyst is present undisguised in more than nine percent of all dreams. Most analysts underestimate this frequency. Moreover, analysts feel a vague discomfort when they appear in their patients' dreams (Rosenbaum 1965). This discomfort stems from earlier accounts which ascribed the mobilization of these undisguised transference dreams either to (1) countertransference in the analyst, or (2) early oral conflicts or major psychopathology in the patient, particularly when the dream was a first or early dream in an analysis. The frequency of undisguised transference dreams (UTD's) can be ascribed to the double role of the analyst in influencing the content of the patient's dreams. First, as a transference figure he may represent any of the significant people of the patient's past. Second, he is a prominent part of the day's residue that contributes to the formation of dreams.

THREE TYPES OF UNDISGUISED TRANSFERENCE · DREAMS

Transference dreams offer access to understanding the course and direction of an analysis. Undisguised transference dreams (UTD's), as

opposed to transference dreams where the analyst is symbolically represented, are a special class of these dreams. In this chapter clinical material
is presented to show how UTD's can serve as a *defense* against deepening
transference. Three types of UTD's are presented: (1) UTD's that appear
in a wide variety of patients in response to a break in the analytic barrier,
(2) UTD's that appear as a defense against an emerging transference
neurosis, and (3) UTD's that reflect a specific character defense. This
paper demonstrates the last in detail in a patient whose first of 300
undisguised transference dreams appeared in the second week of analysis
and continued well into the termination phase.

REVIEW OF THE LITERATURE

Gitelson's paper (1952) on countertransference suggests that these
dreams might result from the analyst's countertransference which evokes
intense transference in the patient. This view has had a more lasting
impact on analytic thinking than any other paper. However, later studies
have demonstrated a wide variety of eliciting factors, many of which
originate in the patient. Several authors have supported the view that if
the analyst appears undisguised in the *first* dream of an analysis, the
prognosis is unfavorable, there is a poor fit between analyst and patient, or
there is serious psychopathology. Rappaport (1959) quoting Blitzten
supports Gitelson's view that either the analyst is in reality too much like a
significant figure of the past or the transference is so erotized that there is
no *as if* between the analyst and the past. The analyst may introduce
something into the analysis that is a repetition of an early interpersonal
situation for the patient, but is not in itself countertransference. In
Bradlow and Coen's (1975) study of undisguised first dreams, the patients
carried diagnoses of borderline, schizoid, or paranoid personalities. Such a
patient's overt wish for the analyst to be a real figure was related to
problems of mistrust and reality testing. One of their series dreamed
literally of the analytic situation "It was this office, I was on the couch
talking. You were sitting behind me."

The earliest report of UTD's is that of Feldman (1945), who described
the typical dream in which the analytic situation is disturbed by the
presence of other people as intruders. In most of these dreams the latent
wish was to cling to the analyst as a mother, to have an uninterrupted
fusion with the mother, or for a nonfrustrating closer relationship with
the analyst. This is consistent with Bradlow and Coen's patients who had

an expectedly high frequency of early parental loss. Harris (1962) concluded from a study of seventeen of his own cases that the bulk of the contribution toward the formation of UTD's came from the character of the patient and the quality of the patient's transference. He was present as himself in ten percent of the patient's dreams. He felt that UTD's represented a primitive oral identification process and were a very early defense in which the image of the mother is called up to cope with anxiety. He reasoned that a countertransference attitude of oversolicitousness or just this quality in the analyst's personal style could provoke UTD's in a hostile-dependent person.

Rosenbaum (1965) found UTD's in forty of forty-four patients in a large statistical study. The analyst appeared undisguised in 9.3 percent of the dreams. Although he found that these dreams represented oral conflicts, he concluded that they were of no prognostic value nor did they correlate with intense transference, countertransference, or highly erotized transference. He felt that each dream had to be studied for its special meaning. Rosenbaum quotes two personal communications that are appropriate to the clinical material presented here: Grotjahn stated that UTD's signify that reality has entered the analytic situation; Seitz concluded that when he stepped out of the classic role (when he was annoyed, angry, or in a hurry) the patient was likely to have such a dream. Gitelson, too, cited a case in which a UTD appeared when an inexperienced analyst became too real to the patient by making an inappropriate reassuring comment.

UNDISGUISED TRANSFERENCE DREAMS
FOLLOWING A BREAK IN
THE ANALYTIC BARRIER

In the author's practice, five patients, two men and three women, responded to breaks in the analytic barrier, where reality entered the analytic situation, by immediately producing a UTD. The patients represented a wide variety of characterological problems, and all had more than one UTD. In two cases the dreams occurred after two of the four weekly sessions were transferred from my office to my home. A third discovered I was on the faculty of a school to which she had applied. Another patient had an undisguised transference dream after I had canceled an hour by telephone because of illness, and a second UTD after driving past my home. A fifth patient dreamed about me undisguised after I filled out a detailed insurance form. It was not clear why these particular five patients responded with UTD's. In some instances their associations revealed previously unreported examples of experiencing the analyst in reality. For example, one had overheard me talking to a colleague. Another had seen me meeting a woman. It is possible that these dreams reflect a mobilization of conflicts by the break in the analytic barrier where the dream occurred before the patient had an opportunity to work through the material in an analytic session. The reality of the encounter with the analyst is preserved, but the dream symbolically portrays the conflicts that were mobilized by the reality experience. Three cases are illustrative.

Case 1

A thirty-year-old social worker, an hysterical character with conflicts over seeing and being seen, who focused on immediate reality to ward off transference feelings, had a UTD after I told her I would be ten minutes late for the next day's session. She consciously forgot this, but the next morning she remembered a dream which then brought to her mind the possibility of my being late: "I was in your office, but it was different. Neither of us said anything. I was naked from the waist up with a long skirt. I was supposed to dance."

The same patient, who had met my office partner at a party and felt very attracted to him, wondered if it was because she was attracted to me. She was reluctant to talk about such feelings, but had the following dream. "I was here on the couch. I had fallen asleep. When I woke up you were not in the chair, but on the couch next to me. I said, 'What happened, did I fall asleep?' You said it was all right."

A third UTD occurred after she had driven past my home. "The whole family was in a motel or hotel bedroom, all in the same room. It was dark; we were stripping the beds and looking for our belongings. Then I was here; I was not feeling well but came because it was the time I was supposed to come. I lay down; then I got up and walked out. The previous patient was still at the elevator. The hall was not yours but like my husband's office building. There was a man waiting. I felt dizzy and could hardly see and came back here, and you were at the entrance of your office, asking, 'Why did you leave?' I was very upset, crying, and you said, 'Sit down.' I couldn't see. You were getting closer and said, 'Everything will be all right.' Then you wanted to kiss me. I didn't want you to; then I let you and I was surprised that you kissed just like my husband."

In association she told that the previous day she had driven down the street where she knew I lived and assumed that she had driven past my home. She had felt very anxious and confused but did not see anything and was worried that she would be seen. She then criticized herself for being too nosy and recalled that as a child she had walked by a boy's house, hoping that he would see her. She had also wondered about calling me at home over the weekend to cancel because she had felt ill.

Case 2

A thirty-eight-year-old accountant with a European background, a masochistic character with obsessive-compulsive neurosis, was told following summer vacation in the third year of analysis that two of our four weekly sessions would be moved to my home. He immediately became concerned that we would become too familiar, and he would reexperience an unsuccessful treatment he had had with a previous therapist. He worried that he would be kicked out of analysis, that he did not belong, and that he was paying less money than he should. His first transference dream was disguised. "There was a city that was supposed to be Geneva, but it was dilapidated, looking more like New York. There was a ferry landing and a man selling tickets. He was not Swiss. He was not you. It was the last trip for the night, but he was selling round trip tickets. I wondered whether I should accept him as a passenger in my car." His next associations had to do with imagining what my house would be like. He recalled how as a child he had learned from his mother not to trust strangers and got the impression that other people had dirty houses and that one must be very careful of the food they serve. He was concerned that he would see things that people were not supposed to see, just as in old movies nobody ever showed toilets or pregnant women. He then reported having seen me with a woman a few days earlier. He felt the transfer was for my convenience, like his mother's enemas that were ostensibly for his own good.

The following day he had a UTD. "I lay on the couch. The couch was near the window and then you threw a cloth over my head. It seemed very real, done as if it were to see my reaction. I woke with relief." His first association was to a childhood event, visiting a Swiss home where the children threw a sheet over his head. It reminded him that as a child he had been very lonely and felt he had to be compliant and do what other children said. He was afraid he would see too much and told me about a woman patient he had seen entering the office as he left.

Following the first session at the analyst's home, he dreamed, "I was at your house and had to wait while you reassured a young psychiatrist patient. Then I went out to my car." There were further associations to distrust of strangers and how people took advantage of one's gullibility.

Case 3

In an inadvertent analytic experiment, six patients' checks were lost in transit when I mailed them for a deposit to my bank. I told each patient that his check was lost and requested each to determine whether his check had cleared and, if not, to issue a replacement check. One of the six patients, a thirty-five-year-old lawyer, responded with a UTD. "I was in this office and other people were here to help me. You encouraged it. The others and I were all lying around with our feet up like a conference though I was still the patient. I indicated that I wanted to talk about something and they discreetly left." The conflict over intimacy (like Feldman's report of "intruder" dreams) was mobilized by the break in the analytic barrier. Associations were to a man who had had incestuous relations with his daughter, but was nevertheless permitted to remain in the home. Later, in the same session when one of my interventions reflected knowledge about his work situation, he said, "You must be hearing this from another patient." To my question of his need to bring in someone else, he replied, "We have each other. It's so intimate."

The unexpected impact of the analyst as a real person mobilizes powerful transference feelings which are represented in the dreams. But the full meaning of the transference is avoided by depicting the analyst as himself.

UNDISGUISED TRANSFERENCE DREAMS AS A DEFENSE AGAINST AN EMERGING TRANSFERENCE NEUROSIS

In these dreams the patient thrusts the analyst forward as a real person to avoid the anxiety of the deepening transference neurosis. The patient's dream momentarily insists on the reality of the analyst in order to repress those memories that are reappearing as transference feelings. The dream is neither a response to any extra-analytic activity or reality nor a result of special pathology in the patient. Probably a large share of UTD's that occur sporadically in the course of an analysis fall into this category.

Case 4

The patient was a twenty-four-year-old single college woman, an hysterical character with some masochism and depression, and a less than optimal tolerance of tension which was handled through missing hours, smoking pot, and a quick succession of intense relationships with men, thus splitting the transference. There was a long-standing relationship with one man that was no longer sexual and had a maternal flavor. Dreams suggested early helpless seduction by her father and sadistic older brothers and seemed related to her fears that attachment and dependence would lower her self-esteem. In the material reported in the second year of analysis there were associations to her mother's principles of acceptance of others, in contrast to the rigidity and strictness of her father. The patient was comfortable picturing the analyst more as the accepting mother who puts up with her acting out and faults without criticism. This, however, was becoming more and more difficult to maintain against the emerging erotic transference. In the two weeks before the undisguised dream, concerned whether I could possibly be interested in her, she had a thinly disguised transference dream. "Dr. M (the consultant who sent her to analysis) and two other analysts were in a restaurant. They were silent. The analysts were silent in their asexual world." The patient then wondered if her interest in her teachers was some sort of substitute for me, at which I interpreted her feeling that if a person is not sexually concerned, he is therefore not concerned at all. She then recalled a promiscuous time in her adolescence when her father hit her, and that was evidence that he cared.

Just prior to the UTD she noticed the wonderful springtime and felt sad that it would be gone. She recalled the lonely summers. I interpreted that she had some feelings about the coming weekend. She responded, "Maybe that's so. I don't know. The weekends keep my resistance up. Maybe we should be meeting five times a week instead of four." At the start of the next week she talked of three or four men that she had been seeing, and I noted that she was shifting from one to the other. To this she became silent, and at length I wondered if the three day interruption had any pertinence. She then spoke of her vulnerability to dependency and contrasted herself to a girlfriend who likes adulation. She was then silent and said that she had been having trouble ever since I mentioned shifting and, in a challenging tone that was unusual for her, asked me to explain myself.

She canceled the next hour without notice, came in the following day, and said, "I knew I would cancel before I left last time. I went out with a girlfriend and stayed out very late." She then reported a dream of the night before. "Things were very good between us [the analyst and the patient]. We had a friendship. I asked you if you had any children. Your wife was in the background. I was like the only child." She then reported another dream that she had had during the actual time of the hour that was canceled. "It was already Monday in the next analytic hour. I was in the session, and the feeling of missing the hour had passed." The patient then talked about how important it was to be the only one. I reviewed how she wanted to be important to me. The patient responded by recounting how she had met her boyfriend over the weekend and had suddenly urged him to spend the night with her despite their agreement to keep some distance from each other. She said, "Now I'll get too involved." I brought up the missed hour and she responded, "I need the freedom to miss."

In this material when I interpreted her shifting displacements she suddenly became aware of the erotic transference and perhaps oedipal memories. She handled this through silence and missing an hour. The frank oedipal dream, in which the analyst appears undisguised, defended against the emerging father transference, and the patient restored her balance by displacing again to the boyfriend and insisting he be closer to her than they had agreed. The sadness over the loss of spring and the sadness that the boyfriend might not spend the night with her suggest that the undisguised transference material defends also against loss of maternal love.

Case 5

The patient was a forty-year-old, compulsive, ambitious business man whose characterological problems interfered with his own success. His narcissism drove him to surpass an ideal of a dimly remembered early father. Prickly aggression warded off passive homosexual trends and tenderness. He could not tolerate working under anyone and had great difficulty working along with his partner. Analysis, now in its second year, was still kept isolated from the rest of his life. In the analytic hour reported, the patient recounted how he needed to keep control of relationships. His associations then turned to his need to impress people: business associates, women, and other tennis players. The analyst suggested that the patient wanted to impress him too. The patient retorted, "I have no emotion here. I have no love for you." He then told how he ran a short marathon in company with some psychiatrists. "I sure want to beat the pants off them." Shortly after the analytic hour, while taking a nap, the patient had the following dream: "I was standing with a group on a grassy hill. You [the analyst] came by in a military gray sports car, zipping along fast." Associations in the hour were first to the phallic quality of the sports car. He then told how he always avoids sentiment and feels embarrassed and weak when he has to tell someone he likes them. He also felt embarrassed as a child when his father told dirty jokes. Then he admitted for the first time that he could not urinate in a public restroom if anyone else was there.

In this case, the UTD appeared in response to the deepening passive homosexual transference. The patient tried to maintain a degraded and isolated father transference, but the admiration of the analyst's phallic power broke through.

UNDISGUISED TRANSFERENCE DREAMS AS A CHARACTER DEFENSE

Case 6

This category is illustrated by one patient who dreamed in a characteristic way beginning in the sixth analytic hour and continued with these dreams throughout a long analysis, well into the termination phase. The dreams seemed to function like screen memories. They often vividly reproduced the content and helpless feelings from early seductions, but were isolated from the patient's waking life.

Depicting the analyst as real in dreams served to defend against awareness of caring for the analyst either as a real figure in a therapeutic alliance or as a transference figure. The discharge into dreams helped her to repress the recovery of the actual memories and helped to isolate feelings from current life. Further, these UTD's seemed to be an attempt to master those childhood traumas whose content was reproduced in the dreams.

The patient was a married woman in her thirties, employed in a day care center, far below her capacity, and avoiding all competition. Her initial symptoms were multiple phobias which prevented her from carrying on many normal daily activities. Frigidity and passivity in sexual relations helped to maintain the repression of vengeful sadomasochistic fantasies. In her childhood she had suffered sexual seductions, followed by oedipal and narcissistic loss before full superego consolidation. Her adaptation was to resolutely avoid caring deeply about anyone, including her husband and children. She did this both to avoid narcissistic hurt and to ward off the helplessness that had accompanied any strong affect in her childhood, stemming from the early seduction experiences and lack of maternal protection. Her vow at the time of her oedipal loss at age five, when her father was called into active military duty, was never to wish for anything or anybody. This became part of her character structure. At the beginning of analysis, she stated that she had heard about the trans-ference, but that she was not going to let that happen to her since she simply would not think about the analyst outside of the analysis.

The patient grew up in a small southern town where her father, the local sheriff, was honored in the community, but treated with contempt by her narcissistic mother who, in turn, never protected the patient from the seductive play of her father and his friends. The third child of seven, singled out for special attention for her beauty and vivacity, she repeated her father's seductions with her younger brother and later repeated her mother's lack of protection with her son. In latency, her exhibitionism and erotic life turned to shyness and guilt, later to phobia. She felt herself to be ugly and renounced pleasure in altruistic surrender to a less favored younger sister. Her outstanding academic record won her a scholarship to a prestigious southern college where she met her future husband. He wooed her so insistently that she was able to marry without having to acknowledge that she cared, and she helped maintain the denial of feelings by keeping her marriage secret for some months. After her children were of school age she found a job far below her training and ability. She sought treatment when an erotic attachment to a male co-worker led to the outbreak of multiple phobias.

This patient was similar to the twenty-six-year-old woman with good ego strength described by Yazmajian (1964). Her first dream in analysis was a UTD followed by several additional UTD's in the first four months of analysis. His patient had an inordinate dread of the unconscious and fear of being overwhelmed by affect derived from childhood visual traumas. She tried to maintain the analyst as a real figure to avoid the deepening transference, but with the emergence of conscious erotic feelings in the father transference after four months of analysis, the transference dreams usually appeared disguised. Yazmajian concluded that the UTD's were a defensive flight into current reality to ward off childhood memories and affects.

In common with my patient was a history of narcissistic hurt from a cold mother and overexposure to a seductive father. Pertinent to this case is Blum's (1973) description of patients whose pre-formed erotic trans-ference reflected sexual seduction in childhood and instinctual over-stimulation, with deprivation of parental protection and support. Many of these patients were exposed to primal scenes along with a general atmosphere of narcissistic injury associated with parental insensitivity and lack of empathy. Savitt (1969) reported a patient whose early UTD repeated a homosexual seduction at age five.

In my patient the original defenses against transference feelings were put forward in the analysis with the erotic transference appearing in the UTD's. The patient's analysis was characterized by a richness of dreams of many types, but for the purpose of this presentation emphasis will be on UTD's.

Opening phase. In an early hour she told of the strong attachment between herself and her father, but how she avoided boys who liked her, as though something was wrong with them. She was the center of attention of her father's friends. She recalled how frightened she was when her father staggered in drunk and said, "Kiss me." After reporting material in which she felt she was liked for her blond hair, but not for herself, she had the following dream. "You [the analyst] said, 'I'd like to ask you a question, but the time is up.' It was right here. I was so disappointed. You were supposed to elicit something, and I would reveal something. I was delaying, and you were over at the desk near the door. I felt embarrassed. I had overstayed the precise time." It reminded her of shy boys who would wait until the last dance before they asked a girl, just as time was up. It also reminded her of how in college she avoided her last conference with a beloved history teacher. She said she had been a star pupil and the appointment did not seem necessary, so she canceled it, but afterwards felt disappointed.

Two months later she reported that she had been feeling depressed and did not seem to be getting any better in analysis. "This morning I took the bus, although I think I would not have been too afraid to drive." She then reported a dream. "It was an analytic session. I went on the couch, but I was sitting up not looking at you. You were lying down on a bed covered with a sheet, a low bed like a Hollywood bed, and I was sitting on a corner of the bed not looking. I knew I wasn't supposed to look and I didn't. You kept moving around and I did too." She associated to her wish to look at me during a session and then to her bed at home where she gets up while her husband is still asleep. It disturbs him, and he gets annoyed when she wakes him to come to her analytic sessions. She was afraid that I would be annoyed too and that she would be abandoned. She worried, on the one hand, that she was too sick and, on the other hand, that she was not sick enough. Her associations led to sharing a room with a sister and how, when they were undressing, they were not supposed to look at each other. However, she would sneak a look at her sister's behind, but never admit it. She then added, "In the dream I saw your leg between your sock and your pants." I asked if she had seen something in reality she felt she was not supposed to. She responded, "No. It was in the dream." Her next associations were to looking at herself in the mirror and how ugly she looks to herself.

In these opening phase dreams the first UTD reveals the narcissistic disappointment that the patient had guarded against for years and defended against in the analysis. The second UTD contains what became a repeated theme of the analyst in bed, sometimes with the patient. Here the theme of looking and being seen is prominent. When the patient does move to the past she is looking at her sister and looking at the behind rather than at the genitals of her father and brothers. As a child she was rashly exhibitionistic and, following her oedipal resolution, she developed a phobia of being seen, and had to hide her work. Her ugliness was a recurrent theme that had to do with ugly and guilty thoughts both of an erotic and aggressive nature.

Middle phase. In the fourth year of analysis, at the beginning of an hour, I handed back the check the patient had just given me, noting that she had failed to sign it. (One of her phobias was that she could not sign her name if anyone was looking.) The patient laughed and said that she was also wearing unmatched shoes. She reported a dream that was thinly disguised. In the dream she was having intercourse with a high school classmate who had the same first name as the analyst, and reached orgasm, although she tried to stop it. In her associations she told about winning the classmate's favor, then avoiding him and feeling humiliated because at that time too she noticed that her shoes were unmatched. She realized that in the dream she had tried to stop the orgasm the same way she tried to stop the check in real life, and I pointed out the connection between her phobia and her sexual inhibitions.

She then reported another dream: "I was coming to my analytic hour, and I was late. Then my mother was driving a VW bus, and she called the shift by another word. It was stuck, and she never got it started." In the next hour the erotic dream was undisguised. "I had a dream. You were being familiar. You sat on the couch, and I complained that you were too familiar and you said that we were looking at television. Then there was a TV set, and my daughter was sitting in front." She then suddenly remembered that the high school classmate did *not* have the same name as the analyst. When I interpreted how much got expressed in dreams, but so little directly, and how much was revealed by the slips and parapraxes, she said, "Yes, during Christmas vacation my husband said, 'How did your analyst spend his Christmas?' And I said I'd never asked." I pointed out how she avoided even the most normal curiosity for fear that she might be humiliated. She then revealed how special she had felt when her sessions were shifted to a later afternoon hour, but then she found out that there was a patient who followed her, and felt deflated.

Three months later she had the following dream. "I had a crude dream. You started having intercourse with me, and I protested that it was not part of psychoanalysis, and you said, 'What do you know?' Then it was my bedroom, and I heard footsteps, and I said, 'For God's sake, stop, my mother is coming,' and you went to hide in the closet and had changed into my husband getting into his clothes."

In this middle phase of the analysis the sexual content is more frankly expressed in the UTD's. The greater acceptance of instinctual urges in the dreams paralleled analytic progress. While the patient could now work analytically, the bulk of the transference feelings remained isolated, denied and expressed in slips and parapraxes. The erotic dream scenes continued to portray the same helplessness and potential for humiliation that characterized the childhood experiences. In her outside life at this time there was a diminution of phobias. She was beginning to be aware of her own wishes and was able to tolerate more the experience of pleasure.

Termination phase. After noting a marked diminution in her phobias and a freedom to assert herself in various transactions, the patient reported the following dream. "I was in the analytic session and you said, 'Why don't you take off your clothes?' So I did. I was putting on my nightgown and getting into bed when suddenly with a feeling of triumph I said to myself, 'This is a dream.' Then it turned back into a couch and I had my clothes on." The patient then remarked how naive and stupid she used to be in reporting dreams. "How surprised I was when you said, 'It's your dream.' These are my wishes." She then reported several instances of an end to her helplessness in social situations and with seductive men.

Somewhat later in the termination period she reported pleasure in activities for which she was previously phobic, and was able to recognize that she would miss the analyst when the analysis was completed. She was much more mistress of her own destiny. She dreamed: "I was doing a dinner party stuffing a pepper. You came over to help me. You were doing it the lazy way, and I realized I would have to do it over. I thought I'd quietly do it over, but then I asked you to do it right and you changed without any protest." In association, she reported several instances in which her marriage had changed because of her assertiveness and her ability to recognize and stand up for her own wishes. She remembered that in the past she had always handled her wishes through denial, passivity, and revenge fantasies.

The dreams in the termination phase show an end to the helplessness and passivity, that she can work together with the analyst, and is sometimes the one who knows more. For this patient, the dream "This is a dream" represents more an integration of an observing ego than a defense (Marianne Goldberger, personal communication). These UTD's are consistent with Oremland's (1973) view that in a successful analysis UTD's in the termination phase portray modifications of the symptoms that the patient had presented at the start of analysis.

CONCEPTUAL ASPECTS OF UNDISGUISED TRANSFERENCE DREAMS

This chapter presents three categories of undisguised transference dreams in a variety of patients. The appearance of the analyst in the manifest dream gives the "sense of the dream" (Sloane 1975), reflecting that part of the preconscious that represents the surface level of a conflict. Sloane states: "The manifest dream can be fully understood only after the patient's associations to it are combined with what the analyst himself can contribute from his knowledge of the patient beforehand as well as from his clinical experience, theoretical background and familiarity with symbols" (p. 62).

The theoretical position taken here is that, in the clinical vignettes presented, the appearance of the analyst as himself reflected the patients' defensive barrier against transference feelings. In the first category of patients are those UTD's which appear immediately after a break in the analytic barrier—whether the break is due to countertransference, necessary arrangements, or extra-analytic events. The sudden reality of the analyst as a person in an otherwise abstinent analysis is a vivid event which in some patients has traumatic impact. The dream appearance of the analyst as himself served both as an attempt to work through the trauma and as an attempt to ward off the impact of the analyst as a transference figure. In at least one instance (Case 3) the barrier break mobilized conflicts over intimacy.

In the second group, the UTD's occurred as a defense against deepening libidinal transference where there was no break in the analytic barrier. The patients insisted on portraying the analyst as real to help ward off the memories from the past that were evoked by the transference.

Finally, the patient who portrayed the undisguised analyst in dreams throughout her analysis combined a characterological need to avoid caring deeply about anyone lest she be overwhelmed by affect with the need to rework childhood traumas. The chief transference position for much of this patient's analysis was a defensive one with the isolated affect appearing in the dreams. The question remains why this patient continued to dream so often in the same mode throughout her analysis. Goldberger has suggested that for patients whose reality testing and perceptions have been entwined in childhood seductions, there may always be subtle realities in the analysis that have the quality of a break in the analytic barrier. Further, the patient was a creative person who perhaps used dreams as a creative vehicle for struggling with conflict. It is possible that the impetus for the continuing UTD's was that she was still working through some very early traumatic events in the termination phase. Finally, as Rothstein (1978, p. 9) emphasizes, there is a "diversity and complexity of meanings that are subsumed under the rubric of dreams of the analyst undisguised." In the termination phase, the analyst appeared as a helper in the therapeutic alliance as well as a transference representative of early trauma.

References

Bernstein, I., and Fine, B. C. (1969). The Manifest Content of the Dream. In Kris Study Group, Monograph III, pp. 59–113. New York: International Universities Press.

Blum, H. P. (1973). The concept of erotized transference. *Journal of the American Psychoanalytic Association* 21:61–76.

Bradlow, P. A., and Coen, S. J. (1975). The analyst undisguised in the initial dream in psychoanalysis. *International Journal of Psycho-Analysis* 56:415–426.

Feldman, S. (1945). Interpretation of a typical and stereotyped dream met with only during psychoanalysis. *Psychoanalytic Quarterly* 14: 511–515.

Gitelson, M. (1952). The emotional position of the analyst in the psychoanalytic situation. *International Journal of Psycho-Analysis* 33: 1–10.

Harris, I. D. (1962). Dreams about the analyst. *International Journal of Psycho-Analysis* 43:151–158.

Oremland, J. D. (1973). A specific dream during the termination phase of successful psychoanalysis. *Journal of the American Psychoanalytic Association* 21:285–302.

Rappaport, E. A. (1959). The first dream in an erotized transference. *International Journal of Psycho-Analysis* 40:240–245.

Rosenbaum, M. (1965). Dreams in which the analyst appears undisguised: a clinical and statistical study. *International Journal of Psycho-Analysis* 46:429–437.

Rothstein, A. (1978). Towards a place for "the analyst undisguised" in the psychoanalytic theory of dream analysis. Presented at the midwinter meeting of the American Psychoanalytic Association. New York, December 14, 1978.

Savitt, R. A. (1969). Transference, somatization and symbiotic need. *Journal of the American Psychoanalytic Association* 17:1030–1054.

Sloane, P. (1975). The significance of the manifest dream: its use and misuse. *Journal of the Philadelphia Association for Psycho-Analysis* 2:57–78.

Yazmajian, R. V. (1964). First dreams directly representing the analyst. *Psychoanalytic Quarterly* 33:536–551.

CHAPTER 3

THE DREAM AS A CURATIVE FANTASY

Roy M. Whitman, M.D.

In the course of a psychoanalysis or during psychoanalytic therapy, most often at the beginning but sometimes after a number of years, patients reveal significantly organized wishes for what they hope to get from their contact with the analyst or therapist (Ornstein and Ornstein 1977). The term *curative fantasy,* mentioned in the title, will be reserved for the psychotherapeutic situation, though it is worth noting that such fantasies are often mobilized during the course of highly intense relationships such as marriage, major crisis experiences, intense friendships or love affairs, or even educational experiences.

Sometimes these curative fantasies are expressed in the form of a directly stated wish; at other times, in the form of a guilt-defined fantasy; but most succinctly in the form of a dream.[1] Though sometimes this wish is clearly stated, in other instances interfering motives, usually self-imposed, present the wish as often in a frustrated as in a gratified way. Nevertheless, how the therapist responds to these wishes is often the content as well as a way to the success of the whole treatment. The transference implied in such a wish and the countertransference it stimulates are often the crux or nodal point of the treamtment relation-

1. Though Schafer (1968) has pointed out that there is a certain logical inconsistency in the use of the term unconscious fantasy, nevertheless common usage in psychoanalytic discussions and literature makes the term "unconscious fantasy" commonly accepted and expressed via dreams or other primary process type thinking.

ship. The recognition of and response to these wishes will be the subject of this chapter.

CURATIVE FANTASY DEFINED

A curative fantasy has three characteristics: (1) an interrelationship with, or emotional response from, another person; (2) something transmitted in this relationship via *(a)* identification, *(b)* teaching or education, *(c)* interactional quality, or *(d)* insight; and (3) the return of the patient to his or her former life and other relationships, now changed in some significant way.

Though every curative fantasy does not have all three characteristics in its ultimate form, they may be identified or inferred. The use of a clinical example will quickly make clear what is meant by this term.

A patient after a period of analysis had the following dream: "My husband brought me to your office and sat waiting for me in the waiting room. Instead of your office it was a large dance floor. You chose me to dance among a number of other women, just a few of whom I recognized. At first we started to dance with you leading, holding each other's hand, much as one dances with a small child. As we continued to dance I watched the way you did it, and you led me in subtle ways by pushing or inclining your head, and gradually I moved closer to you and we danced more the way that a man and woman do. At one point we danced by the waiting room and I was afraid that my husband would see me through the glass door. This made me uncomfortable. Soon the dance was over and you brought me back to the waiting room. My husband and I left together."

Although this dream emerged only after several years of analysis, it is fairly clear even from the manifest content that the patient interacts with the therapist in an emotionally charged way (dancing). The patient learns via identification, teaching, interaction, and perhaps even insight. The end product of these four modes of communication is indicated by her changing from a little girl to a woman in the course of the dancing, and finally and importantly, she is returned to her husband.

REPARATIVE FANTASY AND CURATIVE FANTASY

A reparative fantasy has some of the characteristics of the curative fantasy but in a vastly circumscribed form. There is still interaction with another person, but only a small part of the person is changed. Again, to offer a clinical example, a male graduate student after a number of months of analysis with very little headway in resolving his severe depression presented the following dream:

"I had a large black lesion on my forearm. You were going to cauterize it with silver nitrate. It was amazing. It started to become gray and then lighter and lighter and gradually disappeared. I was very impressed by your skill in applying the cotton swab to the lesion. The lesion was about the size of a silver dollar."

This was a patient who resisted psychoanalysis, could see no merit in depth investigation into his current and past life, and insisted that the analyst give him antidepressant medication. Finally, his depression was getting so debilitating that he was unable to function, and he asked to be hospitalized or given antidepressant medication. Time-released imipramine, 75 mg., was prescribed and the patient immediately started to get better over a period of ten days and remained well at a two-year follow-up. He continued psychoanalysis for another four months, was very pleased with his symptomatic improvement, but showed the same reluctance to make a commitment to the analysis or to get involved in an intense therapeutic relationship.

INFANTILE FANTASY: A PRECURSOR TO CURATIVE FANTASY

A third term that is relevant is the infantile fantasy. The infantile fantasy is often the precursor of both the curative and reparative fantasies. Many patients come in and state quite openly that they want the therapist to "wave a magic wand" and make them well. Other patients, even in the course of the first few interviews, will express wishes of marrying the therapist, having sex with the therapist, or being taken into the home of the therapist and his family. Requests for hypnosis or other forms of symptomatic therapy often are requests for reparation or else hide infantile fantasies of being given the potency or magical powers of the therapist in some incorporative way.

Curative fantasies may be stated either in very direct, simplistic ways or may emerge as extremely subtle forms of interchange as best exemplified by dreams.

DIRECTLY STATED WISHES

A patient came into the V.A. hospital in an acute schizophrenic decompensation. When he reorganized sufficiently to participate in an interview, he began by insisting that he could be helped by any psychiatrist who did not "yell" at him! He related this request very clearly to an overly critical father of whom he had always felt terrified.

Often a patient will make direct statements about wanting a specific therapist, or a therapist of a specific sex because of insufficient fathering, mothering, or other deficient relationships. Implicit in many of these direct requests is the concept, held by patients in these instances, of the corrective emotional experience. Patients seem to understand that if "they could only do it over again" with somebody else who is significantly different from the important other figure in their life, the outcome would be different in a major way.

SUBTLY STATED WISHES IN DREAMS

Kohut (1977), in *The Restoration of the Self,* cites the case of a woman who came to him for a second analysis. During the third year of her analysis she dreamed she was standing over a toilet urinating and was vaguely aware that someone was watching her from behind. Kohut states that the patient had had many similar dreams with a female analyst, and that this woman had repeatedly interpreted the dreams as the patient wanting a penis and wanting to urinate standing up like a male. Kohut, by contrast, pointed out that a more basic wish was to extricate herself from a damaging relationship with a bizarre, emotionally shallow mother and to turn toward a more down-to-earth practical father. This suggestion led to memories that her mother had warned her never to sit on toilets outside their own house. The toilet seat became symbolically the world, a dangerous, infecting, and frightening place. Her wish to have some contact with her father's penis was a sexualized rendition of her attempt to turn to him for a positive, vigorous, nonparanoid attitude toward the world.

This brief case vignette and dream not only demonstrate an extremely subtle wish, but also show that a simple interpretation of an infantile fantasy, that is, the wish to obtain a penis-baby from the oedipal father, may have been operative in the patient, but was only the underpinning for a much more important aspect of herself—a healthy, joyous relationship to the outside world.

It is difficult to determine the source of this self-awareness of what the patient needs from another human being. We see in this example that the hoped for interaction with the analyst is with a male who will get her into healthy, direct, and strong contact with the outside world. This contrasts with the fearful, paranoid attitude that the mother had instilled in her. While Kohut uses this example to emphasize the importance of the self in contrast to the usual oedipal penis-envy concept that is part of classical psychoanalysis, for our purposes it stands as a subtle and sensitive curative fantasy that the person brought into the analytic situation via a dream.

DREAMS AND PSEUDOCURATIVE FANTASIES

In the course of psychotherapeutic work with some patients, the patient may attempt to complete what would seem to be a curative fantasy via the psychotherapeutic process. A patient who had been in analysis several years reported to his analyst the following dream:

"I was driving along a road and there were two farm houses. One was a small one and one was a large one in the background. I drove up to the small one and found out that it had been completely redone inside and outside. I was very pleased." The patient associated to how much he had accomplished in his analysis in redoing aspects of himself. During supervision it was pointed out (to the student analyst by this writer) that the large farmhouse was completely untouched and unmentioned in the patient's associations and that this paralleled the patient's unwillingness to go into large areas of his personality which were probably even more germane to his illness than the area he had redone. In the supervisory discussion we considered this a pseudotermination fantasy, but it has also occurred to me that this could also be considered a pseudocurative fantasy.

CURATIVE FANTASY AND CORRECTIVE EMOTIONAL EXPERIENCE

A patient with extreme phobic anxiety during the course of the psychoanalytic treatment consistently badgered the therapist to give him oxazepam for the various occasions during which he experienced or expected to experience acute anxiety. The therapist stood firm over a number of hours, but finally the patient pointed out insistently that the therapist was exactly like the patient's rigid father who had never given in on any given issue once he had enunciated a stand. The therapist finally agreed to give him five capsules of oxazepam to take with him on a trip to Florida, for extreme anxiety about taking off on both legs of his flight.

In discussing this example with the student analyst, I suggested, as supervisor, that the analyst had a certain justification in yielding at this point to the onslaught of the patient by being different from the totally rigid, nonyielding father. This seemed to make sense on one level, yet on another level an important countertransference was indicated.

The countertransference suggested that the patient was increasing, in larger and larger doses, his attacks on the analyst, and that the analyst had a great need to be "a good guy." In addition, the analyst was willing to share with me that he had lost his own father when he was quite small and experienced that as an ongoing void in his life. It was, therefore, very important for him to see himself as a giving father figure. What would seem to have been an important corrective emotional experience also had this significant countertransference: being the good father and giving the patient what he had not gotten himself.

Nevertheless, the coexistence of the curative fantasy and the corrective emotional experience deserves some attention. Probably, most analysts have appropriately disregarded some of the technical recommendations given by Alexander and French in *Psychoanalytic Therapy* (1946) in playing certain roles or manipulating the transference in a way that would bring about a productive emotional experience. Nevertheless, the concept still exists as a useful one if the role-playing, artificial aspects of the therapist's behavior are eliminated. Only rarely is a specific therapeutic action indicated over and above interpretation, and I have described such an instance in a section of a dream study entitled *The Dream as a Prescription* (Whitman et al. 1970).

Broadly, one might say that many neuroses that Freud faced in the latter half of the nineteenth century involved overstimulation on the part of a closely knit family unit; therefore, the corrective emotional experience was quite appropriately one of nonintrusiveness, respectful listening, and minimal activity. However, the neuroses of the twentieth century seem to be much more of a narcissistic type. In this regard, again in broad terms, there is a question of understimulation in which the child has been brought up vis-à-vis self-absorbed and unempathic parents. The corrective emotional experience in these instances consists of much more activity and more human interchange with the patient, more and freer responses to questions, and a much more natural, spontaneous give-and-take with the patient than was indicated in the neuroses of overstimulation. These, however, comprise a background corrective emotional experience and can be subsumed under the general rubric of the nonspecific effects of psychoanalytic psychotherapy or psychoanalysis.

The specific effects are much more related to the working-through of the curative fantasy or fantasies and the particular wishes which must not be responded to (the rule of abstinence still holds) but must be recognized and empathized with. We can see, therefore, that the concept of the corrective emotional experience may have some usefulness in terms of the overall stance of the analyst, but it has little use in terms of responding to the specific curative fantasy of the patient. In this regard role-playing or deliberate, conscious "acting the opposite of" often hides (as indicated in the earlier example of oxazepam) some specific countertransference stance of the therapist.

SOURCES OF CURATIVE FANTASY

We are faced with the source and organization of the curative fantasy. As Thomas French (1965) pointed out in one of his last studies, Cannon's idea of the "wisdom of the human body" is quite applicable to the wisdom of the human mind. This is also relevant to some of the comments in Spock's book on *Baby and Child Care* (1968) that children given the choice of various diets will choose the one which will be balanced and most beneficial to them.

This whole concept is closely related to an earlier remark that I made in my study on remembering dreams (Whitman 1963) in which I quoted Freud (1915) as saying, "It is not only quite possible but highly probable that the dreamer really does know the meaning of his dream; only he does not know that he knows and therefore thinks that he does not." Other authors such as Anna Freud (1965) have commented on the growth potential of the human being in a psychological sense, and Horney (1939) and Maslow (1954) have commented on the self-actualizing potential in all human beings.

In addition to this, Bettelheim (1977), in his recent book on fairy tales, has alluded to the importance of the fairy tale as offering coping devices for the significant conflicts of humankind. For example, he says that a typical ending of a fairy tale, ".... and they lived happily ever after," does not indicate for a moment to the child that eternal life is possible. But it does indicate "that which alone can take the sting out of the narrow limits of our time on this earth: forming a truly satisfying bond to another." The fairy tale also tells us in this connection that when one has found true adult love, one does not need to wish for eternal life. Bettelheim emphasizes repeatedly that a true, deep, interpersonal relationship enables the human being to escape the separation anxiety which haunts all of us.

ALL PARTS OF CURATIVE FANTASY NECESSARY FOR CURE

Though I intend to elaborate on the misfiring of the curative fantasy in a later study, I would like to give one example as to why all parts of the curative fantasy should be present either in an actuality or by implication.

When I was a student at the Chicago Institute for Psychoanalysis, the advanced diagnostic seminar used the technique of having an initial workup presented to the group. Predictions were then made by the class as to the outcome of the analysis, and the analyst returned to give the course of the analysis and any follow-up material that was available.

One particular analytic case which was presented as a "success" has always haunted me. This was the case of a twenty-eight-year-old single girl who entered analysis, worked through a strong heterosexual transference to the analyst, and after seven years of analysis felt that she had worked through her fear, envy, and dread of men. At thirty-five, the analysis was completed, and a three-year follow-up study, which the analyst was kind enough to undertake for purposes of the seminar, revealed that at the age of thirty-eight, she was leading a quite isolated life although she felt that she was receptive to a relationship with a man. While, of course, the realities and exigencies of life could thwart her "readiness," I could not help but feel that the final part of the curative fantasy was missing—the patient could not return to a real life experience nor did the analyst help her in making that return. She remained fixed in her transference to the analyst, although he felt it had been resolved.

In a similar vein the initial aspect of the curative fantasy, that is, leaving a significant other in order to enter into a relationship with the analyst, must also be present. In this regard I can only mention in passing frequent experiences of many therapists in which the patient is unable to achieve a commitment to the analysis because of a fear or anxiety about the threat that this would pose to another relationship such as to a parent or spouse.

Infantile fantasies, reparative fantasies, and curative fantasies may all be layered in a hierarchical way. They then derive their strength from more archaic and magical infantile wishes which are transformed into realizable, circumscribed (reparative), or widespread, structurally re-organizing (curative) components. Thus, a patient who came into analysis saying that her main complaint was "I am doing all right but *something is missing,"* was found to have (1) an infantile wish for a penis; (2) the hope that the analyst could provide the missing penis or, in a more evolved way, give a baby to her; and (3) at the level of the curative fantasy, the hope that she could engage in a growth-producing interactive relationship which would attenuate and ameliorate the emptiness which had been her response to an unempathic mother (the concept that Kohut [1971] describes as transmuting internalization).

DREAMS AS THE BEST FORM OF CURATIVE FANTASY

This study is a report on the dream as the most striking statement of the curative fantasy. Dreams, above all forms of communication, succinctly express curative fantasies either early or during the course of psychoanalytic psychotherapy. Because of conflicting or even self-frustrating wishes, the specific outlines of the curative fantasy may not become sharply delineated until some time into the therapy or analysis. It is important that the therapist understand and help the patient work through the curative fantasy without feeling that a specific response to it will provide the necessary health-producing growth that the patient envisions. Fairy tales, life experiences, and the innate wisdom of the body provide the impetus for the formation of these fantasies, and it behooves every therapist to pay careful attention to them if he is going to provide more than nonspecific therapeutic leverage toward getting the patient well.

References

Alexander, F., and French, T. M. (1946). *Psychoanalytic Therapy: Principles and Application.* New York: Ronald Press.
Bettelheim, B. (1977). *The Uses of Enchantment.* New York: Alfred A. Knopf.
French, T. M. (1965). The cognitive structure of behavior. Presented to the Chicago Psychoanalytic Society.
Freud, A. (1965). *Normality and Pathology in Childhood.* New York: International Universities Press.

Freud, S. (1915–1916). Introductory lectures on psycho-analysis. *Standard Edition* 15:15–239.

Horney, K. (1939). *New Ways in Psychoanalysis.* New York: Norton.

Kohut, H. (1971). *The Analysis of the Self.* New York: International Universities Press.

—— (1977). The oedipus complex and the psychology of the self. In *The Restoration of the Self.* New York: International Universities Press.

Maslow, A. H. (1954). *Motivation and Personality.* New York: Harper.

Ornstein, P. H., and Ornstein, A. (1977). On the continuing evolution of psychoanalytic psychotherapy: reflections upon recent trends and some predictions for the future. *Annual of Psychoanalysis* 5: 329–370.

Shafer, R. (1968). *Aspects of Internalization.* New York: International Universities Press.

Spock, Benjamin (1968). *Baby and Child Care.* New York: Hawthorn Books.

Whitman, R. M. (1963). Remembering and forgetting dreams in psychoanalysis. *Journal of the American Psychoanalytic Association* 11:752–774.

Whitman, R. M., Kramer, M., Ornstein, P. H., and Baldridge, B. J. (1970). The varying uses of the dream in clinical psychiatry. In *The Psychodynamic Implications of the Physiological Studies on Dreams,* eds. L. Madow and L. H. Snow. Springfield, Ill.: Charles C Thomas.

CHAPTER 4

A COLLABORATIVE ACCOUNT
OF A PSYCHOANALYSIS
THROUGH DREAMS

[Anonymous]

Written accounts of a psychoanalysis are always at least once removed from the living process, the actual experience as it occurs over hundreds of hours in the complex relationship between analyst and patient. It is difficult to express such a personal, emotional, and idiosyncratically symbolized experience in a written report. An additional difficulty is that reports of analyses are typically written by the analyst—though sometimes by the patient—and either way they convey the experience from the point of view of one of the participants and not the other. Yet an analysis is a two-person transaction and a full accounting should ideally present both points of view. Many modern views of psychoanalysis stress the interactive and collaborative nature of the therapeutic process. Thus, while a "case study" written by the analyst-doctor about the patient may have been consistent with the medical origins of psychoanalysis, a collaborative study is more in keeping with analysis as we now conceptualize it, that is, in terms of a therapeutic *alliance* with tranference and countertransference at the core.

For these reasons, it seemed to us that it would be valuable to present an account of an analysis that is, like the analysis itself, a collaboration. But how can this be done? No doubt there are many ways: here is the way we

The names and other identifying material have been altered to protect the confidentiality of the participants. Requests for information should be directed to the editor.

chose. Shortly after we began the analysis we discussed the possibility of a collaborative study. At this early point, it was not clear what the exact form of the study would be, and we did not want it to interfere with the analysis itself. But we thought that dreams might provide a personally symbolic version of the patient's unconscious as it unfolded and changed over the course of treatment. With the present study in mind, the analyst kept a written record of all reported dreams, the major associations to those dreams, and his interpretations. Insofar as possible, we kept the study from interfering with the analysis itself; the dreams and associations were reported by the patient and interpreted by the analyst in accord with standard analytic practice, and we kept in abeyance the questions of if, how, and when we would do anything with the material.

Approximately a year and a half after the conclusion of the analysis it seemed clear that the termination had been successful, the patient was doing well, and we decided to pursue our earlier plan for a collaborative study. Thus, we must stress that this study is *retrospective;* using the dream material as our guide we are now, independently and together, looking back and discussing the state of the patient, the course of the analysis, and the reasons for its outcome.

The analysis covered a period of three years and three months—over 500 hours—with well over 500 recorded dreams. From January to June of the first year we met twice a week in face-to-face psychoanalytic therapy. This will be referred to as the *preliminary phase.* From July to December of that first year we met four times a week with the patient on the couch; this will be referred to as the *early phase.* From January to September of the second year, at the patient's request, we met five times a week, reverting to four times a week from October until the conclusion of the analysis. This second year and the first six months of the third year will be referred to as the *middle phase.* July to December of the third year and January to March of the fourth, when the analysis terminated by mutual consent, will be referred to as the *final phase.* The patient selected one dream from the preliminary phase. We each independently selected six dreams—two from the early phase, two from the middle phase, and two from the final phase—giving a total sample of thirteen dreams. Each of us went through the total sample of dreams and selected our subsample in the following ways: the patient chose dreams that seemed especially vivid and memorable and that were connected with major insights, break-throughs of emotion, or illumination of conflict and unconscious dynam-ics. The analyst was generally guided by the same criteria.

The course of the analysis and the place of the thirteen dreams within it are represented in the following chart. The dreams will be identified by phase and date in the discussion that follows.

TABLE: SEQUENTIAL PROGRESSION OF DREAMS

PHASE	TIME SPAN	DREAMS
Preliminary	January–June, first year	March 3
Early	July–December, first year	June 26, July 1, September 10, October 25
Middle	January–December, second year	April 16, 18, and 29
	January–June, third year	June 13 (all second year)
Final	July–December, third year	August 16, February 18
	January–March, fourth year	March 14, 24

The thirteen dreams comprise the "data" of this retrospective, collaborative study. We put data in quotation marks since it is clear that we both drew on the store of memories, feelings, thoughts, and additional associations that remained with us from the experience. Each of us, working with these thirteen dreams, and other memories, attempted to describe the major unconscious themes and conflicts, the way these manifested themselves in the patient's life and in the transference, and how they were progressively revealed and modified over the course of the analysis. In addition, each of us attempted to describe what seemed to him the major factors that made this particular analysis successful. We each wrote a draft divided into three sections: (1) a description of the patient at the beginning of the analysis, (2) a discussion of the course of the analysis based on the dreams from the four phases, and (3) our different perceptions of what made the analysis a success. When we had independently prepared the drafts of these three sections, we then met, like the coauthors of a book, to compare our drafts, note similarities and differences, and combine our accounts into the collaborative version that makes up the major portion of this paper. For the sake of completeness we could present these separate drafts in their entirety and let the reader judge them for himself. But this, it seemed to us, would produce too lengthy and repetitious a manuscript. So what we have done is this: we have rewritten our independent accounts of the first two sections into a single version that covers all those aspects of the descriptions on which we agree. Points of difference—things that the analyst discussed that the patient left out and vice versa or differences in our views of the same material—are noted and discussed either as they arise or at the end of each of these sections. For the final section, which covers the reasons for the success of the analysis, we present the independently drafted accounts in their entirety and then the discussion from our collaborative meeting.

THE PATIENT AT THE BEGINNING
OF THE ANALYSIS

The patient was a man in his late thirties, married, and the father of three children: a daughter of sixteen, a son of fourteen, and a daughter of eight. He was a professor of literature at a top-ranked university, a successful teacher and scholar, with some additional success with semi-popular writing. (The analyst noted that there were some neurotic inhibitions with respect to writing.) He was an active, athletic individual and a talented amateur carpenter; in addition to his professional work he had remodeled several houses, doing most of the work himself. The patient spoke of the close and enduring nature of his marriage and the deep concern he and his wife shared over rearing their children in the best possible way. He commented, as well, on the resentments and sexual conflicts in the marriage and noted how he unconsciously cast his wife in the role of his mother, feeling angry, rivalrous, and guilty toward her. The analyst noted these same conflicts, which he described in somewhat stronger terms: he saw the patient's unsatisfactory sex life as a major reason for the seeking of treatment. The analyst noted that the patient's wife intermittently "flipped out" (suffered weeklong anxiety attacks with some loss of the sense of reality), and that this frightened the patient—and the analyst. Interestingly, the patient made no mention of these in his account.

Both of us agreed that the chief complaint at the outset of the treatment was *depression.* The patient described chronic, low-level depression, overcontrol of emotions, compulsive overwork, and underlying feelings of guilt and inferiority—all in the face of his outward success and achievements. The analyst's description emphasized depression and pervasive guilt. He described the patient's initial presentation of himself as extremely apprehensive, serious, soft-spoken, gentle, and deferential. We both noted the contrast between the patient's public personality—successful in work and family, insightful about others, seemingly insightful about himself, and psychologically sophisticated—and the inner feelings of guilt, anxiety, and depression.

The patient was the older of two sons of second generation Jewish parents, born and reared in a middle-class community near New York City. His mother suffered from a variety of neurotic-somatic symptoms for most of her life, culminating in a major depression, with attempted suicide, hospitalization, and electric shock therapy when the patient was twenty-five. Another such episode occurred during the period of the analysis. The analyst saw the relationship to the mother as the primary determinant of the patient's neurosis: he spoke of the mother's idolization of the patient, of his being a narcissistic extension of her, and of his symbiotic attachment to her. The patient felt guilty for going away to college and this guilt became enormous following the mother's major depression, which occurred while he was away in graduate school.

The patient described his father as hardworking yet self-defeating and emotionally overcontrolled. There had been much closeness in the early years that had soured from early adolescence onward. The analyst also discussed the loss of the earlier, closer relationship with the father, seeing it as the second most important determinant of the patient's neurosis.

On most of the major dimensions we saw the patient in the same way at the beginning of treatment: the guilt and depression, the major role of the relationship with the highly neurotic mother, the repetition of this in the marriage, and the significance of father's emotional distance. The difference in our description of these dimensions was one of degree: the analyst saw the conflicts, guilt, and depression more starkly while the patient, consistent with his lifelong style of emotional control, tended to dampen them down a bit. The analyst mentioned the wife's anxiety attacks while the patient did not. In our discussion of this difference, we thought the omission by the patient might be due to his resolution of the mother transference, so that, postanalysis, he no longer viewed his wife's difficulties as his.

One final point of difference needs to be noted. The analyst mentioned that he had briefly seen the patient's mother during her first major depression some twelve years before the onset of the present analysis. The attempt at therapy was unsuccessful. The patient did not include this event in his draft. He knew of his mother's short sojourn with the analyst yet felt it had no bearing on his own selection of him, which had been made on the recommendation of other psychoanalysts that he knew through his profession. The analyst speculated that the unconscious meaning might have been: if he (the analyst) could not relate to the mother—if she fled from him—he represented too great a threat to her self-deceptions, and therefore the patient could rely on him in his struggle against the internalized mother. In our discussion of this point, the patient essentially agreed, saying that in his view it made them allies, since no one, including his father, had ever been able to deal successfully with mother. The fact of the analyst's brief contact with the mother seemed to the patient of minor significance, and it did not come up much in the analysis itself.

DREAMS IN PRELIMINARY PHASE

Dream of March 3. "I am riding a three-wheel full-size bicycle, pulling a little wagon-trailer behind with my father and uncle (father's brother) in it. I have some long pieces of lumber balanced on my shoulder. I am riding on the streets approaching the old neighborhood where I lived as a kid. I am biking along rather easily despite the heavy load. I see two young women who are hitchhiking, trying to get to the old neighborhood. They are rather unkempt-looking and not very attractive. Someone says, 'Don't bother picking them up. They can get there with their cunts.' Then the road begins to rise slightly and the bicycling becomes extremely difficult. I am looking down at the ball bearings in the front wheel of the bike which seem to be grinding as I struggle to carry the heavy load up the incline. The feeling is that this seemed so easy when I started but now it's become a terrible burden, almost impossible.

"The scene then shifts and I enter a large beautiful house with a glass roof—so big that trees and plants are growing inside. There are pieces of antique furniture, a round oak table and other pieces, some of which are slightly burned as if there had been a fire. They were a bit damaged but still valuable. I think of sneaking back into this house later to take or steal some of the valuable antiques. Later that night as I sneak in, I see one set of rooms that are lit and have radio music coming out of them. I become very frightened, as if the people in there are going to get me, and the dream turns into a running away and fear scene. I wake up very frightened."

Associations. The bicycle ball bearings and lumber on the shoulder remind him of a hernia that he got from carrying lumber upstairs in one of the houses he worked on in one of his frantic, hardworking, remodeling periods. The beautiful old house looks like the glass building, an arboretum, that he saw in a park. The old furniture reminds him of the furniture from childhood, and the way his remodeling efforts relate to fixing up houses that resemble the house he lived in as a child. He thinks that his father and uncle have never succeeded in life, despite intelligence and opportunity, whereas he is a big success. The furniture with burned edges makes him think of Mother and her electric shock therapy. The room with radio music also connects to Mother—he remembers how she always lay in bed in the afternoons listening to the radio.

Interpretation. None given this early in the analysis.

We both see the first part of the dream as portraying the patient's neurotic character structure: that he will save the world through hard work; nobody else can do it as well as he (father, uncle, the cunts); he can perform almost superhuman (and Christlike, he carries his cross) feats. It also shows how unbearable, how depressing and painful (he is breaking his balls, getting a hernia) this mode of life has become. Entering analysis is a search for relief. The overdone nature of this posture—which the dream captures—suggests it is covering up an opposite set of wishes and feelings.

The second part of the dream reveals more of the unconscious wishes behind the overdone masculine-hardworking surface. The beautiful house and furniture reflect the wish to return to an enjoyable childhood close to Mother. As a young boy he began remodeling furniture for Mommy, and his efforts with houses connect with his search for her love: if he can just get his present surroundings to resemble the old ones, he will recapture a state of bliss. But the "cunts," the stealing, the sneaking around bedrooms at night all suggest the guilty sexual wishes for Mother. The analyst in particular noted that the theme of stealing—reflecting self-depreciation, envy and guilt—was very prominent in the early period of the analysis. The burned furniture–electric shock association is a reminder of mother's present burned-out, depressed state: visible evidence of both his guilt (he should have "saved" her in his Christlike fashion) and the futility of his wishes to return to the past (the old neighborhood).

The dream can also be viewed in its transference meanings. The patient described these as follows: first, he must be the strong one who carries the inept analyst-father on their journey together. Then he wants to give that up and regress to a blissful, childlike state with the analyst as the loving mother. And in anticipation of where this will lead there are representations of the major sources of anxiety and guilt: an intimate closeness with the analyst as mother, with guilt over the sexual and competitive aspects of this wish, and fear that it will once again become a guilty, depressing mess as it did with his actual mother.

Both of us noted the hint of homosexuality in the dream—carrying the men behind, the overdone masculinity, the repudiation of the "cunts," and the "queer" vehicle—suggesting homosexual transference elements. The patient summed up the transference images as (1) the inept father-uncle, (2) the wish for the loving mother, and (3) the wish for a loving father. All three are threatening: either he will have to bear the burden of work himself, or he will feel frightened and guilty or embarrassed and humiliated over incestuous impulses and homosexual wishes. The state of the transference at this preliminary phase is one of aroused threat, anxiety, and danger. The analyst summarized his view in the following way: the dream shows inverted aggression and concealed sexuality along with excellent ego functions, a good capacity for human relationships, and a readiness for transference—with much fear of the transference.

Summarizing the differences in our accounts we note that on most major points we agree. The patient gave a stronger emphasis to his "macho" exterior, and the analyst emphasized self-depreciating feelings and the narcissistic (Christlike) elements which the patient still has some tendency to avoid seeing. On the other hand, the patient (this was true of later times in the analysis as well as at this early point) sees his house remodeling as a part of his neurotic character that the analyst never seemed to fully interpret or analyze. In retrospect, the analyst agreed that this was a countertransference problem; the analyst was in awe of the patient's real skill in this area, in contrast to his own lack of skill, and therefore did not fully appreciate its neurotic components (for example, that it was done to please Mommy-wife, to counter feelings of inferiority, or in place of professional work and writing). The work itself was not neurotic, but the fantasy that he could do everything to his house while simultaneously carrying out all his other responsibilities was.

DREAMS IN EARLY PHASE

Dream of June 26, first year. "My wife and I are going to a group meeting or to dinner with two or three other couples. Someone starts to criticize my table manners and I feel more and more angry, but I squelch it. One guy is the chief critic and I have the urge to flip the table over, but I stop myself. The guy has the same impulse so we both do it together. A fistfight starts and I enjoy hitting and being hit—the give and take—but it also feels inauthentic. I worry how I will explain the bruises on my face to a female student the next morning. The opponent reminds me of my brother and of a male graduate student. I apologize to the other couples for ruining the group meeting with a big fight. I go to the bathroom before leaving. It's very fancy. I feel anxious that I can't lock the two doors while urinating. An older woman, who looks like Joan Crawford, walks in while I am putting my penis back in my pants. I want to leave and am furious with my wife for delaying. I'm about to explode at her when she finally leaves."

Associations and interpretation. Earlier in the hour the patient was anxious about some minor critical feelings towards the analyst. The analyst suggested that the fear of anger to him seems to be connected to family responsibility, as though he does not have the right to enjoy some open anger. The patient then talks about another dream which reminds him of just this feeling. Other associations: he gets very angry in a sexually jealous way when his wife dawdles at parties or with other people and keeps him waiting, and when he feels she ignores him for someone else. In general, there is the feeling that good boys don't fight; good boys are loved. In this dream he comes closer than ever to getting some satisfaction out of fighting.

Dream of July 1, first year. "Cousin Karen is driving a putt-putt that has a bedlike contraption in the back of it. She is driving it around the block. The whole dream has a relaxed, amusing quality. Also, there is a little girl named McNally, from grammar school days, who is there."

Associations. The dream seems to be about pretty little girls. Over the weekend he and his family visited their friends, the Coughlins. Mrs. Coughlin's maiden name was McNally. Today he is being interviewed by a newspaper reporter about his book. He wonders if the analyst has read his book; it's really about himself. He used to have good feelings about his childhood but hardly ever has them anymore; he feels like a happy kid who is now an unhappy adult. Since the analysis more feelings are coming out—but they are largely unhappy ones. If he lets himself go, he would cry. He feels burdened: by so much to do, so many responsibilities, and also by holding so many feelings in.

Interpretation. The dream reflects the wish for adolescent, pubertal-latency carefree days and evenings. Starting to come to the analysis four times a week may evoke these yearnings and may tie up with some feminine aspects of these yearnings. The patient says, "That's interesting." There is a lot regarding the analysis that is uncomfortable. Most of the feelings emerging are uncomfortable, regressive, childlike. The idea of being a girl connects with his "macho" feelings and his denial of emotion. It all converges in the image of being Mommy's little boy—sensitive, easy to cry, and that he must overcontrol himself. Then for the rest of the hour he becomes relatively silent—heavy sighs, talks about being blocked up and filled with emotion, and hopes that coming more often will magically lift these feelings. (In the next hour, there was a big breakthrough of crying, stimulated primarily by associations that led to sadness for his depressed and suicidal mother.)

Dream of September 10, first year. "My wife and I are in a junk yard picking up scraps of wood. It seems like we were there the day before and now there's not as much material. I see a chair on a platform, a basket chair made out of oaken strips with a wrought iron base. It looks very nice and I think it will be a good bargain. I also think how the design of the chair shows how dreams are inventive. Then we are in the palace in Monaco. We are being given a car by the royal family, a gleaming Cadillac. I feel she (Princess Grace) didn't have to give us so grand a car; a Datsun would have been okay. We go on an elevator to a lower level to tell her. There's a whole bank of elevators. We're in a bedroom below, I'm wearing a cordoroy suit, and my wife is still with me. Princes Grace is there, very tall with a flowing gown, and I tell her we don't need a Cadillac. She says, 'Wait until the Prince arrives.' I see him coming and notice how short he is. The scene then shifts to the time of France under Louis XIII, a Three Musketeers type scene. There's an ale house where people are eating; wine is being served; nobility, servants, and dogs are all about; and prisoners are being brought in and thrown into a back room. A fifteen-year-old black kid is brought in, tied up and thrown into the back. He tries to escape by feigning illness, but a big guard with long black hair and a ruffled and dirty uniform grabs him and brings him into the main room and shoves him up against a smoke-smudged wall. I think maybe there will be a firing squad. The guard takes an oaken strip, the same as on the chair in the earlier part of the dream, and starts poking around the kid's body with it. At first, it looks like he is poking with the stick but actually there's a hooked knife on the end of the wood and he's poking holes all over the kid's torso. Blood surges out and the kid turns, mutilated and dying. I wake up with an awful feeling. Now, as I tell the dream, it doesn't feel so bad. I think the dynamic is: something good happens, the gift in the dream, and then something awful."

Associations. The "bank" of elevators reminds him of going to the bank with some extra money earned yesterday. The black kid reminds him of pictures of the young black, Emmett Till, who was kidnapped when he went South and lynched for his uppity behavior. Princess Grace reminds him of the analyst's wife; maybe the analyst doesn't make love to her as well as the patient could. He was looking forward to the analysis, a place where he could be comfortable and direct. In the court of Louis XIII, he has read about all the brutality to children that was particularly rampant at that time, including the children of royalty. (The next day there are some additional associations for the same dream.) The scene in the junkyard reminds him of the Salvation Army Thrift Store where a friend always goes to get bargains. This friend, a woman somewhat older, now has breast cancer and may be dying. He feels guilty that now that he is successful he no longer sees her and her husband. Killing the black boy: he remembers that the night before the dream he was skewering pieces of meat for shish kebab. During this hour he talked about receiving a letter from a very successful colleague (whose first name is Bob) praising his work.

Dream of October 25, first year. "There's a short first scene in a cemetery with my mother and me. The ground is being dug up; a man, a friend of the family when I was a child, is being buried. I am discussing the funeral arrangements with my mother; I'm the expert and she isn't, but she ignores my advice and tells me to shut up.

"In what seems like the main dream, I am driving through the city in my Datsun, trying to get home to my wife who I know will be worrying about my being late. I turn off the expressway down a steep street where the pavement is all torn up. The brake fluid is low and I have to pump the brakes to get friction. At the bottom of the hill is an old village, kind of a restored touristy place with a name like Toonerville. I get out of the car and am walking through the shops when I see a more official entrance, not the way I came in. There is a string of old fashioned taxis bringing tourists in and out this other entrance. I wander through the stores, where the clerks are women with very thin legs and faces. They all look like they are related, inbred, and I think of Appalachia where people inbreed and acquire genetic diseases that weaken them. Outside again, I see one of the taxis being towed up the hill by another; the hood is lifted and I see a very incongruous, fancy, powerful, chrome engine in the small old car. I think how difficult it will be to get home in my own car from this place.

"The scene then shifts and I am home in the bathroom, with no clothes on, with a woman named Kathy who is showering. We're talking; it's a feeling of sexual excitement. I say, 'I'll get in the shower with you,' and she's laughing and embarrassed, but seems willing. There's lots of water splashing on the floor. First I feel I should clean up the water to prevent damage to the floor, but then I realize that the floor is already badly damaged by water so I feel relieved; I don't have to do it."

Associations. Working on the floor of the bathroom: the patient has tended in reality to be much too responsible for fixing up the house, excluding his wife. Kathy: a woman of the patient's age with a cute round face. He had seen her standing out from a group of colleagues at a recent gathering as being the only nonneurotic one. Everyone else in this particular group seemed so obviously nuts. He associates his mother and her neurosis to these other neurotic colleagues. The coffin area in the first short dream reminds him of a place where he dug up around his house to put in cement blocks for a fence, and he thinks the man (who is also a father) being buried in the dream used to be in a cement block business which failed. Death and funerals: in the dream the day before he dreamed about a suicide pact with a brother. Today, a funeral. Why such extremes? He thinks it has to do with recent interpretations of the degree of fearfulness in him. The Toonerville village: the ladies all tall and skinny— the opposite of Kathy in the dream who is normal, healthy looking, short and plump. Again, the switch from bad to good. Genetic engineering: he read an article yesterday. He thinks of defective people from villages in West Virginia. First the woman looked good and sexy and then, as he looked closer, he saw that she was extremely skinny and sick, unattractive. Associates to his mother: she used to be good, then she was sick and unattractive, and even got skinny during her first major depression. Brakes not working in the car: thinks of loss of control. Wanting to enjoy himself—that's the feeling in the bathroom. Just shower with her and forget the water on the floor. Conflict between his guilt and his having to fix things and his wish for pleasure. The cars in the Tooonerville place remind him of the amusement pier where he used to go as a child and ride the little bumper cars, and of his preadolescent dreams of becoming a racing car driver with a powerful machine under his control. The next day he has some additional associations to the John Denver song, "Country Road," which seems to be the stimulus for the dream of going into the old village. He realizes that the girl with the slim legs who looks lovely and then sick is his longing for his mother, knowing he can never have what he wants. Thinks he should have let himself acknowledge these emotions earlier in his life and feels like crying now.

The major themes and conflicts in this series of dreams are fairly obvious from the associations and interpretations. While we did not both describe them in exactly the same words—patient's description was couched in terms of his dynamics, while the analyst's tended to emphasize the evolving transference—our discussion revealed essential agreement on the major points.

The dream of June 26 represents the conflict between phallic assertiveness and sexual guilt. The patient begins to express his real anger (tied
primarily to the hypersensitivity to criticism: mother or wife should not
dare to attack his fragile narcissism) with some feeling that there could be
a safe give and take of anger between men (he and the analyst). But this
changes to feeling anxious over his exposed penis—Joan
Crawford–mother catches him in the bathroom. The regressive pull is
toward his character of early childhood: a "od" unaggressive little boy
who has Mommy's special love. The analyst was struck by how little
evidence of depression was present in the early dreams and was encouraged by the readiness for a transference engagement—a good, clean fight
in which the patient will slug it out with the father-analyst and resolve his
sexual and dependency conflicts with the mother.

The dream of July 1 precedes a major breakthrough of warded-off
sadness. The dream shows his greater readiness to experience the heretofore overcontrolled childish wishes—incestuous sex, the cousin, the
wife of friends—primarily for closeness with Mother. Both of us commented on the emergence of these feelings as the "macho" veneer began
to give way.

The dream of September 10 is more complex. At the center is the
intense conflict between competitive strivings for sexual trimph and
masculine success, on the one hand, and intense fear of retaliation, on the
other. There is, as well, a reference to wood, furniture, and remodeling—
the recreating-something-good-from-junk theme which is a major character symptom—a way he lives out his fantasy of recapturing past happiness
with guilty restitution via hard work. Here is how it works: the patient
wants something wonderful—sex with Princess Grace, his mother, the
analyst's wife—and imagines he can do it better (the prince is short, the
analyst old, bumbling, and so on). He can even be modest about his power:
he turns down the Cadillac in a gesture of humble, moral superiority.
There is a connection to the chair with oaken strips—something beautiful
can be salvaged out of junk—it is a bargain, he can "steal" it. But this then
turns into a scene where emotions of all sorts are much less controlled—
the raucous time of the *Three Musketeers* (his mother was a great fan of
Alexander Dumas) with fighting and wenching (and much open sex play
between children and adults, as well as child abuse, as he knows from his
familiarity with the history of the period).

He is now Emmett Till, the black boy from Chicago who went South
and failed to hide his feelings sufficiently (to show deference to the
whites) and was horribly murdered for being too sexually forward with

the taboo white women. In other words, the patient is extremely frightened of what will be done to him (by Father, by the analyst) if his sexual
and competitive feelings are revealed in their full strength. He fears they
will be turned against him. The oaken strip, first a symbol of a beautiful
"steal," is then used to kill him for his presumptuousness. One sees in this
dream and its associations how the feelings of fear and guilt spread from
their childish core to other areas: for example, he feels guilty for his
academic success, for his talented work as a carpenter, for making money,
indeed, for being an adult man. Again there are hints of the anal (smoke-
smudged wall, junkyard, dirty uniform) and homosexual (the guard's long
hair and ruffled uniform) themes still to come.

While the patient was still caught up in his masochistic version of the
dream, the analyst stressed the sadistic side—after all, it is the patient who
dreams up this horrible torture—and noted that the dream more openly
displays the patient's avarice, competitive rivalry, and sadism. He thought
it particularly important that the good, clean fist fight of June 26 had now
become torture and mutilation. This shift was a sign that, with analytic
progress, the superego was softening and more primitive impulses were
making their appearance.

The dream of October 25 continues the theme of conflict between
wishes for incestuous sex and guilt over the "damage" those wishes have
caused. And, along with these feelings is, again, the grief and sadness over
loss: the neurotic "loss" of the mother who idolized her wonderful little
boy and the real loss represented by mother's current depressed state. The
song "Country Road" came to him as an association and, via reconstruction, it seems as if the dream is a visual representation of that song with its
particular meaning for him.

One line of associations went to the television movie *Sunshine,* seen
the night before, in which this and other songs by John Denver were sung.
The movie concerned a beautiful young mother who is dying of cancer of
the leg bone (the women in the dream with thin legs) and leaving her
young daughter behind. The patient could not hum the song or think
about the movie without crying. In the dream, he leaves the life of the
present for the "country road" of his childhood: things seem pleasant at
first—the attractive women, the festive air—but on closer examination he
sees that the women are horribly diseased. The image and associations
here fuse incestuous sexual wishes (the inbreeding of Appalachia, the
beautiful young mother with cancer from the movie *Sunshine*) and his
own mother, once beautiful and young in his eyes and now ruined by
neurosis and depression. There are references, as well, to the phallic

fantasies of his childhood, the powerful cars. In the second scene, there seems to be a much freer experience of nonincestuous sex. The plump, nonneurotic Kathy represents a healthy wish and hope: if only he can get over worrying about the "damage" this sexual expression will cause, if he can shed his need to symbolically fix up and restore to atone for feelings of guilt, then he could have some fun.

Overall, the four dreams from this early phase of the analysis show a progressive opening up of unconscious content and emotion as involvement in the process deepens. The major unconscious conflict seems a variant of a simple oedipal complex: sexual longings for mother, angry competitive feelings toward other men, and anxiety and guilt over these. There is, as well, a way in which the inhibition of sexual and masculine assertive feelings combines with a blockage of mourning, of the feelings of sadness over the real tragedies in his family. The intensity of his anxiety, most clearly seen in the third dream, was apparent in a number of other dreams from this period. The analyst summed up his view of the work to this point by noting that the softening of the overcontrolling, critical superego was a response, at least in part, to the quality of the analytic relationship. The analyst was unvaryingly kind, respectful, and undogmatic—consistently questioning the patient's attempts to behave in a self-demeaning and unworthy manner. The patient correctly felt liked and valued, and the therapeutic alliance was so strong that the analyst *never* felt the need to euphemize or shy away from the most dystonic interpretations of aggression, incestuous sexuality, homosexuality, pregenital fantasies, and related topics which so often produce analytic squabbles or impasses. In retrospect, he wondered about the validity of some of these interpretations, but they were strong medicine, which the patient swallowed like a man.

DREAMS IN MIDDLE PHASE

Dream of April 16, second year. "In the first scene, I am skiing down a mountain—a whole group fishtailing down the mountain on skis. My mother is at the tail end and I think, 'Oh, they're having fun. It's okay for me too.'

"Then there is a shift in scene or another dream. I am at the university and my chairman's office is in the room where mine really is. He (the chairman) is a contractor and we are in the courtyard in front of the building talking with a student or with a contracting client, something regarding money. I have to check with my boss, the department chairman. There's wheeling and dealing going on."

Associations. The patient expresses a variety of criticisms of his father and his department chairman.

Interpretation. The analyst says, "You have retreated from the homicidal intensity of your oedipal rage of yesterday. [In a dream reported the day before, the patient murdered a man behind him who makes critical remarks—obviously the analyst—by throwing him off a cliff and then bashes in the head of another man to cover up the crime.] You still wish for sex with mother (downhill skiing and fun) and castration of father, department chairman, as a phony wheeler-dealer. The transference attitudes are feelings that the analyst is weak, that he gets sick too often and so on."

Dream of April 18, second year. "A bird cage is suspended in the middle of a room; nothing else is visible; even in the dream there is the feeling that this is a symbol, a symbol of the theory of evolution—the struggle for resources, survival of the fittest—and of psychological growth, in similar terms. There are two parakeets in the cage, and my wife and I put a small tortoise in with them. The animals then undergo evolutionary transformations in competition with each other for survival. At first the tortoise is attempting to kill the parakeets and eat them for food. He is jumping up trying to reach them on their perch and, in the process, his front claws turn into flippers, like wings. But he cannot get them. Then the birds are fighting back, pecking at him, and they manage to peck away virtually his entire shell, leaving him exposed. The larger parakeet has then somehow acquired the tortoise's shell on its own body and the inside of the shell resembles the tire tread of a Michelin X tire. The tortoise is now almost starving. His head and neck are shriveled and thin, but he still has the small bird's head and part of its body in his sharp beak. Then food is thrown into the cage, white crystals like salt, and I think, 'It won't help the tortoise much.' The larger parakeet is then eating the food and, as she does so, getting stronger and acquiring teeth, as if she's becoming a reptile. The tortoise has shriveled at this time and the big bird sucks his head and neck into her mouth like a worm or spaghetti. The tortoise is sucked alive into the bird's stomach where it will be soaked in stomach acid and die. I wake up with a disgusted and horrible feeling."

Associations. The two birds could be the patient and his younger brother. The idea of evolution connects with psychological development: makes him think of a son incorporating his father's strength by identification. In the dream there is the idea that when two enemies are together for a long time, they each take on the other's characteristics. There's the general notion of a Malthusian struggle for survival where one only survives by killing and eating one's adversaries, and this seems also a vision of family life. The Michelin tire is associated to his father who loves these tires so much that he gave a free testimonial, allowing the company to rip him off—which the patient thinks is typical of the father's misplaced affection and bumbling ways. The patient thought: Is he like his father? Yesterday he had the thought that maybe his father would love him if he were some kind of a defective or neurotic person. And then he wonders if he is loving his own son in some kind of perverted way. The tortoise in the dream is associated to a small tortoise that was a pet of the son's which died when his wife mistakenly left it outside in the sun in a glass cage and it was killed by the heat. His son cried over the death of his pet, one of the few times he has allowed himself to cry since he was a young boy. This relates to the way his son, like the patient, has made himself prematurely macho by squelching his feelings.

Interpretation. Analyst discusses with the patient the possible ways in which he has encouraged his son's premature independence and hostility as a part of his own defense against his homosexual feelings.

Dream of April 29, second year. "I feel sexy with my wife, but then she is with our daughters. I am in bed with my son and we are about to have sex; we are both naked and aroused like we will have intercourse."

Associations and interpretation. On awakening, the patient felt guilty and disgusted. He then complains about women, how they demand and reject. Then he thinks how he loves his son, his white, hairless, beautiful body. He then talks about the analyst's beautiful wife. The analyst says, "You're having homosexual longings for me." Patient agrees, recognizing strong feelings of wanting the analyst to love him, but is unaware of any conscious sexual feelings.

Dream of June 13, second year. "Warren Beatty [the actor] is bouncing around on a bed naked. I am sitting at the back of the bed with my back against the wall. Other people are sitting around on chairs and on a couch. I see Beatty's naked ass from behind as he jumps all around. I am afraid that he will accidentally, or even intentionally, put his ass on my face. Then the scene shifts to a school classroom. Mr. M (a history teacher of my son in reality) is standing in front of his class. I am a student in the class, and he is giving us a mathematics puzzle—something about 28 + 3, then a series of equations which are permutations of 28 + 3 = 31. I realize it's a trick; these are just a distraction. I'm the only one in the class who knows that the real answer is 30 instead of 31, since there are two nostrils rather than three!

Associations and interpretation. The previous night he saw a movie on television in which the good-guy sheriff, in tracking down the bad guy, becomes transformed into the bad guy. There's a con game in the movie. Mr. M, in the dream, presents the math problem in a tricky or conlike way. Warren Beatty's ass: he sees Beatty as a wild, sexually irresponsible person. Analyst says: "This is a sexual-anal fantasy." Patient goes on that yesterday he had sex with his wife. A friend of his met Warren Beatty one time. The friend, at a different time, reported having a homosexual dream about the patient. Associations to the numbers: trickery, and maybe he's being sarcastic about the analysis.

The analyst says: "The first dream is a homosexual wish for me and the second dream a defensive depreciation of me to ward off the homosexual wish. The three nostrils refer to holes in the human body. Women have three—urethra, vagina, anus." Then patient and analyst discussed the patient's childhood neurotic symptom: his inability to touch his own anus with toilet paper.[1]

The dreams of this phase show the transisiton to deeper layers of conflict. The unconscious shows through the dream symbolism with crystal clarity. The analyst emphasized that this period was the turning point in the most important task in the analysis of an obsessive-depressive patient: the transformation of the superego. While there had been oedipal dreams earlier, the patient's competitive rage had been muted. In the dreams preceding that of April 16, the patient murders the critical analyst—throws him off a cliff, bashes in his skull—and the next night glides down the mountain with his mother. The father-analyst (in the form of the department chairman) continues to be demeaned—he is a crooked wheeler-dealer in contrast to the morally superior patient.

The dream of April 18 was one of the most vivid and memorable of the analysis, for both of us—though the patient's discussion of it was in terms

1. In retrospect, we can see that the dream derives from Freud's close relationship with Wilhelm Fliess, whose theories tied together nostrils, sexuality, the female menstrual cycle (28), and the days of the month (31). In other words, this is another root of the homosexual theme—emotional closeness between Freud and Fliess (which the patient had been reading about) connecting with his wishes for closeness with his "Freud," his father-analyst.

of family-history and the analyst's in terms of the transference. In the abstract quality of its symbolism it is like a surrealist painting and, indeed, may have been partly stimulated by a painting by Magritte, *The Therapeutist,* that depicts a man whose upper body consists of a bird cage with two white doves inside. The dream can be viewed in several different ways. It shows the patient's feelings about his closeness with his mother and father and his identifications with each of them. As the analyst noted, it is a dream of oral incorporation which reflects the now permissable deep oral regression in the service of the ego, a dream which reveals the deepest roots of the patient's symbiotic tie to his mother, the hunger which her hypocritical love never really relieved, and the incorporation of strength by absorbing the analyst, his love, his strength, his masculinity, and his femininity.

The dream shows the patient's intense conflicts over closeness and identification with both parents. If he identified with his father he would become stupid and susceptible to exploitation (as well as "henpecked"), but closeness with Mother means a sickening involvement with her neurotic character (in reality she constantly complained of acid stomach, hence the image of being destroyed in the bird's stomach). His involvement in the analysis has already exposed him (the turtle shell pecked away) to these sides of himself—the sides derived from his masculine and feminine identifications. And the more threatening feminine side is coming increasingly to the fore as the analysis moves to earlier levels beneath the competitive-oedipal material. This comes out most strongly as the wish for Father's (and the analyst's) love and the fear of love between men (he and his son, he and the analyst). If he becomes a sick person (or cries or shows his feelings), the father and analyst might love him. But this arouses the danger of being a woman—and a sick one like mother, at that. This is also connected to his feelings for his son: he was able to be physically affectionate when the son was little, but the son soon became hypermasculine like him (repeating the pattern with him and his father) and it takes the death of a pet for the son to show his feelings.

The analyst noted that he interpreted this dream in terms of father-son homosexuality (father-patient, analyst-patient, and patient-son). While this interpretation intuitively captured the central meaning, it might have been interpreted more clearly and thoroughly.

In the final two dreams from this phase (April 29 and June 13) the homosexual wishes become much more open. In this period a dream of first being attracted to his wife and then to his son seemed to mean an attraction to the analyst's wife and a deeper wish to be in her sexual role vis-à-vis the analyst along with the theme of receiving his strength.

The dream of the actor Warren Beatty shows the manifestly homosexual feelings—looking, possible physical contact, and smell (the reference to nostrils)—all of which are simultaneously interesting and repugnant to the patient. In addition—as the analyst noted—Beatty's indirect link with a close male friend of the patient mobilized competitive strivings.

A word about the childhood neurotic symptom mentioned in the interpretation of this dream, for its derivatives were fairly prominent during the middle and later phases of the analysis. Until fairly late in his childhood the patient had an inhibition against wiping himself after a bowel movement, and specifically against touching the shit or his anus with his fingers. Consciously, he felt this a form of "goodness"—of moral superiority—as if he had incorporated his toilet training so completely that he could not bear to touch the filthy stuff. Thus he guarded, in a compulsive-neurotic way, against the wish for anal pleasure and an interest in anal smells and touching. And, like any neurotic symptom, there was a disguised gratification and punishment. His inhibitions left him with shit on his underpants about which he felt guilty and embarrassed. While he had overcome the specific inhibition at the beginning of adolescence, faint derivatives remained, such as not always washing his hands after going to the bathroom—(good boys save soap and water) with vague guilt feelings. The conflict was very active in the unconscious and many dreams and associations led to the image of the dirty, ashamed little boy exposed in his shitty underpants. In other words, it was a major focus of unconscious guilt.

The connection of the anal symptom with the homosexual themes was probably by way of similar symptoms in his father, who was guilt-ridden and compulsive, on the one hand, yet a great saver of dirty old clothes and junk, on the other. Thus, another side of his childhood symptom was an identification with his father and an unconscious attempt to draw father's attention to his anus. In one way the wish was, "Love me, I am a nut like Mother" (who, since she washed the clothes, must have known of the problem and done nothing about it). And in another way the message was "I need you to wipe me," to show me how to strike a better balance between active-rebellious and passive-submissive feelings. Thus, the symptom was partly a narcissistic denial of his helplessness and inferiority relative to adults and authority. Similarly, now the patient depreciates the analyst to ward off his frightening receptive, absorbing impulses toward him.

The analyst commented, and the patient agreed, that they were both very absorbed in the analysis during this period. He looked forward each day to the next installment and the promised episode was always available.

DREAMS IN FINAL PHASE

Dream of August 16, third year. "I came to your office, but it's not here, it's near my old neighborhood. We meet in an outer office and decide not to have a regular hour. I feel okay and like I don't need a session, so you say, 'I have some errands to do.' We start off together to go to your mother's house and we go into Greenwich Village. You are in a car and I am following on a bicycle. I don't see where you turn, and I get lost. Then I'm in my underwear, but I don't feel too anxious or embarrassed. I find you and we go into a crummy old apartment building. You say, 'I bet you can't tell my mother's age.' I expect someone in her seventies and am surprised to see a woman in her forties, with dyed blonde hair, in the bedroom. There's a covered figure in the bed that I first think is her lover, but she says it's her ten-year-old daughter. Then we leave. I have no bike and I'm running through Greenwich Village in boxer shorts, with the many creepy village characters around, but I feel fairly comfortable even though I have a hard-on some of the time."

Associations. The patient says the dream seems to deal with guilt over sexuality, Mommy and Daddy, but feeling less upset about it. He is less embarrassed about dirty underwear, hard-ons, and so forth, more able to accept his sexual feelings for his mother and to accept her as crazy (as always trying to act younger than her age). He can see more firmly what the end of the analysis will be like: writing more and better; more mature with his wife; more open to his tender, soft, and tearful feelings; an acceptance of his life as it is, not a fantasy of something else that will be wonderful. Associations to following the analyst in a lesser vehicle and getting lost: disappointment that nothing wonderful will happen. Sees the analyst as ordinary. He feels superior as a writer, just as he feels superior to his own father.

Interpretation. "So to deal with your superior attitude you portray yourself as inferior to me." Patient agrees. By being inferior and subordinate he makes himself Christlike and superior. Analyst says, "You have still got neurotic, competitive, and guilty feelings in relation to your father."

Dream of February 18, fourth year. "I am threading film onto a projector but the film is toilet paper. It then becomes a lacy ribbon and then changes into lasagne noodles. Anne [an older female colleague of the patient and the wife of another colleague] and you are both there watching."

Associations. The patient mentions the Magritte painting, *The Thera-peutist:* Anne gave him a card with that picture as a thank-you note. Other associations: the toilet paper—yesterday the patient reported an embar-rassing fantasy of smearing shit on my white rug by rubbing his asshole in it. This will be very embarrassing to him to include in a book about dreams. The homosexual feelings were present in the last dream. Maybe he and I colluded to avoid analyzing this problem. He is having warm feelings toward me because I like him and have helped him; regret over having to give up being a kid here with me.

Interpretation. The analyst says, "It's nice to come here, lie down and be taken care of and talk about your homosexuality, but you continue to feel guilty over being loved and given to as well as giving to others." Patient goes on with confirmatory associations.

Dream of March 14, fourth year. "We are in bed and my wife is mad at me for farting and for taking so long to come during intercourse."

Associations. Actually his wife has been very sexy lately. She has just begun the first week of her own analysis. He and she are fucking a lot. She's having sexual feelings regarding the patient's analyst and another male analysand. He goes on to talk of how positive his wife is and how lucky he is to have selected me as an analyst.

Interpretation. The analyst says, "The dream suggests some wish not to give up the connection with the hostile, negative parents."

Dream of March 24, fourth year. "I am in a town called Pye (I think of Rye, New York) high in the Swiss Alps. To get there, we had to go very fast on winding, twisty roads. I am in a bus that is made from a converted jet plane with the wings off. It's going down the mountain roads very fast and I am feeling frightened and worried about whether the driver knows how to get down from here safely. Then the scene shifts. I am with an old friend, Les, and feel rejected by him. The scene shifts again and I am having sex with my wife. She's fucking me, lying on top, kissing me; we are very excited, with deep kissing, a very enjoyable feeling."

Associations. The patient thinks of a series of connections to Pye: he saw the name of the political scientist Lucian Pye in a book the day before, and Lucy is the first name of his wife's analyst. His wife is just increasing her psychotherapy to analysis as he finishes his analysis, and he hopes she will be able to work through her neurosis and love him in a mature way, in contrast to the neurotic love that went on between him and his mother. Pye in the Alps also refers to pie-in-the-sky and the feeling that he is completing analysis and there is no pie in the sky, no gratifying fantasy. Association to being let down too fast, by the driver of the plane, the analyst, rejected by a male—his friend Les—but achieving some more satisfying closeness with his wife in the third scene.

Interpretation. The analyst says the first two scenes express his disappointment in the analysis, no pie in the sky. But there's the happy ending, bliss with his wife, so that he has moved from certain homosexual preoccupations to a more clearly heterosexual feeling.

A number of themes in this series of dreams are portrayed in the associations and interpretations, and it was relatively easy for us to agree on them. There were, as well, some differences in our comments which will be noted.

The main theme of the first dream from this phase (August 16, about seven months before the actual termination) is anxiety over being left alone by the end of the analysis (no regular hour, getting lost, embarrassed without clothes on). The dream then portrays certain of the patient's typical means for dealing with this anxiety. The scene with the analyst's sexy "young" mother in bed with her daughter fuses two of the patient's neurotic-regressive wishes that dominated the transference: (1) the wish for sexual-intimate closeness with the analyst-as-mother, and (2) the homosexual wish for love between him and the analyst (a daughter in bed with the mother symbolizing him and analyst in bed together). The dream also shows the oscillation between inferiority and superiority feelings to the analyst—the second defending against the first—which is aroused again by the impending termination. The analyst was most struck by the self-demeaning attitude in which the patient experiences himself as Christlike in his humble (following behind) superiority. The dream ends, however, with the patient on his own, feeling less menaced by his inner conflicts.

The dream of February 18 (about six weeks before termination) is a creative recapitulation of the major unconscious themes of the analysis. The presence of Anne—an older woman, married to a colleague, who had given him a gift (and the Magritte picture at that: see dream of April 18, middle phase)—symbolized the simple oedipal wish: "Mother loves me more than she does father or brother." The movie film that changes to toilet paper, lace ribbons, and lasagne noodles (lasagne was one of his mother's better dishes) symbolizes the anal symptoms, the feminine-homosexual feelings, and the oral wishes as these emerged in the course of the analysis. The patient experienced the dream as a relaxed review of the analysis, as if he were saying, "Now I can look at these previously frightening sides of myself in a calm way." The analyst, while seeing this aspect of the dream, continued to press the interpretation of its neurotic side. He noted the wish to remain in analysis and the guilt over feeling loved and given to by the analyst. The wish to remain is paradoxically evident in that the recapitulation reveals various problems as though they require indefinite continuation of the analysis.

The dreams of March 14 and March 24 are from the final two weeks of the analysis and show both the hopes and continued fears related to termination. In both dreams the patient is openly sexual with his wife, and the first contains anal aggression (farting) as did the associations to the previous dream. And, while both show pleasure and progress, the anxiety stimulated by termination is portrayed in a variety of ways. There is the sexual holding on: the wife on top in sex symbolizing the patient's wish to continue to lie on the couch and enjoy the passive experience with the analyst. And there are almost direct portrayals of the end—the driver of the bus-plane taking him down too fast and the rejecting friend, Les.

The patient's wife, throughout the analysis the most prominent recipient of real and projected feelings, appears in both of these final dreams. This mixture of real and fantasied hopes in the relationship with her is intertwined with the patient's loss of fantasied hope that his analysis would give him pie-in-the-sky. The wife had sought psychotherapy for her own problems and, with the conclusion of the patient's analysis, she was able to afford an increase in her hours. The patient supported her in her therapy, yet behind this support lay the complexities of his own neurotic wishes. If she could resolve her neurosis with her analyst Lucy, then maybe he would be given the pie-in-the-sky, passive-childlike love that he seemingly renounced in the first dream of the sequence. Put another way, the three scenes of the March 24 dream can be viewed like this: there is no pie-in-the-sky; the analyst is letting you down without your neurotic wishes for love being gratified. The rejecting friend, Les, had gone through an analysis in another city with an analyst that the patient viewed as cold and ungiving, an analysis that seemed of little benefit. Hence, he and his rejection symbolize the fear that there is no love, no gratification to be had. But happiness, love, and sexual gratification return in the third dream which combines neurotic with realistic wishes. Analysis will "cure" his wife, as his mother was never cured, and she will give him the love he seeks. While this dream sequence shows that the patient's old neurotic wishes are still active, they are much closer to consciousness and their recognition more likely to provoke laughter than frustrated anger and guilt. In our discussion of this final dream it was the patient, interestingly enough, who picked up the remaining neurotic elements. The analyst—who commented on the mature sexual relationship with the wife—had an investment in idealizing the patient's condition at the end of their work.

In addition to our agreement on the main issues active in this final phase, the analyst made several comments of a broader nature. He noted that earlier in the analysis there were a number of dreams in which persons close to the patient—his wife, daughters, and so on—were in danger of attack by snakes or other hazards, and he had the task of rescuing them. The analyst felt that these rescue fantasies paralleled his waking overprotective attitudes to most persons who entered his life, especially his immediate family. When the hostile components of his unconscious were brought to consciousness and integrated, the need for these nocturnal fantasies subsided, and the aggression became more directly portrayed in the dreams.

More generally, the analyst noted an important shift in the expression of both sexuality and aggression which he attributed to the modification of the patient's superego. Sexual expression became freer, more overt and less guilt-ridden, on the one hand, and aggression eventually became less brutal, sadistic and/or masochistic, on the other. In other words, with a less severe superego no longer stifling both the wish for sexual pleasure of all sorts (passive, childlike, hetero- and homo-) and competitive, angry, and rebellious impulses, there is less frustration, less shunting of the feelings into guilt-ridden and more "perverted" forms of expression.

COURSE OF THE ANALYSIS AND REASONS FOR ITS SUCCESS

As we noted at the outset, both of us independently wrote our descriptions in three sections: (1) The patient at the beginning of the analysis; (2) discussion of the analysis based on selected dreams from the major phases; (3) our perception of the overall course of the analysis and the major reasons for its success. While we blended our accounts of the first two sections, for the third it seemed to make more sense to present each account separately, in the form it was originally written, and these accounts follow.

PATIENT'S PERCEPTION OF THE
PSYCHOANALYSIS

1. I'll begin by noting certain of the commonly described features that make for a successful analytic or therapeutic experience. I experienced the analyst as calm and accepting, as noncritical, and as seeing things that I did not see. That is, despite my initial tendencies to perceive him like many other authorities in my past life, as weak and ineffective parent figures, he in fact emerged as quite strong and perceptive. I was able to criticize him, to expose my deprecating, superior feelings—for instance, that he's always sick and I'm always healthy. In fact, he helped bring these feelings out and to show me how frightened I was about them. Crucial to all this was the essential accuracy of his interpretations. He was not always right; he made mistakes for which I was mostly forgiving; but over the long run his perceptiveness and intelligence led to the construction of a basically accurate picture of the unconscious themes. One final comment here: All of this material just presented, as well as these comments on the effectiveness of the analysis, is being presented in an intellectual way. When it happened it was experienced in a very different way. That is, in the relationship with the analyst I felt him to be initially weak, sick, and unable to take care of me; then angry with me and potentially retaliatory because of my own rivalrous feelings; later seductive, attempting to lure me into some horrible homosexual trap; and eventually loving and accepting. Again, all of these were felt, dreamed about, associated to, and experienced by me as the analysis progressed. It is only subsequent to this experience that they have become the subject matter of intellectual constructions such as this paper.

2. The crucial feature for me was giving up some emotional control. The most striking examples of this were the few occasions (and they were not many) during the analysis when I was able to cry openly. This always led to great feelings of relief, recognition that what was bottled up inside me was simply sadness about the real tragedies and unhappiness of my family and friends, and the feeling that I was able to share with the analyst and others the real pain of the world rather than bear this pain in a silent, hypermasculine, suffering manner.

3. Later in the analysis there was the exposure, with much embarrassment, of the dirty, ashamed little boy feelings—with their corresponding needs for love and approval. The analyst, with his acceptance of these feelings and even encouragement of them, was able to bring them out and make them seem much less awful. This included, of course, the anal material as well as the homosexual wishes.

4. Let me summarize here some of the changes in personality as these are seen approximately a year and a half after the conclusion of the analysis.

Changes with women. I feel basically more comfortable. Where before there was the underlying feeling that any sexy, attractive woman who was nice to me could get me to do anything, because I felt so deprived and guilty, I now feel much less guilty, more able to enjoy positive feelings—sexual or other—but also more able to see particular women that I interact with for what they are, whether they are intelligent or not, sad or happy, seductive, hostile, loving, or genuinely friendly. My perception is much more differentiated and my reactions much more comfortable.

Authority figures. In general there is a diminution of fearfulness. I feel more able to say what I think and do not feel I am a secret revolutionary for harboring ideas that may, in fact, differ little from those of others.

Male friends. I am much more able to be intimate and close, to share a confidence; I have less need to see men as younger brothers that I must surpass; and I am less threatened by the homosexual implications of male friendships.

My wife. There's a much greater separation of her neurotic problems from mine. The fights that we used to have are much less frequent, and when they do occur they are miniversions of our old patterns. Where, in the past, I would become silently hurt and enraged, feeling that she was depriving me of sex and love, and go around for several days in a state of depressed suffering, this now either does not occur or, when it does, passes in a couple of hours. On the other side, I am much more able to feel real love for her and sadness when she is unhappy.

5. Not all is roses. I am basically the same person that I was before the analysis. All the central features of my character and the basic patterns of my reactions are there, in modified form. It is as if my strengths have been turned up—I can work more effectively with less feelings of a guilty struggle, enjoy the company of others (both men and women), take more pride in my accomplishments—while the neurotic side has been turned down. I feel less like a dirty little rebel who must sneak around respectable people and less like a person whose real accomplishments are somehow counterfeit.

6. Some final thoughts on what made this particular analysis successful. First, I had a lot going for me from the very beginning. I was intelligent, sophisticated psychologically with the capacity for stable long-term relationships, with my wife especially and with my children; and there was a good deal of real success to counter unconscious feelings of

inferiority. The strong feelings of guilt and compulsive "goodness" led me
to treat the analysis with the utmost serious dedication. This also was a
part of the emotional control that was my foremost resistance. And,
second, there seemed to be a good match between analyst and patient. The
analyst's special interest in dreams, his affection for radical politics and,
maybe most important, the fact that his real character was more like that
of a loving mother than a critical father, countered my massively self-
critical superego. A more hard-line psychoanalytic stance might have
unwittingly played into increasing my tendency to be a "good boy" by
outwardly obeying rules and inwardly keeping the superego problem
hidden. In a related way the "loving" nature of the analyst made my own
fear of closeness more evident.

ANALYST'S PERCEPTION OF THE PSYCHOANALYSIS

This section is complex and difficult. My remarks will adhere as closely
as *possible* to the information and ideas derived from the dreams.

1. The high level of motivation in the analysand elicited a corresponding therapeutic, intimate and investigative response in the analyst. This
fortunate convergence resulted in an alliance which was established with
speed and solidity. Upon this platform, the analytic action occurred.

2. The patient quickly regressed in a beautifully therapeutic fashion.
Almost from the outset the therapeutic split in the ego was established,
so that he was experiencing and observing with optimal consistency
throughout most of the analysis.

3. The analyst's role in the above is, of course, essential. A multitude of
shared values, interests, and activities promoted commonality as well as
competition, envy, jealousy. But the productive sharing for the most part
prevailed, permitting an optimal climate of exploration of the negative
sentiments. On occasions when my analytic empathy lapsed (as in an
instance when I erroneously revealed a painful personal concern), the
therapeutic split could not be sustained, and negative feelings flooded the
analysis for a brief period. Although some good was salvaged from this
episode, it was basically an interference in the analysis. At another time
when a personal ambition threatened the analysis by the possibility of my
leaving practice, mostly realistic anger and apprehension in the analysand
temporarily disturbed smooth analytic progress. Here again, my empathic
listening was not sustained, because I was distracted and torn by the reality
issue.

4. The copious dreaming and the abundant associations and the available affect were very important sources of analytic work and progress. At times dreams were perhaps excessive in number and length, and were sometimes so interpreted. *If* the association and affects had not been available, then I would have assessed the many, many dreams differently.

5. We each learned from the other. For example, the analysand expanded the experiential dimensions of his insight; conversely I accumulated knowledge from him—both enjoyable and useful to me. The basic mutual work contributions and benefit enhanced the analytic richness which then increased the mutual rewards in a benignly circular and cumulative manner.

CONCLUDING NOTE

The observations, impressions, and interpretations presented in this paper speak for themselves and need not be repeated or summarized here. Let us just note a few additional points.

One of the consistent differences between the patient's and analyst's accounts was the greater tendency for the patient to focus on his dynamics, history, and inner conflicts while the analyst was more attuned to the transference. The reasons for this seem obvious: the patient is experiencing the process from inside himself, as it were, while the analyst is more the outside observer of the interaction between them. This difference should serve as a reminder that the role of each person in a psychoanalytic situation will be a crucial determinant of his perception and evaluation of the process. In addition, we must emphasize again that the differences in perspective were only partial; in many respects our views of the process overlapped or were identical. On most essential points we drew the same conclusions regarding major conflicts, defenses, and dynamics, and we shared the same view of the general analytic progression. This is to be expected, of course, since almost by definition a successful analysis involves arriving at some agreed upon view of these matters.

It is worth commenting on the special value of this retrospective research effort. Having completed this project, we both concluded that we now had a more complete picture of the analysis then we previously possessed. We feel we can recommend this procedure as a valuable adjunct to an analysis, to be used when a thorough analysis has been completed and where an active, self-analytic capability has been established in the patient. The teaching potential of this process is significant—both patient and analyst learn new things about the analysis when viewing it in this new way. It seems to us that a method such as this would be particularly suited to training analyses and related psychotherapy of psychotherapists. One must plan in advance, of course; some form of records must be kept; and, in this regard, we can strongly recommend the method we used—dreams along with associations and interpretations. As the present study shows, the dream material contains a record of the progression of unconscious themes, unfolding transference, and historical antecedents, while the interpretations convey a clear sense of the type and level of the analyst's interventions. By recording all dreams, associations, and inter-pretations, analyst and patient have a *sample* of the progress through the analysis which they can use later in a retrospective study such as the present one. While this whole process involves a considerable amount of time and thought, our own experience has been that the harvest in understanding is well worth the investment of time and effort.

CHAPTER 5

THE PRIVATE LANGUAGE
OF THE DREAM

Ramon Greenberg, M.D. and Chester Pearlman, M.D.

> "If we don't ever sleep again, so much the better," Jose Arcadio Buendia said in good humor. "That way we can get more out of life." But the Indian woman explained that the most fearsome part of the sickness of insomnia was not the impossibility of sleeping, for the body did not feel any fatigue at all, but its inexorable evolution toward a more critical manifestation: a loss of memory. She meant that when the sick person became used to his state of vigil, the recollection of his childhood began to be erased from his memory, then the name and notion of things, and finally the identity of people and even the awareness of his own being, until he sank into a kind of idiocy that had no past.
> —Gabriel Garcia Marquez, *One Hundred Years of Solitude*

CORRELATION BETWEEN NEUROPHYSIOLOGY AND PSYCHOLOGY

We hope to demonstrate that data about dream physiology can help us to understand more clearly the process of dreaming. A basic premise of our work is that hypotheses about various aspects of nervous system function should be consistent. Findings in the area of neurophysiology should not contradict or be contradicted by psychological hypotheses. For example, evidence that activity in the pons was necessary for the occurrence of REM sleep (the phase of sleep associated with dreaming) led some investigators to equate REM sleep with this pontine activity (Jouvet 1962). On the other hand, the imagery of dreaming seemed indicative of cortical activity, which was inconsistent with the pontine hypothesis. Accordingly, subsequent studies of the role of the cortex in REM sleep demonstrated that cortical damage altered one of the major physiological markers of REM sleep—the eye movements (Greenberg 1966). Lesions of visual association areas markedly diminished these eye movements. Thus, it seems unlikely that pontine structures alone account for all the activity that we call REM sleep.

THE IMPORTANCE OF DREAM LANGUAGE

As for the contribution of REM physiology to theories of dreaming, a large body of sleep research has shown that REM sleep is involved in the processing of new information in both humans and animals (Greenberg and Pearlman 1974, McGrath and Cohen 1978). In animals, this seems to involve the integration of unusual experiences into the animals' behavioral repertoire. In humans, experiences with a traumatic or otherwise emotionally arousing quality have been connected with the process of REM sleep. These observations led us to reexamine dreaming with two questions in mind. One question involves the traditional psychoanalytic theory of dreams. Might the perspective of information processing change our understanding of the meaning of dreams? The second question is whether the manifest dream indicates the nature of information processing during REM sleep. In other words, does the dream language which portrays the integration of new information give clues about the mechanism? An analogy would be the understanding about the organization of a computer which might be gained from study of its programming language.

INVESTIGATORS' REASONS FOR USING THEIR OWN DREAMS

In an earlier study, we recorded dreams in a sleep lab from a man undergoing psychoanalysis (Greenberg and Pearlman 1975). Comparison of this material with transcripts of his analytic hours revealed that the manifest content of the dreams presented undistorted portrayals of his major emotional concerns during the preceding analytic hours. Upon examining the dreams for evidence of how this emotionally significant information was being processed, we found that the dream was often an attempt at resolution of a problem. The analytic material following a night in the sleep lab suggested that when resolution of a disturbing issue had occurred in dreams, the patient's waking mental state also showed restoration of emotional equilibrium. This finding was consistent with the hypothesis of French and Fromm (1964) that dreams involve solution of focal conflicts. We then reexamined Freud's Irma dream in the light of additional information provided by Schur (1966). Again, the manifest dream showed undistorted incorporation of emotionally important waking concerns and a solution which defended against these concerns (Greenberg and Pearlman 1978). In both studies, knowledge of what was currently important in the dreamer's waking life made the dreams readily comprehensible.

These studies involved single individuals and were also limited by the impossibility of returning to the dreamer for further information about the source of the dream material. Patients would also be unsuitable for such an exploration because a careful attempt to ferret out the various day residues might not always be consistent with the therapeutic process. We decided, therefore, to collect our own dreams with the hope that a large sample, about which we could question each other, would allow us to expand the understanding gained from the previous studies. Because each of us had been analyzed and because we also felt comfortable with each other, we hoped to be able to retrieve information about the source of our dreams and their patterns of organization. Neither of us was able to spend time in a sleep laboratory, so we decided to write down our dreams and the day residues during summer vacations. In this fashion, over a period of three years, we each collected a large sample of dreams. One of us found that after a short while he was awakening three to five times during the night with a remembered dream, which was consistent with the conventional pattern of three to five REM periods during a night. That these were REM awakenings was confirmed by the presence of erections, which occur only during the REM phase of sleep. We then spent the rest of the year reviewing the dreams, the day residues, and the past memories that were associated with the dreams. This paper will be devoted to the nature of the dreams we collected, our observations, and the implications of this material in answering the questions with which we began.

MANIFEST DREAMS PORTRAY
CURRENT LIFE ISSUES

With respect to the issue of whether the manifest dream is meaningful in itself or just a pastiche of perceptions disguising underlying meaning, our dreams left little doubt that the manifest content was meaningful. The answer became apparent with the first dreams we examined. Two current issues were obvious. The first involved leaving our patients and our responses to their concerns about our vacation. The second had to do with our investment in and skepticism about our efforts to discover more about dreaming, as illustrated by dreams of searching detectives, binoculars, keys, and taking things apart, perhaps more than intended. While the importance of this project to us was easily seen in the manifest content, the dream material also indicated deeper sources than our professional and academic interests. These involved personal issues reflecting such themes as competitiveness with older men (former teachers in the manifest content) and narcissistic themes representing us in comparison with colleagues and teachers.

Other issues from our waking experiences which appeared in the manifest content included feelings about parents as they came to visit during vacation, feelings about one of our children visiting colleges in preparation for going off next year, issues involved in books we were reading, problems of becoming accepted by the group at a camp one of us attended, and at the end of the vacation, overt concerns about going back to work and the problems awaiting us. Sometimes the dreams portrayed the actual situations in which we were emotionally involved and sometimes they seemed to present a picture of certain thoughts with which we had been preoccupied. This was most dramatic in the dreams of one of us after his father died at the beginning of the vacation. The preoccupation with grief and attempts to cope with it pervaded both waking and dreaming. One waking effort at self-consolation involved thoughts about Dr. Semrad's [1] comment that one cannot really help people grieve until one has known grief. One night, the following part of a dream seemed to portray this thought quite clearly.

"Some kind of religious gathering—something happened where I became convinced to become religious. A rabbi had me repeating prayers *'ha motzi lechem.'* Some comment about how I was in a better position to

---

1. Dr. Elvin Semrad was a highly respected psychoanalyst and a teacher in Boston. Both of us had been his students.

help others because I had been nonreligious, so I could understand the feelings of those who weren't religious better than someone who had always been religious."

In addition to the depiction of Dr. Semrad's observation, the dream shows changes which illustrate the role of dreaming in coping with emotionally important problems. There seems to be a conversion of the passive experience of loss into one where the dreamer has some sense of choice; he is persuaded to become religious (rather than being forced to become a mourner) and could then use this experience to help others. Yet the elements of the actual experience were very much in evidence because the religious rituals associated with mourning and the struggle about participation had been a central part of the mourning period.

INDIVIDUAL LIFE STYLE SHAPES MANIFEST DREAM

This dream fragment also demonstrates another factor which became apparent in our review. While some issues, such as our feelings about the study and the wish to solve the problem of dream formation, were evident in both our sets of dreams, portrayal of these issues was as different in style and content as each of us is from the other. On hearing each other's dreams, a typical response was, "That's you" to the other but, "That's not me" to oneself. It was like hearing one's voice on a tape recorder and finding it strange to the self but familiar to one who knows you. Thus, one of us characteristically, in waking life, rejects the passive role and tries to become active, as in the dream above. The other often would make a joke about a serious issue. On the day his father was leaving after a visit, he had the following dream which clearly illustrates this characteristic.

"Meeting of supervisors and residents at hospital—with Semrad (who resembled his father) as chief. He was running a benignly autocratic meeting. One joking resident jumps in his lap and lies there—half sarcastically."

PROBLEM-SOLVING FUNCTION OF DREAMING

In these examples, a present problem was clearly portrayed, as well as an attempt to manage the troublesome feelings in a manner acceptable to the dreamer. At other times, the same problem appeared in a series of dreams over a period of days. In these dream series, one could see continuing attempts at solutions, even though unsuccessful. These attempts seemed to reveal the nature of problem-solving in dreams. There was recurrent drawing on memories of similar situations which might suggest a resolution that seemed to fit the dreamer's individual style. For example, one of us, when feeling helpless, would turn in dreams to images of fixing things, a process more tangible and capable of solution than the actual situation about which he was feeling helpless and one to which he often turned in waking life. The dreams seemed to express both the helpless feeling (not knowing how to make a repair) and a means or guide showing how to feel better (one must fix this dial or that part of the car in order to get things going).

Another solution was evocation of past memories of similar situations which had worked out well. Thus, at the end of a period when his mother was visiting and he was struggling to gain some emotional distance from her, one of us dreamt of being back in a group singing madrigals, a reference to an experience where he had started as a rank beginner and had developed real competence at that activity.

Solutions did not always come with undistorted memories, however, but showed evidence of rewriting history in the effort to deal more effectively with disturbing feelings. One example was seen in coping with the continuing concern about our quest for the answer to the riddle of dreams. One dream indicated a childhood root of this wish for an answer and a characteristic (for the dreamer) method of dealing with the frustration of not knowing. The dream occurred on the night of his four-year younger brother's birthday, following a series of dreams filled with obvious concerns about our attempt to understand or uncover the secrets of dreams.

"Had moved into a new house—somewhat like the house at 73 Lewis [childhood house]—had cut through floor of kitchen and put stairs into cellar, stairs had been brought in sections which folded into each other, so were quite compact. Then assembled them in kitchen—my parents there—father wondered how stairs got in and I explained. Try to figure out the best place to put table."

It does not take much imagination to see a four-year-old boy wondering about the secrets of pregnancy and birth, but here it is turned around and father is asking the questions. It is also of interest that one of the day residues had been a discussion about the expansion of the dining room so there could be room for more people to eat. We had inspected the addition. In this dream, one might say that the memory triggered by the combination of the present situation (searching for answers about dreams) and the brother's birthday was that of the child's efforts to understand pregnancy and birth and his struggle to deal with the frustration of not knowing. The dream, however, is not just a portrayal of the problem but also shows changes which make the situation more acceptable to the dreamer.

BLENDING OF PAST WITH PRESENT IN MANIFEST DREAM

This blending of past with present was repeatedly seen. The proportions varied and seemed, in part, related to how arousing the present stimuli were. In effect, when a present situation or problem touched on emotionally important conflicts, the past would emerge more clearly. Otherwise, the manifest dream contained more material from the present. This observation may clarify an inconsistency between dream reports in the clinical and experimental literature. For example, in a clinical situation with a well-developed transference, implying active contact with the past, one might find a great deal of past memories in the dreams. On the other hand, laboratory studies of dreams have usually reported content much more related to the present. The laboratory subjects may be mainly concerned with their present lives and reflect this in their dreams.

Another dream was a particularly good example of the dual function of memories, both as a vehicle for expression of feelings, analogous to drawing a picture of how one feels, and as a portrayal of some kind of past solution to the current problem.

"In some kind of building—try to find way out—across some kind of roof or third story—can't find—then leave door open behind me so can go back and find way through number of rooms—something like a museum—get out and can't find way back—realize that from front of building the shape is such that is easy pathway—disconnected in back but connected in front." A later dream involved trying to buy some searchlight bulbs; then came dreams about the frustration of trying to fix things. The symbolism of this series of dreams seems to reflect past concerns about anatomical connections combined with the theme of searching for knowledge.

EACH DREAMER HAS HIS OWN "VOCABULARY"

Other aspects of dream content involved things we had heard or thought or read. As we began to appreciate the varied nature of the sources of manifest dreams, we realized why it is so difficult to develop a set of rules for dream language. In contrast to the fixed vocabulary of each spoken language, often formalized in a dictionary, each dreamer has his own "vocabulary" made up of his personal experiences and concerns. While the problems we struggle with may be common human ones, our ways of expressing them in dreams will depend on our own personal memory files. That these are indeed files became clear as we noted changes in dream content with changes in situations. Thus, when one of us visited his old university for the first time in years, not only did the dreams portray the feelings stirred up by this trip, but also the content contained people from college days with whom there had been no contact over the years and who were rarely thought of. It was as if the pressure of the present stimulus had opened that file drawer and those memories were now accessible for use in dreams. These changes in dream content may present some picture of how the filing system used for memory storage is organized. It should be also noted that a large sample of dreams from one person may be necessary to develop a clear sense of that dreamer's "vocabulary" (memories) and his "grammar" (style of organizing his experiences). This is like deciphering a new language or a coded message where one must have a large enough sample in order to translate it.

PSYCHIC PAIN NECESSARY FOR DREAM RECALL

Another aspect of memory concerns the ability to recall dream material. Studies of dreams in the laboratory have emphasized physiological factors in dream recall. Thus, awakenings from REM sleep usually lead to good dream recall. On the other hand, awakenings from NREM sleep lead to less recall or more thoughtlike content. In this study, two other aspects of dream recall emerged. One had to do with a sequential ebb and flow of memory. Thus, there would be a series of dreams over several nights in which there was evidence of a struggle with a single problem. One of us had a series of dreams involving portrayal of a sense of danger and issues of attachment to Mother, who was visiting. Gradually, there was a sense of resolution of the problems and then a period of no recall of dreams, suggesting that a certain intensity of disturbance was necessary for recall. The other aspect involved times when there was a sense of having dreamed, but there was no recall. Then, some waking observation would suddenly remind one of the dream and it would be recalled in more and more detail. This phenomenon is frequently seen in the clinical situation where an interpretation will suddenly lead to recall of a dream. Our observations suggest that the dream itself has been recorded as an experience. The problem in recall is not one of registration but one of retrieval. Something, a perception or an interpretation, may then lead to the proper focus of attention on the appropriate memory area with a rather clear recall of a dream and a sense of recognition of this as part of one's experience. It is as if, once attention is focused on the right place, one can pull out more and more of the memory, one piece connecting to the next as if they were all strung together.

OVERALL PICTURE OF THE DREAM PROCESS

We have presented a series of observations based on a large number of dreams that we have collected and discussed. None of these observations are new (Breger 1967, Faraday 1972, French and Fromm 1964, Jones 1970, Stekel 1943), but we feel that an overall picture of the dream process has begun to emerge as we put them together. This allows us to answer some of the questions we raised earlier in the paper. An overall view would suggest that dreams are made up of a combination of present and past experiences. These experiences are meaningfully connected by the emotional tone of the present experience. The past is either a way of expressing this meaning or may be an issue stirred up by the present experience. Our present experience can either be illuminated by the past or may be a repetition of the past. With respect to our dreams, our memories seem stored in clusters or file drawers, so that a particular issue in the present will draw on memories that are related by time, place, or emotional meaning. These memories may portray either the issue or an old solution to the problem with which we are struggling. Because dreams are made up of each dreamer's unique memories, there can be no universal dream vocabulary. This does not mean that someone else's dreams cannot be understood. We can understand an artist's painting without knowing all about the artist because common symbols may reflect experiences which we all have shared. But we must consider that the tools and raw material for the construction of a dream are unique to each dreamer. As a therapist becomes more familiar with a patient and his dreams, certain patterns lead to a rather quick recognition of the meaning of a dream. It is as if the therapist has become fluent in this particular patient's language. If an obscure dream then occurs, it may well represent some new aspect of the patient's vocabulary of life experiences. More significantly, what we portray in our dreams is a reflection of our unique concerns and interests based on what is important to us now and what was important to us in the past. It is this which makes dreaming a dynamic process which provides access to the emotional life of the dreamer.

RECONSIDERATION OF THE PSYCHOANALYTIC MODEL

We began this study with a model derived from REM physiology, and we have found a consistency between the dream material and the conclusions drawn from physiological studies. This consistency does not require, as some would have it, that dream content arises from efforts of the cortex to make sense of random neuronal firing in the pons (Hobson and McCarley 1977). Rather, it seems to require reconsideration of the psychoanalytic model of the dream as a mode of drive discharge or wish fulfillment. Dreams are dynamic because they are a part of our struggle to make emotional sense of our experiences. They vary from person to person and from time to time in the same person. They may show only the problem, as in a traumatic dream, or when a major emotional event, such as loss of a parent, occurs, as in our samples, they may show a process of grappling with a problem and then the finding of a solution—that is, making sense of it. The problems we struggle with may be based mainly in the present or may be mainly from the past, although the content of dreams shows again and again that we approach the present or color the present with our past. In this process, we obviously maintain or develop a sense of continuity with our past selves. One might wonder whether an important, disturbing feature of the traumatic dream is the loss of contact with our past selves. The present experience is too different from the past to be assimilated.

CLINICAL USE OF THE DREAM

We will conclude this examination of dreaming by considering what it can tell us about the clinical use of dreams. Most obvious is that the dream can show us and can show the dreamer the problem he is struggling with and how the present problem fits with the past. In order to understand this, we must have some familiarity with the dreamer's language. Associations to the dreams may provide us with the source of the images—the memories that make up the manifest dream—either recent or remote. Here, we should distinguish between associations revealing the source and those which allude to related experiences. When a patient describes a life experience which is portrayed in a dream, we should assume that this is what he is dreaming about. On the other hand, when the dreamer's associations lead to memories of similar conflictual experiences, these are not the source of the dream but may help us to understand the meaning of what is portrayed. The dream can also alert us to the fact that the dreamer is having trouble fitting the pieces together. This may be reflected by a disorganized dream or series of dreams or by the fact that in the dream the present is overwhelming the past or vice versa. On the other hand, over a series of dreams we may see a gradual resolution of a problem with increasing organization of the dreams. By understanding which memories from the past have been tapped, we can get a clearer picture of what is coloring the dreamer's present perceptions. In effect, the dreamer may in his dream be saying that this experience in the present is "like the one I had when . . ." or "I will try to deal with this experience the way I did when . . . , and therefore, now I can understand it and perhaps feel differently about it."

This last statement is, in our opinion, the core of trying to understand dreaming. It seems to be a process in which the dreamer struggles to make sense of and thereby master his life experiences, while maintaining a continuing sense of himself in relation to the world. It begins with high levels of REM sleep at birth and persists throughout life. It shows evidence both of success and of failure and is an accurate portrayal of life as the dreamer experiences it.

References

Breger, L. (1967) Function of dreams. *Journal of Abnormal Psychology.* Monograph 641.

Faraday, A. (1972). *Dream Power.* New York: Coward.

French, T. M., and Fromm, E. (1964). *Dream Interpretation: a New Approach.* New York: Basic Books.

Greenberg, R. (1966). Cerebral cortex lesions: the dream process and sleep spindles. *Cortex* 2:357–366.

Greenberg, R., and Pearlman, C. (1974). Cutting the REM nerve: an approach to the adaptive role of REM sleep. *Perspectives in Biology and Medicine* 17: 513–521.

——— (1975). A psychoanalytic-dream continuum: the source and function of dreams. *International Review of Psycho-Analysis* 2:441–448.

——— (1978). If Freud only knew: a reconsideration of psychoanalytic dream theory. *International Review of Psycho-Analysis* 5:71–75.

Hobson, J. A., and McCarley, R. W. (1977). The brain as a dream state generator: an activation-synthesis hypothesis of the dream process. *American Journal of Psychiatry* 134:1335–1348.

Jones, R. (1970). *The New Psychology of Dreaming.* New York: Grune and Stratton.

Jouvet, M. (1962). Recherches sur les structures nervenses et les mecanismes responsables des differentes phases du sommeil physiologique. *Archives Ital-ieene Biologie* 100:125–206.

McGrath, M. J., and Cohen, P. B. (1978). REM sleep facilitation of adaptive waking behavior: a review of the literature. *Psychological Bulletin* 85:24–57.

Schur, M. (1966). Some additional 'day residues' of 'the specimen dream of psychoanalysis.' In *Psychoanalysis: A General Psychology.* New York: International Universities Press.

Stekel, W. (1943). *The Interpretation of Dreams: New Developments and Technique.* New York: Liveright.

Part II

THE DREAM
IN THE VARIOUS
PSYCHOPATHOLOGICAL
STATES

CHAPTER 6

THE DREAM IN SCHIZOPHRENIA

John S. Kafka, M.D.

PROBLEMS IN ASSESSING THE DREAMS OF SCHIZOPHRENICS

When I was asked to contribute this chapter on schizophrenic patients for *The Dream in Clinical Practice,* I agreed to do so only if a somewhat personal, partly impressionistic contribution were acceptable rather than a more scholarly paper which would include a review of the literature. So many questions about schizophrenia and its treatment remain unanswered that I consider a chapter dealing with the clinical use of dreams something of a *tour de force.* Nevertheless, despite vast areas of ignorance and uncertainty, we are working clinically and psychotherapeutically with schizophrenic patients, and therefore some thoughts which have crystallized out after several decades of experience are perhaps worth reporting. Two further initial cautions are in order: (1) Since areas of uncertainty tend to foster the influence of idiosyncratic factors, elements of one's personal work history must be spelled out; (2) I do not *generally* consider the clinical use of dreams of central importance in the therapeutic work with schizophrenic patients. Some thoughts about when it may be important, the extent to which it may be important, and similarities and differences between ways of using dream material in the treatment of schizophrenic and other patients will be explored below.

The following elements of my work history are pertinent to my perspective on the psychotherapy of schizophrenia and the use of dreams in this context. For many years I spent a significant portion of my time working with extremely ill schizophrenic patients in a psychoanalytically oriented hospital. I continued to work with a few of these patients after I stopped my formal affiliation with this hospital and concentrated on a psychoanalytic practice and teaching activities. My views thus largely result from observations of a few patients with whom I have had contact, and usually fairly extensive contact, for up to two decades. Consultative work on a schizophrenia research unit, which in recent years has concentrated more on biological questions, has also contributed to my perspective. Prior to medical, psychiatric, and psychoanalytic training, I was educated as a psychologist, and I am aware that an interest in some perceptual problems, which dates from that period, still contributes to my approach. I also wish to state emphatically that psychoanalytic treatment of neurotic patients and also of patients with character disorders is radically different from "psychoanalytically informed" psychotherapeutic work with schizophrenic patients.

DREAMS AND THE "BRIDGING" THERAPEUTIC APPROACH

In referring to the personal work history, I want to stress the continuity of my work with schizophrenic patients during acute phases, during prolonged states of regression or "decompensation," and during long periods when there is no psychotic state, at least of the kind which requires hospitalization. The attempt to provide continuity, to offer a bridge from the flagrantly psychotic to the other stages, has always been a major component of my therapeutic strategy. This is not to be taken for granted even for therapists who are psychodynamically and psychoanalytically oriented. Federn (1952), many of whose insights I profoundly appreciate, thought, for instance, that it might be better for some patients to have another therapist take over after the patient emerged from an acute psychotic state. His view had something to do with the thought that the first therapist might be in a sense "contaminated" with the terror of the psychotic experience, and that this contamination would interfere with the treatment in other phases. The fact is that even if one works with them long enough, *some* relapses for *some* of the patients occur, whichever of the now available treatments are used. Furthermore, some of these relapses are not, at this point, understood, whether we try to understand them "biologically," psychodynamically, or through combined approaches.

If I had written this article earlier in my career, I would have announced some "understandings" which I do not now claim. This is because over the years too many different "understandings" were required for the same kind of relapse in the same patient. Overall it is my current opinion that a "bridging" therapeutic approach has played a part in avoiding relapses in some patients, very probably in diminishing their frequency in other patients, in diminishing their duration, and certainly in diminishing the impact of recurrences on their lives and also on the lives of family members. It is in connection with the bridging approach in the work with schizophrenic patients that dreams have their most explicit application.

The topic of the continuity of the content of the psychosis in dream material was developed by Douglas Noble (1951) and by Clarence G. Schulz (1969). While I wish to refer the reader to such discussions of the etiology of schizophrenia as are summarized in the two-part article by James S. Grotstein (1977), some relatively simple ideas have determined many aspects of my day-to-day therapeutic work. Clarence Schulz (1969) writes about his work with a severely disturbed schizophrenic patient who began to relate dreams after about five months of psychotherapy: "As his behavior began to improve, his psychotic thinking decreased and he began to report dreams" (p. 20). Three themes which were prominent in this patient's psychosis were: "(a) Violence and Fear, (b) Depression, and (c) Identity Diffusion . . . " (p. 53). One aspect of the history of Schulz's patient was that his two siblings had died under tragic circumstances in separate accidents. I will return shortly to the use of dreams in the psychotherapy of schizophrenic patients with a fairly obvious traumatic history of this kind.

EVACUATION FUNCTION OF DREAMS IN SCHIZOPHRENICS

I would like to refer to a few other ideas in the literature which have evoked an echo in my own clinical experience. One concerns the function of "evacuation." I have found applicable in work with schizophrenic patients, at times and with reservations which will be spelled out gradually, what André Green (1977) says about work with borderline patients:

dream analysis . . . is, as a rule, unproductive. . . . Dreams do not express wish-fulfillment but rather serve a function of evacuation. . . . The dream

barrier is an important function of the psychic apparatus. . . . Even though
the dream barrier is effective, the dream's purpose is not the working
through of instinct derivatives, but rather the unburdening of the psychic
apparatus from painful stimuli. . . . The dreams . . . are not characterized by
condensation but by concretization. One can also observe dream failures in
these patients: wakening in order to prevent dreaming or to find themselves
surrounded by a strange, disquieting atmosphere, which constitutes a
transitional dream state akin to a nightmare. In more successful instances,
dreams are actualizations of the self in the dream space, attempts to
reformulate traumatic experiences. . . . In such instances, the most significant thing in analyzing a dream is not the dream's latent content but *the
dreamer's experience* [p. 38].

TRAUMA IN THE LIFE AND DREAMS
OF SCHIZOPHRENICS

Whatever our eventual understanding of the etiology of various
schizophrenic disorders, for immediate therapeutic and practical working
purposes, I do find that I function as though I believed that trauma was
etiologically more important for some schizophrenic patients than for
others. I think, for instance, of a patient, Eleanor M, who had her first
acute episode after she had obeyed her mother's request and arranged to be
present in the operating room in which her mother was "opened up" and
found to have a widespread malignancy. Eleanor was also the main
caretaker of her dying mother, and the notion that a sedative which she
gave her mother killed her was at times an important element in her
delusions. Without giving a more complete case history, I do want to
indicate that she was diagnosed as schizophrenic on the basis of all the
usual criteria by the staff of several hospitals and showed particularly
flamboyant pathology. Hallucinating, wildly agitated, she was denudative,
smeared herself and the walls of seclusion rooms with menstrual blood,
and was destructive of property and sometimes assaultive. During more
than fifteen years of psychotherapeutic work with her, I found the role of
dreams in treatment an important one, as I shall describe below. She was
eventually able to leave the hospital, the frequency and the severity of
acute episodes diminished radically, and during the last eight years only
one brief hospitalization was necessary. (Medication, on the whole, did
not play a significant role in her management and treatment.) When she
did not need to be hospitalized, Eleanor's functioning was usually of a
rather high caliber as a wife, mother, and participating member in

community affairs. Her preoccupation with violence in her waking life was limited to a fascination with crime and criminals, wars, and catastrophies. Her selection of movies and television shows, her reading of newspaper and magazine articles, was almost exclusively based on such interests. Her dream life was characterized by prolonged periods during which she reported hundreds of more or less repetitive dreams dealing with amputations, mutilations, and bloody scenes.

Thus, Eleanor presented the contrasting picture of being prim and proper when not psychotic, but of having a dream life and psychotic periods full of gore. Over the years of working with her, I developed a technique of using "gory" language in talking about her dreams and impulses. I also commented, however, again and again about my reasons for doing so, spelling out the idea that the attempt at compartmentalization of such material in her case might contribute to the psychotic episodes. I would like to repeat that I draw a sharp line between doing psychoanalysis and conducting psychotherapeutic work with such schizophrenic patients, although there may be times when the technique of working with such a patient has some superficial resemblances to psychoanalytic technique. A thorough grounding in psychoanalytic concepts is important for understanding both the analogous techniques and the approaches that might be useless or destructive.

In this instance there were long periods when the therapy resembled some of the therapeutic work done with cases of "battle fatigue" during and after World War II. I am referring, for example, to the actual showing of war movies to soldiers who had experienced major dissociative episodes in battle. Showings of these movies were interrupted from time to time, and when the lights went on Red Cross girls offered the soldiers tea. Despite the use of such techniques, recognition of transference elements and the genetics of the conflict had their place in the treatment. The emphasis was, however, as André Green put it, "not [on] the dream's latent content, but the dreamer's experience."

REPAIR OF PSYCHOSIS THROUGH DREAMS

From the literature on dreams in schizophrenia and psychosis, I will cite one further notion which is in harmony with my own clinical use of dreams with these patients. In Eissler's paper, "The Effect of the Structure of the Ego on Psychoanalytic Technique" (1953), there is a reference to a psychotic patient, who in her dreams repairs the psychosis, so to speak. It is as if the dreaming ego were nonpsychotic while her waking ego was psychotic. Eissler also refers to similar observations made by Freud. Furthermore, Eissler refers to Freud's notion that "reality" appears like an instinct derivative in dreams of psychotics. That is, it was Freud's belief that the psychotic individual had constructed for himself a world which was so different and distinct from "reality"—I would now (Kafka 1977) say commonsense reality— that ordinary reality broke through into dreams in the same way in which material related to "instinct" broke into the dream of the nonpsychotic individual. Although oversimplified, these references to Eissler's and Freud's notions are related to the following clinical observations.

I accidentally discovered many years ago that when I woke a hospitalized schizophrenic patient with a complex paranoid delusional system, for five or ten minutes he was apparently free of delusions. I could never obtain from the patient any confirmation that he was dreaming, and any possible "repair" of the psychosis could have been the work of merely the "sleeping" and not necessarily of the "dreaming ego."

I would also like to refer to the work with another male patient, John M, who had been diagnosed as schizophrenic during several prolonged hospitalizations and who had at one time prior to my acquaintance with him, received a series of electroconvulsive treatments. Without getting into a discussion of diagnostic criteria, I would simply like to say that some clinicians would consider him as having a severe borderline disorder with pronounced narcissistic features. He did have frankly psychotic periods during my years of work with him, and brief hospitalizations were required, although drug abuse made it difficult to identify the precipitating factors. Dreams were also important in my work with John; but in this instance I worked more analytically, and my clinical use of dreams did not differ significantly from psychoanalytic dream interpretations. One feature of his reporting of dreams may, however, relate to Eissler's observation. He often spoke with great emphasis about the fact that his dreams now contained some "distortions." A room in which he lived or a landscape which he remembered from his childhood differed from the way it "really" was. Ordinarily, *nonpsychotic* dreamers consider such distortions as part of the *usual* fabric of the dream. John emphasized these distortions, for him "unusual," which he compared with what he considered his *normal* dreams. During psychotic episodes, he had apparently experienced dreams in which there was much "undistorted" reality. Clinically he was able to use my observations relating to such fluctuations in his dreams in a "bridging" fashion. My observations served as an introduction to part of normal living, namely, normally distorted dreams. Furthermore, I learned to use the degree of distortion reported by him about his dream material as an indicator of his "distance" from a psychotic episode, and such observations helped in his "management."

On the other hand, I have also encountered in a patient, Robert S, specific fear of a psychotic reaction when the vividness of the dreams was extreme—for instance, when he not only saw his own face as that of an animal, but also in his dream touched his face and discovered that his skin possessed the texture of an animal's skin. Robert never actually was psychotic, but several family members had been hospitalized with a diagnosis of schizophrenia, and his fear of psychosis was never far from the surface.

Another patient, about whose schizophrenic diagnosis there was no doubt but who lived most of his life outside a hospital, found that he had made all kinds of commitments, had pledged charitable contributions, and had accepted invitations when he had actually answered the telephone, but had believed that he was dreaming the whole thing. By the time I started working with him, he had already developed a method to circumvent this problem. Since he did not know if he was awake or dreaming—he had multiple dreams within dreams—and since "pinching himself" didn't do the trick, he had learned to always ask, "What is your number? I'll call you back."

"INTELLECTUAL" APPROACH TO DREAMS

Some of the above observations tend to move away from the clinical use of dreams in the therapy of schizophrenic patients. They are nevertheless pertinent. For some patients there seem to be common elements in dreams and psychotic experience, or at the very least, there are fears that certain dream characteristics herald psychotic experiences. In working therapeutically for prolonged periods with such patients, the therapist is likely to discover characteristics of dream reports which are indices of the closeness to the surface of some psychotic phenomena. An index may be valid for only one particular patient because it depends not only on general characteristics of schizophrenic and dream processes, but also on such personality variables as intelligence and intellectual style, and various characteristics of patient and therapist which determine their relationship and communication. If one works long enough, even with deeply re-gressed, chronic or "deteriorated" patients, one often discovers periods of

relatively greater accessibility during which both content and formal
elements of dream experiences can be considered collaboratively with the
patient. Despite my overall recognition of the general uselessness of too
much "intellect" in therapeutic endeavors, I have become less afraid of an
"intellectual" approach with some patients at such junctures. It connotes a
respect for formal characteristics of the patient's thought—a respect
which has a therapeutic function in itself.

My goals are often rather modest and frequently turn out to be only
a hope for better self-management of psychosis. Such better self-
management occurred with a patient who on previous occasions had been
brought to the hospital in a police ambulance, with sirens wailing and half
a dozen aides needed to restrain her agitated behavior. After a prolonged
therapeutic effort, this patient experienced herself as disturbed while on
vacation, hallucinated my office in her vacation home, heard me telling
her that she had better go to the hospital, and did so on her own initiative.
Discussion of form and content of dream material has been, for me, one of
the tools useful in facilitating such a development—that is, previous
discussion with the patient of form and content of dreams enhances the
patient's ability to observe critically some of the psychotic experiences,
even with the therapist only psychologically present.

PRIMARY PROCESS, DREAMS, AND PSYCHOTIC PHENOMENA

I do not wish to enter here into a more theoretical discussion of the
degree to which the primary-process concept may have different explana-
tory power in elucidating the formation of dreams and of psychotic
thought content. Nevertheless, an understanding of primary process can
clarify for the therapist such practical problems as, for example, the
equivalences and fusions of various family members in the mind of the
waking schizophrenic patient (Kafka and McDonald 1964).

Certain characteristics of the dreams of schizophrenic patients can also
give the therapist information about the patient's control techniques or
methods of self-management. Robert S—the patient with the telephone-
answering difficulties—on many occasions had "geological" dreams.
While geology was one of his daytime interests, it was the immensely long
and slow time scale of geological events that was the clue to his self-
management style. One day I told him that I was reminded of the puzzle
which one citizen of Berne—whose inhabitants have a reputation for

slowness—poses to another. "What is this?" asks the Swiss from Berne, while very slowly drawing an angular line in the air. The correct answer is "lightning." Very, very slowly the patient dared to break—or, should I say, "melt"—into a smile. After this it was possible for me to comment on certain catastrophic geological events in his dreams and to relate them in a therapeutically meaningful way to events in his life.

While one could discuss the nature of the obsessive elements in the defensive structure of Robert S, I would like to focus on the relative *completeness* of his slow-motion perception and his slow-motion self-perception, and the relative completeness and appropriateness of his gradually developing affective responses. Elsewhere I have developed the notion that perceptual acts recapitulate the development of perception, so that what is perceived in and as a "flash" by the adult corresponds to what a child may perceive in a more "lingering" perception (Kafka 1977, 1979). I have also developed the idea that certain qualities—for instance, "suspendedness"—can have for certain patients and under certain conditions an "object constancy" which is in a sense more "solid" than the objects which we usually associate with the notion of object constancy (Kafka 1979).

CONCRETENESS VERSUS ABSTRACTNESS IN DREAMS AND THOUGHTS OF SCHIZOPHRENICS

This work has a possible connection to the question of concreteness or "concretization" versus abstract qualities in dreams of schizophrenic patients—and perhaps also in schizophrenic thinking generally. In writing about "abstract expressionist dreams" (Kafka and Gaarder 1964), we gave an example in which a reported dream consisted of a continuous line with a small squiggle. It was perfectly clear to the dreamer, a "normal" individual after an LSD experience, that the line represented the course of history, and the squiggle represented the holocaust. I have come to believe that this kind of dream experience corresponds in large measure to the waking experience of many schizophrenic patients for whom certain "abstractions" carry a bewildering but convincing richness of meaning or meanings. As I indicated earlier, I have been impressed by the contrasting concreteness and vividness—"the reality"—of certain "schizophrenic" dreams (always remembering that in the most acute phases dreams are not reported and the question is thus irrelevant for therapeutic purposes). If "abstract expressionist" elements in waking experience have been recognized by the therapist, this may facilitate the patient's reporting, at stages of considerable improvement, the reversal in dream characteristics that I mentioned earlier—namely, a dream "atmosphere" in dreams and more "concreteness" in daily living.

As an elaborated example of this kind of reversal, one month after a psychiatric hospitalization a schizophrenic patient, Amanda T, reported dreaming that her mother was dead, her father was alive, and another woman was embracing him. The patient's actual life situation was that her *father* was dead and her *mother* was living. She emphasized that the scene reminded her of some Picasso paintings of the Blue Period, and further commented, "It's an interesting dream; the female figure is of undetermined age." Her sexual interest in her father had been an explicitly recognized theme in my prolonged work with her. During acute psychotic episodes she also was fused with, transformed into, or partially blended with her father. At one time, for instance, she made a point of not shaving her legs because "I have father's legs." I want to underline in the present context the patient's emphases on the Blue Period and the atmospheric qualities of the dream. Some of her other associations involved her daughter who liked Picasso, a period in her daughter's life when she was developing breasts, a visit to a relative who was divorcing her husband, and the patient's wish that her father had divorced her mother. In many respects these dream elements were understood by Amanda and were interpreted by her in a fashion similar to that in which a neurotic patient after prolonged insight-oriented therapy or analysis might comprehend her own dream material. She explained, however, that she could have such a dream now "because last month has been going very well. My husband did not go on any trips. He cooked a lot of dinners." She then talked about her father's flirtations, but discussed "love" very explicitly in terms of who fed whom. Mother did not feed father well; therefore, she did not love him. Amanda made precise equations in energy terms. She could have this dream now because she was well fed during the last month and consequently had enough energy to work on the old problems of her father's death.

"DREAMLIKE" DREAMS AS A SIGN
OF IMPROVEMENT

In my experience, when a schizophrenic patient can talk about atmospheric conditions—that is, in essence the *dreamlike* qualities of a dream—and does not see everyday reality as the intruder in the dream, then the patient is most removed from a psychotic ego organization. In prolonged psychotherapeutic work with a schizophrenic patient such a period should not be ignored. That is, the therapist can at such a moment explicitly deal with the apparently "neurotic" conflicts which are being presented and dealt with in the dream, but the therapist can also at such a moment introduce a discussion of the changes which such material undergoes during psychotic episodes. With Amanda, for example, the topic of her wish to be close to her father, to be with her father, and its shading into her wish to *be* father or at least to have *parts* of father, could be introduced in an effort to form the bridge between the current and the psychotic states. It is my belief that such an approach in the long run permits the patient to utilize the image of the therapist in the "bridging" management of her own psychosis.

PHARMACOLOGICAL INTERVENTIONS AND DREAMS IN SCHIZOPHRENICS

Thus, despite our uncertainties in understanding schizophrenic phenomena, despite the observation that the most clearly schizophrenic patients—*when* they are most clearly schizophrenic—do not report dream material, it is apparent that dreams can be used in the treatment of schizophrenia. Recently, as a psychoanalytic consultant on a biologically oriented schizophrenia research unit on which various vigorous pharmacological interventions are being studied, I have noted that in some patients whose condition changes and fluctuates rapidly, the reporting of dreams can occur almost immediately after emergence from the most severe disorganization. Dream material may be reported when delusions are still very active. The overlapping of acute psychotic manifestations and the reporting of dreams is greater here than I have observed where no such forceful pharmacological interventions are attempted. I would, therefore, not exclude the possibility that the study and perhaps the therapeutic use of dreams in schizophrenia may become of interest to clinicians with a variety of theoretical orientations.

References

Eissler, K. R. (1953). The effect of the structure of the ego on psychoanalytic technique. *Journal of the American Psychoanalytic Association* 1:104–143.

Federn, P. (1952). *Ego Psychology and the Psychoses.* New York: Basic Books.

Green, A. (1977). The borderline concept. In *Borderline Personality Disorders,* ed. P. Hartocollis. New York: International Universities Press.

Grotstein, J. S. (1977). The psychoanalytic concept of schizophrenia: I. The dilemma. II. Reconciliation. *International Journal of Psycho-Analysis* 58:403–452.

Kafka, J. S. (1977). On reality: an examination of object constancy, ambiguity, paradox, and time. In *Thought, Consciousness, and Reality. Psychiatry and the Humanities,* vol. 2, ed. J. H. Smith. New Haven, Conn.: Yale University Press.

——— (1979) Psychic effort, drift and reality structures: Observations from psychoanalytic work with neurotic, borderline and schizophrenic patients. In: *Psychotherapy of Schizophrenia,* ed. C. Miller. Proceedings of the 6th International Symposium on the Psycho-therapy of Schizophrenia, Laussane: *Excerpta Medica,* Amsterdam-Oxford.

Kafka, J. S., and Gaarder, K. R. (1964). Some effects of the therapist's LSD experience on his therapeutic work. *American Journal of Psychotherapy* 18:236–243.

Kafka, J. S., and McDonald, J. W. (1964). The latent family in the treatment of hospitalized schizophrenic patients. In *Current Psychiatric Therapy,* ed. J. S. Masserman. New York: Grune and Stratton.

Noble, D. (1951). A study of dreams in schizophrenia and allied states. *American Journal of Psychiatry* 107:612–616.

Schulz, C. G., and Kilgalen, R. K. (1969). The treatment course of a disturbed patient. In *Case Studies in Schizophrenia.* New York: Basic Books.

CHAPTER 7

THE DREAM IN MANIC-DEPRESSIVE PSYCHOSIS

Ping-nie Pao, M.D.

Do dreams by manic-depressives show certain specific characteristics which distinguish them from dreams by schizophrenics, neurotics, or "normal" persons? Lewin (1946) has indicated that "structurally, manic dreams do not differ markedly from the general pattern. The blank dream is an exception" (p. 119). The same can actually be said about the depressive dreams. The dream by manic-depressives, like the dream of "normal" persons, represents the compromise formation between disturbing impulses and affect and the censuring forces. However, on account of the varying ego organization during a full manic-depressive cycle, the dreams during the manic, the depressive, and the normal phases could show some differences. These differences can be explored through the study of all the dreams of two manic-depressive patients during one full (or nearly full) manic-depressive cycle. Inferences from this clinical material can be made.

THE DIAGNOSTIC TERM "MANIC-DEPRESSIVE"

In the sixth edition of his textbook, Kraepelin (1899) first introduced the term "manic-depressive," which comprised the entire group of the so-

I am grateful to Dr. Joseph D. Lichtenberg for his comments and criticism in the preparation of this paper.

called periodic and circular psychoses and most of the simple manias. Kraepelin intimated that in the course of years he had become more and more convinced that all of these pictures are but forms of a single disease process. According to Kraepelin, the manic-depressive psychosis and schizophrenia (or, in his terms, dementia praecox) were two discrete disease entities, both of constitutional-hereditary origin. The differential diagnosis between the two was based on their clinical courses: the manic-depressive psychosis was episodic and self-terminating whereas the schizophrenia tended toward and ended in dementia. In his subsequent writings (seventh to ninth editions of his textbook), Kraepelin seems to have broadened the scope of manic-depressive psychosis to include, in addition to the above-mentioned mixed types, an involutional melancholia. With respect to those cases which showed schizophrenic symptomatology, Kraepelin would determine whether the patient was a manic-depressive or a schizophrenic in accordance with the subsequent absence or presence of mental deterioration.

Bleuler (1911) indicated that Kraepelin's effort to delineate manic-depressive psychosis and dementia praecox was important. For, in the process, the boundaries of the diseases were not only "drawn unilaterally from within but also solidly from without" (p. 7). While accepting Kraepelin's classification of major psychogenic psychoses into manic-depressive and dementia praecox, Bleuler (1924) felt "it is nevertheless impossible to base a classification of morbid picture only on the course of the disease" (p. 174). To emphasize diagnosis based not on the course of the disease but on the symptomatology, Bleuler arrived at a viewpoint of manic-depressive which was somewhat different from that of Kraepelin's. He suggested that "every man then has one syntonic (cyclothymic) and one schizoid component. . . . Either both or one of the reactions may be morbidly exaggerated in the same individual. The extreme cases then belong to the pure manic-depressive and the pure schizophrenic diseases. Frequently, however, we find distinct mixtures; preponderating manic-depressive types with schizophrenic accessory symptoms and the 'reverse' " (1924, p. 175). In accordance with this viewpoint, the manic-depressive and the schizophrenic are two discrete disease entities only insofar as the symptomatology is concerned. As Jelliffe (1931) succinctly put it, "When Bleuler states that it is of little value to ask is it manic-depressive or is it schizophrenic? but rather how much manic-depressive and how much schizophrenic? one can see that the entity platform of the Kraepelinian synthesis has markedly shifted in accent" (p. 12). From the clinical point of view, this shift is of pragmatic importance, because a case of manic-depressive psychosis may change its clinical picture to that of schizophrenia and vice versa. Often, affixing a diagnosis is not simple. W. W. Elgin (in the mid 1950s) often told the story that during the 1930s the clinical picture and, therefore, the diagnosis of many patients changed from manic-depressive psychosis to schizophrenia in a matter of months when they were moved from Phipps Clinic to Sheppard and Enoch Pratt Hospital—two prominent treatment centers in Baltimore.[1]

Psychoanalytic studies of manic-depressive psychosis have left an indelible imprint on the concept of this psychosis. Because of the importance which psychoanalysis lays on the "disposition-experience unity" (Freud 1914), the concept of "disease" is altered. From the psychoanalytic point of view, manic-depressive psychosis is not a disease because of the existence of certain non-identifiable but specific constitutional-hereditary defects in the patient, but rather because the patient shows deviational human behavioral patterns resulting from the interaction of constitutional-hereditary endowments with the environment during the early phases of life.[2] The psychoanalytic study of human development—more specifically, the developmental lines—offers an explanation of the possibility of mixed or alternating clinical pictures of manic-depressive psychosis and schizophrenia. The theory of anxiety (Freud 1926) and the "best possible solution" (cf. Sandler 1969) explains why there might be a marked shift of symptomatology such as described by Elgin above. The psychoanalytic scrutiny of symptom formation with respect to mania and depression further allows a dynamic understanding of the structure of the illness (cf. Lewin 1950, Pao 1968).

CLINICAL EXAMPLES OF DREAMS
IN MANIC-DEPRESSIVES

The clinical material I will present describes two cases in which dreams were related to the therapist during the course of treatment of manic-depressive psychoses. I will convey the general nature of the illness and the timing during the phases of illness when the dreams were related. The manifest content will be described along with whatever sparse

1. Personal communication
2. Bleuler might have specifically had this in mind when he spoke of cyclothymic and schizoid components.

association the patient provided. In no instances were the dreams able to be subjected to a detailed analysis and interpretation as would have been done with a psychoneurotic patient.

Case 1

A diagnosis of manic-depressive psychosis of the circular type was established in Mrs. A during her late thirties. After several years of excessive anxiety, Mrs. A became severely depressed and suicidal. The depression was soon followed by mania which was again followed by suicidal depression. At the height of her third manic episode she was admitted, for the first time, to a psychiatric hospital from which she soon signed herself out. The manic episode lasted for several months, driving the family to total distraction. As she was about to plunge into the depressive phase, she finally accepted a recommendation from her family and psychiatrist and admitted herself to Chestnut Lodge. Upon admission, she was still flighty and overactive, although she felt depressed. She was seen four times a week. During the initial interviews, she was asked to tell freely of her thoughts; she was not specifically asked to report dreams. (How the dreams were used by her two previous therapists was not known.)

The first dream (dream 1) was reported during the fourteenth hour when she was still very flighty, but considered herself very depressed. The dream: "I, my husband, and my previous therapist were on a boat, touring the world. I gave advice to this previous therapist that he should acquire some lightweight clothes like my husband's. The scene changed, and my husband and I went to a movie on the boat; I chose the seats. The scene changed again. I was shopping ashore, was concerned about how much time I had. While shopping, I told myself not to be extravagant. I bought only some cheap trinkets."

Her associations to the dream were meager and mere elaboration of the manifest content. Furthermore, she ran back again and again to the theme of depression, hopelessness, and suicidal preoccupations. Transference connection was completely denied, even though she admitted that she had entertained thoughts of leaving the hospital and that she did not think she would get much from her treatment there.

In the nineteenth hour, while talking about her life with her husband, she reported another dream (dream 2): "I opened the door and saw my husband and another patient in bed under the covers. I closed the door and fled." Initially her association was to her husband's alleged affairs with other women, but later it was directly to her conversation with another of the therapist's patients.

In the twenty-second hour, while talking about her vow not to have children with her husband because of his affairs, she dreamed (dream 3): "I was going away—I prepared the meal for the cat before I went away." She talked about a cat which she had for twelve years and about how different her life might be if she had had a child. As she went on, she expressed her fear of vindictiveness which might spill over to her therapist.

Steadily, her depression deepened. She was less careful about her appearance. She dragged around. Even lifting a little finger seemed to be performing a monumental task. Her verbalization was confined to despair, futility, and a desire to die.

Slowly and definitively, her depression improved. During the seventy-first hour, she reported a dream (dream 4): "I was lying on my stomach, like a child." She had no association whatsoever. She continued to show clinical improvement. During the ninetieth hour she reported another dream (dream 5): "I was talking to Kim," who was her best friend before her marriage. While her association began with the good times they had had, it ended on the note that, by comparison, Kim was far better off and more successful than herself.[3] She admitted her envious feelings toward her therapist because of his profession and his capacity to give.

She continued to talk about feeling depressed and futile. And she had frequent physical complaints such as headaches, backaches, and so on. Yet, she participated in all the activities in the hospital and was able to do analytic work. In the treatment hours she dealt with her feelings of being empty-handed and of her needs ungratified by her therapist upon leaving the office; her dilemma of having a bad object and being afraid to leave it. This attitude was duplicated in her contact with her husband. At various times, she talked about her past. Although such talks appeared to have been used to avoid rather than to illuminate the present, they had profound emotional impact on her. For instance, when she spoke of her wish to drown her younger sibling in the bathtub, she was guilty and agitated. When she spoke of her inability to match her deceased oldest brother, she felt self-depreciating.

By the 180th hour she said she was getting well and was no longer depressed. She talked freely about stories her mother told her, which indicated that her mother was deeply depressed following the death of her

---

3. Months later, she revealed that Kim had two children. Thus, the dream seemed to pick up where she had left off before the incapacitating depressive phase supervened.

favored son, the patient's oldest brother, when the patient was barely two years of age. She reported in the 191st hour (dream 6): "Both [living] brothers of mine were in a new car, which had a nose like an airplane. I was sitting on the hood. My younger brother was driving, at the speed of a hundred miles per hour. I asked him to slow down and he ignored me. We drove through Canada, via small tortuous roads. He finally stopped on the shoulder of the road. There were several beer joints. Pointing at one, I said I knew this place. I walked in. I saw a fat woman standing there. I woke up." Upon awakening she went for some orange juice. After this, she went back to bed and then she recalled a tune—the tune was from the movie "High and Mighty."

The following hour she reported another dream (dream 7): "I was looking for a hatpin in my husband's factory. Men there, very brawny, tried to attack me. I ran." The associations of the two dreams were to her devaluation of femininity, her envy of men, her wish to fit into her deceased oldest brother's shoes, her effort to help her husband to be more manly so that he could make her more womanly, and so on. Following these dreams she continued to feel good. Instead of complaining, she became very self-sufficient. In this, she enacted out in treatment the mother's wish for her to be independent and to be the deceased eldest brother to get things for the mother.

Now seventeen months had elapsed since her admission. When her therapist went on a summer holiday, she arranged with her husband to take a trip to a summer resort. The trip turned out to be a fiasco; they played hot and cold, tested each other's love, and ended with both feeling frustrated and enraged. Immediately upon resuming treatment, she said that she was "going high" and she did soon have a manic episode. During mania, she enacted out her lifelong fantasy as Cleopatra, the queen. The mania lasted for three months. As she was coming down from the mania, she reported (in the 307th hour) the following dream (dream 8): "I was estranged in a motel with my dog. I was afraid." She never had a dog, and the dog was associated to barking and biting. Further association revealed her concern with her aggressivity during the manic episode, lest she had offended the people around her, including her therapist.

Her treatment continued, but the above material is sufficient for the present purpose.

Conflict and Ego Organization in Manic-Depressive Dreams: First Example

A dream must be understood within the total context of a session as well as the ongoing therapeutic process; the dreams of manic-depressives are of no exception when reported. The dream reveals the patient's conflict of long past and how it is being reactivated in the present therapeutic situation. It also reflects the patient's ego organization at that particular moment. With respect to the conflict, in the case of Mrs. A, dream 1 bespoke her fear of involvement with the therapist and her derogatory attitude of a defensive nature toward all men, including the therapist. In dream 2 her rageful thoughts about her husband's infidelity corresponded to her similar thoughts about the triangular relationship in the treatment situation. In dream 3, her lifelong vindictive tendency was exposed; this tendency hurt others as well as herself. Dream 4 showed her concealed childish needs, and dream 5, her propensity for envy. Dreams 6 and 7 footnoted grandiose fantasy through the identification with her deceased oldest brother in order to compensate for her feelings of being unloved and unloveable. Because of these feelings, she devalued herself and consequently her femininity. In dream 8, she expressed her conflict over aggressive impulses. In these eight dreams, her basic conflicts were well articulated within the context of the material presented.

As for the ego organization, its integrity can usually be taken for granted in neurotics. But in psychotics, the ego functions may be severely impaired and along with the impaired, reality testing the capacity to distinguish night dreams as such may be interfered with. In the case of Mrs. A, dreams 1, 2, and 3 showed a relatively well organized ego. These dreams were like those of neurotic patients. The relatively well organized ego also offered adequate association for the understanding of the dreams. The short dreams (4 and 5) reflected the poorer ego organization at the initiation of the "incapacitating depressive phase."[4] Emerging from the incapacitated depressed phase, she was in better ego organizaton and had the lengthy and more self-revealing dreams 6 and 7. This was soon followed by the manic phase during which she did not dream. Then, the manic phase subsided. As her ego organization improved, she had dream 8.

Case 2

Miss B was twenty-five upon arrival at Chestnut Lodge. During the previous four years she had had two full cycles of manic-depressive psychosis and was twice hospitalized during the manic phase. Six months before her admission to Chestnut Lodge, she made a suicide attempt and

---

4. For a fuller definition of this term, see the section below on dreams in the four phases of the manic-depressive psychosis.

was hospitalized elsewhere, where she was described as very depressed and retarded. She moped around and showed no interest in anything.

Miss B's father had been diagnosed as manic-depressive. Several times it was recommended that he enter a psychiatric hospital, but he had refused to do so.

At the time of her admission to Chestnut Lodge, Miss B was not as depressed as she was during the earlier hospitalization, although she was still considered a high suicidal risk. Obviously, she was emerging from the incapacitating depressive phase. At that time, she said, "I have to be in a hospital, otherwise I might kill myself. I don't like myself and I wish I were someone else." Although she still felt like a blob, she was dressed neatly in style and used a lot of makeup. She was seen four times a week. When first seen, she was asked to freely tell her thoughts and her bodily experiences to her therapist. No special request was made for her to report dreams.

During the sixteenth session, she started the hour by saying that she had nothing to say, but immediately she said she woke up from a dream (dream *a*): "I was going downstairs. The stairway was long, winding and endless. I was in shepherd clothes. I had a staff in my hand." Her association was immediately to her fifteenth year when her father remarried. Her stepmother's mother moved into their house and into her upstairs bedroom. She and her brother, two and a half years younger, were forced to move downstairs. She also talked about her brother and herself as inseparable. She described the person (herself) in shepherd clothes with a staff in her hand as the boy who cried wolf. She said that her father always ridiculed her when she felt distress. "No one ever cared."

The next session she was listless, very depressed, and complained endlessly about restrictions she experienced in the hospital. Then toward the end of the hour she said she had dreamed of "bundles of paper her father sent over" (dream *b*). She explained that in recent years she lived away from home. Her father, who lived in the same city, would periodically send her bundles of clippings to read. She elaborated further on how her father was heedless of her own interests and psychological needs. She agreed that meeting with the therapist and talking about herself bore a similarity to getting assignments from her father's bundle of clippings.

No dream was reported until the thirty-second session. After talking about her uneasiness at the ward meetings, she said she had dreamed of "taking examinations. In the classroom I saw some girls from high school" (dream *c*). She said the examination dream was a recurrent dream. She couldn't specify when such dreams began. Examinations had another important meaning, for toward the end of her sophomore year in college, she first became manic while preparing for a year-end examination. (Later it was revealed that the mania occurred a few months following the break up of her relation with her step-uncle.) From girls of her junior high school days (twelve to fifteen years old), she moved on to talk about her mother who was discovered at that time to have cancer and who died a year later; she was twelve and thirteen. Because of the death of her mother, she did not enjoy her high school years as other girls did.

Clinically, she felt better and began to participate more in hospital activities. She was quite attached to her therapist and often talked about him with others in positive terms. She reported no dreams until the seventy-seventh session. Following a long weekend, she began the hour by complaining about feeling lonely and bored. She was an insomniac and had the following dream (dream *d*): "I was at a dance party in a big hall. There were a lot of people there but I didn't know them. The scene changed. I was shopping with the mother of a girl. The mother was in a purple velvet dress, plain but dressy, and I was in a similar dress in blue. The scene changed again and I was rushing to take an examination."

The first part of the dream reminded her of the dance the other night in the hospital. At the dance, she felt very ill at ease as she had always been at such occasions. The girl in the dream was a classmate of her brother's, two years her junior. Miss B met this girl's mother once at a football game, who had impressed Miss B as being very nice. This girl recently had married the boy across the street from Miss B's family home in the old neighborhood. Further association led to the time when they were living in that home, where her mother died. Then her father began to court her future stepmother and gave many fancy balls. She and her brother were left to themselves. As soon as her father married her stepmother, she became, at fourteen and a half, involved with the stepmother's married brother. Because of him, she did not associate with boys of her own age. When the relation with this uncle terminated five years later, she had her first manic episode. She cried and said that if her mother had lived, she could be married like the girl in the dream and probably would not have been psychotic. She further expressed her fear of being involved with the therapist, since this involvement could place her in a vulnerable position.

Six weeks later, upon learning about her therapist's forthcoming summer holiday, she reported a dream during the ninetieth session. "Father urged me to leave. I left with the feeling too soon. Then the scene changed and I was at home. It was perhaps Christmas; Stepmother and I decorated the tree. A black thing over me" (dream *e*). She was ready to admit that it was not her father who wanted her to leave but she herself wanted to leave treatment before her therapist's vacation. The Christmas scene reminded her of her "formal" relation with her stepmother. She couldn't go back to live with her father and her stepmother. The black thing was related to her "depressive mood." Anticipating getting depressed again, she felt that she should not leave. During the next session she reported another dream (dream f): "I was with my stepmother, father, and brother. The Japanese invaded. My brother and I were walking in the street, confronting the Japanese soldiers and feeling panic, while my father was playing golf and my stepmother was partying. I woke up in a sweat." She clarified that during the second world war she was still a young child, and her mother had often expressed fear that the Japanese might bomb or invade their home state on the West Coast. Further associations led to her thoughts of being together with her mother, even though together they worried about the Japanese invasion and the dissolute loneliness of a fragmented family life following her mother's death. She spoke resentfully about the therapist's forthcoming vacation and spoke of him in terms of Japanese invaders who had the potential for undermining her emotional equilibrium.

During the therapist's vacation, she got drunk when she was given a pass to be away from the hospital grounds. She ran into difficulties with the police. She made attempts to sign herself out of the hospital. When reunited with her therapist, she reported these events matter-of-factly. During the therapy hours, she appeared "shallow" emotionally, used a great deal of denial, and tended to chit-chat. She was no longer as psychologically minded as she had been. Three days later (104th session), she reported having dreamed that her "mother was alive but my brother was dead" (dream g). Her mood was noted to be euphoric, and she was not able to talk much about the dream. Promptly, without consulting the clinical administrator, she acquired a job off-grounds and bought herself a new car. When her decision was questioned, she identified the administrator with her father who, to her, was dogmatic and opinionated. She threatened to leave the hospital, while telling everyone how important it was for her to stay with the treatment. In this predicament she became increasingly hyperactive and flighty.

It took several weeks or so before she entered a full-blown mania which lasted for four months. As she calmed down, she first made an effort to change her therapist. After she talked herself out of making this change, she reported the following dream during the 204th session. "I was driving my stepmother's car over a wooden bridge in my hometown. As the car landed on the bridge, the bridge fell apart. I woke up" (dream h).

Her first comment on the dream was about the fallen bridge which actually had been replaced in recent years by a concrete structure. The fallen bridge was soon equated to her father, who was described as more dependent on her than she on him. Because of his severe mood swings, he had been "weak" and leaned heavily on his three "women"—the patient's mother, the patient, and the patient's stepmother. With bitterness Miss B said, "Following my mother's death and before my stepmother married him, I had to look after him. He was depressed and pathetic. But I helped him to get his strength back. He married my stepmother." She felt that her stepmother's married brother was like her father in the sense that he came to her when he was unhappy and depressed. As soon as he regained his strength he returned to his own wife. She concluded that all men were equally bad; her therapist was no exception.

The treatment went on, but the above is sufficient for our present purposes.

Conflict and Ego Organization in Manic-Depressive Dreams: Second Example

As in the case of Mrs. A, the eight dreams revealed Miss B's preoccupation as well as her ego organization at the time of dreaming. With respect to her conflicts, dreams *a* and *b* disclosed that because of her relation with her father she feared becoming involved with her therapist. Dream *a* also revealed her confusion about her sexual identity. Dream *c* brought forth her feelings of having missed a developmental phase of her life following her mother's illness and death. Dream *d* elaborated on her feelings about men. In dream *e*, she revealed her conflicted feeling toward her therapist with a tentative desire to leave him before being left. Following her decision to stay with her therapist she sensed in dream *f* a more severe conflict and a possibility of disaster. In dream *g* she resorted to a magic solution to her conflict by reviving her mother. Dream *h* again depicted her conflict over the therapist, who in her view was like every other man in her life.

With respect to ego organization, dreams *a, b, c, d,* and *e* were products of relatively well organized ego. Dream *f* was dreamed at a time when she experienced severe anxiety. At dream *g* she was markedly regressed. She did not dream during the manic phase when her ego organization was greatly impaired. By the time of dream *h*, the ego organization had improved, and she was again concerned with her feeling about men.

MANIA AND DEPRESSION AS PARALLEL STATES

With respect to manic-depressive psychosis, prior to Lewin's insightful contribution, melancholia was regarded as the primary illness and mania as secondary to depression. Lewin (1950, 1959) stressed that mania and melancholia are two independent ego reactions to extreme anxiety, in the form of fear of dying. Both in depression and in mania, the patient is regressed. But in mania the patient is further regressed, to the earliest ego state—the pleasure ego capable of world mastery. In a previous clinical report on the study of the causative factors in the transition of states (1968), I concluded, as Lewin did, that mania and depression are indeed two parallel states. When disappointed by the contemporary libidinal object, the patient experiences great mental pain. This pain is a complex affective experience;[5] it is an admixture of unbearable feelings of helplessness and hopelessness described by Bibring (1953), tension resulting from an insuppressible urge to discharge aggressive impulses, and guilt derived from the superego censuring such discharge. In the face of this pain, the patient regresses and loses much of later-acquired ego function. As reality testing becomes impaired, boundaries between the internal and external experience become obliterated. Thereupon the patient associates the disappointing contemporary object with the infantile "bad" affect and attempts to flee from it. If a new object is available—by which is meant not only the physical presence of the object but also its willingness to be libidinally responsive—the patient takes flight to the new object, succeeds in shaking off the "bad" object or "bad" affects, makes use of "good" affects to eliminate the "bad" affects, and simultaneously identifies with the idealized omnipotent primary object (the idealized "good" mother)—this constitutes the manic psychosis.[6] If, however, a new object is not available, the patient has to "stay" with the disappointing "bad" object and as in the further interaction with it, he holds back his aggressive impulses, turns them inward against himself, and creates a clinical picture of melancholia. Mahler (1966) observes that the basic mood of elation is crystallized during the practicing period par excellence, and the basic mood of depression is crystallized during the succeeding rapprochement period. Elsewhere (Pao 1971a, b) I have suggested that mania is related to the basic mood of elation as described by Mahler and may have its fixations

5. Corresponding to what Lewin conceptualized as fear of dying.
6. From recent observations, I would add that with the new object, the patient does not need to feel as restrained as with the original object in the expression of aggression. The direct expression of aggressive impulses facilitates the precipitation of manic psychosis.

at the practicing period par excellence when the basic mood of elation was crystallized. Considering the similarity that melancholia is related to the basic mood of depression and may have a fixation point at the rapprochement period,[7] I suggest, as Lewin did, that in mania the ego is more regressed.

DREAMS IN THE FOUR PHASES OF THE MANIC-DEPRESSIVE PSYCHOSIS

I have also made the observation (Pao 1968) that the depressive phase of the manic-depressive psychoses may be distinguished into two phases: (1) the functioning depressive phase during which the patient feels depressed and appears depressed, yet can perform daily chores without much problem and functions well enough to do analytic work; and (2) the incapacitating depressive phase during which the patient seems to be completely weighted down by his depressive mood, and is physically and intellectually retarded and cognitively preoccupied with thoughts of badness, death, and suicide so that he cannot do any analytic work at all. Thus, during the course of psychoanalytic treatment, a full cycle of the manic-depressive psychoses may be distinguished into four phases instead of two,[8] namely, (1) from the functioning phase of the depression to the mania; (2) the reverse; (3) from the functioning phase to the incapacitating phase of the depression; and (4) the reverse. Moreover, I have

7. Of course, early traumatic experiences are contributory to the causation of the fixation point.

8. In "Elation, Hypomania, and Mania," I have said (Pao 1971b): "The clinical importance of distinguishing between normal and pathological mood elevations may be illustrated by the following brief account. In the case of circular psychosis, at the conclusion of a prolonged depressive psychosis, there is usually a brief period of elevated mood; just as in following a manic psychosis, there is a brief moment of sadness. The sadness following the mania is actually an expression of mourning over the loss of all the glories experienced in the manic fantasies. It is not to be thought of as depression proper, which clinical picture, as Bibring (1953) described, constituted the basic depressive ego state plus manifestations of various defense and secondary gains. Likewise, a brief period of elevated mood following emergence from a prolonged depression is an expression of self-satisfaction for having accomplished the task of overcoming a long spell of depression. It is an expression of achievement, and it is an experience akin to elation as a basic mood. At such a moment, the ego is not concerned with the denial of loss and the containment of destructive impulses. Consequently, it would be erroneous to conceptualize this brief period of elevation of mood as mania proper" (p. 795–796). In speaking of four phases here, I have not taken into account the "normal" mood responses.

suggested that the "functioning depressive phase" would be a product of the treatment—if the patient were not in treatment this phase might be what we considered "normal interim." That is, instead of the cycle of the functioning depressive phase, the manic phase, the functioning depressive phase, the incapacitating depressive phase, there would be only the normal interim, the mania, the normal interim, the depression, and so on. With respect to the two illustrative cases, the aforedescribed four phases were easily distinguished in one full cycle of manic-depressive psychosis. Mrs. A was in the functioning depressive phase upon admission. Soon she slumped into the incapacitating depressive phase which was followed by the functioning depressive phase, the manic phase, and again the functioning depressive phase. In the case of Miss B, she was admitted at the tail end of the incapacitating depressive phase, which emerged into the functioning depressive phase, then the manic phase, and subsequently the functioning depressive phase again.

Quite coincidentally, Mrs. A and Miss B each reported eight dreams. In the case of Mrs. A, dreams 1, 2 and 3 (during the fourteenth, nineteenth and twenty-second hours, respectively) were dreamed during the functioning depressive phase; dreams 4 and 5 (during the seventy-first and ninetieth hours, respectively) were dreamed while emerging from the incapacitating phase; dreams 6 and 7 (during the 191st and 192nd hours, respectively) were dreamed shortly preceding the manic phase; and dream 8 (during the 351st hour) was dreamed toward the end of the manic phase. In the case of Miss B, dreams a, b, and c (during the sixteenth, seventeenth and thirty-second hours) were dreamed during the functioning depressive phase succeeding the incapacitating depressed phase; dreams d, e, and f (during the seventy-seventh, ninetieth and ninety-first hours) were reported during the middle of the functioning depressive phase; dream g (during the 104th session) was reported at the outset of the manic phase and dream h (during the 241st hour) was the first dream reported when a full blown manic phase was over.

It is of interest to note that in both cases all of the eight dreams were dreamed during the functioning depressive phase. During both the incapacitating depressive phase and the manic phase, Mrs. A did not dream or did not report dreams. Similarly Miss B reported no dreams during the manic phase (she was not under our observation during the incapacitating depressive phase). This phenomenon of not dreaming or not reporting dreams during the more severely psychotic periods may suggest that dreaming and reporting dreams are ego functions and are closely related to level of ego organization. For instance, during the incapacitating depressed phase, Mrs. A seemed so totally consumed (defensively) by her delusional thoughts about badness, death, suicide, and so on, that in order to keep out the even more unpleasant conflictual feelings she was like Lewin's (1946) depressed woman patient who could not sleep and was fearful of dreaming because of her need to frustrate the intrusion of a wish to die into visual content of her sleep. During the manic phase, Mrs. A's sense of reality was so impaired that she could not distinguish fantasy from reality.[9] She believed that she *was* Cleopatra and therefore had the power to assign her therapist as the Egyptian premier who looked after the well being of the people and the country. She was not able to discern the difference between daydreams and reality—she was *living* in the dream.

Overall, neither Mrs. A nor Miss B demonstrated adequate willingness and ability to study their dreams as most neurotics do. While ability was handicapped by their potentially psychotic egos, their lack of willingness seemed to be related to their life styles, which involved not revealing themselves to others or, more specifically, not revealing their narcissistic vulnerability. Still, during the middle of the functional depressive phase,[10] Mrs. A and Miss B did show more capacity and willingness to work on these dreams than they did at the beginning or the end of the same phase. This may very well speak in support of Abraham's (1911) observation that the manic-depressives can do collaborative, analytic work during the "normal" intervals (i.e., functioning depressive phases) between the mania and the incapacitating depressive phases.

In general, in the treatment of Mrs. A as well as Miss B, dreams and reporting of dreams were valuable indicators of the nature of the conflict, the extent of regression, and the extent of ego organization. To a certain degree, they were even more useful than dreams of neurotics in treatment, where the therapist's main concern would be the content of the conflict only.

THE BLANK DREAM DURING MANIA

In the literature, studies have been made on the manic dreams and the depressive dreams. Lewin (1946) observed that manic dreams are not

9. See Lichtenberg and Pao (1974) in regard to the difference between delusion, fantasy, and desire.

10. Inasmuch as the patient's ability for analytic work is greatly curtailed during the manic and incapacitating depressive phases, I have noted in a previous paper (Pao 1968) that the verbal and nonverbal products of the patient during these periods are rich in content and in meaning, and that it may prove useful for the therapist to stay with the patient during such severely psychotic moments.

structurally different from dreams in general except for the blank dream. He has also postulated (Lewin 1946, 1950) that dream content is to be projected on a dream screen. A blank dream is one in which the content is blotted out, and the dream screen is the only thing that is present and discernible insofar as the patient is concerned. The blank dream indicates the fulfillment of the wish to sleep or to die, and the mania which follows the blank dream represents the attempt at a denial of the dangers inherent in the fulfillment of the wish to sleep. Following Lewin's lead, Rycroft (1951) suggested that the dream screen is not present in all dreams but a phenomenon that occurs in the dreams of patients who are entering a manic phase. It symbolizes the manic sense of ecstatic fusion with the breast and a denial of hostility towards it. Studying dreams preceding elation, Levitan (1967, 1968, 1972) noted that such dreams were characterized by the revival in the manifest content of an extremely painful life experience. At the height of reexperiencing the trauma, the dreamer failed to awaken as he would be expected to. Instead, he regressed further to the pleasure ego capable of world mastery—this appears in the manifest content in the form of a sudden magical resolution of the traumatic experience. He explained, "Although during dreaming there is always some disconnection between the body and the hallucinated body image, the increased depth of sleep in these instances reduces this connection more than usual and thereby reduces the capacity to experience pain and painful affect which reduces the capacity to test reality" (1972, p. 54). When this dream experience is carried over to the waking life, mania prevails. As for the regression to a deeper sleep, it is based on a wish to sleep identical with the wish leading to formation of a blank dream. In a sense, such dreams with regressive shift to deeper sleep are blank dreams "with regard only to affect rather than to both affect and manifest content; this fact may indicate that we are dealing with a precursor to the true blank dream involving only partial fusion with the breast from a state of light sleep" (1968, p. 59).

Mrs. A had not reported "true" blank dreams such as described by Lewin. Nor did she report exactly the kind of transitional, turn-to-mania dream as described by Levitan. At the time of dreams 6 and 7, Mrs. A was talking about one of the most tragic traumatic experiences of her life.[11] As

11. When she was one and a half years old, her oldest brother died and her mother plunged into a profound depression that lasted for months. The experience of living with the unarousable mother, as was learned in the later course of Mrs. A's treatment, had reenforced her belief of being unwanted and it had initiated many adaptive and defensive maneuvers in living with a depressed mother—*for example,* extreme identification with the mother and with the brother, flight to good object, and so on.

much as the recalling necessitated regressive living out rather than talking out her experience around the trauma, she could still maintain ego organization enough to dream and to cope with the painful experience. In the midst of this, she learned of her therapist's vacation. Her anxiety and aggressive impulses intensified, and mania gradually evolved in the next few weeks. In the case of Miss B, she did not report the "true" blank dream as described by Lewin. However, her dream g approached what Levitan described as turn-to-mania dream. Some weeks before this dream, Miss B was talking about the tragic loss of her mother during one phase of her life when she needed her the most. It was then that her therapist announced his vacation. She reacted with increased anxiety and resorted to some "acting out." Subsequently, upon reuniting with her therapist, there could be a reactivation of fantasy pertaining to a very early experience wherein she felt deprived of her mother because of the arrival of her younger brother. Dream g seemed to be a direct translation of this fantasy. Dream g seemed to bring forth additional stress and regression, resulting in the manic solution.

MANIFEST CONTENT IN THE DREAMS OF DEPRESSIVES

The dreams of "depressed patients" were studied from a quite different standpoint. They were, for instance, not studied in the analytic situation but were studied mainly statistically in terms of the manifest content. Beck et al. (Beck and Hurvich 1959, Beck and Ward 1961) reported that the manifest content of dreams of his *neurotically* depressed patients contained with relatively high frequency a "masochistic theme"; that is, the dreamer experienced himself as the recipient of a painful experience such as being rejected, thwarted, deprived, or punished in the dream action. Kramer and Whitman et al. (1965) claimed a higher frequency of "depressive theme" in the manifest content of their *severely* depressed hospitalized patients. The "depressive theme," according to their observations, was characteristically "a desire to escape" and "the subjective feeling of hopelessness-helplessness." Langs (1966) found that the dreams of his group of *severely* depressed patients are brief and barren and do not show the "masochistic" or "depressive" theme as described by the other authors. These dreams center on family members and appear to reflect an extensive decathexis of external objects and a pervasive utilization of defensive denial. Langs' study supported Lewin's observation (1946) about a depressed woman who couldn't sleep for fear of dreaming and visualizing her wish to die in the dream. But when she did dream she dreamed all about her mother and was herself a passive, submissive child to be taken care of. Another study on depressive dreams was by Miller. From her study of a group of hospitalized depressed patients, Miller (1969) concluded that most dreams of patients in a "deep depression" showed an absence of threat of harm from other people or the environment and an absence of inner conflicts, danger or worry, whereas most of the dreams of "improving patients" were characterized by "troubles," conflicts, and their being hurt by others. Miller suggested that

> the dream data from [three previous studies] shows points of confluence. . . . We would say that the patient emerging from deep depression begins to dream that others may harm him . . . and he becomes angry and anxious. . . . He tries to act, but people block him and coerce him. . . . Perhaps if he cannot handle these types of problems, he eventually becomes depressed again and gives up active and independent functioning. He then dreams that people are positive toward him or at least neutral and his experience is pleasant or innocuous . . . [p. 565].

Inasmuch as these research studies on depressive dreams are interesting, the importance of the manifest content must be placed in proper perspective. Spanjaard (1969) proposed that "the manifest dream content usually has a subjectively conflictual aspect, and that the aspect offers us the opportunity to evaluate the most superficial layer of the conflict and thus to arrive at a construction of the potentially most useful interpretation" (p. 224). Still, in the clinical work, the necessity for the patient's associations to the dream and the determination of the latent ideas is important. Representing the ego's best attempt in its synthesis of instinctual wishes and of censuring countercathexis, the manifest content is the resultant compromise formation. Through dream work (i.e., symbolization, condensation, displacement, reversal) the latent dream thought is disguised. On one hand, a tiny bit of latent thought can be hidden behind an elaborated story; on the other hand, a massive amount of latent ideas and affects may be represented in an insignificant fragment of the manifest content of the dream. "Interpretation of manifest content alone is arbitrary, simplistic, speculative and unjustified" (Blum 1976, p. 318).

CONCLUSION

In the above, a study of the dreams of two manic-depressive patients (during one full or nearly one full cycle) was made. Such a study, placing dreams in the context of the therapeutic situation, provides material for interesting clinical research. These dreams not only offer clues to the conflict besetting the two patients at the time of dreaming, but also to the organization of the dream, as well as the patient's association to the dream, revealing the ego organization and ego's ability to do analytic work.

From the findings of the study I do not feel the state of knowledge of (1) the illness and the general psychodynamics, and (2) the analysis of dreams from their manifest content allows me to confirm or refute the conclusion drawn by previous groups of researchers. I note that the same "royal road to the unconscious" that dreams provide for psychoneurotic patients does not follow for manic-depressive patients because the nature of their illness does not allow them to associate and does not encourage the therapist to enter into the same "penetration" he would with a non-psychotic patient. In treating the manic-depressive patient, the therapist's empathy tells him to "sense" off the surface of the narcissistic hurt referred to in the dream, and not to add to the hurt by pressing to analyze. Perhaps because of this reason, the research potential of dreams in manic-depressive patients is markedly reduced. Any attempt to formulate a "theory of depression" (e.g., Kramer et al. 1965) through the study of the manifest content of dreams by "depressed" patients is certainly hazardous.

References

Abraham, K. (1911). Notes on the psycho-analytical investigation and treatment of manic-depressive insanity and allied conditions. In *Slected Papers on Psychoanalysis.* London: Hogarth Press, 1949.

Beck, A. T., and Hurvich, M. (1959). Psychological correlates of depression. *Psychosomatic Medicine* 21:50–55.

Beck, A., and Ward, C. H. (1961). Dreams of depressed patients: characteristic themes in manifest content. *Archives of General Psychiatry* 5:462–467.

Bibring, E. (1953). The mechanisms of depression. In *Affective Disorders,* ed. P. Greenacre, pp. 13–48. New York: International Universities Press.

Bleuler, E. (1911). *Dementia Praecox or the Group of Schizophrenias.* New York: International Universities Press, 1950.

——— (1924). *Textbook of Psychiatry,* trans. A. A. Brill. New York: Macmillan.

Blum, H. P. (1976). The changing use of dreams and free association. *International Journal of Psycho-Analysis* 57:315–324.

Freud, S. (1914). On the history of the psycho-analytic movement. *Standard Edition* 14:3–66.

——— (1926). Inhibitions, symptoms and anxiety. *Standard Edition* 20:87–172.

Jelliffe, S. E. (1931). Some hysterical phases of the manic-depressive synthesis. In Manic-Depressive Psychosis, ed. William A. White, Thomas K. Davis, and Angus M. Frantz, pp. 3–47. Vol. 11 of a series of research publications by Association for Research. In *Nervous and Mental Diseases*. Baltimore: William and Wilkins.

Kraepelin, E. (1899). *Manic-Depressive Insanity and Paranoia,* trans. [from *Psychiatrie,* ed. 8] R. M. Barclay. Edinburgh: Livingston, 1921.

Kramer, M., Whitman, R., Baldridge, B., and Lansky, L. (1965). Depression: dreams and defenses. *American Journal of Psychiatry* 122:411–419.

Langs, R. (1966). Manifest dreams from three clinical groups. *Archives of General Psychiatry* 14:634–643.

Levitan, H. (1967). Depersonalization and the dream. *Psychoanalytic Quarterly* 36:157–171.

——— (1968). The turn to mania. *Psychoanalytic Quarterly* 37:56-62.

——— (1972). Dreams preceding hypomania. *International Journal of Psycho-Analytic Psychotherapy* 1:50–61.

Lewin, B. D. (1946). Sleep, the mouth and the dream. In *Selected Papers of Bertram D. Lewin,* ed. J. Arlow, pp. 87–100. New York: Psychoanalytic Quarterly, 1973.

——— (1950). *The Psychoanalysis of Elation.* New York: Norton.

——— (1959). Some psychoanalytic ideas applied to elation and depression. *American Journal of Psychiatry* 116:38–43.

Lichtenberg, J., and Pao, P-n. (1974). Delusion, fantasy and desire. *International Journal of Psycho-Analysis* 55:273–281.

Mahler, M. S. (1966). Notes on the development of basic moods: The depressive affect. In *The Selected Papers of Margaret S. Mahler,* vol. 2. New York: Jason Aronson, 1979.

Miller, J. B. (1969). Dreams during varying stages of depression. *Archives of General Psychiatry* 20:560–565.

Pao, P-n. (1968). On manic-depressive psychosis. *Journal of the American Psychoanalytic Association* 16:809–832.

——— (1971a). Pathological considerations of a case of recurrent manic psychosis. *British Journal of Medical Psychology* 44:239–248.

——— (1971b). Elation, hypomania and mania. *Journal of the American Psychoanalytic Association* 19:789–798.

Rycroft, C. (1951). A contribution to the study of the dream screen. *International Journal of Psycho-Analysis* 32:178–184.

Sandler, J., and Joffe, W. G. (1969). Toward a basic psychoanalytic model. *International Journal of Psycho-Analysis* 50:79–89.

Spanjaard, J. (1969). The manifest dream content and its significance for the interpretation of dreams. *International Journal of Psycho-Analysis* 50:221–235.

CHAPTER 8

THE DREAM IN THE DEPRESSIVE PERSONALITY

Walter Bonime, M.D. with Florence Bonime

There exist only a few studies, relatively recent, that focus specifically on the dreams of depressives (Beck and Hurvich 1959, Beck and Ward 1961, Kramer 1969, Kramer et al. 1965, 1968, 1969, Kramer and Roth 1973, Langs 1966, Miller 1964, 1969, Hauri 1975). This chapter will correlate the personality dynamics of the depression-prone individual with the metaphors and affects of his dreams.

The individual prone to depression, because of the way he functions, is constantly experiencing frustration, anxiety, needless failures or underachievement, isolation, low self-esteem, and other agonies. With these patients the psychotherapeutic approach is often abandoned. They may gain repeated symptomatic relief by way of other modalities, but they are left with their established self-defeating, symptom-engendering ways of dealing with their lives. Finding with a patient, in his or her dreams, the reflection of the depressive personality functioning and affect can increase and maintain the effectiveness of psychotherapeutic help.

There is no universally accepted concept of depression. Wide variation characterizes most of the recorded views of the disturbance (Beck 1967, 1973, Ascher 1952, Mendelson 1974, Grinker 1961, Bonime 1976b). I shall use the description of the depressive personality from other of my publications (Bonime 1960, 1962a, 1962b, 1965, 1966a, 1976a, 1976b, 1978), in which the basic depressive psychodynamics are manipulativeness; hypersensitivity to and reaction against coercion, coupled with a tendency to interpret the attentions of others as efforts to coerce; unwillingness to enhance others; anxiety; and an emotional core of variously expressed anger (the subdued mode of depressive anger is eloquently conveyed by Philip Roth [1960, p. 117] in the phrase "then he exploded into silence"). I shall delineate this profile as it is symbolically set forth in the dreams of two patients.

DREAMS REFLECTING DEPRESSIVE ANGER

The creator of the following dreams, a woman in her mid-thirties, had had what appeared to herself and others a relatively good marriage for ten years. On starting analysis the only problem which she gave definition was a sense of shame over her lack of maternal feelings toward her two children. During an extensive time in analysis she sporadically revealed healthy assets such as a capacity for lively responsiveness, a genuine sense of humor, and an appetite for living. Most of her existence, however, was colored by discontent, grudgingness, sulkiness, and irritability.

Not much change had occurred during more than two and a half years of analysis preceding the period of the following dreams, which themselves, however, marked a period of salutary transition.

She came to a session depressed, and filled most of the hour detailing her general feeling of *not wanting to make the effort* to take part in activities in her community groups, *not wanting* to enliven herself with the pursuit of her many intellectual interests, *not wanting* to organize enjoyable experiences for her family. These were all undertakings in which she had been intermittently successful, but she resented having to propel herself in these directions.

After she had talked extensively about what an awful "bitch" she felt she was, how unwilling she was to do anything for anybody, how unhappy she was, I reminded her of her demonstrated capacity to enjoy life and make others feel good. "But," I added, "as we've seen so many times, you get sore as hell because this happiness doesn't come to you without your having to work for it."

At this moment the patient said, "I had a dream. I had a sort of screened-in porch, something that we had seen in a magazine for attaching to a house. A neighbor was saying to me, 'It's no good. It has hydrogen and it will burn.' Then it is burning and I call the fire department, but right while I'm on the phone the fire starts going out and I say, 'Never mind, I'll call again if it's necessary.'

"Then a neighbor comes with a pot of water to throw on the small flame that's left. I say, 'Thanks, never mind,' but she says, 'It's perfectly all right. Let me do it for you,' and she throws the water on the flame. *I was so pleased that someone else was doing it for me.* That's what I thought of when you said, I don't want to work for my own happiness. *I want to be happy but I want you to do it.* I don't want to have to change, I don't want to have to work for it myself. *I want to yell and scream and fume* and be a prima donna. I want to spit venom and not have anyone interfere."

That ended the hour. Her depression appeared dissipated. Over the following weekend she initiated small congenial family activities that further improved her mood.

Her spirits always lifted when she was willing to reach out for what she wanted. She was a prime example of one of those individuals who, because they sullenly maintain their grievance at having been deprived of a nurturant childhood, rebel against the responsibilities of adulthood and consequently miss its pleasures. A year earlier she had energetically pursued and achieved the family's move to a new home. Homes were recurrent dream symbols of her life and her analysis. In the dream just reported she sat in an extension of her life. The added porch seemed to represent her recent affirmative efforts. That this porch was a prefabricated structure may also have reflected her statement, "I want to be happy but I want you to do it." If the expansion of her life (the porch) is threatened (the fire), she wants someone else to remove the threat. She calls the fire department, but contributes no emergency activity of her own. Then she invokes good luck forces—"the fire starts going out." Finally her dream conjures up intervention by a solicitous neighbor. The patient was *"so pleased that someone was doing it for me."*

All this interpretive conjecture is further supported by the patient's recapture of the dream in response to a specific remark of mine. The patient herself later spontaneously noted the moment of her dream recall: "It was when you said I don't want to work for my own happiness."

In the dream a constructive aspect of her life begins to be consumed by flame. During the session she says, while discussing her dream, "I want to yell and scream and *fume*. . . ." Thus, in both the initial depressed mood of the analytic session and the fire metaphor of the dream, the patient expresses the emotional core of anger.

DREAMS OF SELF-RESCUE FROM DEPRESSION

After this hour of recognized and felt anger, of insight into her demand for help, she had another positive, pleasant weekend, and a new dream. In it she and her husband were before a fireplace in their living room. They were going to put a baby on the fire. (The real children were of school age.) He was going to do it; although she felt horrified at the idea, she did not protest, but walked out of the room. She had the feeling in the dream that rescuing the baby was her husband's business. Suddenly, however, she made up her mind that she couldn't let this go on, that she herself would have to do something about it. She returned to the living room and rescued the baby from the flames.

Work on the dream suggested that the baby represented herself, who so often felt "burned up," angered by her husband. Her feeling at the start of the dream was that her husband had to do whatever was necessary to save her (the baby) from being "inflamed," because he was the cause of her "fuming." (He was responsible for burning the baby and should therefore be responsible for saving it.) This was like her attitude in the previous dream and the previous session, expressed as her not wanting to make efforts to deal with her self-consuming flames, her depression, her anger.

In the dream about burning the baby there was, however, also the promising metaphor of self-rescue. The patient used her own resources to prevent herself from being burned up. The initial walking out, followed by her return and salvage operation, reflected her ambivalence; notably, ambivalence here was the beginning of change. The particular quality of her therapeutic movement was her evolving willingness to make use of her own resources. This development constitutes the essence of the curative process for the depressive.

DREAMS AND FIVE FEATURES OF DEPRESSIVES

The weekend following the session was again gratifying, and included the best sexual experience she had yet enjoyed.

Then came the negative therapeutic reaction. Particularly for such a patient this was itself an episode of depression, because I had "coerced" her into improvement. The reaction was augmented by her failure to manipulate a teacher in an adult education course at the local high school. The patient had tried to get some equipment without paying for it. She summed up the situation by saying, "I think the whole relationship with the instructor has been phony. That reminds me of a dream.

"Some woman was telling me about *her child*. I wasn't listening. I was just going through the motions—smiling, saying 'yes,' nodding. At the end I asked her a polite question to imply that I had been going along with her, but the question revealed that I hadn't been listening. By her answer she showed that she recognized I hadn't paid attention, and I immediately tried to cover up with all kinds of double-talk and then I woke up, feeling extremely embarrassed."

In a seeming *non sequitur,* the patient added, "I like something if it's a bargain. If I have to pay, I'll think twice, even if I like it."

She elaborated on this subject, recounting shopping incidents. I interrupted and asked her what she thought the dream meant. She answered at once, "This double-talk, this pretended listening. I didn't go back to work on my other dream, though I said I would. And with this one I was too tired and too busy, and when I first woke up, I was too sleepy. So I didn't write down this one or do any more work on the others." Sitting behind the couch, I mused to myself that the metaphor seemed to be a picture of the analyst as a garrulous mother talking about her child—the patient (in one of her dual roles in the dream) is the analyst's child. What he's involved with is "his baby," no concern of the patient's. She continued, "I don't care what people say. I'm really not interested in what people are trying to tell me. I just pretend that I'm listening."

I interrupted again: "The person who is talking in the dream then might be me."

She associatively responded, "My sister-in-law recently signed up for a slenderizing course. She goes up there and spends ten dollars having somebody massage her and then she goes out and eats a huge lunch. She won't put any effort into losing weight. She wants somebody to do it for her. She'll never get anywhere. I just thought of all the hours I've lain on this couch expecting someone to do something for me."

I correlated her recent negative behavior and feeling in analysis with the "not listening" dream and contrasted this with her more constructive behavior and feeling during the preceding ten days. I finally said, "You know your analysis is not *my* baby."

Viewed in context, the dream presents a rich constellation of the features of the depressive personality. It was dreamt in an emotional setting of anger. The anger had been provoked by an episode of frustration following a period of salutary struggle. The patient had again lapsed into an unwillingness to draw upon her own resources—she assigns responsibility for this "child," the baby, analysis, to the analyst, to whom she is reluctant even to pay attention. By not listening *she avoids coercion, his influence.* During the dream episode the patient reveals *manipulative* social techniques, pretenses, to avoid detection of her indifference and to avoid rejection. Not listening is itself partly an expression of the depressive *unwillingness to gratify another*—even minimally, by paying attention. Finally, being "extremely embarrassed" when her fraudulence is detected may indicate *anxiety*. Depressive individuals often experience anxiety when they strain the tolerance of others to the point of jeopardizing the relationship. This seemingly simple dream metaphor of "not listening," with its accompanying affect, thus reflects all the described cardinal elements of the depressive personality.

DREAMS COMBINING DEPRESSION AND RESTITUTION

The following week the patient had been sick on the day preceding her session and planned to cancel the next morning's analytic hour. But she did not cancel and that night had the following dream.

"I was in the subway. I had just gotten out of the train and I was going up some stairs to change trains. I felt that the train was already on the upper platform, and it actually was. I had indecision about whether I should run for it or whether I shouldn't bother. I decided at once, of course, I should. It's silly not to. There was another girl with me running for the train, but she was running for it only half-heartedly. I decided to make a real run for it, but it was a tremendous effort to run. *Every step was a great effort. My legs and feet were leaden. I felt that I was getting old.*

"Just as I was reaching the train, the door started to close. The girl was right in front of me, not going fast enough, and I rushed forward and either pushed her in with me or I pushed her out of the way in a determined effort to get in. I got into the train. . . .

"I felt very good about this dream. I was *really struggling hard to miss the boat, I was holding back,* and the fact that I made it anyway made me feel very good. My association with my feeling very old is that 'it's hard to teach an old dog new tricks.' I don't want to change.

"This girl who was in my way, the girl who couldn't hurry, or wouldn't hurry, she was me, too, but I didn't let her keep me out. I pushed through and was very determined and glad. I've been very happy these last few days, especially with my children. *With my husband I sometimes feel like the leaden feet* in my dream."

The patient's grasp of her emotions and her effort to overcome her depressive problem is dramatically represented here. Not only is there the dream metaphor of deciding to and straining her own resources to catch the train (to get on with her life), but there is also the striking affective metaphor of depressive psychosomatic retardation, *the leaden feet,* which she reinforced by her insightful waking metaphoric expression, "I was really struggling hard to miss the boat, I was holding back."

As the session proceeded, she spoke more spontaneously and honestly than ever of her difficult relationship with her parents.

Toward the end of the hour, thinking of the recent negative therapeutic reaction, I brought her back to the dream. "Let's see more about the reluctance to work *here,* the leaden feet in analysis, even when you've resolved to work."

Her response was a recollection that had come painfully at an earlier time, but which was reported now histrionically and with good humor. She said, "I can hear my mother getting her teeth set and saying, 'Stubborn devil!'—I'll show her stubbornness!" Her mother's threats, the real coercions, were an important part of the genetic milieu of the patient's character. As the child grew, she came to experience and resist ordinary expectations as coercions. A few days later, speaking again about the dream, she said, "My resistance to coercion, that's what the dragging feet is. Nobody is going to force me to do anything. . . . "

A further significance of her dragging feet arose in a new context a few weeks later. She had been initiating gratifying activities with family and friends. Then she came in one day and said she'd been thinking "about taking a vacation from analysis. I'm tired . . . maybe I'd better quit. I'm wasting my time." There was a pause and then, "I just thought of my 'dragging feet.'" After further silence, she revealed, "I don't want to give myself to my husband."

I thought about that and said to her, "Perhaps you would sacrifice your own joy in being healthy rather than let your husband enjoy a happy, fully functioning woman and wife." She indicated that her husband had lately become much more agreeable and responsive. Deeply serious, she added, "It's really that I've been keeping myself away—he's trying hard—we have a better marriage than we've had. It's me."

Her depressive resistance was expressed in this reluctance to enhance her husband's life, and her reluctance extended to her children and to the broadening circle of people who enjoyed her. Her now expanding pleasurable interpersonal existence conflicted with her lifelong begrudgingness. Her problem applied too, I speculated, to the pleasure that might be accruing to her analyst as she improved. Cumulatively all this could make her "tired" and give her the feeling she'd "better quit."

DREAMS AND MANIPULATION IN DEPRESSIVES

Another dream indicated not only her desire to be provided for, but also a correlated characteristic—manipulation to elicit solicitude or special service from others.

"I was going into a high school cafeteria to get lunch . . . I was on line and about to be served. I recognized a woman behind the counter . . . somebody I knew . . . since she knew me I felt she would give me something extra for the same money. . . . When she asked me which vegetables I wanted *I said nothing,* kept quiet, and she gave me servings of all the vegetables. When I got to the cashier she started to charge me for all the vegetables and I argued that I had not asked for all of them. . . . Finally she took the spinach away. I paid her but when I turned back, my tray was gone. It was stolen. I started looking for the thief and woke up angry. . . . "

The metaphor may be stated: The world is a cafeteria where if you are quiet and appear naive you may get a larger portion; if this tactic fails, however, you're the victim of robbery. (We might add: and then you may justifiably become angry, depressed.)

Associating to the dream, she thought of a young woman in an Italian movie, someone "who has been hungry all her life" and wolfs down two dinners that are paid for by someone else. The patient elaborated, "*All my life I've taken things if they're for free* . . . I'm like my mother. She always wanted something for free. She always feels that you're a nice person if you don't ask for things and that they're nice people if they don't ask for payment. But—*if I expect to get something without asking and I don't get it, then I'm furious.* And I get furious too when I'm asked for payment at a time when I've expected something for free." Her next association was the incident in the adult education class where she was "furious" at having failed to manipulate the instructor into endowing her with equipment. There, too, uncertainly hoping not to have to pay, she had silently accepted something for which she was later charged.

The depressive's universally described "dependency" is much more than a desire—it is an expectation, a demand to be subsidized. In daily functioning he or she maneuvers—by seductiveness, naiveté, special pleading, silent waifishness, pitiable or punishing gloom, among other techniques, all calculated, awarely or unawarely—to bring about the solicitude he wants.

ANXIETY WITH DEPRESSION

Another patient, a gifted underachiever, illustrates the anxiety which is an important element of the depressive way of life. This was a man in his mid-forties, a Master of Social Work and psychotherapist, who had come for analysis because he had been bogged down in his attempts to gain his doctorate.

He had a highly seductive charm and earnestness with which he maneuvered people into sponsoring and supporting him professionally, academically, and domestically. Throughout his life he placed obstacles before his required work, *hating the coercive pressure* he sensed from any responsibility, including his analysis. He entertained fantasies of being presented with a D.S.W. without writing a dissertation. He expressed *fury* over his need to change through analysis—fury at his wife for not getting into treatment to relieve his burden, and fury at me for not responding to his cues to recommend that she enter therapy. He shouted, "Why do I have to make a life for myself, my wife, my children!" He could not bear his contributions to his family's happiness and *constantly sabotaged what pleasures he did bring about*—such as outrageously delaying the fulfillment of generous promises, or scolding his children when he engaged in play with them. A characteristic incident was one in which he came home with a bottle of champagne to celebrate an anniversary and then ruined the evening by upbraiding his wife for a scratch on some new furniture.

The patient had fouled up many opportunities in life. He entered analysis after procrastinating six years over his doctoral preparations. Over a long period of his life he had experienced a recurrent anxiety dream. In it he has climbed to the uppermost step of an outside stairway attached to a tall building. At the top of the building is an iron railing. "I am precariously holding on, trying to pass my leg over the railing to reach the safety of the solid ledge, to gain footing and escape the pull of gravity." With each recurrence of the dream he somehow fails to get his leg over the railing and onto the solid roof. He strains nearly the whole way but can't seem to make the final effort that would fulfill his commitment. He feels anxious during the dream and wakes up with anxiety.

Anxiety haunts depressives regularly because their fears are rooted in reality. Their refusal to carry out responsibility, and their taxing the patience of the solicitous near to or beyond tolerance—these behaviors put depressives in real jeopardy occupationally, academically, maritally, and socially. This man had for years veered toward disqualifying himself for a doctorate. His resultant anxiety in the recurrent dream is expressed in the exquisite anxious metaphor of the long steep climb and then the failure to take that last and securing step.

This patient's dream links in an interesting way with one of the dreams of the first patient, who represented her "holding back" with the psychosomatic metaphor of leaden feet. The second patient represents his unrecognized unwillingness with the psychosomatic metaphor of feeling *the pull of gravity*.

DREAMS AND CONTACT WITH FEELINGS

The second patient, in another dream, offers a striking example of depressive affect. It graphically portrays his unwillingness to take responsibility for his life. In addition, it is an analytic excerpt that demonstrates the crucial role of the dream in an individual's ultimately making contact with feelings.

Very early in treatment I had suggested that in spite of his constant avowals of deeply wanting to do the things he put off or aborted, his work problem might be a real unwillingness. He had an immediate association to my word *unwillingness*—an incident with a dog he had owned years before. One day the animal lay down in wet snow and refused to move. No matter how the patient cajoled, threatened, commanded, or punished it, and no matter how uncomfortable it was, the dog would not stir. He recognized the possible aptness of his association, but on a "purely" intellectual basis.

Several months after the dog memory, he arrived one day with a dream. The session, almost in entirety and verbatim, follows: He lay down and said: "I woke up from a dream at 3:00 AM this morning and wrote it down. It is similar to daytime experiences. I was in front of a disassembled vacuum cleaner. I was surprised there were so many pieces. Before I started working on it, I thought it would only have to be cleaned, it would be a snap. But then I felt frustrated. It was not something I wanted to do. It would take so much time. It would be a distraction."

He went on spontaneously: "I thought of when I have to do something around home, when there's a door or window to fix. It takes more time than I intended. I feel I wasted time. Now, as I report it to you, I think it refers to my analysis. There's much more to analyze in myself than I thought. It is more work. It also refers to my problem with Grace [his wife]. I used to think much of my problem had to do with what *she* does. Now I'm beginning to discover that regardless of what she does, I have my own problems, and it will be a lot of work. I feel the same way about my dissertation. I feel it will be a snap. But when I'm working on it . . . [a brief silence here] . . . will I come to a point in analysis when I feel I have a solid base from which to go on? It's like the pieces of the vacuum cleaner. There are so many pieces. Will I be able to figure it out?

"Why a vacuum cleaner? [he asks himself]. It's my reaction to women. Saturday and Sunday I was aware—I feel a tremendous attraction toward *any* woman. I'll cross the street just to pass a woman approaching on the other side. On buses, subways, I try to make contact. I look at them, try to catch their eyes.

"A vacuum cleaner is indiscriminate: It's like me wanting to have all the women. Then I think—but I have a woman. I have a family. If I'm to have a relationship with a strange woman, what will it be? But the impulse to have them all remains. I have a feeling of not grasping anything. Everything is a free-floating frustration.

"In analysis I seem to go from one thing to another. I feel particularly frustrated with dreams."

At this point I said, "You rarely risk dreams with me. Today's dream has something you do not recognize." (I had in mind, but did not say, two of his statements. The first was his statement of *feeling* in the dream: "It was not something I wanted to do." The second was his comment immediately after telling the dream: "Now as I report it to you I think it refers to my analysis." Combined, they suggested: Analysis is not something I want to do.)

In response to my remarks about his not risking dreams with me and about today's dream containing something he did not recognize, he retorted, "I don't know what you mean. My first association is last session—competitiveness with you—I'm not getting the benefit of your understanding of dreams.

"I had an image this morning before I left the house: One of the children's [miniature] turtles was walking into our bedroom. I took it back to the living room and felt: I almost stepped on it. I had a fantasy of stepping on it. I have a creepy feeling now. What does it mean? Symbolically my squelching any beginning." Here, in another form, the morning after the vacuum cleaner dream, his fantasy echoes his squelching of motivation, his unwillingness.

He went on: "I'm aware of wanting to avoid these associations. I didn't use the weekend to work on my dissertation at all. I was aware when I was with Grace that I was enjoying being with Grace and the children. But I felt I shouldn't be with them. It is time for me to be working. I should leave this for later. I'm always indecisive; deciding for pleasure with Grace and the children. I should be a little more mature—I could say to them: 'I have work to do.'

"I'm feeling I always have indecision between getting my work done and being with them. I can't divide time—be with them and also do my work.

"The *feeling* through these dreams is suspense; always directed on something up in the air—vacillating—going back and forth.

"Another thought. On Thursday, after I left here, I didn't go back to what we talked about. I thought about your book on dreams. Some cases in it are similar to my problems. But if I go on with your dynamics, I'll miss somebody else's. It's the same with people: If I'm with this person, I'll be missing being with someone else. If I read this article, I'll miss reading something else. If I become expert in this, I'll miss being expert in something else. *In the end I have nothing.* Then I saw I better try to stay with something, not flit around. How do I choose?"

The session ended here. Three days later he returned to fill the hour with fury at his wife for her domestic inadequacies and her not being constantly loving toward him. He had threatened his wife with being cold to her from then on, would even help her enter an affair—let her get her pleasure from someone else. He was furious at me, too, for not recognizing his wife's need for analysis and concluded with the sullen statement: "That's the way I feel; that's the way I am and I can't change."

DREAM METAPHORS OF ANGRY
UNWILLINGNESS

A week later he started a session, saying, "In a dream I was identifying with a patient of mine—a patient who is very resistant. [*New dream*]: I was fucking things up like this patient. I was going around with bundles of clothes under my arms—not free to use my hands. I was awkward. I was revealing myself."

I asked what he was revealing about himself.

He responded, "My clothes are like my defenses—they're a cover-up. I don't have things in my life in proper order."

Here I intervened with an interpretive hypothesis: "These bundles are like the crap you burden yourself with that interferes with your important activities—all the irrelevant magazine and newspaper articles you read when you're about to get to work on your thesis. It's like your taking a thermos of hot chocolate to your family in the playground when they've gone there on a Sunday specifically to let you work without interference. It's like your defrosting the refrigerator when they leave you home alone to do your own work, or like the Sunday they went driving with neighbors all afternoon and you stopped your thesis work early to prepare a surprise supper for their return. These seem to me to be the bundles you load yourself with, to prevent yourself from getting to work."

"I thought of those things, too, in connection with the dream."

"It would have been valuable for you to have reported these associations. Referring to the bundles as 'defenses' was very vague."

I then told him why I called his vacuum cleaner dream important. In that dream, with his words: "It was not something I wanted to do," he had for the first time designated his *felt unwillingness.* He had often spoken instead of "indecisiveness," "procrastination," "vacillation," or of being somehow unable or "I couldn't seem to. . . . " Even with his association to the pitiful dog in the snow, he had always emphasized that he could not contact the feeling of unwillingness. But in this dream with the difficult task of reassembling the vacuum cleaner, he felt the recoil, the squelching of energy, the unwillingness to tackle the job. He experienced, in a dream, the global nature of his recoil from getting his life together.

He went on associatively to enumerate many life circumstances affectively analogous to the dream, and these included reluctance toward analysis and toward writing his dissertation.

In the course of the last month of the therapeutic year, the period following the vacuum cleaner dream, he fluctuated considerably in his commitments both to work on his dissertation and to work in analysis. It was, nevertheless, the most productive month of his three years in analysis and was filled with more of his honest expressions of feeling, particularly anger, than he'd manifested cumulatively in the past. There was also a greater openness in revealing his feelings toward me—both positive and negative.

About the middle of the month, after one of several brief surges of activity on his thesis, he came in and, following a report of his accomplishments, said intensely, "I'm angry I have to buckle down. *I* have to change without getting *my* claims." It was like the end of a long tantrum.

Referring on one occasion to the vacuum cleaner, he said: "This is very relevant, the symbol of a vacuum cleaner—taking everything in—making suckers of everyone—taking them in, sucking them in. But why putting together a vacuum cleaner? I have analyzed myself but haven't put it together to function . . . to put it together would be to make it function—it need not be a sucking-in instrument, but an instrument for useful work. [Then he described thesis work he'd first put off over the weekend, but successfully tackled on Monday.] Monday I realized and accepted there is no way of avoiding steady work, continuous work—that's what's new, my accepting the amount of work rather than as in the dream, *not wanting to do all* that's required."

And then, after three years of analysis, he finally said, "My refusal to work is like the pull of gravity."

The following session he started by saying: "You said that day of the vacuum cleaner dream, it was the most important I'd had in three years. I was shocked and surprised that it had such importance and I'd missed it. I worked hard that night and the next morning on my dissertation. I felt my reluctance to do it: my reluctance remained the same. I have made enough effort to do my research and writing, but I have not yet been able to get rid of the reluctance itself. In the dream the disassembled vacuum cleaner parts were neatly arranged, as in a display case. All the intellectual insights I have—they are not put together and functioning as a whole. It's a display of things that are not functional. That refers not only to my work but to the rest of my life and to what I've neglected. It refers to my analysis, too. The effort to recover dreams is something I've *refused* to do most of the time. I'd rationalize it by saying to myself that 'it's not important—only a fragment.' Then the fragment would disappear."

In the last session of the year he openly expressed the most intense anger he'd ever manifested in analysis. He had received a special delivery letter granting permission, after long negotiation, to use an institutional population for data gathering, the final step for his thesis. Guessing its content, he didn't want to open the letter. He tried to think of how he could pretend he'd never received it.

He exploded: "Damn it! Why do I have to make a life for myself, my wife, my children? I feel definitely: damn it, I don't want this!"

This patient and his vacuum cleaner dream illustrate well one of the central affects of the depressive: *unwillingness*—to take responsibility for making a life for himself, to fulfill requirements; and unwillingness, even indirectly, to enhance others by self-fulfillment. All acceptance of responsibility, all appropriate responsiveness, is subjectively misperceived and experienced as submission to coercion. The emergence of this patient's dream feeling and the focus upon it generated a crucial breakthrough in the analysis. He had avoided bringing in dreams chiefly because of his fear and reluctance regarding exposure of his feelings. *Without concentration on the accompanying affect, the impact of the vacuum cleaner metaphor would have attenuated into merely another graphic intellectualization and would never have produced the turbulent and productive therapeutic movement that followed.* The *idea* of unwillingness had been developed during three years in connection with innumerable life situations. The bodily feeling of unwillingness had for the first time been captured, as affect, in a dream.

DREAMS AS REFLECTIONS OF DEPRESSIVE TRAITS

In summary, this chapter correlates psychodynamic concepts with the content and feeling of the dreams of depressive patients. Taking the author's view of depression as a conceptual framework, material from analytic practice has been presented to demonstrate that dream metaphors of depressive patients may be recognized and used as reflections of characteristic depressive personality traits and feelings. The dream metaphors of two depression-prone individuals have been shown to reflect the depressive's *anger* (the fumes and flames of the first patient); her *manipulative* practices (indirectly seeking something for free in the cafeteria); her *unwillingness to enhance others* (in not listening as her friend [the analyst] talked to her, and in "dragging her feet" which she associated with not wanting to give herself to her husband or continue in analysis). In the second patient, *anxiety* was evoked by his not exerting effort toward fully meeting his responsibility (not exerting himself to achieve sure footing after climbing the tall tower); and finally his *reaction against coercion,* expressed as unwillingness to accept responsibility for his own life (to put together a vacuum cleaner into a functioning whole). Attention has been focused upon *angry unwillingness* as a basic affect of the depressive. And lastly, emphasis has been placed on the importance of concentrating on dream affect for finding, with the patient, this living emotion underlying much of his depressive practice.

References

Ascher, E. (1952). A criticism of the concept of neurotic depression. *American Journal of Psychiatry* 108:901–908.

Beck, A. T. (1967). *Depression.* New York: Harper and Row.

——— (1973). *The Diagnosis and Management of Depression.* Philadelphia: University of Pennsylvania Press.

Beck, A. T., and Hurvich, M. S. (1959). Psychological correlates of depression: I. Frequency of "masochistic dream content in a private practice sample." *Psychosomatic Medicine* 21:50–55.

Beck, A. T., and Ward, C. H. (1961). Dreams of depressed patients: characteristic themes in manifest content. *Archives of General Psychiatry* 5:462–467.

Bonime, W. (1960). Depression as a practice: dynamic and psychotherapeutic considerations. *Comprehensive Psychiatry* 1:194–198.

——— (1962a) Dynamics and psychotherapy of depression. In *Current Psychiatric Therapies,* vol. 2, ed. J. Masserman, pp. 137–146. New York: Grune and Stratton.

——— [with Florence Bonime] (1962b). *The Clinical Use of Dreams.* New York: Basic Books.

——— (1965). A psychotherapeutic approach to depression. *Contemporary Psychoanalysis* 2:48–53.

——— (1966a). The psychodynamics of neurotic depression. In *American Handbook of Psychiatry,* vol. 3, 1st. ed., ed. S. Arieti, pp. 239–255. New York: Basic Books.

——— (1966b). A case of depression in a homosexual young man. *Contemporary Psychoanalysis* 3:1–20.

——— (1976a). Anger as a basis for a sense of self. *Journal of the American Academy of Psychoanalysis* 4:7–12.

——— (1976b). The psychodynamics of neurotic depression. *Journal of the American Academy of Psychoanalysis* 4:(3), 301–326.

——— [with Florence Bonime] (1978). The cultural approach. In *Dream Interpretation: A Comparative Study,* ed. J. Fosshage and C. Lowe. New York: Spectrum Books.

Grinker, R. (1961). *The Phenomena of Depression.* New York: Hoeber.

Hauri, P. (1975). Dream content in patients remitted from neurotic depression. *Sleep Research* 4:185.

Kramer, M. (1969). Manifest dream content in psychopathologic states. In *Dream Psychology and the New Biology of Dreaming,* ed. M. Kramer. Springfield, Ill.: Charles C Thomas.

Kramer, M., Baldridge, B., Whitman, R., Ornstein, P., and Smith, P. (1969). An exploration of the manifest dream in schizophrenia and depressed patients. *Diseases of the Nervous System* 30:126–130.

Kramer, M., and Roth, T. (1973). A comparison of dream content in laboratory dream reports of schizophrenic and depressive patient groups. *Comprehensive Psychiatry* 14:(4) 325–329.

Kramer, M., Whitman, R., Baldridge, B., and Lansky, L. (1965). Depression: dreams and defenses. *American Journal of Psychiatry* 122:411–419. (Discussion: W. Bonime.)

Kramer, M., Whitman, R., Baldridge, B., and Ornstein, P. (1968). Drugs and dreams. III. The effects of imipramine and the dreams of depressed patients. *American Journal of Psychiatry* 124:1385–1392.

Langs, R. (1966) Manifest dreams from three clinical groups. *Archives of General Psychiatry* 14:634–643.

Mendelson, M. (1974). *Psychoanalytic Concepts of Depression,* 2nd ed. New York: Spectrum Press.

Miller, J. B. (1964). Structure and content of the manifest dreams of depressed patients. University of Syracuse School of Medicine. (Unpublished).

——— (1969). Dreams during varying stages of depression. *Archives of General Psychiatry* 20:560–565.

Roth, P. (1960). *Goodbye, Columbus.* New York: Meridian.

CHAPTER 9

THE DREAM IN OBSESSIVE STATES

Arnold Namrow, M.D.

> Let us go then, you and I,
> When the evening is spread out against the sky
> Like a patient etherised upon the table;
>
> . . . .
>
> And indeed there will be time
> To wonder, "Do I dare?" and, "Do I dare?"
> Time to turn back and descend the stair. . . .
>
> . . . .
>
> For I have known them all already, known them all:—
> Have known the evenings, mornings, afternoons,
> I have measured out my life in coffee spoons. . . .
>
> . . . .
>
> Shall I part my hair behind? Do I dare to eat a peach?
> I shall wear white flannel trousers, and walk upon the beach.
> I have heard the mermaids singing, each to each.
>
> . . . .

In 1917, T. S. Eliot's "Love Song of J. Alfred Prufrock" captured poignantly the existential anxiety of modern man; the passage of time has not diminished its truth. Throughout the poem Prufrock repeats his refrain: he is the observer, the onlooker, the detached one, yet he is the orchestrator of his fate, a fate governed by an escape from responsible action. The poet's deftly sketched portrait of an individual torn by

indecision and irresolution is one that is familiar to us in clinical terms—
the obsessionally neurotic person. Ambiguity in the experience of hurt
and the avoidance of passion speaks to him; and so it is with our
obsessional patients.

In the analytic situation, and to the world at large, the obsessional
person presents himself as imperiously driven. All the cognitive forces at
his command are enlisted in the task of self-justification and self-
explanation; his precarious sense of worth lies in the balance. He attempts
to contain the turbulence of his inner world with concretized, affect-free
abstractions, intellectualizations, reaction formations and, centrally, a
steadfast isolation of his emotions.

The analyst is confronted with a prodigious task: how to be an effective
aide in reducing the formidable array of defenses; further, how best to ally
himself with the growth of a responsible observing ego freed from the
pseudosincerity of the patient's usual detachment and vigilance, particularly devoted to the difficult task of meeting drive derivatives directly.

No matter the good will and high motivation of patient, no matter the
giftedness of the therapist or his temperamental fit, the treatment course
can be long and arduous. The dream is neither the royal road, nor the only
road, to unconscious infantile conflict—but it may be a touchstone for
therapeutic movement.

THERAPEUTIC MOVEMENT THROUGH
DREAM-WORK

Andrea G, an attractive thirty-five-year-old married woman, conducted her suburban matronly life with the highest degree of organization,
smoothness, and efficiency. To live a life of unruffled harmony and control
was her goal. The years of marriage had widened the gulf between her and
her husband. Tensions were strenuously defended against and, for the
most part, were neither in her awareness nor discernible to those around
her. Her husband was of different character: overtly phallic, forceful,
impetuous, masculine, and assertive. He dealt with his anxieties with
increasingly heavy drinking. In the glow of alcohol he showered her with
protestations of their idyllic mating, their valued children, splendid home
and other blessings.

This confused her; she felt revulsion at his effusions and his increased
drinking, and she avoided his sexual advances. All in all, she mused, life
was difficult, filled with burdens and rigors to be borne with grace and

control. With one unexpected blow this whole structure was shattered; her husband, Charles, moved out of the family home to live with his girlfriend. She then entered analysis.

An only child, she recalled being surrounded with love and affection throughout all the developmental phases. A large extended family (from cousins to grandparents) helped to solidify the high value placed on conformity, adherence to the proprieties, and the need to excel, both socially and academically. Her mother was the force and power in the home. She bound her daughter to her as confidante and derided her husband for ineptitude and lack of ambition. An ambiguous and strongly ambivalent message was conveyed to the patient: father was good, loyal, the support of the family, and the carrier of important values; and, yet, was he not a weak, castrated man who allowed his brothers to walk over him in the family business? The theme was unmistakable: if only I had the privileges of a man, a chance to finish an education, a chance of business or academic success, then, and only then, would I feel complete and fulfilled. In her early middle years, the mother committed suicide during the course of a severe depression.

The course of treatment was characterized by the usual measured caution, ambivalence, and intellectualizations. The early transference paradigm centered on her never allowing herself to be controlled—that the analysis had been foisted on her by unwanted life circumstances and that I would feel the full force of her obstinacy. She experienced treatment as an indignity, a shameful exposure; she was not brought up to be open and unreserved.

After a four-month separation, Andrea's husband returned. Her not unexpected response was matter-of-fact: life goes on as usual—no angry outbursts, no upheaval, no rancor; icy calmness—yes.

Increasingly the transference became erotized. The jolting separation from her husband intensified the libidinal attachments to me. Entwining herself with me as an ally against loss and abandonment, she experienced a degree of protection; equally present were countervailing forces that emerged from primitive fears of violation and penetration. Rapid regressive swings from oedipal material to pre-phallic oedipal levels were clinically evident. Several interesting dreams at the end of the first year of treatment illuminated these themes. In reporting the first dream the patient stated, "I had an odd dream. I've gone over it carefully, and there is no place where you fit in."

In the dream "I wanted to be alone so I could masturbate before Charles came home. My cousin was in the house. I pushed her out rudely. I put on a satin nightgown with a lace top. My first thought was how pretty my breasts were. The nipples got darker and darker and suddenly they ejaculated white fluid over the nightgown. I went to a small house and father was there. I got in bed with father. He said that Charles should take better care of me. I said 'If he won't, why don't you?' He started to caress me in a sexual way. I thought how much better it was than with Charles."

Spontaneously she commented, "You're going to tell me that there is something masculine about liquid coming out of my breasts, you stupid, idiot man." In recent months this type of epithet had often been used, delivered in a dry, hostile, teasing manner. "It was forcible, not a trickle. I keep dreaming about old clothes so much of the time it must go back to the past." I asked for her ideas about the nightgown, and she replied, "It was my wedding night nightgown, a sexy one, but there was no sex that night, I was menstruating. Charles didn't seem to mind. What are your thoughts about the nightgown?" I replied, "You wish to be pregnant, to have mother's milk, but you wish to have power and be in control of men." She then said, "I thought you would say something about that, but during the time Charles was away I thought that if I had been pregnant Charles would never have left, it would have held him, ensnared him. And father did come to visit when Charles was away. Maybe I was angry at Charles' leaving. I've often thought of leaving, but where would I go, and what would I do?"

The next dream was the following week: "At a bowling alley. Charles was gone. I went through all the motions of bowling. I took the right steps, etc., but I had a plastic bag instead of a bowling ball. I felt foolish and made up a story that I was practicing."

Her thoughts about a plastic bag substituting for a bowling ball went, "I feel very handicapped not having the emotional equipment other people have, I feel that something is missing, that I lack force. Oh yes, there was another part to the dream, two lawyers there. The younger one put his arms around me and I was covered by a blanket. He caressed me. I told him that my first husband was dead and that I took care of him for a whole year and now I wanted fun. I felt that the sides of my mouth and lips were cracked and dry."

I said to Mrs. G, "You make great efforts in treatment, as in your life, to order and to organize, but your feeling that you lack the proper equipment stirs great anger and resentment." She answered, "I think you mean a penis," and she went on to describe in greater detail masturbation fantasies that she had previously alluded to in a fleeting fashion.

The governing theme of these fantasies usually involved an older, fatherly man and an older brother: they forced her to undress, spanked her buttocks, degraded and humiliated her, and forced her to perform all manner of sexual acts usually prohibited by her weighty superego. Occasionally, the fantasies involved a group of strange men who would inflict their will upon her in similar fashion. The escape from the sense of responsibility, the disclaiming of superego censure, was patently clear.

In the first dream, the manifest content, "pushing cousin out rudely," and the subsequent associations spoke for her unconscious wishes for domination and destruction of her mother. These latent destructive impulses made their dangerous claim; anxieties about mutilation were pronounced; the wish for pregnancy and alliance with father/analyst were in the service of reparation and the modification of anxiety.

These themes were continued in the second dream. Penis envy and concern over mutilation were clearly stated. Her associations led to an important addition in regard to the two lawyers: she condensed her wishes for maternal nurturance, her strivings for father, husband and analyst, reversed her husband's leaving, engaged her sense of omnipotence in the powerful "taking care of him for a year" and, finally, displaced upwards her fears of waning femininity and decreasing desirability.

A dream in the third year was of particular significance: "I'm sitting on a public toilet in a cubicle. There is a long row of them, the doors are unlocked. I sit on one, then the next and so on down the line."

The previous night she had been angry with her husband for bringing unexpected guests to dinner. While everyone else was having after dinner drinks, Mrs. G slipped away to an upstairs bathroom, crouched over the toilet bowl, and masturbated to intense orgasm. She fantasied with her usual sado-masochistic imagery: a series of men humiliating her, sexually abusing her and spanking her buttocks. She stated, "I had the double pleasure of thinking I won't tell Dr. Namrow about this tomorrow and no one downstairs knows what I'm doing." I asked for her ideas about sitting on a public toilet. She said, "You probably think I'm saying something about you or treatment." I replied, "You do shit on me as you wanted to do on your husband and his guests." She agreed laughingly, was quiet for a moment, and said, "There is something more." She continued with a vivid remembrance of the daily bathroom drama she had undergone as a child, the unyielding ritualized inspection of her stools by her mother. This had continued until the grade school years and was often combined with enemas if production, according to mother's standards, was insufficient.

She recalled the struggles, her sense of outrage, and the fascination, excitement, and abhorrence at the enemas. The overriding perception was one of violative assault on her body, her self, her integrity. This was expressed in the manifest dream elements "public toilets" and "unlocked doors."

The residue of the previous evening, the manifest elements, and the subsequent de-repression highlighted significant issues in her neurotic structure. The desire for submission, to be the recipient of controlling aggression, was commingled with the wish for merger with an internalized, supplying good mother. Countering these urges was a limitless quantity of unneutralized aggression, expressed in identifications with an attacking, assaultive figure. Thus, compactly expressed in her fantasies and dreams were aspects of her self as victor/victim and conqueror/vanquished. Withal, her cognitive functions held sway. She functioned deliberately, tensely, and indecisively and vacillated in her accountability for the omnipotent destructiveness within.

The above dreams spanned a three-year period in the continuing analysis of a complex human being. They did not herald dramatic breakthroughs or major changes. The indicators of movement and maturation, as is so often the case in psychoanalysis, were more subtly shaded.

As was noted, the earlier dreams—"nipples got darker and darker and ejaculated white fluid" and "I had a plastic bag instead of a bowling ball"— contained crucial components of her oedipal struggles and the regressive, preoedipal wishes for fusion with the internalized mother. A clearly marked outline of her psychopathology could be delineated. Notably absent was any strong sense of emotional conviction in her associations; the elements of intellectual contrivance were still in ascendency.

Particular attention should be given to the association, "I think you mean a penis" in the second dream. The derisive component was scantily concealed but was spoken in careful, academic, textbook cadences. At this juncture the dreams and the associations fitted in with her overall resistive pattern; my interpretations seemingly fell on deaf ears. This was all true; but I also perceived the rudimentary anlage of her introjection of the analyst's work ego. Her curiosity was engaged; she reflected on the work between the hours and began to sense the flow and continuity that is at the core of the psychoanalytic process.

The dream of the third year, "I'm sitting on a public toilet," showed further movement in the analytic work. The associations were emotionally alive and were spoken with conviction and a concomitant diminution of the intellectual constraints. Andrea had instituted the important work of bridging the gulf between her traumatic, anxiety-laden past and her current self-defeating patterns. A more effective observing ego had split from her experiencing ego: where id was the analytic work ego would be.

DREAM PRODUCTION AS RESISTANCE

The obsessional patient not infrequently uses dream production as the handmaiden for resistance. Perceiving the analyst's interest in dreams the patient reacts compulsively and compliantly in the offering up of his dreams as gifts. The unconscious wish states: This is my production, my pride, a treasure which I offer to you; my expectation is unconditional love; if not forthcoming I will exert ruthless control. A centrally important meaning in the patient's compliant posture is his unremitting commitment to disclaiming and abnegating any responsibility for the pain and suffering in his life. He is innocent and powerless in the face of forces beyond his control. The ground is set for future dry runs when the therapist responds to these overtures with a matching overintellectuality and countercompliance. Tracing the associative minutia of each dream element may yield a high order of enthrallment with each other's intellectual powers; higher yet is the risk of shifting the emphasis from affective, conflict-laden areas and, in effect, sterilizing the analysis.

Sophisticated patients who have been exposed to the popular lore of the use of dreams in analysis need little prompting in the introduction of their dreams. This is particularly true with obsessional patients. A repeated hearing of "I had a dream last night" as the session begins should flash warning signals that an important resistance has been introduced.

Many years ago I worked with a young, homosexual, obsessional man, Robert S, who started each hour reporting a dream. I was entranced with the rich manifest content and the thick symbolic imagery. The patient was similarly beguiled with the process of tracking each element to its root source. And thus we proceeded, locked in a shared illusion, with the analysis suffering accordingly.

Robert S was the youngest of two brothers reared in a tradition-rich and money-poor Southern family. He was enveloped by a demanding, domineering, anxiety-ridden mother, abetted by her two maiden sisters. The father was ineffectual and unsure; in dealing with his wife, he fled, concentrating his energies in guiding his older son to his ideals of strength and manliness. To the patient the father represented a stony-faced, fearsome figure to be held in awe and hatred; to consult him in matters of emotional importance was unthinkable. Robert presented a picture of

troubled, uncommitted homosexuality; despite constant references to his
shame and guilt, the accompanying affect was strikingly absent.

In the second year of treatment the following short dream was
reported, unusual in light of his customary dream prolixity:

"I am going on a journey. I am going to Budapest."

Robert S associated easily in his usual flat, dry tones. "There's something strange about this dream, my dreams are usually so much longer,
much more detail. I'm not sure what it's saying, but the journey must
allude to the analysis. It seems to me that a journey often means that."
While he spoke my thoughts flashed to the death of his favorite uncle the
previous week and his expressed concern over an inability to feel sadness
or grief. He had been puzzled at this; his uncle had been the one male who
had shown any interest in him. At this stage I had begun the recognition
that our daily dream exercise was leading to sterility and a floundering of
the analysis. My piece of self-understanding was not unmixed with
chagrin and dismay; I thus felt pleased at his show of emotion.

I said, "You are speaking of death and loss." Robert was quiet for
several minutes and then replied, "I'm not sure where you got that, oh, you
mean Uncle George. Yes, well yes, I miss him. I know I must but I still feel
nothing." And his thoughts meandered into their usual dead ends.

When I asked him his thoughts about Budapest, he answered, "Well,
you know I'm planning a trip to Europe this summer but nowhere in the
vicinity of Budapest." I replied, "You mean more in my vicinity, whom you
pester with your hostility and envy while wearing a Buddha-like mask."
Robert burst out, "What!" and was silent for several minutes. He finally
spoke, "I think you just might be right. I remember a sudden headache the
other day when you didn't answer my questions. But that's my way, it's so
hard for me to feel my feelings." This was the first undefended, spontaneous display of emotion since the start of treatment.

In the two previous hours he had strongly denied any competitive
jealousies toward his father and brother. He had revived a memory of his
brother brushing him away as a "tag-a-long" when he attempted to join in
his brother's games. In the session on the day of the dream he had asked
me several times to give him a treatment progress report; to my silence he
spoke with the slightest edge of irritation, "Why are you silent? Why don't
you answer? You let me flounder. You act like a Zen master." The
atmosphere in my consulting room thickened with his strained, muted
anger.

A symbolic representation of the death of his uncle with its attendant
sadness, loneliness, and grief was contained in the element "going on a

journey." The primitive libidinal yearning for his ambivalently held, idealized mother was slated for future work; at this juncture the nascent state of the therapeutic alliance warned against premature intervention; I said nothing. The manifest dream thought "Budapest" condensed his latent oedipal rage towards his father and, in transference, manifested in complex projective identificatory processes with me. I felt the preconscious derivatives of this material had at least a fighting chance at accessibility, and thus, my comment.

It is important to bear in mind that these areas had previously been approached from a number of different angles. The sexualization of his aggression was evident in the acting out of the transference and in his narcissistic object choices (younger men, lower social status).

These activities embodied his destructive impulses towards me linked with denial of any meaningful, dependent attachment. Thus, the full panoply of his behavior, his ego state, the therapeutic alliance, his confused sexual identifications, the drives, affects, and their defenses all required balanced attention. The interpretation of the dream and his associations was a useful adjunct.

CIRCUMSTANTIALITY AND INDIRECTNESS IN DREAMS AND ASSOCIATIONS

Circumstantiality and a circuitous avoidance of direct statement—often to a tortuous degree—recurs throughout treatment. Verbal interchange with an obsessional person, particularly in the anxiety-charged atmosphere of the therapeutic encounter, often results in both parties feeling chained together, as in a convoluted Chinese puzzle. What starts off as reasonable discourse soon becomes tangential and elliptical; what seemed communicative becomes chopped, interspersed with fragments of new ideas or reduced to meaninglessness by a sudden shift in direction. This disjointed misuse of the cognitive process does not suffuse the listener with uncanny feelings as induced by schizophrenic patients; the bizarre quality is lacking. All has the appearance of calm and reason—the ambience of secondary process syntactical thinking is disarming.

This curious style of proceeding has its inner method for the patient. It provides him with a bearable, steady state of tension despite the often distressing force of the ego-dystonic symptoms. Whether inexperienced or more seasoned, the therapist often finds himself baffled and perplexed. How did we get over here when we started over there?

Assailed by an inability to make or stick with a decision, Mr. Frank N, thirty years old, sought analysis. His rising professional career was seriously interfered with by discomforting tension and the preoccupying obsessional thought, "I am to blame for the death of my father." His father had been harshly despotic; he tyrannized the family with a mixture of verbal and physical abuse. The father's early death, when the patient was thirteen years old, was violent and unexpected. The family was stripped of financial support and the load fell on the young mother to raise her four children. She was long-suffering, readily aired her grievances, yet held steady in the face of heavy reality pressures.

In early adolescence Mr. N pledged himself never to be a hostage to an inconstant fortune; he would insulate himself with wealth and the praise, love, and affection of all about him. A core of effective reaction formations was early established. He learned to be adaptive and achievement oriented: an exemplary student, he avoided excessive roughhousing with friends, played an optimal amount of sports, and became the conciliator and mediator in family quarrels. Fleet of foot, he physically avoided his father's rages—strengthening his already present sense of omnipotence and omniscience.

His whole mode of being was staked on being good to all; affability, conformity, and an even temper were devoted to the task of maintaining unending narcissistic supplies. The compromise formations worked well in the reality sector; he married the daughter of a wealthy businessman, had three thriving children, and his own career was promising. Nonetheless, the press of instinctual forces had their say.

Following the death of his mother in his middle twenties he experienced short-lived grief; a year later he felt the full force of his obsessional thoughts. These were accompanied by headaches, base line tension, and premature ejaculations.

Slights to his self-esteem—from office help who dared question his judgments, from a parking attendant who frowned at a tip, to his wife's lack of sexual response—all were sufficient to evoke a surge of self-blame and self-castigation and, in short order, the leap to the magical, talismanic thought, "I am to blame for my father's death."

In the first six months of treatment I had commented on his "goodness" pattern as indicating compelling needs to manage and control others in order to achieve his goals. He would receive my remarks as reproaches or, alternatively, would convert them into action programs for self-reform. In one session he had mentioned lending large sums of money to acquaintances of dubious integrity. I remarked that it must make him feel not only good but also strong and powerful. In the next hour he reported a dream.

"I'm in a basketball game. Oh, I do remember a game, [pause] a game in a gym in high school. I went to a relatively small high school, you knew everyone there, it's different today, [pause] everything is so impersonalized, so cold. I knew everyone in my senior class, [pause] did you hear that noise out there? That must be trucks bringing in building material for that empty lot on the next block. In the dream the referee was rough looking. I don't know why the referee should be rough looking. I've known some hard looking men in my life who were decent and kind when you got to know them. The high school kids I used to know, well, some were rough and some weren't. I wouldn't exactly avoid the tough kids in class, but I certainly didn't make it a point to mix with them and get into fights. Fights can lead to both physical injury and hurt feelings. Maybe I am too much of a peacemaker, but even though it sounds like a cliché I do believe in doing unto others what I would want done to myself. I was reading a book last week that brought home that idea to me with such clarity, [pause] things in life can be simple but still true. This morning at the office I was saying to my secretary . . . [and so on]."

Several minutes later I interrupted to say, "You know you started to tell me a dream." He answered, "Well, I am doing that." I said, "Notice how you veer off in different directions all at once." He was silent for a few minutes and then said, coolly, "I would like to continue with the dream," and he did.

Mr. N reported, or more precisely did not report, his dream in his own fashion: stingy, retentive, parsimonious. He deposited a piece here, a bit there, held back a feeling here, allowed a sliver of emotion to emerge there. Following the session he completed his work at the office in a frenzy and on his drive home reflected on the hour. He felt that I had criticized him unfairly, that he was doing a conscientious job in reporting the dream, that he was doing the best he knew how to do, maybe I wasn't the best analyst for him. He thought I was capable but maybe I didn't know what I was doing, but then who was he to say, he wasn't an expert, he was in no position to judge, maybe he wasn't cooperating enough. And within minutes his self-reproaches had turned into, "I am to blame for the death of my father."

Here, in capsule form, were his psychodynamics, the state of the transference, the impulse/defense balance, and his cognitive style of maintaining self-regard.

As a complex human being, the obsessional patient reflects this structure in his attitude towards dreaming as part of his overall behavioral repertoire. Patients often regard recreation time as a dangerous lacuna to be cram-filled with activities, work, and so on. I recently saw, in consultation, a young obsessional woman who had reached an impasse in treatment. Among the variety of obsessional behaviors that impeded her progress she regarded her open time periods (weekends, etc.) as moral injunctions that mandated work. With the grave seriousness that stamps the obsessional posture, she tensely and single-mindedly dedicated each waking minute of her recreational time to the detailed scrutiny of her dreams and fantasies. She looked at me with earnest candor and said, "I know it seems like too much but this is what I feel I should do to make the analysis progress." It was a labor of Sisyphus.

CONCLUSION

Freud was appropriately affected by his insight into the workings of the latent dream thoughts and the dream-work; it was, indeed, monumental. The core object-related conflicts of infancy and childhood, the drive forces and their accompanying affects, the pressures of reality—all are shaped and filtered through the dream work. Condensation, displacement, symbol formation, visual representation, and secondary revision all work synchronously. There is a blending, a coalescing of the past, the present, and aspirations for the future. The resultant is that unique intrapsychic phenomenon—the manifest dream.

Yet, one must be chary of overvaluing the obsessional dream in its manifest form. It is a clinical truth that our patients—whether those undergoing psychotic decompensation or those in the range of the psychoneuroses—do not manifest clearly distinguishable diagnostic, dynamic, or genetic characteristics in their dreams. More to the point, understanding dreams removed from the context of the therapeutic alliance, without associations, without knowledge of the patient's impulse–defense position or the state of the transference and countertransference can only be, at best, an exhilarating form of educated guesswork. From the economic point of view, levels of anxiety can be roughly assessed or intuited from manifest content; but a word of caution: the obsessional person often represents intense, libidinal or aggressive affect-filled experiences in his dreams, only to reassume his mechanical, fretful, passionless posture upon awaking or reporting in his session.

In the clinical vignette of Robert S it was shown that the recognition of dreams used to further resistance was singularly useful. The patient was faithful in bringing forth his daily dream; with equal fervor he visited the bathroom daily after breakfast and religiously produced a stool that was remarkable in its invariance: small in quantity and spheroid and pelletlike in form. This is the obsessional mode, whether in the cognitive style of dream reporting or in the realm of bodily function. Mr. Frank N's method of dream reporting was distinctively his own. His scatter, circumlocutions, and anxiety-containing way of speech yielded a niggardly therapeutic harvest for a long period of time. Andrea G, although of well-defined obsessional character structure, showed a good analytic aptitude with strong reflective and self-observing capacities. Her dreams and the associations were fruitfully used and helped to achieve significant character change.

Openness, spontaneity, understanding with conviction, responsible freedom—the goals of treatment—are danger marks to the obsessional patient. With good will, good sense, and a degree of tolerance, the patient, in concert with his therapist, can productively use his dreams and disengage himself from the thankless task of moving the mountains of the world.

References

Altman, L. L. (1969). *The Dream in Psychoanalysis*. New York: International Universities Press.

Eliot, T. S. (1917). The love song of J. Alfred Prufrock. In *The Complete Poems and Plays: 1909-1950*. New York: Harcourt, Brace and World, 1952.

Fine, B. (1969). *The Manifest Content of the Dream*. Kris Study Group, Monograph 3. New York: International Universities Press.

Freud, S. (1900). The interpretation of dreams. *Standard Edition* 4:1–338 and 5:339–627.

——— (1909). A case of obsessional neurosis. *Standard Edition* 19:221–228.

Greenson, R. (1970). The exceptional position of the dream in psychoanalysis. *Psychoanalytic Quarterly* 39:519–549.

Rappoport, E. A. (1959). The first dream in erotized transference. *International Journal of Psycho-Analysis* 40:240–245.

Waldhorn, H. F. (1967). *The Place of the Dream in Clinical Psychoanalysis*. Kris Study Group, Monograph 2. New York: International Universities Press.

CHAPTER 10

THE DREAM IN DISSOCIATIVE STATES

Stephen S. Marmer, M.D.

CONCEPTS OF MULTIPLE PERSONALITY AND DREAMS

Psychoanalysis had as its earliest focus the study of hysteria and the investigation of dreams. In the "Dora" case, Freud (1905) used each to help unfold the mysteries of the other. Today, the recent publication of a number of celebrated cases of multiple personality (Ludwig et al. 1972, Schreiber 1973, Thigpen and Cleckley 1957) calls our attention again to patients with dramatic hysterical symptoms. Many of the case reports on multiple personality are primarily descriptive and few offer psycho-dynamic speculations. None to my knowledge deals specifically with dreams or dream interpretation or the unique problems of handling dreams in the therapy of this group of patients. In this clinical paper, I will discuss the role of dreams in the treatment of patients with multiple personality and other forms of dissociation. My emphasis will be clinical and I will not be making the kind of theoretical inferences Freud could make in his case studies. I will simply be setting forth some of the techniques I have found to be helpful in my work with this group of patients and some of the metapsychological assumptions I make in these cases.

This chapter is written for the practitioner who has treated patients with dissociation and for the therapist who may be looking for guidance with a current case. For those who have never seen such a patient, I refer you to the numerous case studies of multiple personality as well as to my own paper (Marmer 1980), in which some of the case material mentioned in this chapter is considered in greater detail. But let me emphasize again that at this stage my work is empirical, and if it raises questions or stimulates further work by other investigators, this chapter will have fulfilled a useful purpose.

DISSOCIATION, SPLITTING, AND MULTIPLE PERSONALITY

The four classical dissociative reactions are fugue states, amnesia, somnambulism and multiple personality. These are characterized by the presence of behavior disconnected from the mainstream of the patient's actions and identity and often disconnected too from his awareness. Amnesia can exist for specific events or for the entirety of prior life experiences of the patient. Fugue states are generally brief episodes of flight behavior, though frenzied or violent states are also known to occur. Somnambulism is often thought of as simple sleepwalking behavior, but it can also consist of psychologically significant complex activity often carried out night after night in a trancelike state. Multiple personality is the presence of separate identities within the same person, which function alternately or sometimes simultaneously. Ellenberger (1970) divides multiple personality into three groups:

1. Simultaneous multiple personality
2. Successive multiple personality
   a. mutually cognizant of each other
   b. mutually amnesic
   c. one-way amnesic
3. Personality clusters.

In my clinical experience, where dissociative phenomena are not generated by organic pathology, all of the classical varieties have turned out to be variations of multiple personality. For example, in amnesia the forgotten history of the amnesic patient usually constitutes one personality, while the new experience becomes a second personality. For this reason, I am going to focus in this paper on the treatment of the dreams of a patient with multiple personality. I believe that the techniques useful in this case have applicability to the other forms of dissociation which, in turn, I hold to be multiple personality variants.

A feature I believe to be common to all forms of dissociation is the splitting off of the dissociative experience. When the dissociation is brief, this splitting is difficult to distinguish from repression; but when the dissociation is well organized and exists over a period of time, something more far reaching is at work. I hold that this mechanism is splitting of the ego described by Freud (1894, 1896, 1927, 1940a, b). The notion of splitting is used by different authors to mean different things. In this paper, I am adhering to the specific concept of splitting of the ego as articulated by Freud.

In the following section, I am going to offer a series of dreams and selected data from a case of multiple personality. The principles by which the dream material was analyzed are applicable, however, in my opinion, to all forms of dissociation.

CLINICAL EXAMPLE

Anne B was a forty-year-old married woman with four children when she came into analysis. She was a college graduate, housewife and painter, and conducted art lessons in her home and at a local community college.

She came into analysis because of what she described as the start of "an emotional breakdown," with symptoms including "physical memories which I could 'live' through, but for which I had no verbal or visual recall: like putting my own hand on my shoulder and rocking myself until I was shaking myself, until it felt like someone else was shaking me and I was whimpering. I could not say what incident this was connected with, where it took place if it took place at all, or really what I was doing. It was a strong physical message to myself that needed translation." These would intrude on her at unexpected moments. She also had anxiety attacks, crying spells at the contemplation of her father's death (he died when the patient was eight years old), and a variety of psychosomatic symptoms such as headaches, galactorrhea, sore breasts, and sore neck. There were also occasional fuguelike episodes in which she would run around the room but from which she could emerge instantly should someone unexpectedly confront her. Finally, she reported many episodes of automatic writing in which various parts of her personality would conduct written dialogues.

In spite of her difficulties, the patient was able to continue with only modest loss of efficiency in her activities as housewife and mother, art teacher, creative artist, and citizen active in the affairs of her community. There were, however, throughout the apparently stable marriage, signs of sexual difficulty and fears of any conflicts which might result from too much intimacy. Similarly, in the aggressive sphere she and her husband seemed to collude in maneuvers which would avoid conflict, even if the price was a reduction in intimacy.

Fifteen years earlier a prior "breakdown" had occurred. The patient then had successful therapy, twice a week, with a woman psychologist for a year and a half. During this therapy the patient kept a notebook of the conversations between the various parts of herself which she presented to me early in our work. This notebook revealed a "yellow person" who wrote in a naive fashion about childhood happenings, a "red person" who warned of imminent and remote dangers, a "green questioner," and a "gray or blue observer." Imagined dreamlike scenes became the background for interaction and conversation between various of these "personalities," all of whom would reemerge in our work as "yellow Child, red Witchy, green Jane, and gray Observer."

During the years between "breakdowns," the patient used her artistic work and her dance for self-analysis. For example, shortly before beginning analysis to overcome a block against the color green she forced herself to paint a green picture of a young girl in a forest, which became transformed, as if beyond conscious control, to a wounded monster hiding behind the bushes. On seeing what she had painted, she became horror-stricken and then compassionate, saying "What have they done to you?" She then proceeded to smooth over the painting and turned it into a Christ's head. In fact, the process by which paintings emerged from the canvas with a minimum of foreplanning was typical of her most creative and best work. During the course of the analysis, the patient's artistic productions were frequently discussed and were often extremely revealing.

The principal event in the patient's youth was the death of her father, by brain tumor, when she was eight years old. The patient recalled having invented several scenes of father's death which she believed to be true at various times in her life, all of which included her disappearance for three hours after hearing the awful news.

The attribute of shielding herself against the immediacy of experience was present in the analysis, particularly in the early phases. The patient defended against her experience of the transference by diffusing, minimizing, and delaying their direct experience, often responding to my transference interpretations by talking about peripheral things, coming back minutes or hours or sometimes days later to respond to my interventions. At times she appeared to be ignoring my interpretations, only to reveal later that she had in fact taken them in, worked on them, and was able to give a delayed, but nevertheless highly meaningful, response. In this fashion she demonstrated her dissociative style within the transference.

One aspect of the analysis that further revealed the patient's unique dynamics was the emergence, particularly through automatic writing, of her multiple personality pattern. In our fourth session, the patient recognized the presence of the multiple personalities during her prior psychotherapy and that this was recurring mostly in the form of automatic writing dialogues that she would have at home. This time she identified the different parts of herself by names as Jane, a sexy, lusty, carefree, aggressive, but also practical, straight-thinking part of herself; Witchy, a "lady disaster" person, who was concerned lest any harm come to her through an overly dangerous action and who represented society's conventions, but who also embodied graciousness, tact, and style; and Child, who was a dreamy, wistful, and sad character with playful and vivid imagination and a sense of deep appreciation for art, nature, and all kinds of sensory images. At first the analysis focused on Jane's, Child's, and Witchy's productions only insofar as they were revealed in automatic writing that the patient would first have at home. Later, the patient was able to produce the automatic writing during the sessions and in the third year of the analysis Jane, Child, and Witchy were able to speak directly to me in the sessions.

While the patient was not amnesic during her dissociative episodes, she would nevertheless become fully controlled by her multiple selves. For example, early in the analysis Child one day leaped from the couch and ran frantically around the room, finally huddling in the corner, upset over a dream whose associations led to a discussion of her father's death. A few minutes later the patient regained normal control and finished the hour. Later in the analysis, while recovering the memory of the three "lost hours" that followed her father's death, the patient went through very eerie and moving reenactments of those horrible times in similar dissociative fashion. It was nevertheless a sign of her basic ego strength that she was conscious during these episodes and always consciously accepted each of these characters as part of her, even if unconsciously she was at the same time dissociating them.

One of the problems in the analysis was how to accept material which was produced by the patient in a way which allowed the dissociated elements of the patient to express themselves, while at the same time encouraging integration. As the patient brought in more and more increasingly disorganized and regressed material, mostly automatic writing, the major defensive styles of each of the personalities emerged with increasing clarity. This permitted me to establish interpretations tailored to each of the personalities, which in turn promoted the uncovering of additional material. Soon the material of the analysis converged onto an important incident of childhood, which shed crucial light on the genesis of the splitting. For a period of approximately two weeks, the patient had a series of dreams which we finally decided dealt with different versions of a primal scene trauma. What distinguished our work on these dreams was that our prior work with the automatic writing had taught both of us to be alert to the specific styles of each of the personalities. When we looked at the dreams, asking the question "Which one of these personalities dreamed this dream?" we were able to view them differently, both individually and as a series. They became a collection of dreams which expressed the different ways in which the split aspects of her ego had experienced and processed the trauma.

DREAMS OF A MULTIPLE PERSONALITY

Dream 1: "I was dreaming of a path in the woods. I didn't follow the path, but went across the bridge to the city instead. It was a leafy path which got dark."

Dream 2: "I passed the spot where the green house was supposed to be but instead there was a patch of grass. I climbed a rock and looked through the trees, over the lake through the moonlight. It was beautiful. It was very dark, or maybe my eyes were closed. I held out my arms and felt the damp leaves and ran over the path. I came to a place like a Rousseau painting, or like illustrations in a child book called *My Father the Dragon.* There were brown dogs barking. They were mouthing my hands on my way home. They were playful dogs, maybe they were doggies."

Dream 3: "There were beautiful sinewy, slimy, dark people sliding on each other. It was the same location of the other dreams, but it was like there were Roman columns and ruins."

Dream 4: "I was riding on a horse bareback. I was on a sandy path and I walked up to the rear of the horse. It wanted to bite me. I backed off and it ran off, but didn't go into the corral."

Dream 5: "I was riding a bicycle along the path to our old house. There was a long snake in the driveway. I was not frightened of snakes, but I looked to see if it was a rattlesnake. It was very fat around and it was the length of the driveway. It had horizontal stripes, very odd; it gave one big ripple. I went past it on my business. I don't recall the other parts of this dream."

Dream 6: "I was with my sister, riding on an old merry-go-round, sitting on the bench because we were too small to ride the horses. We were peering over the bench; we had our arms around each other."

Dream 7: "You were making sexual advances toward me and I was dismayed and pleased at the same time, but I wasn't frightened. It was not a relationship I was going to be party to, it was more like physical closeness, like hugging."

Dream 8: "I am walking very snugly with my husband. 'I really do love you,' he says. 'I love you, too,' I say back. It was a cross between our local market today and the house where I grew up, that same leafy area. It was evening. I was worried about our safety, though my husband was not scared. It was not summer, it was more like early fall. A darker section of the path made me feel hesitant. Out of the corner of my eye I saw the suggestion of a male figure and let go of my husband and sat behind a tree. But my husband went on and I did too. We crossed the street and saw some construction. I walked around it. My husband said it was what he was doir.g at work. We saw some stairs and I have the cleverest stairway in the dream. Then we were in L."

Dream 9: "I found a baby. I loved it. I brought it into the apartment. The baby was wrapped in a blanket, sucking. I wondered where it was. I saw her sucking on her sleeve. I picked her up. I had to get important information from her. I shaked it and banged it gently. There was conflict in my feelings. I really wanted to smash it, but I also wanted to love it."

Dream 10: "There was a hunk of land washed against the rest of the land by a current. It was flying into pieces and coming down. I saw it from a distance. Then, in a building underneath, it was coming down. Maybe it was a medical building. Pieces were coming down. I expected the building to be smashed and crushed, there were lots of vibrations, but it was okay. One room had dusty-looking people on the floor, lying there looking dead. I said, 'You're not going to lie there, are you?' Then they got up and went to look for others. Then the scene changed. I was walking along a path to a country club house. I went inside and sat down, it seemed nice. Sis came in wearing a revealing petticoat, carrying a letter. She was young and strong-looking. She sat on my lap and she was reading this letter, taped together in odd pieces like the automatic writing I've given to you. The top of her petticoat opened, revealing her breasts. They had inverted nipples. It embarrassed me, though not her, but the letter kept her covered. I couldn't read the letter in the dream."

Dream 11: "I was having a dream of dancing and I was doing the splits and marveled at how I was held together by my body."

Dream 12: "A long snake was in a tree. It was in the top of the tree and then went into the tree trunk and came out through a hole in the tree trunk. The pattern on it was very much like the pattern of the rug in your office."

Dream 13: "The house was rocking, slowly and carefully, in an earthquake. I wondered if the house was holding up and the toilet was breaking. I wanted to see it from the outside. People were pretending nothing was happening. A friend from childhood who now lives near me, I guess it was her house. The dogs were running around, scared. They came out with me. I petted and reassured them. My friend was not sure about earthquakes. She was more curious than afraid."

Dream 14: "We were walking along the stairs on the walkway at the university. There was a black girl with me who I remember from childhood who had a neck tumor. Then we were walking by the park near the ocean. We went down the stairs to the beach. At one point she decided that the quickest way was to jump. The stairs were green with a blue railing. She jumped and landed on the beach. Some people came up to see if she was okay and I shouted down to them that they had to help her and meanwhile I knew that I had to walk very carefully down the rest of the stairs."

Dream 15: "A man was spanking his child for masturbating and asked my advice. I told him that he didn't have to worry because it was normal for children to masturbate."

DREAM ASSOCIATIONS AND RECONSTRUCTIONS

One of the interesting features about these dreams is that they all led to associations of a primal scene trauma. Through the analysis of these dreams and a careful sifting through of the associations, the patient and I were able to arrive at a reconstruction. Around Christmastime, when the patient was about a year and a half old, she was restless and awoke and walked to her parents' bedroom to observe her parents in intercourse. Her father discovered her standing in the door, leapt from the bed wearing a nightshirt, his penis still erect and exposed, grabbed her by the right arm and marched her off to bed stiffly, and told her to leave, shouting at her loudly. This upset her greatly, and she turned to her stuffed doggie for comfort, masturbated while playing with the doggie. She chewed on the doggie's ear while masturbating, gagged herself, vomited on the doggie, aroused her parents' further attention by the sound of the vomiting and was cleaned up. But in the process of being cleaned up, she was told that the stuffed animal would have to be thrown away. It was this primal scene which the patient believed she was dreaming about again and again during this period of analysis.

The dream of a path in the wood (dream 1) and the dream of the dark place where the green house was supposed to be and where the brown dogs were barking (dream 2) were both felt to be dreamed by Child. They were very visual; they were primarily pictorial as compared to dreams consisting of actions or concepts. Simply seeing them was to see a beautiful scene. They were full of Child's characteristic defenses of idealization, reversal, and denial. The idealization was exemplified by the beauty of the scenes, and the reversal was shown by the dogs' mouthing her hands in the manifest content, while her associations led to the latent wish to mouth her father's penis. The denial was revealed by the way she made her angry father into a playful dog. These dreams were poetic, filled with dreamy imagery, sensuous, simple, innocent.

The dream of the beautiful, sinewy, slimy, dark people, sliding over each other (dream 3) was less clear. The patient felt it might be another Child dream with the theme of sneaking around and peeking with no real knowledge of what people were doing. On the other hand, the direct sensuous contact between the two people might indicate that undisguised sexual expression was the subject. In that case it would be a dream such as Jane would dream. In this sense there was much less denial, which was also a characteristic of Jane.

She said that riding the horses bareback (dream 4) was a Jane dream and a Jane image of intercourse. The themes of biting and refusing to go quietly into the corral also expressed Jane's aggression and independence.

The dream of riding the bicycle along the path to the old house and observing the long snake in the driveway (dream 5) was a condensation by Child of an enema experience in which the long orange thing was inserted into her, combined with the primal scene experience. These two events would frequently become condensed with one another in the course of the analysis. Confusion of sexuality with a traumatic enema and other anal experiences was also characteristic of Child.

The merry-go-round dream (dream 6) was seen as representing Child and Jane as the two children, both peeking over the bench into something that they really shouldn't be involved in because they were too small.

The dream in which I made sexual advances toward the patient (dream 7) was an Anne dream. This was not a dream produced by a split-off part of herself but was rooted in her current transference feelings.

The dream that started with the walk together with her husband in her present community, and changed to the location of her old house, and then to L (dream 8) was a Witchy dream. In this dream, dire consequences would take place if she were without daddy. L was the city where her mother-in-law was vacationing when she heard the news that *her* father had died. The end of summer and the beginning of fall was the time of the year in which the patient's father died.

The dream about the conflict over love and aggression experienced toward the orphan baby (dream 9) is believed to be a recapitulation of the masturbation following the primal scene trauma and also of her frustration at the various parts of herself as symbolized by the baby for getting into trouble. This was an Anne dream *about* her split selves and not a dream *produced* by the splits themselves.

The two-part dream of the cataclysmic earthquake–tidal wave and her sister's exposed breasts (dream 10) represented two themes. One part was dreamed by Witchy, full of all the danger and cataclysmic forces that could be unleashed against her. The second part was dreamed by Jane. The patient believed that the second half of the dream was in an entirely different set of colors, a different location with many sexual innuendos and expressions of direct sexuality, consistent with Jane.

The dream of doing the splits (dream 11) was an Anne dream, a beautiful metaphor of her integrated personality and how the integration was proceeding.

The dream of the snake coming out of the tree (dream 12) led again to associations which pointed to primal scene preoccupations. In this instance, however, it was not possible to assign this dream with clarity to any one of the personalities.

The dream of the house rocking slowly and carefully in the earthquake (dream 13) was yet another reference to the primal scene. The toilet breaking up was associated with the vomiting and with the enema which in her mind had often been confused with the primal scene. This particular example was a Jane dream because it was characterized by action exceeding passive imagery. In addition, the objective view of the friend was a sign of Jane's old useful role in assessing real danger.

The dream of the stairway with green and blue and with a black companion who jumps to danger (dream 14) was a Witchy dream warning Child, Jane, and Anne to watch where they were going. Jane was sometimes represented by the color green and Anne sometimes by the color blue.

The dream of the man spanking his child for masturbating (dream 15) is another primal scene reference, this time showing that considerable integration had taken place. In this dream, the trauma was reenacted: the man represented father who was scolding the young Anne for her sexual curiosity, for her masturbation and for her intrusion into the primal scene. By this time an integrated patient was able to reassure all of the parties that the situation could resolve in a healthy manner. This was an Anne dream of advanced form.

GENERAL APPROACH TO DISSOCIATIVE PATIENTS

Patients with dissociative symptoms are persons who, for defensive and adaptive reasons, maintain multiple personalities and splits in their egos. In treating such patients, I have found it helpful to accept communications from any personality who wishes to participate in the therapy. Going one step further, I believe that the establishment of a therapeutic alliance with each personality affords the patient perhaps his first opportunity to have every aspect of his defensive organization come into relationship with another person. Different transference configurations with each personality illuminate the conflicts those personalities were created to solve, and the acceptance by the therapist of each different dissociated aspect of the patient provides the precondition for acceptance by the patient of his disowned parts. Throughout this process the therapist must adhere to the principle that the patient is a single unitary person who has pressing psychological reasons for existing in a split state.

These splits ordinarily interfere with waking life, and it is the disorder caused during the day by the patient's dissociations that typically brings such patients into treatment in the first place. I believe that Anne and other similar patients have helped me discover that the same splits in the ego continue through the night and affect mental life during sleep as well as during waking.

DREAMS AS EXPRESSIONS OF SPLIT EGO

Analyzing dreams of dissociated patients as expressions of split ego can significantly advance the work of analysis. With Anne, we were able to understand which parts of the patient dreamed which dreams and then to see how the conflicts, struggles, and adaptive styles were expressed. The therapeutic alliance with the patient was strengthened, and during this phase several therapeutic alliances seemed to exist. It was crucial to the ultimate successful outcome in this case that we were able to establish therapeutic alliances *between* each of the separate personalities and me, and also for the first time, a therapeutic alliance *among* the various personalities. Hitherto, they had seen themselves as fighting for control, or seeking to eradicate each other, or needing to save themselves from the mischief wrought by the others. By focusing interpretations in the way in which I did, the personalities saw that they all had to deal with the same material, that they had all experienced the same traumatic events, that they each had their unique defensive styles, and that these became recognized as reactive instead of being regarded as primarily destructive as had previously been the case. They were forced to recognize each others' existence and legitimacy as never before, which, of course, was very beneficial to the work. This permitted them to begin to have empathy for each other for the first time, which then became the turning point toward integration, as they saw more and more clearly that they had a common interest in Anne's whole existence.

Their differing symptoms during waking hours had been seen as intrusions or distractions or interferences. They each had important things to express through dreaming and this made it possible for them to see themselves as allies and ultimately connected within Anne.

It is basic to the understanding of dreams to assist the patient to see that he is the author of his dreams, and that his dreams express his repressed infantile wishes according to his defensive organization. With patients who use dissociation as a chief defense, such an approach with dreams can form a highly useful vehicle for helping them to see their dissociated and disowned experiences as their own creations. This becomes a building stage for psychic reunification. The splits are allowed into the analysis, are experienced in the transference, are seen to exist both asleep and awake, are gradually accepted as the patient's defensive and adaptive creations, and can then be interpreted. Reintegration of the formerly disavowed split ego organizations can be seen to be worked through within the transference, and within the dreams.

References

Ellenberger, H. F. (1970). *The Discovery of the Unconscious*. New York: Basic Books.

Freud, S. (1894). The neuro-psychoses of defense. *Standard Edition* 3:43–68.

——— (1896). Further remarks on the neuro-psychoses of defense. *Standard Edition* 3:43–68.

——— (1905). Fragment of an analysis of a case of hysteria. *Standard Edition* 7:3–111.

——— (1927). Fetishism. *Standard Edition* 21:149–158.

——— (1940a). An outline of psycho-analysis. *Standard Edition* 23:141–207.

——— (1940b). Splitting of the ego in the process of defense. *Standard Edition* 23:273–278.

Ludwig, A. M., Brandsma, J., Wilbur, C., Bendfeldt, F., and Jameson, D. (1972). The objective study of a multiple personality. *Archives of General Psychiatry* 26:298–310.

Marmer, S. S. (1980). Psychoanalysis of multiple personality. *International Journal of Psycho-Analysis* (in Press).

Schreiber, F. R. (1973). *Sybil*. Chicago: Henry Regnery.

Thigpen, C. H., and Cleckley, H. M. (1957). *The Three Faces of Eve*. New York: McGraw-Hill.

CHAPTER 11

THE DREAM IN PHOBIC STATES

Sydney L. Pomer, M.D. and Robert A. Shain, M.D.

This chapter is in the nature of an inquiry into the relationship between phobic patients and their dreams. Are there features in such dreams which are specific to phobic patients? A brief historical survey of the literature is followed by clinical examples and conclusions.

OVERVIEW

Phobic anxiety accompanying conflicts of the phallic-oedipal phase has been inextricably bound to the case of Little Hans (Freud 1909). In this landmark exposition, psychoanalysis was applied successfully for the first time in the treatment of a child by means of discussions between Freud and the boy's father. Hans's dream demonstates the evolution of his symptom: the fear of being bitten by a horse. A dream several months prior to the onset of his phobia conveyed the lad's pleasure at having someone unbutton his pants to help him urinate by holding his "widdler" (p. 7). He often asked his mother to touch his penis after his daily bath. Later, close to age five, the usually cheerful youngster awoke weeping, "When I was asleep I thought you were gone and I had no Mummy to coax with [to caress]" (p. 23). How Hans first became preoccupied with horses and their widdlers, and then subsequently developed an intense fear of being bitten by a horse is well documented. This case clearly conveys the classical psychoanalytic position, namely, that the oedipus complex and its vicissitudes are at the origin of anxieties and phobias. Symptoms are seen to be connected with forbidden sexuality, and they form a compromise between the dangerous incestuous wishes and the repressive defenses. By means of a still unexplained phobic mechanism, instinctual drives are displaced onto an object which becomes irrationally feared. Thus, the danger of castration, which is a threat because of phallic drives, is averted. Lorand (1946) noted that patients with phobias were the subject of Freud's early investigations leading ultimately to his basic psychoanalytic theory and principles as well as to the evolution of psychoanalytic technique. The exact etiological mechanism of phobia remains obscure, but Anna Freud (1977) noted that

> when fantasy activity has failed to protect against massive unpleasure, a different mechanism comes into operation, namely, condensation, which precedes externalization. This means that fears and anxieties do not remain diffuse but are compressed by the child into one encompassing symbol which represents the dangers left over from preoedipal phases as well as the dominant ones due to phallic-oedipal conflicts. It is, then, this symbol (animal, street, school) which, as a supposed part of the outside world, is dealt with by avoidance [pp. 87–88].

Of the famous dreams in the annals of psychoanalytic literature, the anxiety dream of the Wolf Man, at age four, must rank high. Freud's patient, as an adult, recalled the childhood dream in the first weeks of his therapy (Offenkrantz and Tobin 1973). From the analysis of this nightmare, Freud (1918) was able to reconstruct that the eighteen-month-old toddler had experienced great fright at witnessing his parents in coitus *a tergo*. Freud's later formulation (1926) was that the patient's phobia, an irrational fear of being eaten by wolves, was based on his fear (and unconscious libidinal wish) to be castrated and devoured in the course of seeking homosexual gratification from the father. It was Lewin (1952) who argued that anxiety dreams of phobic adults frequently conceal the fear of being devoured, and that the clinical picture of phobic patients is based on significant contributions of pregenital as well as oedipal features. The Wolf Man's wish to be eaten was aroused due to the genetic tie to his wish to sleep, a defensive reaction to having been awakened by the noise of the primal scene. The case was reviewed by Blum (1974) in light of present ego psychology and structural theory, utilizing various sources now available about the Wolf Man's extremely disturbed childhood. These experiences included swaddling, severe anorexia, frequent separation from the parents, punishment for masturbation, and threats of castration by a vengeful governess. In his carefully documented contribution, Blum sees the overwhelming phobic anxiety as related to the Wolf Man's conflict over symbiotic fusion and a regressive tendency to global identification involving merger with the object. That the primal scene trauma and subsequent nightmare occurred during the rapprochement subphase of separation-individuation is basic to Blum's study. It is now widely agreed that the Wolf Man suffered from a borderline condition. His later history revealed a panoply of pathology: debilitating obsessional neurosis, extreme narcissism, fragility, impairment of object relations, poor impulse control, bizarre hypochrondrical trends and impoverishment of affect, all clustered around a central paranoidal core. At the time, however, except for the wolf phobia, the nightmare itself offered no more than a hint at the forthcoming pathological symptomatology of the patient. Gedo and Goldberg (1973) see the nightmare of the wolves as creating the "actual core" (p. 50) of the Wolf Man's condition.

In the course of treating a thirty-eight-year-old man with a doll phobia, Rangell (1952) demonstrated the usefulness of regarding the phobic object as the hub of a wheel from which radiates numerous spokes representing origins, motives, causes, and other determinants connected to the hub. Rangell reported the following dream of his patient.

> I am in a bathtub. I have an erection and touch it. I show it to my wife, who wants to take a picture of it. Then my penis is detached, floating around. But I tell myself it is nothing, as this always happens [p. 183].

Rangell explains that the wife-mother has seen the forbidden erection, and castration has resulted. But the patient reassures himself, "It is nothing." The doll which is avoided is the detached penis, an unwelcome reminder of castration. The use of the term "nothing" was encountered frequently in both the literature and in our clinical examples.

Lewin also addressed the relationship of dreams and phobias, and described how Freud stated that the symptoms of phobias were analogous to the manifest dream. Erikson (1954) in a paper distinguished by its clarity and instructive style wrote of a young woman with agoraphobia who dreamt only of an image of the word: S(E)INE. Analysis of her dream was to prove the solution to the riddle of the hysterical patient's symptom and to provide the critical point of origin for the therapeutic course of events which were brought to a successful resolution. Greenson (1959) noted that in over nineteen years of clinical experience he analyzed only four patients whose symptoms were mainly phobias. All were anxiety-ridden individuals who were essentially pregenital neurotics. Phobias, then, may be seen in all diagnostic categories. Altman (1969) stated that the grouping of dreams under any classification is misleading, whether under transference diagnosis or any other heading. However, Levitan (1974) sought to find a relationship between the symptoms and dreams of a phobic patient, offering the hypothesis that the displacement which results in a phobia takes place initially in dreams. He analyzed a patient with agoraphobia whose dreams demonstrated conflict and anxiety over restraint of movement coupled with heightened muscular eroticism, a characteristic of agoraphobia. Sexual affect was present only when the manifest content of her dream was nonsexual. Her dreams showed that it was easier for the dream ego to disguise the sexual fantasy than the sexual affect. Levitan posits that this split between content and drive is crucial in the development of a phobia, and hence the characteristic sexualization of an asexual situation can be seen in phobia. He added the possibility that the patient becomes phobic for a specific situation which is associated with sleep and dreaming. The closer one is to the awakening state, the likelier one is to experience anxiety of a phobic nature. Curtis and Sachs (1976) quote Kernberg as stating that patients experience emotions in dreams in keeping with their pathology. Kernberg reported that patients with disturbed object relations have an increased tendency to feel persecutory anxiety in their dreams, and even more disorganized patients may have dreams with terrifying affects related to emptiness.

Stamm (1978) reported the dream of a patient with agoraphobia which returned after over a year of being symptom free. When her husband's salary was reduced, the patient dreamt their two beds were thrown onto the street. This dream reactivated humiliating childhood memories of evictions her family had sustained, lowering her self-esteem. The return of the agoraphobic symptom was ushered in with this dream which included again the patient's fears of loss of love, separation, and prostitution fantasies. Projection, displacement, and symbolization resulted in her agoraphobia, as a repressive reaction. Stolorow (1978) in reporting the dream of an agoraphobic patient emphasized the utilization of the manifest content in delineating the genetic and current diagnostic determinants.

DREAMS IN A CASE OF MULTIPLE PHOBIAS

Beset by incapacitating phobic symptoms, anxiety, depression, and stomach-aches, a small young woman came for analysis. Although only twenty-seven years old, Anna felt doomed to be an old maid, caring for her parents with whom she lived. She was very isolated and had never dated. Indeed, her drab, unattractive clothing, braided hair, and colorless face unconsciously conspired to hide any spark of sexuality. As a first-year pharmacy student, Anna was phobic about sexuality, men, blushing, having her hair cut, not to mention her fear of germs. She had made two unsuccessful attempts to live alone but each failed after night terrors.

Although talented and artistic, her mother was a confirmed alcoholic who alternated between seductive sweetness and angry tirades. Her chronically depressed father, a pharmacist himself, encouraged the patient's devotion to the family, making clear his expectation that she take over his pharmacy. He enjoyed her doting affection as a substitute for his wife's coldness. Her older brother had married six years earlier and lived in another city. The patient was raised by her parents to mistrust outsiders and had been indoctrinated to be secretive and seclusive.

Her typical analytic posture was that of a remote, polite, superficially cooperative woman who would remain in a high state of resistance. She appeared affectively frozen or else mildly depressed, and was either silent or complained of boredom. When apparent transference feelings were interpreted, she would withdraw and dismiss the analyst as stupid.

Her dreams, although filled with frightening images, were often reported with characteristic detachment. Nevertheless, she would allow the analyst's interpretations to penetrate her otherwise marked defensiveness and to be therapeutic. It was this work, within the obvious but unacknowledged positive transference, that provided the main impetus for subsequent change and progress. Paradoxically, Anna would rationalize these islands of clarity by disclaiming their relevance. These were just her dreams, she would explain. As such, they just did not count and could be safely worked on.

She reported her first dream in the fourth session. "I am at the wedding of my friend, Pat. While there is a wedding to take place, the groom is dead. The wedding is also a funeral. The groom has been in an accident. He drives a bus and is being removed from it. Someone suggests that they give him potassium cyanide to end his misery, while others say that he might survive. They take him out of the bus but he dies anyway. Then I am at the wedding reception in the kitchen. I am poaching a salmon. I think of a coffin which is also present. I feel sad, and notice that the wedding cake is in the sink. I reassemble the cake in which I place galdiolas which remind me of death. I join the rest of the guests who are sitting at a long table. They taste the cake and burst into joyous song. I am unable to sing because there is cake in my mouth."

For the first time she mentioned the imminent marriage of her only girlfriend, whose friendship with the patient was now in jeopardy. She had been upset about this event for months and had become so inexplicably anxious when attending religious services that she decided not to go to her friend's church wedding. She admitted being angry with her, and then added with uncharacteristic laughter, "Well, I guess if he [the groom] were to die, there would be no wedding." She found the groom uninteresting and boring, like a salmon she would like to poach. She had been angry at her brother for getting married and recalled having dreams about her sister-in-law being killed. She felt frightened about her own mortality and that of her parents. Now she expressed surprise, and some pleasure, at having so many feelings about which she was also fearful. This dream was a harbinger of Anna's dynamics. It expressed her ambivalent struggle between murderous, aggressive wishes, sexual longings and unrelenting prohibitions against them. The resulting anxiety was transformed into the development of phobic symptoms.

During the first three months of analysis, the patient would tediously describe the difficulties with her parents. She spoke in a flat monotone, her body stiff and still. Feeling responsible for the welfare of her disturbed and depressed parents, it was impossible for her to move out. Besides, she further rationalized, her parents were wonderful people, and her father was more mature than any man she might meet. At other times, she described feelings of being trapped and depressed about living with them, expressing envy of women who had active social lives. At the end of this period, Anna began anatomy class and became terrified that she might be left alone with the dead bodies.

She then presented a series of dreams in one session.

1. "I am walking with my sister in a park. We find three bodies in three plastic bags with ties. One I recognize as A.D., a male classmate. I was frightened."

2. "My sister and I are sleeping in a room. I flop my hand into hers, and she becomes angry. 'For God's sake . . . just moving my hand. I am not used to sleeping with someone.' Then I look out of the door and see three bodies in the hallway. I say, 'Can't you move the bodies farther away?'"

3. I stumble over the body of A.D. I ask him how he died. He tells me that he was diving for pearls and got caught on the shelf in the back of the knees. He became hysterical and ripped his own leg open.

After a thoughtful pause, the patient recalled many events of her childhood. As a little girl, she shared a bedroom with her brother but, "Something happened," and from then on, her brother slept downstairs.

She knew of the deaths of friends of her parents and also of several of their children. One died in a motorcycle accident in which a leg was severed. There were a number of suicides. She spoke of her concern about her depressed father and his accident proneness. Could he survive her moving out? She equated suicide with mental illness and reported that her mother had been in a psychiatric hospital two years earlier. Anna felt that her mother's psychosis was due to what a psychiatrist had told her. She fantasied that any understanding of herself could plunge her into a psychosis as she imagined had occurred to her mother.

The resulting terror was defended against by a phobic avoidance of the therapist and of the therapeutic alliance. The dream of the three bodies represents the death of her parents and of herself. It is the result of her wished-for emancipation experienced in its most literal sense. In the last dream, the patient is represented by her friend. Diving for pearls symbolizes the doing of the forbidden intimate exploration and enjoyment of herself and of others. Death, suicide, psychosis, loss, and castration are all seen as the punishments for seeking intimacy, sexuality, and autonomy.

On successive days, Anna reported the following dreams.

1. "I find the cops at my house, I can't go in. I know my parents are murdered."

2. "I am in our house. My father has shot someone on the stairs. I worry about what I would say to the police and know that I would tell the truth, and my father would have to go to jail. I tell them to leave the country."

3. "I am in a building in a city. I am talking to a woman, who is a judge. My mother is in prison. She is to be executed Saturday at 1:00 PM. I was relieved but scared."

4. "I am in the kitchen with my father. He was looking into the swimming pool where I had seen my mother with her face up dead. My father said, 'It's just junk in the pool.' 'But mother's dead in the pool.' 'OK,' he said, 'She is dead, just forget about her.' I woke up frightened and felt that there was someone in my room."

In this dream series, the patient revealed undisguised solutions to her dilemmas of rage, guilt, and quest for autonomy. Her parents are murdered and her father blamed. In the third dream, her mother is executed by the legal authorities as justifiable punishment. In the last dream, getting rid of mother seems more important than the obvious oedipal victory, that is, having father to herself. The last dream also offers a clue of explanation for her night terrors and anticipated their development. Someone (mother) will get her for wishing to be free of her parents.

These dreams were cautiously interpreted, for example, "You seem to have strong desires to be free of your parents but feel you can only do so if they no longer exist." "Your dreams seem to say 'If only my parents didn't exist, I would be free to pursue my own life,'" or "You appear to be angry, even have murderous feelings toward your parents which frighten you." The patient would react with irritated surprise or outright negation. In spite of this denial, progress was achieved and she was able to complete her anatomy class with manageable anxiety. With the diminution of separation anxiety from her parents, her autonomous strivings emerged with the decision to move away from her family and she began to look for an apartment. She made new friends and spent more time away from her parent's home. Anna claimed that she felt well and that there wasn't anything more to be discussed.

At this time, Anna began a pharmacology class which utilized white rats for the demonstration of medication effects. In a detached manner, she reported her increasing discomfort and later, her terror of these animals. Anna took to avoiding the lab. She had resisted efforts to explore this phobic symptom for several hours when she reported the following dream.

"I am alone in my friend's apartment. She had a chinchilla who claws out of the cage. She is all dirty and shows me her long teeth. I am scared. 'Oh, my God,' I think, 'I forgot to feed her.'"

Her associations were to her mother, who when drinking heavily would hurl insults at her and throw glasses at the wall. Mother was furious at her for preferring the company of friends. Anna remembered returning from a play several weeks earlier to find the kitchen full of broken glass. She recalled, as a child, seeing her mother throw beautiful crystal from her bedroom window. If her mother could smash things that she claimed to love, Anna could also be destroyed. She remembered her terror and determination to avoid anything that might be disagreeable. Anna accepted the interpretation that the same anxiety had reappeared: the fear of her mother's destructive rage. She is no longer feeding her mother, as in the dream, but rather ignoring her in the service of expressing her own emerging aggressive and sexual strivings.

She was able to see that she had condensed her fear of and identification with her sadistic mother which was projected onto the white rats to which she responded with phobic avoidance. Evidence of a maternal transference was interpreted, that is, she fears the analyst's attack and criticism, and defensively hides her spontaneity. This was dismissed by the patient as ridiculous and "Freudian." Nevertheless, the phobic symptoms melted away. Anna resumed her previous effective level of class work and successfully found a place of her own. She was supported by several friends and by her brother.

With considerable apprehension, Anna moved into the apartment and immediately began to experience anxiety over sounds from neighboring apartments at night. She complained of television noises and peoples' voices which she felt were too loud. She could not sleep and would cover her ears by burying her head under the pillows. She wrote notes to the neighbors asking for quiet after 10 PM and spoke to the landlady. Now her complaints focused on a woman who lived one floor below. Desperate and on the verge of returning home, the patient had this dream.

"I am in the hallway of a familiar house and I hear disturbing loud noises coming from the bedroom. I am frightened. The noise stops and I open the door to look inside for Bill, a classmate, and he isn't there. I open the closet and find the decomposing body of a woman."

Anna then realized the noises emanating from the apartment below were of a man and a woman. Indeed, they were sexual sounds. She recalled her fright of the similar sounds coming from her parent's bedroom and agreed with the analyst that they must have been the sounds of sex and violent arguments, creating both confusion and fear. In her fantasy, Anna saw violence as inextricably part of sexual activity. The noises not only recreated primal scene anxiety but they also forced her to confront her own warded off "dangerous" sexuality. Following this hour, fear of the noises disappeared but Anna still complained of anxiety and difficulty falling asleep.

A week later, she reported two dreams.

1. "A man is found in his apartment. He is murdered with lots of blood."

2. "I am asleep. There is a knock on the bedroom door. I awake with fear. I slowly open the door and see my mother who motions to me. She looks wild. I follow her to the living room where my father is bending over my dead body covering it with a blanket. My mother says, 'Get your coat. We have to go home.'"

She felt that her parents' recent polite acknowledgment of her independence belied their anger and she feared her mother's retaliation. For many years she had felt that independence was bad, a crime against her parents which would be punished. Her parents were too powerful, she felt, and in the end, they would "win out."

The first case demonstrated typical phobic symptoms as well as the patient's avoidance of the analytic process. Both are in the service of defending against the experience of unconscious anxiety and meanings. Fortunately, Anna's dreams would give her away. They presented an open window through which affects and meanings were visualized, permitting the understanding of her terrifying symptoms. Frightening dead bodies appeared everywhere in her dreams. The dead body is a symbol of her murderous and sexual wishes together with the feared retaliation if drives and needs were to be expressed. Separation, aggression, and sexuality, including oedipal and preoedipal strivings, will kill or bring others to kill her. The death of others was seen as making possible psychological life for herself. While the analytic leverage achieved proved efficacious, it had to be dismissed consciously. It is noteworthy that Weiss (1964) reported that the wish for the death of a parent is, through identification with that parent, turned into a fear that the patient herself might die on leaving home.

A DREAM IN A CASE OF CLAUSTROPHOBIA

A young physician came to treatment because of symptoms of severe anxiety, hypochrondriasis, and a phobic state which markedly interfered with his personal and professional life. Although accomplished in his field, he had difficulty concentrating and was increasingly haunted by frightening homosexual preoccupations. Claustrophobia was a main inhibiting feature. He would avoid entering elevators, tunnels, and closets at all costs. The idea of traveling by airplane resulted in a reaction of cold shuddering anxiety. "What will I do when they close the door of the plane? I'll lose control. Even if I load up on tranquilizers and alcohol, it won't work." He was concerned with fleeting physical symptoms. "I have this throbbing pain over my eye. Do you think I have a brain tumor?" "This chest tightness of mine—I feel a sharp pressure right here. Could I be having a heart attack?" Bracing himself early in the analysis for what he saw as an ordeal, an attempt to penetrate a chamber of horrors, he determined to plunge on. He dreamed profusely and reported his dreams with faithful concern. It was an early dream which conveyed his anxiety over heterosexuality, and, in effect, a phobia of female genitalia.

"Word had gotten around the hospital that there was a cat in the pathology refrigerator which had come back to life. I thought, 'That's surprising—the cat was dead when I put it away. I must have misdiagnosed it.' Someone was sticking something into the cat's chest, and I was angry at whoever was doing this. The instrument looked something like a screwdriver. Then someone was sewing up the cat. At another point, one of the legs of the cat was almost off, and the cat was walking around with the leg just hanging on, dragging behind. All the time, I could feel the cat's claws on my hands."

He immediately associated to his fear of a situation in the hospital when he is asked to confirm that a patient is dead. He has to listen and check again and again to see if there are any vital signs. Maybe, he thinks, he will miss a sign only to have the patient return to life. He used a screwdriver to fix a radio on the evening of the dream. He loves to assemble radios, clocks, to put things together and fix them, if he can. Now the idea of resurrection comes to him. The cat has come back to life. He thought of the clawing wounds on his hands as the stigmata on Christ's hand. A frequent fantasy, he now revealed, was that analysis would find him guilty of a heinous crime and crucifixion would be the inevitable result. The wounds were a punishment he deserved for what he did to the cat. The cat was alive again, born again. Early memories surfaced: his mother telling him how he had damaged her in his difficult birth. He knew the birth was protracted and that there had been postnatal complications. His mother had to return to the hospital for several months, while he was cared for by a nursemaid. Further, the nearly amputated leg of the cat was his mother's leg which had bled profusely when, as a small child, he kicked at her during a quarrel. Now he was able to talk of his horror at the sight of female genitalia especially during menstruation. The bleeding cat was his mother's injured gentalia. That the central issues were thinly disguised did not necessarily result in a shortening of the anlytic procedure but the dream did afford the analyst the opportunity to more readily comprehend the core conflicts of the patient.

A DREAM IN A CASE OF AGORAPHOBIA

For another patient, a teacher in a small college, an anxiety attack accompanied by phobic fear of leaving her house was triggered by a feeling of trauma rooted in praise. When an ex-pupil achieved a major success, her significant contribution was belatedly acknowledged. For a few hours she felt pride and exhilaration, but soon there followed anxious dismay and phobic symptoms forcing her to take to her bed.

A profile of the woman gradually emerged. She tended toward excessive mannerisms and was aware of her tendency to engage in undue theatricalism, and she repeatedly told the analyst of her efforts to hold these traits in check. Nevertheless, the mask she wore would slip when her anxiety came close to a state of terror, and she would find herself on the brink of losing total control. A defeatist attitude now pervaded everything as opposed to her previous demeanor of being able to "rise to any occasion." To illustrate again the relative clarity with which such phobic patients can reveal their essential dynamics, an early dream is presented.

"I am in a car with a man who resembles B [a favorite writer]. We are driving in the country on a lovely evening. Then I am surprised to see we are both naked. We come to a rustic lodge and put on blankets to cover ourselves before we walk into the lodge. There are many couples there. Are they making love? There are beds and also attendants who apply ointments to our bodies and hair. I could feel the warmth going through me. We sit on a large bed. I say to the man, 'What about your wife?' I look in a mirror and see my lovely long black hair. I ask him or I think I ask him, 'Why would you leave her?' I am uncertain now and I turn to ask again, 'Won't this affect our relationship?' I tell him I must go home. My husband is at home alone. I look in the mirror again and my hair looks dreadful."

She awoke with a pain in her stomach. The dream was erotic and for a while she felt very sexually stimulated but then felt cheated. Her husband "is the basis of my frustration." She can't count on him any longer except as a provider. Her thoughts turned to the ex-student who reminds her of the man in her dream. Her envy of him and his success had never been so experienced before. There followed a halting expressed sexual interest in the young man. The drive in the country related to the course of her analysis which resulted in an early reduction of her phobic anxiety. Erotic transference elements included her feelings toward the analyst/writer and her fear of retaliation from the wife/mother. Combined with the patient's envy of the successful young man was her sexual attraction to him. The catastrophic implications of such an encounter with her analyst pene-trated the dream. Thinly disguised are prostitution fantasies, wishes, and fears centered around exhibitionism and fright at loss of love. The subject of her hair turned out to be very important during the ensuing months. The patient was unusually concerned with her hair, fearing that it would be badly cut, and she worried about punishing herself by destroying her "crowning glory." The analysis of the dream led to the recovery of primal scene experiences including memories of her mother's rejection of the father's sexual overtures. Her phobic symptoms were successful in bind-ing much of her anxiety but only after the fusions of libidinal and aggressive cathexes of the envied object failed.

DREAMS AND THE DYNAMICS OF PHOBIAS

In seeking to answer the question initially posed—are there features in the dreams of phobic patients which are specific to their symptomatology?—we were confronted with the experience that the classical phobic patient is an elusive individual indeed. While nuclear phallic-oedipal problems predominate in these patients, conflicts remaining from the preoedipal period are still present. In the dreams of our patients, phobic anxiety based on achievement of the phallic-oedipal stages of development is directly tied to forbidden oedipal incestuous wishes and their vicissitudes, as seen most clearly in the agoraphobic patient. Even where relative phase appropriate functioning and organization was achieved prior to the phobia, we found, in terms of objects, derivatives of earlier preoedipal introjects. These aspects were demonstrated in the first two cases, where murderous aggression is revealed.

The process of change from free-floating to phobic anxiety in our patients showed features closely parallel to the experience of a dream, namely repression, condensation, displacement, projection, and symbolization.

If dreams are, as has been so often emphasized, the single most important window to what is repressed (Freud 1900), then the dreams of phobic patients are especially valuable to the analyst. Mindful of Freud's expressed dismissal of the manifest content in order to attend to the latent dream meaning, we find in phobic patients that the manifest content of their dreams conveys less disguise and more readily available access to the reality and unconscious conflicts with which the patients are dealing.[1] Recent authors (R. Langs 1971, Greenberg and Pearlman 1978, Spanjaard 1969) have placed increasing importance on the manifest dream content.

While phobic patients tend to exhibit clarity in the manifest content of their dreams, they also tend to compartmentalize the insights gained, to parry the implications of understanding by typically dismissing the dream as unimportant or as a "nothing" dream. Not unusual is the gambit: "It's only a dream." The attempt to refute the message can often occur as part of the dream content or will be an immediate association to the dream, including lengthy discourses on devaluing dream interpretation. An illustration of this may be found in the case of Anna or in the case presented by Rangell, noted in our survey of the literature.

1. Personal communication from R. R. Greenson, November 18, 1978.

SUMMARY

A review of the relevant literature has shown the central importance of phobic patients and their dreams in the history of psychoanalysis. Increasing emphasis on the manifest content of these dreams is based on the demonstration of their usefulness to the analyst in comprehending the symptomatology. In many instances the dreams of phobic patients, in manifest and latent content, show a distinct clarity and relative lack of disguise which unwittingly reveal nuclear conflicts and the dynamics of the phobia. It is characteristic of these patients, having in effect given themselves away, to then dismiss out of hand the significance of the revelation which they have just presented to the analyst, by disclaiming the importance of what they have just revealed. In spite of such protestations, the analytic work holds as revealed by subsequent movement toward resolution of phobic symptoms and, ultimately, toward emotional growth and autonomy.

References

Altman, L. L. (1969). *The Dream in Psychoanalysis,* rev. ed. New York: International Universities Press.

Blum, H. P. (1974). The borderline childhood of the Wolf Man. *Journal of the American Psychoanalytic Association* 22:721–742.

Curtis, H., and Sachs, D. (1976). [Report on] Dialogue on 'The changing use of dreams in psychoanalytic practice.' *International Journal of Psycho-Analysis* 57:343–354.

Erikson, E. H. (1954). The dream specimen of psychoanalysis. *Journal of the American Psychoanalytic Association* 2:5–56.

Freud, A. (1977). Fears, anxieties and phobic phenomena. *Psychoanalytic Study of the Child* 32:85–90.

Freud, S. (1900). The interpretation of dreams. *Standard Edition* 4:1–338 and 5:339–627.

—— (1909). Analysis of a phobia in a five-year-old boy. *Standard Edition* 10:3–152.

—— (1918). From the history of an infantile neurosis. *Standard Edition* 17:3–122.

—— (1926). Inhibition, symptoms and anxiety. *Standard Edition* 20:87–172.

Gedo, J., and Goldberg, A. (1973). *Models of the Mind.* Chicago University of Chicago Press.

Greenberg, R., and Pearlman, C. (1978). If Freud only knew: a reconstruction of psychoanalytic dream theory. *International Review of Psycho-Analysis* 5:71–75.

Greenson, R. R. (1959). Phobia, anxiety and depression. *Journal of the American Psychoanalytic Association* 7:668–674.

Langs, R. (1971). Day residues, recall residues, and dreams: reality and the psyche. *Journal of the American Psychoanalytic Association* 19:499–523.

Levitan, H. L. (1974). The dream of a phobic patient. *International Review of Psycho-Analysis* 1:313–323.

Lewin, B. D. (1952). Phobic symptoms and dream interpretation. *Psychoanalytic Quarterly* 21:295–322.

Lorand, S. (1946). *Technique of Psychoanalytic Therapy*. New York: International Universities Press.

Offenkrantz, W., and Tobin, A. (1973). Problems of the therapeutic alliance: Freud and the Wolf Man. *International Journal of Psycho-Analysis* 54:75–78.

Rangell, L. (1952). The analysis of a doll phobia. *International Journal of Psycho-Analysis* 33:43–53.

Spanjaard, J. (1969). The manifest dream content and its significance for the interpretation of dreams. *International Journal of Psycho-Analysis* 50:221–235.

Stamm, J. L. (1978). The meaning of humiliation and its relationship to fluctuations in self-esteem. *International Review of Psycho-Analysis* 5:425–433.

Stolorow, R. D. (1978). Themes in dreams: a brief contribution to therapeutic technique. *International Journal of Psycho-Analysis* 59:473–475.

Weiss, E. (1964). *Agoraphobia in the Light of Ego Psychology*. New York: Grune and Stratton.

CHAPTER 12

THE DREAM IN REGRESSED STATES

John E. Gedo, M.D.

Among the manifold accomplishments of Sigmund Freud in creating psychoanalysis, only two have stood the test of time without need for modification. The standardization of the psychoanalytic situation as the characteristic observational tool of depth psychology is the more funda-mental of these contributions. The other aspect of Freud's work that has required no change was a greater intellectual feat: his discovery of the method of dream interpretation, based on deciphering the language he named the "primary process."

Psychoanalysis as a method of treatment has been applied with increasing effectiveness in a steadily expanding range of psychopathologi-cal conditions. Although some investigators advocate departures from the classical analytic technique in what they consider to be "borderline conditions" (e.g., Kernberg 1975, 1976), many others—including myself (Gedo 1975, 1977)—have attempted to use the classical technique to treat all personality disorders with the exception of the psychoses (see also Kohut 1971, Settlage 1977). In the context of this more radical approach to the psychoanalytic management of archaic transferences, systematic dream interpretation retains its traditional role as the royal road into the realm of unconscious mental life.

If the topic of dreams in the treatment of severe personality disorders merits fresh consideration, such an effort is justified by the overall evolution of the psychoanalytic theory of mental life rather than by changes in our actual approach to the translation of the meaning of any particular dream into discursive language. More specifically, recent emphasis on the developmental perspective in the clinical theories of psychoanalysis (A. Freud 1965, Gedo and Goldberg 1973) has made it possible to refine our theories of therapeutic technique. This evolution has moved in the direction of conceptualizing separate modalities of treatment for each of those distinct aspects of an individual's psychopathology that result from the vicissitudes of various phases of early development. One classification of appropriate treatment modalities was proposed in my collaborative work with A. Goldberg, *Models of the Mind* (Gedo and Goldberg 1973, see especially chapter 11). In order to provide a framework for further discussion, I shall summarize the schema here. It should be kept in mind through this account that the technique of interpreting one specific dream remains the same, whatever overall therapeutic strategy is being pursued. Moreover, it must be stressed that every analytic patient will sooner or later present behaviors referable to the poorly resolved sequelae of each phase of development. Hence every analytic procedure must consist of the application of all possible modalities of treatment in various combinations. This point of view may seem novel, but in fact it simply articulates the logical consequences of an epigenetic theory of psychological development.

HOLDING ENVIRONMENT: THE APPROPRIATE TREATMENT MODALITY FOR REGRESSED STATES

In accord with this hierarchical schema, it is appropriate to use interpretations about intrapsychic conflicts and their childhood genesis when dealing with material organized in the psychological mode characteristic of the oedipal phase of development. In other words, for the "transference neuroses" proper, it is optimal to use the model technique of psychoanalysis. However, the free associations produced by all analytic patients contain material not only in this mode but also in more mature and more primitive ones. The mode that reflects postoedipal phases of mental organization permits the analysand to apprehend his internal life through introspection, that is, without the interpretation of defensive operations. In such circumstances, the role of the analyst is optimally confined to lending his presence to the procedure as an empathic witness. In more archaic modes of psychic organization, on the other hand, more active modalities of intervention are required, in line with the relative lack of autonomy in self-regulation prevalent in those states. Borrowing a phrase from Winnicott, Modell (1976) summarized the proposals about the optimal therapeutic handling of these regressed states that we put forward in *Models of the Mind* as the provision of a "holding environment." We specified a series of psychological issues that must be dealt with in these conditions; the principal ones are those of tension regulation, of the establishment of a single and coherent hierarchy of aims, and of the correction of unrealistic illusions, either about oneself or about the persons around one. In circumstances of stimulus overload, the appropriate therapeutic modality is that of "pacification"; when the cohesion of the self has become compromised, the analyst must address himself to its reunification; for the illusory thinking characteristic of pregenital disturbances, efforts at optimal disillusionment are indicated.

I should like to reemphasize that the necessity to employ any or all of these aspects of a "holding environment" in a particular psychoanalytic procedure has no implications, in and of itself, with regard to diagnosis. Nosological categories based on psychoanalytic principles cannot be established through focusing on such cross-sectional samples of behavior; diagnosis must take into account long-term progressive and regressive sequences, particularly as they occur in the transference relationship within the analytic situation. In other words, regressions to the various modes of psychic functioning that may temporarily require the provision of a holding environment will occur in the course of specific transference developments no matter what the ultimate overall personality diagnosis may turn out to be. On the other hand, this point of view also entails the conclusion that only those conditions are to be regarded as derivatives or sequelae of difficulties during the earliest years of life (what was formerly designated as the pregenital era) in which the central and predominant issue of the analytic process continues to be the quality of the setting as a holding environment.

IMPLICATIONS OF THE HIERARCHICAL MODEL OF PSYCHIC LIFE

What are the implications of this hierarchical model of psychic life for our view of dreaming? In 1925, Freud added the following comment to his discussion of wish fulfillment in *The Interpretation of Dreams:*

Experience has shown that distorted dreams, which stand in need of interpretation, are already found in children of four or five; and this is in full agreement with our theoretical views on the determining conditions of distortion in dreams [1900, p. 127, n. 1].

Freud also provided a series of illustrative children's dreams in which the wishes represented as fulfilled are quite undisguised; among these, the most memorable was that of his daughter Anna, dreamt at the age of nineteen months:

Anna Fweud, stwawbewwies, wild stwawbewwies, omblet, pudden! [p. 130].

In 1911, he added some examples of undisguised wish fulfillments in the dreams of adults exposed to circumstances of extreme duress.

DISGUISED WISH FULFILLMENT RETAINED IN REGRESSION

However archaic some of the transferences we encounter in the analytic situation, adult patients in our consulting rooms are never exposed to external stresses of sufficient magnitude to produce dreams of undisguised wish fulfillment, and they never seem to do so purely on the basis of their psychopathology. In other words, whatever their ultimate diagnoses, patients who can be expected to be analyzable have invariably matured sufficiently to distort the infantile wishes that are represented as fulfilled in their dreams. Even dreams that are thought to be typical as expressions of infantile grandiosity, such as those in which the dreamer transcends the laws of gravity (see Kohut 1971, especially pp. 4–5), cannot be taken literally. Dreams of flying do not signify that the analysand would like to be able to perform acts of levitation; even when the associations do lead to some kind of infantile grandiose ideation, the ability to fly symbolizes the wish to be omnipotent with regard to some current activity of a more serious import. Candidates at psychoanalytic institutes, for example, often represent their wishes to be able to perform analyses without supervision in this guise—especially so after they have read about the common significance of flying fantasies. I would therefore contradict Kohut's assertion that certain "typical" dreams containing overtly grandiose ideation can be understood as direct expressions of the dreamer's "self-state" (see Kohut 1977, pp. 109–110).

ABSENCE OF PATHOGNOMONIC SIGNS OF FUNCTIONAL REGRESSIONS IN DREAMS

The profoundest functional regressions in psychic organization are not characterized by changes in the inner structure of the dreams reported in analysis; there are, in fact, no specific pathognomonic signs of such regressions referable to dreams or dreaming. Quite the contrary: the very capacity to fall asleep and to dream implies some degree of reintegration; one indication that the regression to the most archaic modes of organization did not persist during the night may well be the report of one or more dreams. To be sure, one cannot find such reassurance in the occurrence of unsuccessful dreams, that is, in nightmares. And yet anxiety severe enough to awaken the dreamer is not necessarily a sign of actual regression to an overstimulated state, especially if it is promptly relieved by the interruption of the dream. The principal point I wish to make here concerns the need to focus on the analysand's current mode of organization in the here and now of the session, instead of allowing oneself to be diverted to his state at some point between sessions. There are, of course, exceptions even to this sound precept, but their enumeration here would take us too far afield.

PACIFICATION INTERVENTION FOR TENSION REGULATION

From the vantage point of monitoring the occurrence of severe regressions within the analytic setting proper, it should be kept in mind that such contingencies are almost invariably accompanied by strenuous efforts to recover. At the very moment of trauma, we may witness a period of stunned and empty "absence"—but, in properly conducted analyses, iatrogenic incidents of that kind should be rare indeed. Much more frequently, the regression is set in motion before the start of the analytic hour, and the patient will attempt to use the analytic relationship to effect his reintegration.

One manner of promoting recovery from trauma is self-soothing through analytic business-as-usual, and this tack may often involve the recital of one or more dreams. In general, it is less than helpful to interfere with such efforts, although, as we might expect, they seldom eventuate in the successful interpretation of the latent meanings of the dreams reported. In any case, the primary analytic task in such circumstances is not the interpretation of content but the detection of the traumatic state and its management through "pacification."

FRANTIC PATTERN OF DREAM REPORTING

The analyst may be led to the proper diagnosis by noting, among other phenomena characteristic of traumatic states, shifts from the analysand's customary style of narrating his dreams. Possibly the most common change consists of pressure of speech, often with marked obliviousness about the value of the resultant message as comprehensible communication. Another variation involves changes in pitch and volume. In traumatic circumstances, however, one does not feel that the stream of words or the muttering is being aimed against one in a provocative or sadistic manner. A tactful comment about the impression of frenzy or excitement given by the analysand's manner of speaking may have a powerfully calming effect in these emergencies. We must forego a discussion of the reasons for the pacifying results of such interventions; from the viewpoint of our focus on dreams, it must suffice to underscore that it is essential to avoid behaving like a machine programmed to uncover unconscious meanings. The analyst must be an empathic and sentient person, ever alert to the potential need to assist the patient with disturbances in tension regulation.

LIFELESS PATTERN OF DREAM REPORTING

The potential variety of ways in which dream narratives may betray traumatic states defies classification. I shall therefore content myself with mentioning only one additional pattern that is fairly common. If the frantic style I have just described might be likened to stepping on the accelerator while the car is not in gear, the next pattern might be compared to the sound of an engine one cannot quite get to turn over because of a weak battery. The tone is lifeless and flat; speech is halting and slow. There may be a startling discrepancy between the affectively charged material implicit within the dream content and the detached manner of its presentation.

In these circumstances, as in the states of overexcitement, it would be gravely unempathic to proceed with dream interpretation instead of focusing on the analysand's actual emotional state. The appropriate measures may be somewhat easier to carry out in this variety of reaction to trauma than in excited states because one can address oneself to the fact of the disorder and expect to be understood without first having to re-establish conditions conducive to meaningful communication. Noting the paradoxical affect may suffice to direct the analysand's attention to his hitherto overlooked traumatic episode, and some correlation between the meaning of these events and the regression that followed them may succeed in restoring the patient to his usual mode of integration.

COHERENT HIERARCHY OF GOALS OUT OF FRAGMENTED STATES USING DREAMS

Once reintegration has taken place, it is generally quite illuminating to go on to decipher the latent means of the dreams themselves, should the associations make this possible. The foregoing statement may seem like a truism; however, I mean something beyond the self-evident proposition that every fresh look into the depths will increase our insight. The nature of the new information we sometimes obtain in these circumstances may be quite specific. The bits and fragments of dream available in such conditions, sometimes called "fractionated dream narratives," may reflect a variety of uncoordinated and irreconcilable personal goals and values. These internal contradictions are generally concealed from view through defensive distortions and, even with manifest dreams, seemingly (albeit falsely) "compromised" through operations which have sometimes been designated as the "synthetic functions" (Nunberg 1930). In traumatic regressions, these confusing defensive epiphenomena fall away, to reveal the chaos of the basic aims of the individual in their naked irrationality. In another context, I have called such subsets of personal goals and values "nuclei of the self" (Gedo and Goldberg 1973, chapter 5).

In terms of the dreams reported in regressive states, each nucleus of the self continues to find only distorted representation in the manifest content. Primitive aims are generally disclaimed in the course of later development, and their potential reappearance mobilizes anxiety, shame, or guilt. Hence, as Freud (1900) demonstrated in convincing detail, infantile wishes are transformed by the dream work. From the structural viewpoint, even the latent content always contains not only the archaic wish (the id) but also the countervailing repudiation from more mature sectors of the personality (the ego). Hence, each discrete dream will be

completely conventional in its organization in these regressive states, but
dreams in pairs or series may reveal not merely conflict about one or more
wishes, but a multiplicity of uncoordinated and mutually exclusive wishes
of that kind (cf. Alexander 1925). A relatively simple example may help to
illuminate this issue.

Following a short interruption of his analysis, a young psychotherapist
returned for his next session in a state of panic focused on his bodily
integrity. He talked in a feverish and disjointed manner but eventually
revealed that he had, in fact, experienced seemingly objective signs of
illness. He had, however, taken no steps to obtain medical attention and
conceived of the problem, confusedly, as something to be handled within
the analysis. He began to calm down after I differentiated the physical
signs that had to be evaluated by an internist from his hypochondriacal
preoccupations. In the following session, the patient calmly reported a
number of dreams of the intervening night: (1) a big fat rat had come out of
the woodwork; (2) an alligator was sitting in a tree, happily eating a bunch
of Concord grapes; and (3) the patient boarded a westbound bus driven by
a very nice person. Associations to all three dreams were given in a
scattered way in the course of the remaining sessions of that week. For the
sake of clarity of presentation, I shall systematize these by recounting all of
the associations most directly relevant to each dream sequentially.

1. During my absence he had lost his appetite and his weight had
diminished precipitously. His children own a gerbil, but they have lost
interest in this pet rodent since the family acquired a cat. From his reading
of one of my publications, he knew about my special interest in Freud's
case histories, including that of the "Rat Man." He felt that something
very disreputable about him was about to come into the open.

2. The second dream reminds him of Aesop's fable about the fox and
the grapes. Except that Concord grapes are not sour—they are blue. He
read a story—it was a satire about psychoanalysis—in which a tiny dog
opened his enormous jaws and swallowed a much bigger opponent. The
dog belonged to a little boy who recounts that it had been called an
alligator before his father cut off its tail and painted it white. Perhaps he is
thinking of the account in my book about the "Wolf Man" and his dream
of wolves sitting on a tree. But an alligator could only get up on a tree by
magic, and grapes do not grow on trees. As a therapist, he does *not*
practice magic.

3. The only bus he rides is the one he takes to my office. However, that
ride does not involve going west. His wife picked him up in her car after a

professional meeting; they drove west from there. They had been chatting, but she gradually lapsed into silence. When he asked her what was the matter, she told him that his conversation bored her. However, over the weekend, he had received a call from a former patient who is about to move west. She confessed her love for him and was clearly hoping that he would invite her to have an affair. He had to struggle to overcome this temptation.

On the basis of these associations, the latent conflicts in each dream might be summarized in the following terms:

1. The unacceptable infantile wish expressed by the first dream is that of being fed and cared for by the analyst as a favored pet. The reference to Freud places this within the context of the father transference; there have been numerous indications that the patient is extremely uncomfortable about the homosexual implications of these passive wishes. They are therefore disguised through projection (into the rat) and reversal (instead of being a pet, he is an aggressive predator).

2. In the second dream, the archaic wish is for the attainment of omnipotence: the automatic satisfaction of his needs without reliance on anyone else. In this situation, the primary need was for instant relief from feeling blue and from the murderous hostility aroused in him by the interruption of my caretaking functions. The day residue was the seductive offer by his patient—she is the victim he is swallowing like an alligator, precisely because he is *not* anybody's pet. In fantasy, he can magically cure himself (and her!) through sexual acting out. The various threatening affects at issue are successfully warded off in the dream through humor, and the grandiose ideation is disavowed, once again, by externalization (unto the alligator and ultimately the Wolf Man).

3. The last dream represents the most unacceptable of his infantile wishes, his desire for a soothing, ever-attentive maternal presence within the transference. The wish is repudiated through representation by its opposite (he is going away from my office) as well as disavowal of its frustration (everything is pleasant, and any stranger can soothe him).

In spite of the unavoidable imprecision of brief summaries of this kind, they do demonstrate that every infantile wish in the latent dream thoughts was adequately disguised in the manifest content in order to satisfy the requirements of various countermotives. To review, the mutually exclusive early childhood goals represented in this trio of simultaneous dreams were (1) to be the favored pet of an honored father; (2) to be omnipotently self-sufficient and immune to frustration; (3) to have an ever-helpful maternal surrogate at his service.[1]

Although each of these wishes probably originated at somewhat different developmental stages, clearly they had not *succeeded* each other on one developmental line, so that in adult life they continue to exert an active influence on behavior simultaneously. However, when this person has been at his best level of integration, it has not been possible to discern *any* of these sets of infantile goals in his psychic life. At such time, the patient was generally preoccupied with his adequacy (in the sexual and professional spheres), barely aware of some concern about the implications of his need for analytic assistance in this regard. In such a state of integration, even the latent content of his dreams reveals only wishes that are derivatives of a later phase of development, when the infantile goals I have attributed to his dream trio had already been fused into one common final pathway and their basic discordance had been covered over.

The last point may best be illustrated by a dream reported several days later in the same analysis:

> He and his wife were shopping for rings, but they could not decide whether to look at Marshall Field's or Carson's. He associated that Carson's is a substandard store; Field's carries adequate merchandise. When he was about to get married, he had allowed his future wife to select their wedding rings. He has just received his first copy of a psychoanalytic journal and was surprised to discover my name among its editors. He has obsessional doubts about everything—Is Memorial Day really a public holiday? He feels similar uncertainties about his marriage and his analysis.

To put the interpretation of this material briefly, he wishes to re-cement his relationship to his wife and to the analysis; his ambivalence has been displaced to a trivial aspect of the arrangements, and its origins are attributed to questions about my professional status. I shall not belabor the transparently oedipal cast of this material.

The detection of various nuclei of the self through dream interpretation may occur in the stage of recovery from traumatic regressions, as in the illustration I have just provided; on the other hand, certain individuals

---

1. It is not self-evident that the first and third of these wishes are mutually exclusive. Their coexistence does not violate the law of contradictions, as the second wish does in relation to either the first or the third. In other words, these specific wishes were incompatible only in terms of the particular historical circumstances of this person's childhood, i.e., in view of the fact that he could not gain his father's approval as long as he depended on his mother.

(most frequently they are considered to be "borderline personalities") are permanently organized in a mode characterized by such lack of integration into one hierarchy of aims. Alternatively, regressive episodes in the course of analyses of better integrated individuals may not eventuate in actual traumatization; in many instances, they involve only loss of the capacity to maintain a single hierarchy of personal goals. At the bottom of regressive swings of this kind, the clinical picture will resemble the one I have presented to illustrate the recovery phase from traumatization. As I have stated earlier, in all of these circumstances, the immediate analytic task is to promote the reestablishment (or the initial construction) of a unified schema of goal-directed behavior. Interventions designed to accomplish this are the measures designated as "unification" in my previous work, and it is a unified schema of this kind that I would propose to call the "self."

How can the analyst utilize dream material to promote unification of the personality? There is, in fact, no special prescription to this end to be followed with regard to dreams: their latent meaning should be used in the same manner as any other information in the service of helping the analysand to establish a workable hierarchy of goals and values. In practice, by reference to dream material, the analyst may focus the patient's attention on the multiplicity of his mutually exclusive wishes and on his failure to make choices among them. The principal technical requirement in these contingencies is to counter the patient's tendency to lose sight of the totality of his personal aims through isolated preoccupation with the dominant wish of the moment. Consistent attention to the need for a global view may be succeeded by explicit awareness on the part of the analysand of the nature of this psychobiological deficit in adaptation and its eventual correction through self-awareness.

CORRECTION OF UNREALISTIC ILLUSIONS USING DREAM MATERIAL

The third component of a holding environment we defined in *Models of the Mind* (Gedo and Goldberg 1973) was the modification of those erroneous beliefs about one's person and about the milieu that grossly interfere with adaptation—the process we called "optimal disillusionment." Insofar as patients harbor conscious illusions about the world contrary to the laws of nature, we need no confirmation of that fact through dream interpretation. More often, however, these unrealistic beliefs have been repressed or disavowed, and active analytic intervention

is required to demonstrate their continuing significance for the analysand's inner life. Dream material can obviously serve as a principal avenue
for insight into these problems—I need only cite the familiar and
ubiquitous example of disavowed credence in the phallic woman as it
shows up in the latent content of dreams. This illustration may also serve
as a reminder that optimal disillusionment does not necessarily involve
the analyst in the correction of misinformation; it is often sufficient to
throw the light of consciousness on an archaic belief system to bring it into
line with public standards.

In a certain sense, it might be legitimate to look upon the fulfillment of
infantile wishes characteristic of all dreams as a regression to a mode of
mental organization that partakes of illusions. However, I am inclined to
take a different view in this matter, starting from an aspect of dreams that
usually does not find explicit representation in the way they are reported. I
am referring to an implicit awareness on the part of the dreamer that his
experience is "only a dream." It is rather the occasional absence of such a
sense of differentiation between dreaming and actual waking experiences
that patients tend to report, often by stating that a particular dream had a
special quality of seeming "real." We are not concerned here with the
latent meaning of such a dream element (see Freud 1900); I cite this issue
only to demonstrate that most of the time dreamers do have an implicit
sense of the reality that they are dreaming. Imagining the fulfillment of
various wishes in such circumstances, however unrealistic hope for such
outcomes might be, does not mean that the person has regressed into a
realm of illusion.

In other words, I think we are only entitled to conclude that an
analysand holds erroneous beliefs about the nature of things on the basis
of assessing the premises about reality contained in the *latent* meaning of
the dream. To return to the concrete illustration of belief in the existence
of phallic women: the appearance of a woman with a penis in the manifest
imagery of the dream does not prove that the dreamer has illusions about
the anatomical distinction between the sexes. It is more than likely that
such dream material merely expresses the wish that this painful reality
were nonexistent. By contrast, the fetishist will assert his belief in the
maternal phallus as a reality in indirect ways that defy immediate
comprehension—even in his dreams. A specific illustration from clinical
dream interpretation may help to sharpen our focus on the kind of illusory
thinking that should be corrected by psychoanalytic treatment.

The analysand whose trio of dreams I reported in the previous
vignette continued to demonstrate unaccountable passivity in relation to

his difficult spouse for a long time. After considerable work focused on this issue without any alteration in his behavior, I gave an unmistakable sign of impatience, to which he responded with the following dream:

> He was trailing after the best friend of his adolescence who led him through the back door of a restaurant. The place was filled with rows of folding seats, like the grandstand at a ballpark. He made his way across the space with much difficulty. When he got to the street entrance, he wondered why he had done the whole thing backwards.

He experienced some reluctance to associate to this material. In response to my inquiry, he revealed for the first time that his ball-playing friend of the teenage years had been a clever, manipulative child of the streets who had tried to make his way as a gambler. He then veered off into complaints about his wife, starting with her lack of cooperation about buying the proper foods for his special diet, but going on to matters with no seeming connection to the dream. Eventually, I commented that his approach to the analysis of this dream reminded me of his friend's attitude toward life: it was cavalier and lacking in attention to detail. He agreed with obvious enthusiasm and quickly added further associations. These concerned his unwillingness to comply with what he had learned about getting along with his wife through the analytic work. He had refused to share her bed for several nights; he had slept on a folding cot instead. The folding seats of the dream also reminded him of a movie theater; he had recently seen a science fiction film in which a man with magical powers was engaged in rescuing a regal woman.

The latent meaning of this dream might be stated as the expression of the wish to rescue his sick wife without having to suffer the consequences of devoting himself to such an impossible effort. But the illusion on which this hope was based was hidden, projected onto a dream screen that was not even reported explicitly in the manifest content. The patient's belief in magic was disavowed; in fact, however, it was the controlling factor in determining his behavior in actuality. Hence, the image of following in the footsteps of a gambler signified the patient's adherence to the same system of magical beliefs that underlies a reliance on "chance." This meaning was not evident from the initial account of the dream, of course; the analysand's adolescent companions had in the past come up in his associations in the context of fantasies of liberating himself from his family responsibilities, as he had fled from his parents earlier. Interpretation of the dream as an expression of persistent unconscious efforts to improve his relationship with his wife by means of magic produced a feeling of helplessness and depression in the patient. Disillusionment thus took place automatically and in this case did not prove to be traumatic.

CONCLUSION

I have now provided examples of the most important types of intervention required to make the psychoanalytic treatment setting into an adequate holding environment. Although, as I have repeatedly stated, such measures are occasionally necessary in specific circumstances in every analysis. In the treatment of persons with disturbances centered on pregenital developmental vicissitudes the issues of tension regulation, of the correlation of personal goals, and of the relinquishment of illusions are invariably crucial to the therapeutic task. I have tried to give clinical illustrations of the manner in which dreams can be used in the service of pacification in overstimulated states, of the unification of a hierarchy of goals in states of fragmentation, and of optimal disillusionment when patients hold erroneous beliefs about the nature of things. I have chosen these examples from the analysis of a single patient in order to attempt to show how the analyst should shift his focus from one area of difficulty to another and how he must vary his tactics among the therapeutic modalities available.

The process of reaching an understanding of the latent meaning of particular dreams was established by Freud before 1900 and has required no revision. However, the analyst's use of these latent meanings should be guided by his determination of the specific mode of psychic organization implicit in the material of a given session. Focus on the intrapsychic conflict represented in the dream is most appropriate when there is no problem about autonomous self-regulation. In more primitive modes of organization, the analyst should use his grasp of the total context, including the latent meaning of dreams, to supplement the patient's limited capacities to regulate tension, to correlate personal goals, and to renounce illusions.

References

Alexander, F. (1925). Dreams in pairs and series. *International Journal of Psycho-Analysis* 6:446–450.
Freud, A. (1965). *Normality and Pathology in Childhood.* New York: International Universities Press.

Freud, S. (1900). The interpretation of dreams. *Standard Edition* 4:1–338 and 5:339–627.

Gedo, J. (1975). Forms of idealization in the analytic transference. *Journal of the American Psychoanalytic Association* 23:485–505.

———— (1977). Notes on the psychoanalytic management of archaic transferences. *Journal of the American Psychoanalytic Association* 25:787–803.

Gedo, J., and Goldberg, A. (1973). *Models of the Mind.* Chicago: University of Chicago Press.

Kernberg, O. (1975). *Borderline Conditions and Pathological Narcissism.* New York: Jason Aronson.

———— (1976). Technical considerations in the treatment of borderline personality organization. *Journal of the American Psychoanalytic Association* 24:795–830.

Kohut, H. (1971). *The Analysis of the Self.* New York: International Universities Press.

———— (1977). *The Restoration of the Self.* New York: International Universities Press.

Modell, A. (1976). "The holding environment" and the therapeutic action of psychoanalysis. *Journal of the American Psychoanalytic Association* 24:285–308.

Nunberg, H. (1930). The synthetic function of the ego. In *Practice and Theory of Psychoanalysis,* pp. 120–136. New York: International Universities Press, 1955.

Settlage, C. (1977). The psychoanalytic understanding of narcissistic and borderline personality disorders: advances in developmental theory. *Journal of the American Psychoanalytic Association* 25:805–833.

CHAPTER 13

THE DREAM IN ACTING OUT DISTURBANCES

Doryann Lebe, M.D.

ACTION FOLLOWING DREAMS: THE FUNCTION OF PREVERBAL CONFLICTS

Acting out disturbances are characterological disorders in which the ability to tolerate anxiety and stress is poor. Anxiety and stress are briefly tolerated, not easily sublimated, nor intrapsychically worked through, and are instead acted out through behavior. A simple example: a man is angry with his wife. Rather than verbally express his anger, or think about his anger and later discuss it with his wife, or go out to his workshop and hammer out a project, he hits his wife. Diagnostically, antisocial personalities, impulse-ridden personalities, addictive personalities, as well as infantile personalities, and some oral characters and narcissistic personalities, would be included in acting out disturbances. All these acting out disturbances arise from problems in the preverbal phase of development. The patients have frequently been fixated at a preverbal level of development, or if they have continued beyond the preverbal level will easily regress to this level under stress. Hence, their feelings come out in action or behavior rather than verbally. In the last ten to twenty years, psychoanalytic theory and treatment have focused more on preverbal and preoedipal development. Even the most classical psychoanalytic patients, those with hysterical personalities, obsessive-compulsive personalities, and depressive-masochistic personalities will at times be dealing with preverbal material and may act in therapy rather than verbalize. Preverbal material never entered the ego organization in verbal form. The early preverbal issues most often become available first in the form of behavior or action. Then, it may later become available in the domain of verbal, conscious awareness. Dreams are filled with early, preverbal material. In the process of analyzing dreams, the preverbal material is brought into conscious awareness and discussed in verbal form. Sometimes this is not readily possible. A dream association may be an action rather than a verbal expression. A dream may be understood and analyzed using a patient's behavioral associations.

ALTERED CONSCIOUSNESS IN DREAM STATES PERMITS ACTION

I have found it useful to closely investigate and observe behavior and actions following dreams of my patients. I have also found it useful to observe my own actions following a patient's dream. This is true of all my patients, but especially for those with acting out disturbances. Their unconscious and my unconscious are communicating without words. It is the analyst's job to observe and verbally clarify these processes.

Freud wrote in great detail about the material and source of dreams. He felt there were three main sources: the day residue, the infantile neurosis, and the adult conflicts. He elaborated about how an event, word, or sight during the day will set off memories from childhood and adulthood. This was the model I used for many years. I now think further information needs to be added to analyze and interpret dreams more completely. I do not feel, however, as do some of the members of the Kris Study Group on Dreams (Waldhorn 1967), that dreams are only further free associations in analysis. I think they have special impact and meaning because they are a product of an altered state of consciousness. The usual discharge outlets of the waking state—action, waking thought, and fantasy—are not available for expression. Dreams are elaborate, symbolic, condensed material from this altered state of consciousness. During this altered state, primary process thinking and unconscious material are more dominant than in the waking state. Free associations in psychoanalysis contain unconscious and primary process material to a greater degree than any other activity in the waking state. Discharge outlets are reduced to a minimum and channeled into fantasy and further free associations. However, free associations are still in the waking state, there are discharge outlets available, and the ego and the superego are actively censoring and editing unconscious material. This is not true in the altered state of consciousness when we dream. The dream censor edits dreams, but differently and not usually as thoroughly as in the waking state. There are no discharge outlets available in sleep, except interruption of sleep and limited physiological responses.

There are times when the impact of the unconscious wishes, drives, or conflicts is so strong in dreams it compels action in the waking state. This is particularly true in patients with low tolerance for stress: acting out disturbances. An uncomplicated dream-action is a type Freud mentioned. These are dreams of convenience. These dreams try to continue sleep by filling a need such as the desire to urinate. A person dreams he is urinating. He wakes and has to urinate. The dream was unable to preserve sleep.

VARIOUS BEHAVIORS FOLLOWING DREAMS

A person's action or behavior following a dream can be seen in a number of ways. It can be (1) entirely unrelated to the dream, (2) a continuation of a dream, (3) an association to a dream, or (4) a resolution of a dream. An unusual behavior following a dream may be acting out the manifest or latent content of the dream. This is a further association to the dream and essential for clarification. A behavior immediately preceding or during narration of a dream can be a continuation of the dream.

I want to focus on behavior following dreams of patients who are in analysis, or psychoanalytically oriented psychotherapy, but where the behavior is an association, continuation, or resolution of a dream.

DREAMS OF CONVENIENCE

First, I want to discuss two common types of behavior following dreams. Number one is what Freud called a dream of convenience. The dream attempts to take the place of action and act as the guardian of sleep. It attempts to resolve the conflict or need but is unable to do this, and the person awakens and puts the dream into action. I will use as an example Freud's dream from his *The Interpretation of Dreams* (1900, p. 123):

If I eat anchovies or olives or any other highly salted food in the evening, I develop thirst during the night which wakes me up. But my waking is preceded by a dream and this always has the same content; namely, that I am drinking. I dream I am swallowing down water in great gulps, but it has the delicious taste that nothing can equal but a cool drink when one is parched with thirst; then, I wake up and have to have a real drink.

This type of dream is common to us all and usually is set off and resolved in action by caring for a bodily need, thirst, urination, feeling cold, or sex. They are even more common in children, perhaps because they cannot tolerate as much delay in their bodily needs and because their dreams are more purely wish fulfillment.

DREAMS OF PREPARATION

The second common type of action following a dream is more delayed and connected with waking thought and fantasy. This second type of action can be called a dream of preparation.

An eleven-year-old boy dreamed he was water skiing on a lake where he had spent his summer vacation. The next day he told his parents about the dream. He continued to plead that they take him back to the lake until they finally consented to take him water skiing the following weekend.

A young woman decided to go on a diet after she dreamed she had gained ten pounds. She had felt for several weeks she was gaining weight and should diet, but the dream dealing with her concern prompted a change in her behavior.

The same eleven-year-old boy worried because he did not understand a math concept and feared he would get behind in school. He dreamed he understood the math and could do all his work perfectly. The next day, he surprised himself in school by knowing all his math and by not being nervous.

Dreams may be trial or preparatory action, just as thought can be trial action. The preparatory dream can invoke subsequent waking action and subsequent behavioral changes. This same preparatory action also seems true in the creative process, although I think most creative people have the facility in their waking thoughts and fantasies to shift into primary process preverbal and verbal thinking. There are also times when a dream by its preparatory action will help resolve a creative problem. A young successful dress designer was having particular difficulty designing her new spring line. She could not identify with the fashion trend in the country; it did not seem right to her, but she could not define in her mind what she wanted to express. She had a dream in which she went to a party where almost all the women were wearing sexy *femme fatale* dresses, but one woman was wearing a demure, soft, high-necked dress that reminded her of the 1940s. Upon awakening, she realized the dream defined what she had been unable to express in her waking thoughts. She put this into action, resolved her problem about her spring line, which became demure, soft, high-necked dresses in contrast to her previous *femme fatale* designs of past years.

BEHAVIORAL CHANGE IN CONTRAST TO ACTING OUT

As patients change in analysis, their behavior and actions change. This is one way of judging the success of analytic insight. It is part of the process of working through. It follows slow, thorough repetition, extension, and deepening of the analysis of the resistances, which results in altering the modes and aims of the instinctual drives. The change in behavior is consciously planned and somewhat predictable. This is in contrast to what we call acting out behavior. In acting out, the behavior is without conscious awareness or recognition and is a reproduction of forgotten memories, attitudes and conflicts. The acting out disturbances have the highest percentage of this behavior. Freud's definition is more specific. He was not defining acting out in terms of personality disturbances. It was acting out in the process of therapy. It is action rather than words. Freud's definition of acting out in 1914 in "Remembering, Repeating and Working Through" was "the compelling urge to repeat the forgotten past and to do so within the analytic setting by actually reliving repressed emotional experiences transferred on to the analyst and also on to all the other aspects of the current situation." Acting out was understood to replace the ability or willingness to remember whenever the patient was in resistance.

ACTING OUT AS A PRELUDE TO REMEMBERING

In Freud's time, there was a fairly even balance between remembering and reliving or acting out in the transference. As analytic interest shifted from the phallic oedipal phase to preoedipal phases and early mother-infant interactions, there was a shift in the balance between remembering and reliving. More feelings were expressed in action and behavior. The forgotten past if it refers to the preverbal period never entered the ego organization in verbal form. It could not be remembered in memory or verbal memory, but only in relived or acted out behavior.

Unfortunately, the term acting out has developed a pejorative connotation in the psychiatric and psychoanalytic literature. It has come to denote bad behavior characterizing some patients in therapy. However, for some patients, it is the only way of expressing forgotten events. It is communicative and an attempt at mastery. However, in the process it can be destructive and harmful. It is a technical problem when to tolerate acting out in analysis and when to try to quickly control it. There are many times when we have no choice. We either tolerate it or stop seeing the patient. Sometimes it may be better to stop seeing the patient rather than allow further self-destructive acting out.

There are times when I have told the patient before a possible acting out behavior that if it happens again I will not continue to treat him. I have done this with a patient who signed out from a hospital against medical advice, and again with one who continually failed to keep appointments. At times it stops the acting out behavior; at other times it does not. When it doesn't, I help the patient find another therapist, with a personality different from mine, in the hope that a better therapeutic alliance might be possible. Sometimes, my refusal to participate in self-destructive acting out has been therapeutic; the patients have felt that I cared enough to try actively to stop the behavior. Other times it has been felt to be a rejection. Perhaps in those cases I should have tolerated the behavior longer, or, as I suspect, a better therapeutic alliance would have developed with a different therapist.

ACTING OUT AS RESISTANCE

When I do tolerate the acting out behavior, I continually bring it into the sessions, often despite the reluctance of the patient, and work at analyzing and interpreting the meanings. Often the patient cannot take in or retain the interpretations for extended periods of time. The acting out behavior is an attempt to throw off the interpretations and feelings associated with them. Finally, after some destructive activity, patients will gradually be able to retain my interpretations and the meaning of their behavior. It is then reassuring for them to find that I have retained the past work. The analyst attempts to contain and retain the work and insight which the patient was unable to use during that time of acting out.

The analyst may have to be like the good mother: let the patient experience, live, and relive, but prevent serious harm and contain the feelings and insight until the time when the patient can take them inside himself.

In order to get them into therapy, the behavior of patients with acting out disturbances has to be dislodged from the external world and brought into the transference. When they act in the transference rather than act outside the transference, they become classical analytic patients. However, it is very difficult to restrict their transferred strivings to the psychic sphere and exclude motor expression. There is little chance that they will not act outside the transference as well as in the transference. An example of acting in the transference rather than outside the transference is: the patient now comes late to sessions but is on time for all other appointments. Greenacre (1950, 1968), Ekstein (1965), Limentani (1966), and Rosenfeld (1965) have all stressed the communicative and adaptive nature of acting out patients, but only Nathan Roth (1958) and Richard Sterba (1946) have written specifically about acting out and dreams. Roth stated: "Acting out of the manifest dream occurs with consistent regularity whenever the resistance of the analysand is too great to permit the interpretation of the dream." He uses acting out in Freud's definition: a painful action motivated by unconscious repetitive impulses in the patient's neurosis. He feels the patient is compelled to act out the manifest content of the dream because of a powerful incentive to analyze and gain comprehension of his dreams. He thinks dreams, in addition to a wish fulfilling function, serve the efforts of the psyche in its strivings for fuller living and better adaptation. He believes neurotic behavior, following a resisted or unanalyzed dream, is acting out parts of the manifest content of the dream. It should be analyzed as part of the dream. He states that manifest parts of a dream strongly opposed by the superego will not be acted out. I have found this to be true also, but with the analysis of acting out characters there is less that is strongly opposed by the superego. This makes acting out the dream even more common, sometimes even when the dream is adequately analyzed.

Richard Sterba (1946), in a brief article, gave four examples of acting out incidents immediately preceding the narration of the dream in the analytic hour. He felt after the narration of the dream the dream and the behavior were immediately understandable; the acting out functions as a preceding dream association. One example he gave was of a man who came to the office without the spectacles he always wore. He had never forgotten his spectacles in the two years of analysis. He then told a dream from a preceding night. He dreamt he was in an argument with another man and had removed his spectacles before getting into a fist fight in order to prevent his eyes from being injured by glass if the man struck him.

The dream and forgetting the spectacles explain each other to a great extent. The other man is the analyst, and the aggression of the dream is acted out in diminished form by forgetting to bring his spectacles to the appointment. It is clear that the acting out closely preceding the narration of the dream is unconsciously connected with the dream content. The acting out functions like an association to the dream.

TWO TYPES OF BEHAVIOR FOLLOWING DREAMS

I now want to describe behavior following dreams of patients in analysis and treatment with me. I will describe them in two categories. The first category is behavior that is acting out, not consciously thought through. It is compulsively driven and self-destructive. Category two is conscious behavior that is connected to feelings or awareness aroused in the dream and is part of the process of working through. I will then describe behavior of the analyst, myself, following patients' dreams, also in two categories, acting out and working through. I think this is particularly important. We look for countertransference reactions during the hour, but may forget about countertransference actions. A patient's dreams—their unconscious—will set off reactions in the analyst's unconscious that may only come out in nonverbal form. Particularly, this will occur if we are working in preverbal areas.

CASE EXAMPLES

I will give two examples of category one. Mr. G was a lawyer who had been in analysis with me for two years. He had a history of compulsively driven, self-destructive behavior seemingly occurring around successes and separations. He had forged a check just prior to law school graduation, knowing he would be caught. He had forged a check in the name of a lawyer with whom he worked, bought unnecessary items, and when he was not caught had turned himself into the police. He was involved in a hit-and-run accident, again getting himself caught. He had been involved in a number of other minor thefts, as well as polymorphous perverse sexual behavior. He had managed to extricate himself professionally and legally from all this by using his seductive, charming personality. The analysis had progressed well, despite these activities. He expressed an intensely ambivalent, eroticized transference with me. I was either his brilliant, attractive analyst or cold, rigid, and dumb. He would, at times, refuse to be analyzed, not use the couch, and threaten to leave; at other times he would lie quietly on the couch and freely associate with no motor activity. As the analysis progressed, I had become more active and less anxious, and he could control me and the sessions less. He told me the following dream two years into analysis, just after his WASP (like myself) girlfriend had stopped seeing him. He told me it was a nightmare; it woke him up.

"People were celebrating in a dark street. A wealthy Jewish girlfriend was there. I was on my way to exchange paper money for gold. All the people were stoned and controlled by drugs. She said,'Come along with us.' I was torn and anxious and woke up."

What he did not tell me until the next session, two days later, was that following the dream, at 11:00 to 12:00 PM, he had walked into a closed outdoor garden shop on a busy street and started to walk out with large table tops. The owner caught him and told him to put them back. Two nights later, he returned and did the same thing. This time the police came and the owner told them to arrest him. Although he brought in a number of associations to the dream when he first told it, he had left out his behavior following the dream, an essential association.

He also left out an association to this behavior, that he was thinking of seeing me five times a week rather than four. We were unable to fully analyze the dream, probably necessitating further action until he was caught and controlled. We finally analyzed the dream as follows: he was thinking of leaving me and seeing a male analyst. He was unable to control his recent girlfriend or me. I was the girlfriend in the dream who was trying to get him stoned and controlled. He was turning his paper money (dollars for the analysis) into gold—the successful end to analysis. Maybe I wanted to keep him controlled and drugged, in analysis forever, rather than help him toward a successful outcome. He was afraid of committing himself further to me, yet he wanted to be guided. His unconscious connected guidance with control. In retrospect, the behavior had an adaptive, therapeutic effect. He felt scared, thought he should be controlled by me and the police, and so thereafter began five sessions weekly. The behavior was a further communication of the dream. It clarified the splitting of the transference feelings and ended by propelling him further into analysis. It is interesting that he never had any further acting out episodes and terminated a successful analysis.

The second example, Larry, was a handsome, bright, interesting man in his mid-thirties who had just begun a successful career after many years of seeing himself as a rich man's son. He had been referred to me after years of analysis by male analysts, hoping the experience with a woman would change his homosexual orientation. Several of his other analysts saw him as borderline and unable to change. It was very difficult for me to tell whether insights were really internalized. We would have what seemed like an insightful session, full of rich associations and interpretations, followed by his completely forgetting the session. No movement seemed to occur. He described himself as frozen, and it appeared true. He could not allow me or anything from the analysis to unfreeze him.

After several months, I had an interesting observation. Several times after an hour rich in associations where childhood connections and interpretations were possible, most often centering around a dream, he would nonchalantly mention he had gone homosexual cruising. He would feel depressed, guilty, and forget the events of the previous session, rich in meaning. As I became aware of this, I interpreted his need to undo any insights we had made by cruising. I also learned that his cruising signified we had gotten through his frozen character armor. I could use it as a barometer. He was letting a woman enter him, but tried to deny it by homosexual cruising. Here is an example. He dreamed:

"I and a man I admire and genuinely like go into a room. He tells me he's tired, and the remark has a sexual overtone. We make love without fucking. It is done with abandon and guiltlessness. I'm in Chicago. I'm making love to an aggressive woman. It is very intense, but without fucking. I go to her house, I'm afraid her husband will see us. A male taxi driver with a young waif, prostitute, girlfriend then tries to kill us. I don't run too fast because I know it's a dream and I'll get away."

His associates were numerous. The man he makes love to is successful, but right now the patient is more successful. The man represents himself. He is making love to himself, but it is a better image of himself than usual. He is feeling free, but he does not fuck because his cock is a weapon that will destroy like a razor blade. He turns to an aggressive sexual woman, can be sexual with her, but not fuck her. The taxi driver is the destructive, angry part of him that kills people like the character in the movie *Taxi Driver*. He kills for his deprived, prostitute girlfriend. He felt unfrozen in the hour. He left saying that this analysis was working: "I'm turning to women in my dreams."

He came in the next sessions saying he was depressed, felt ten years older, never could change. He told me that the previous evening he had wanted to embrace his male dinner companion. He was unable to do so, because he thought it might be considered homosexual. He then went cruising till 3:00 AM and could not successfully pick anyone up. I interpreted the events of the evening as further communications about the dream, as well as a behavioral reaction to our dream interpretations. He saw his cock as a destructive weapon. He felt close to his friend and wanted to embrace him but held back to protect him, just as he felt close to me in the previous hour, but held back to protect me. He then went cruising, which made him feel depressed, inadequate, and powerless. His cock was no longer a dangerous weapon. He had turned his destructiveness onto himself. He castrated himself. He returned to me the following day feeling castrated, protecting me from his destructive cock. Larry was unable to contain his aggressive feelings as well as his loving feelings toward me. In the dream, he knew he would get away so he did not have to run fast. This is not true in analysis. It is not easy to get away. The more he understands, the more he feels, the more anxious he becomes. He had to experience his love and his hate. His hate is seen as extremely destructive, killing. This necessitates dissipation of the anxiety by cruising, as well as splitting of his love and hate. He turns the hate onto himself, making himself powerless and inadequate. He is then unable to hate (be destructive toward me) or to love me (fuck me and take me inside). The homosexual cruising occurs because he is unable to contain the anxiety experienced with loving and hating me at the same time. As the need to split these feelings decreases and he sees his aggressiveness as less destructive, the need to cruise should decrease. Despite constant interpretations, until he can contain his ambivalent feelings toward me and others, cruising will persist.

Conscious Working-Through Behavior

I would now like to give a few examples of behavior after dreams that are not unconscious or ego-dystonic. These are examples of category two. Laura was in the beginning stage of analysis. She was developing a very eroticized transference toward me which she was having difficulty expressing. She dreamt she was making love to another woman. The woman looked nothing like me. She said it could be me, but thought it was an old girlfriend. At the end of her hour, I found a bowl of violets in my waiting room. She had put them there before the session but hid them from me.

This behavior, of course, fostered our talking about her sexual feelings toward me. What she could not verbally express in her associations to the dream she expressed in her behavior.

A woman patient of mine presented this dream:
"I saw my old thesis professor. I kissed him goodbye and went across the street. There were two crosswalks. At first, I resented the crosswalks. Then I realized they were there for my own protection. I crossed in a crosswalk."

While she was relating the dream, she ate a peppermint lifesaver and offered me one. She immediately realized these were the kind her favorite grandfather had given her as a child. This behavior was preconscious, immediately accessible to consciousness. She often chewed gum or hard candy in the sessions, but always sugarless because she would not allow herself the calories. This was the first time in six years she had even allowed herself the comfort of sugar candies. This behavior immediately made the dream clear to us. She could now protect and give to herself. She could see a crosswalk as a protection, rather than a limitation. She had been talking about termination for several months, but had not felt ready to set a date. Now we both knew she could be her own lifesaver and protector. Shortly afterwards, we set a termination date. This is an example of how behavior during the narration of the dream makes the dream immediately understandable. It is only slightly different from Richard Sterba's (1946) examples where the acting out closely precedes the narration of the dream. However, in this case, the action was preconscious, then immediately conscious and functioned as a further association and resolution to the dream.

ACTING OUT BY THE THERAPIST

It would be incomplete not to mention behavior by the analyst following his, or her, patient's dreams. They are countertransference actions rather than reactions, but they can be used to provide clues to the meaning of the patient's, as well as the analyst's behavior, feelings, and thoughts. Countertransference actions can be conscious, partly conscious, or unconscious. They can occur in the process of therapeutic working through or as acting out by the analyst. I will give examples of both from my personal experience.

The first example is from category one: acting out behavior. I was analyzing a bright, attractive young man who was in the midst of a highly eroticized transference. I was partially aware of my sexual attraction toward him and had several fantasies and dreams about him. I was personally struggling with serious problems in my own life. I had recently separated after eleven years of marriage. I felt needy and guilty. During this period, my sexual fantasies and dreams about this man became more frequent and intense. One session, he related this dream to me:

"I had called and cancelled a session because I was ill. You came over to my home because you were concerned. I was lying in bed thrilled. You sat on the bed and asked me how I was feeling. I said better, now that you are here. You reached out to me, we touched and kissed and had our arms around each other."

I was immediately aware that the dream made me uncomfortable. I wondered if any of my countertransference feelings had accentuated his feelings and this dream. None of his associations suggested this. I managed to interpret and handle the session.

At this time, I was involved in a colloquium, in which I was the only psychiatrist. I felt my role as somewhere between member and therapist. A man in the group developed a very sudden, intense, erotic-dependent transference reaction to me, and I to him. We became involved in a brief, intense, sexual affair which was uncharacteristic of either of our previous patterns. It was driven ego-dystonic behavior for me. In retrospect, it occurred shortly after the session where my patient narrated this dream. It was only later, with further self-analysis and supervision, that I realized I had acted out my countertransference feelings to my patient through my affair with this man. It served as a further communication to me about my feelings toward the patient and the dream. It perhaps was a necessary action that enabled me to continue to be an effective analyst to him. It provided me with a behavioral discharge outside of the analysis that enabled me to continue the analytic work without countertransference interference. Otherwise, I may have avoided analyzing the eroticized countertransference feelings and confused my patient and the analysis or caused some acting out in him. I think this was avoided by my extra-analytic action and my further self-analysis.

Conscious Working-Through Behavior by the Therapist

Now I would like to give an example of an action I took following a patient's dream that was more consciously thought through. I had been analyzing a young woman, using the couch, for two years. Neither of us was happy with the progress. From the beginning, she frequently came twenty to thirty minutes late. It was difficult for her to free associate. I felt we were struggling in a negative therapeutic reaction. She could not let me help her because I would then be too powerful and she would have to depend on me. She had to keep me powerless and push me away. I interpreted this over and over in a variety of ways. Her response usually was "I don't know, maybe." We did not see any progress. I continued with the interpretation of what I saw as resistance. Her response became intense. "I wasn't trying to keep you away, I'm feeling desperate and I told you that." She then brought in this dream:

"I'm in my mother's apartment. My mother and husband were also there. An ambulance came. The attendant said I was going to a mental hospital. I said he had the wrong address. I appealed to everyone there to help me. No one did."

This was a frightening dream to me and to her. I finally believed how desperate she felt. I really was abandoning her. I suggested that she sit up during the next session and told her I had finally heard her. The dream made me aware it was not resistance, but a protection against her own disintegration. I had to give her more of a sense of herself. I had to fill her up, not take her covering away. We continued to work face to face. I focused on her fear of abandonment and disintegration. Slowly she began to come on time and slowly improved. She is now feeling a sense of herself, but has not yet accepted that self as worthy of love and respect.

NECESSITY OF ANALYZING ACTIONS FOLLOWING DREAMS

Action following dreams needs to be considered in the analysis of dreams, particularly in patients with acting out disturbances. They are unable to contain their anxiety. They also have less rigid superegos. Material is expressed behaviorally, rather than verbally through free associations. Their actions can be further associations to a dream, a continuation of a dream, or an attempt to resolve a dream.

Actions by the analyst or therapist need to be considered as well. He can consciously, preconsciously, or unconsciously act because of a patient's dream. If he notices an unusual ego-dystonic action, he should reflect on his countertransference feelings toward his patients and try to recall any of their recent dreams. His unconscious may be responding to the patient's unconscious. The unconscious material is clearer and more elaborate in dreams than in other material, hence easier to pinpoint. This may clarify his behavior and help his effectiveness with patients.

Sometimes action following a dream may signify working through a dream. The patient is taking conscious action rather than unconscious action. It is ego-syntonic, logical, and constructive rather than ego-dystonic and destructive. It is action following preparatory or trial action in the dream.

The therapist or analyst may also consciously and constructively change his behavior or response to a patient's dream. A dream may successfully reach the therapist where other material in sessions fail. He may then decide to consciously change his behavior, as in the case I mentioned.

Actions following dreams can be valuable clues to the understanding and analysis of dreams. They are particularly valuable in patients with acting out disturbances, or when we are dealing with preverbal material in our patients. Material is expressed in action rather than verbally by free association. The therapist's job is to understand the action, transform it into verbal form, and interpret it to the patient. Through repeated understanding and interpretation, eventually the acting out, ego-dystonic action will lessen or stop. This requires constant monitoring by the therapist of his own and his patient's actions.

References

Ekstein, R. (1965). A general treatment philosophy concerning acting out. In *Acting Out,* eds. Abt and Weissman. New York: Grune and Stratton.

Freud, S. (1900). The interpretation of dreams. *Standard Edition* 4:1–338 and 5:339–627.

——— (1914). Remembering, repeating and working through. *Standard Edition* 12:145–156.

Greenacre, P. (1950). General problems of acting out. *Psychoanalytic Quarterly* 14:455–467.

——— (1968). The psychoanalytic process, transference and acting out. *International Journal of Psycho-Analysis* 49:211–217.

Limentani, A. (1966). A re-evaluation of acting out in relation to working through. *International Journal of Psycho-Analysis* 47:275–282.

Rosenfeld, H. (1965). An investigation into the need of neurotic and psychotic patients to act out during analysis. In *Psychotic States.* London: Hogarth Press.

Roth, N. (1958). Manifest dream content and acting out. *Psychoanalytic Quarterly* 27:547–554.

Sterba, R. (1946). Dreams and acting out. *Psychoanalytic Quarterly* 15:175–179.

Waldhorn, H. (1967). *Place of the dream in clinical psychoanalysis.* Kris Study Group, Monograph 2. New York: International Universities Press.

CHAPTER 14

THE DREAM IN
PSYCHOSOMATIC STATES

Harold Levitan, M.D.

FAILURE TO EXPERIENCE FEELINGS

In the last few decades the investigative approach to the psychology of patients with psychosomatic disease has shifted drastically. Previously the focus of attention had been placed upon the etiological significance of a single conflict, such as between dependence and independence (Alexander 1950), or upon a single emotional state such as hopelessness–helplessness (Engel 1968). By contrast the recent studies have been attempting to delineate the broad personality characteristics of this type of patient. Two teams, one in Boston (Nemiah 1973, 1975, Sifneos 1974) and the other in Paris (Marty, de M'uzan and David 1963, de M'uzan 1974) have been in the forefront of this research.

The new wider approach has led to the important finding that a large percentage of psychosomatic patients fail to experience fully their own feelings. The failure to experience feelings may be partial or complete. If the failure is complete, the patient experiences no feelings regardless of provocation. If the failure is incomplete, the patient, though aware of some feeling, is unable to describe it well or to localize it within his body. The Boston group has used the Greek word *alexithymia* which literally means "no word for emotion" to refer to this phenomenon. The Paris group has used the term *pensee operatoire* to refer to essentially the same phenomenon. The French term is intended to emphasize the cognitive style of the psychosomatic patient, which tends to be concrete and devoid of feeling.

The partial or complete absence of the driving force of conscious feelings in these patients helps to explain many facets of their behavior including their failure to fantasize, their tendency to reject the psychotherapeutic relationship, and their low rate of suicide. However, a significant issue remains unsettled; namely, is feeling absent in these patients? Or is it present in the patient's mind yet somehow excluded from awareness?

PROJECTION OF INTENSE AFFECT ONTO ANOTHER DREAM CHARACTER

It is often true that when information from waking life is difficult to comprehend, data from dreams can be helpful. Indeed, in previous papers (Levitan 1967, 1968, 1969, 1970, 1972, 1974, 1976–1977) dealing with the syndromes of mania, depersonalization, phobia, traumatic neurosis, and obsessive neurosis, I have presented data which strongly suggest that dreams, because of the prevalence of primary process mechanisms, actually play a role in producing the shift in the structural and dynamic forces which results in symptom formation. As will be seen, the same relationship between dream and symptom formation appears to hold true in the psychosomatic syndromes as well.

In the present paper I will provide examples of a particular type of dream reported to me by many psychosomatic patients which bear directly upon the crucial issue of the missing affect in their waking life. In this type of dream a character other than the dreamer is depicted as experiencing the affect while the dreamer himself is actually expressing it. For example, in the case of a dream involving grief, a dream character other than the dreamer is represented as crying during the dream but when the dreamer awakens he finds his pillow soaked, indicating that he himself has actually been crying. It is evident that the dreamer in this type of dream is able to avoid the affect by displacing it onto another person who acts as his proxy in this regard. This data supports the second alternative cited above, which states that feeling is present in the patient's mind but excluded from consciousness.

In my series this type of dream involving the affect of sadness was reported at one time or another by six asthmatic patients, eight arthritic patients, three hypertension patients, and one ileitis patient. These groups made up, roughly and respectively, 65, 60, 50 and 15 percent of my patients. In many patients the dreams occurred repetitively. It is possible that further search will turn up more examples in these patients as well as in other patients with psychosomatic diagnoses. The dreams were remarkably similar in the several patients. In fact, it was this feature of similarity which initially alerted me to the possible significance of this type of dream. In my experience this type of dream has not been reported except by psychosomatic patients.

I encountered only one instance of a dream in which an affect other than sadness was displaced. In this instance the affect was terror and the displacement of it occurred in a patient with regional ileitis. This dream has considerable heuristic significance since it suggests that a variety of affects may be displaced.

Mind-Body Split Contributes to Psychosomatic Illness

The projection by the dreamer of his feelings onto another dream character illustrates the narcissistic relationship which exists between the dreamer and his characters. The configuration which has been described, in which a dream character experiences the feeling while at the same time the dreamer himself expresses it, demonstrates a total split between the mental and physiological components of affect. As will be discussed, it is very likely that a split of this type contributes to the production of the physiological changes responsible for illness.

EXISTENCE OF FORMED UNCONSCIOUS AFFECT

Furthermore, these dreams have significance as regards our general theory of affects. Freud and most workers after him have held the opinion that there are no unconscious affects in the sense in which there are unconscious ideas because, while an idea consists of cathexes of memory traces, an affect corresponds to a process of discharge which, if it is unconscious, exists only as a potential disposition to discharge rather than as an entity with concrete properties. In fact, this very difficulty in conceptualizing the existence of unconscious affect has constituted one of the major stumbling blocks in the development of our understanding of psychosomatic mechanisms. The configuration in these dreams demonstrates at least one way in which affect can flourish in a fully developed form and yet remain outside of consciousness.

CLINICAL EXAMPLES

As already noted, the dreams which demonstrate the phenomena under consideration are very similar. I will present several representative examples in association with a very brief description of each dreamer's situation at the time the dream occurred.

Arthritis and Dream of Object Loss

Mrs. F is a sixty-year-old secretary with rheumatoid arthritis. Her symptoms developed twelve years ago following a series of defeats dealt her by an older woman who was her superior at the office. Under most circumstances, she lacks awareness of her own feelings. For example, during our first consultation she complained repeatedly of "wet eyes" in addition to her joint symptoms. On questioning, it turned out that her eyes became wet only in certain situations, as for example, when she was saying goodbye to a helpful co-worker who was moving to another country. She truly had not recognized the fact that she was crying and she was very surprised when I brought it to her attention.

In the midst of our therapy her mother died. Though she was deeply attached to her mother she gave few signs of sadness. The following dream which occurred very shortly after her mother's death illustrates the process by means of which she was able to avoid awareness of grief: "We were all at mother's funeral. . . . Suddenly my brother Jack burst into tears . . . I never saw anybody cry so hard . . . I felt very sorry for him . . . ." Though she noted during the dream how sorry she felt for her brother whose suffering was intense, it is clear that her grief on behalf of his grief was easier to bear than would have been her own grief at first hand.

On awakening from this dream her pillow was wet. This dream sequence serves to emphasize how wide may be the split between the mental and physiological components of emotion: while she was simply an observer in process of watching someone else cry, her own body was actively shedding tears.

It is interesting to note that in waking life, as in the dream quoted, she experiences her own feelings in situations in which she can identify (i.e., empathize) with the feelings of another person. For example, she experienced tremendous sadness at the funeral of an adolescent boy who was a stranger to her because "his parents seemed so sad." Likewise, she regularly cried in the car after leaving the home of her parents because she imagined how lonesome they must feel rather than because she felt lonesome herself. However, her parents were not lonesome at all; they had many other children at home to occupy them. It is evident that she had projected onto her parents her own feelings of sadness of which she was unaware and then she reexperienced them at second hand.

Asthma and Dream of Separation

Marcel Proust (1934) was a great novelist who suffered from severe asthma. His asthma began when he was nine and persisted with few interruptions throughout his life. Like many asthmatics he had severe problems separating from his loved ones. In fact, a key portion of the first part of his autobiographical novel deals with his inability to separate from his mother, even for an evening.

In *Swann's Way,* the protagonist Swann, who is clearly the author's alter ego, has the following dream while he is trying desperately to separate from his beloved.

> He was going away for a year . . . leaning from the window of the train towards a young man on the platform who wept as he bade him farewell, he tried to persuade him to leave also. The train began to move: he awoke in alarm and remembered that he was not going away, that he would see Odette that evening [p. 271].

Later the same type of dream occurs as he is once again obliged to consider separating from his beloved:

> The strange young man in the fez bursts into tears . . . Swann tried to console him saying . . . 'why be so distressed'. . . . " [p. 290].

Presumably, Proust had dreams of this type himself. It does not seem likely that he could have invented such a sequence of events.

Proust did not manifest restricted awareness of his feelings in waking life: on the contrary. Yet his dreams contain the same mechanism for dealing with feeling as do the dreams of patients who manifest marked restricted awareness of feelings in waking life. It has been difficult to provide an explanation for the fact that a certain percentage of psychosomatic patients demonstrate restricted awareness of affect while a certain percentage of patients fail to do so. Perhaps the dream contains the link between the psychology of these two subgroups of psychosomatic patients.

It is not at all clear why a person who has direct access to his feelings in waking life would resort to such a drastic mechanism to avoid awareness of feelings in dreams. However, it is possible to speculate that since the ego is weaker during dreams than during waking life, it therefore tolerates feelings less easily at that time. Also, as noted earlier, the mechanism of projection of feeling away from the self is especially available during dreams due to the naturally occurring narcissistic relationship which exists between the dreamer and his characters. It is interesting to note, while on the subject of Proust, that the same type of narcissistic relationship exists between a novelist and his characters as between a dreamer and his characters.

Arthritis and Dream of Traumatic Events

Mrs. G is a forty-four-year-old woman with severe rheumatoid arthritis. She developed rheumatoid arthritis in her late thirties after being struck by a succession of traumatic events. Her husband, upon whom she was very dependent, was sent out of town on a new job, and at practically the same time her two sons were sentenced to prison for antiwar activities. She was very sad and cried a good deal in this period. Like Proust, she is one of those persons with psychosomatic illness who do not lack awareness of feeling in waking life. The following dream occurred following our discussion of her persistent loneliness for her mother who had died twenty-four years earlier: "We were all at a funeral. My children were crying profusely. . . . I am trying to comfort them."

Like Patient number 1, she found her pillow wet when she awoke.

Arthritis and Dream of Object Loss

Mrs. H is a fifty-nine-year-old woman with severe rheumatoid arthritis of forty years' duration. Her condition worsened sharply six years ago following her husband's suicide. At the time I met her she was aware of very little feeling. She was completely bedridden and would lie immobile for hours with her mind quite blank. The following dream occurred the night after she had been "floored" by news of her daughter's imminent departure to start a new life in a distant city.

"A neighbor is crying. I rush up to her, I say, 'Why are you crying? . . .' She says, 'Because your daughter is going on an airplane'. . . . I say casually, 'Why be frightened about that? She often travels. . . .'"

It is important to note that her response to the news during the day was one of shock, that is, she was "floored." It was only in the dream succeeding the event that true feeling, albeit projected, appeared.

Arthritis and Dream of Denial of Illness

Mrs. E is a thirty-six-year-old woman with a galloping arthritis of six years' duration. She showed little affect and attempted to deny ever-increasing limitation of her activity. The following dream occurred during the night following a visit to her surgeon, when he gave her the discouraging news that she would require further surgery. It is of particular interest because the figure chosen as the proxy is her doctor. This relationship in the dream was actually the first step in the development of a narcissistic transference which shortly thereafter made a full appearance in waking life as well.

"My doctor was going to give me a gold injection. . . . He was crying. . . . His face was wrinkled and he looked very old. . . . He said he had been sick . . . I said I was sorry . . . I wanted to take his head and put it against my shoulder, but I didn't dare. . . . " It is obvious that she gained a measure of respite in her dream by changing places with her doctor.

Asthma and Dream of Object Loss

Mr. S is a sixty-three-year-old advertising executive who has had moderately severe asthma since early childhood. He tends to be quite unaware of his own feelings. This inaccessibility to his own feelings enabled him to separate from four wives in the course of his life without difficulty. The following dream occurred during a period of therapy in which we were reviewing his attitudes regarding the deaths of both his parents, which had occurred within a short interval ten years earlier.

"I am in a room with a noisy radiator . . . steam is coming out . . . I am worried because the steam is under such strong pressure. . . . Then I think it's okay . . . but Pa enters the room and says: 'It's not okay!' . . . I look at the valve closely and see that a piece of ice is blocking it. . . . Suddenly Pa falls over onto the floor. . . . It's obvious he is dead . . . an old friend appears who is very sad because of Pa's death . . . he is crying and moaning loudly . . . I attempt to console him but all the time I am consoling him I am aware of the fact that I feel no emotion whatsoever."

His own manifest lack of emotion in the dream is an accurate reflection of his attitude at the time of his parents' death in real life. At that time he had been estranged from them for several years. As far as he had been concerned, the funerals were a "damned nuisance." Until I pointed out to him the projected grief in the dream, he had had no awareness of a reaction to the loss.

The work with this dream marked a turning point in his therapy. In the weeks after our initial discussion of it, he began to remember positive aspects of his relationship to his parents. He supplied the interpretation that the steam under pressure in the first part of the dream represented his suppressed emotion which was about to burst out. He also felt that the ice which was blocking the valve represented his own icy heart which prevented him from experiencing his feelings.

Essential Hypertension and Dream of Defeat

Mr. K is a thirty-year-old executive with moderately severe essential hypertension. Over the years he has made several serious suicide attempts related to failures in his family life brought on by his own illicit activities. At the time of the following dream he was devastated and once again suicidal because his wife, who had become completely fed up with his activities, had just left him.

"I met the Prime Minister on the street . . . he was very sad because of his standing in the public opinion polls . . . he was crying and I felt very sorry for him."

The difficulties of the Canadian prime minister were very much in the news at the time he had this dream. He felt that the prime minister was "at the end of his rope." This dream demonstrates that on occasion the psychosomatic patient may reach outside his immediate personal sphere to find a figure onto whom he can project his grief. It is interesting to note that one of my patients with regional ileitis, whose own life had taken a sudden turn for the worse, had a nearly identical dream involving a political figure who had just lost an election.

Regional Ileitis and Dream of Terror

Mr. D is a thirty-year-old engineer with severe regional ileitis. The degree to which he lacks awareness of his feelings in waking life is remarkable. He leads a more or less robotlike existence with only minimal interpersonal contacts. It was not possible, perhaps because of his reticence, to discover the provocation for the following dream:

"There is a violent thunder and rain storm in progress . . . I am crossing a hall which has large door-windows at the end. I become aware of loud knocking on the window. . . . It is my ten-year-old nephew who has walked along an outside balcony to this location because he is frightened of the storm. I let him in. Then I awaken . . . I am trembling with terror . . . my heart is racing . . . and I am covered with sweat."

It is interesting to note that long into his childhood he had many repetitious nightmares involving similar situations in which he himself was the character experiencing the fright. This shift from the direct experience of emotion to the projection of emotion suggests that the capacity to project affect onto another dream character requires some degree of maturation of the mental apparatus. As noted in the introduction, this dream is the only one in my series in which an affect other than sadness was projected.

DREAMS AS SUBSTITUTES FOR GRIEF IN WAKING LIFE

It is evident that the dream ego in these examples possesses a paucity of defensive resources. A dream ego equipped with a more powerful range of defenses might have been able to prevent the affect of grief from appearing in the dream at all. The projection of the experiential aspect of the grief reaction onto another dream character seems to represent a last ditch defensive effort which accomplishes the warding off of awareness of the affect after it has already undergone considerable development. The fact that the dreamer continues to cry during the dream is a clear indication that the only aspect of the affect complex which has been altered by his defensive operations is his awareness of it.

All but one of the dreams which have been presented deal with the management of the experience of grief. This focus on the vicissitudes of grief in dreams of patients with psychosomatic illness is in accord with observations reported from the waking life of the patients. To illustrate; there are many similarities between patients with asthma and patients with melancholia. The similarities include the cyclic occurrence of symptoms, the predominance of oral factors, and a persistent sad mood (Knapp, Mushatt, and Nemetz 1966). Also, asthma attacks are often associated with an urge to cry which is abruptly prohibited. The urge to cry seems to be related to a powerful longing for the missing mother (Weiss 1922). As for rheumatoid arthritis, it is often preceded by a major loss which would be expected to produce a severe grief reaction but which, in fact, fails to do so (Ludwig 1954). This observation is especially interesting with regard to the findings I have presented in this paper. The projection of the experience of grief onto a proxy which is demonstrated in the dreams provides an example of a method for handling grief which may explain its puzzling absence in the waking life of these patients.

ROLE OF THE DREAM IN ILLNESS FORMATION

The configuration described in which affect is present and operative, yet removed from the awareness of the patient himself, seems ideally suited to produce the overstimulation of the physiological systems which leads to illness. The feeling component of affect, apart from its role in interpersonal communication, is essentially a medium for feedback between the lower brain centers which produce the physiological components of affect and the higher centers which interpret it and tame it. It is obvious that this signalling function of feeling cannot be working properly in these dreams because the dreamer himself is not receiving the message—that is, he is not the one who is experiencing the feeling. These dreamers are presumably, therefore, incapable of regulating either the intensity or duration of the physiological output associated with grief which may under the circumstances pass beyond the limits compatible with healthy functioning. It is important to remember, as regards the factor of duration of affect, that a traumatic affect such as grief usually causes the dreamer to awaken. However, in these instances, because the dreamer himself is not experiencing the affect, he fails to awaken from the episode which continues for an unduly long time. These dreamers, without awareness of their ongoing grief, can be compared to patients without awareness of pain who are often injured because they do not receive warnings of ongoing danger.

Other characteristics of dreams also favor the hypothesis that the physiological overstimulation which sets the stage for the development of illness occurs during dreams. Firstly, it is well established that the autonomic and hormonal systems are more labile during dreams than during waking life; and, secondly, significant dreams (including a few of the examples in the present series) tend to be repetitive, which greatly enhances their potential for pathological sequela. Empirical data in support of this hypothesis is provided by Ravenscroft and Hartmann (1968), who demonstrated that nocturnal asthma attacks are more likely to occur during REM periods than during NREM periods.

Greene (1958) described a mode of adjustment to loss in the waking life of certain psychosomatic patients in the pre-illness period which is rather similar to the process which occurred in these dreams. His patients projected awareness of the significance of loss with its associated feelings onto another person who had experienced the same loss. According to Greene, this mode of grieving by use of a proxy was very effective in maintaining the psychological and physiological equilibrium of the future patients as long as it could be used. The trouble started when the person who had been acting as a proxy was, for one reason or another, no longer available as a target for the projected feeling. At this point the traumatic feelings were deflected back onto the patient himself, causing him to fall ill. However, it is important to note that there are important differences between my formulation and Greene's. His data, taken from waking life in the pre-illness period, led him to emphasize the long-term restitutive and compensatory aspects of the new configuration of object relationships produced by projection of grief onto a proxy. He notes, for example, that the bereaved patient can provide comfort for himself by comforting his proxy. On the other hand, my data taken from dreams during the period of ongoing illness lead me to emphasize the more immediate benefit of avoidance of awareness of grief which is achieved by projection of it onto a proxy.

References

Alexander, F. (1950). *Psychosomatic Medicine.* New York: Norton.

de M'uzan, M. (1974). Psychodynamic mechanisms in psychosomatic symptom formation. *Psychotherapy and Psychosomatics* 23:103–110.

Engel, G. (1968). A life-setting conducive to illness: The giving-up, given-up complex. *Annals of Internal Medicine* 69:293–300.

Greene, W. A. (1958). Role of a vicarious object in the adaptation to object loss. *Psychosomatic Medicine* 20:344–350.

Knapp, P., Mushatt, C., and Nemetz, S. (1966). Asthma, melancholia, and death. *Psychosomatic Medicine* 26:114–143.

Levitan, H. (1967). Depersonalization and the dream. *Psychoanalytic Quarterly* 36:157–171.

——— (1968). The turn to mania. *Psychoanalytic Quarterly* 37:56–62.

——— (1969). The depersonalizing process, I. *Psychoanalytic Quarterly* 38:97–109.

——— (1970). The depresonalizing process, II. *Psychoanalytic Quarterly* 39:449–470.

——— (1972). Dreams preceding hypomania. *International Journal of Psychoanalytic Psychotherapy* 1:50–61.

————— (1974). Dreams of a phobic patient. *International Review of Psycho-Analysis* 1:313–323.

————— (1976–1977). Dynamic and structural features in a case of compulsive neurosis as revealed in dreams. *Psychotherapy and Psychosomatics* 27:125–132.

————— (1976–1977). Observations on certain catastrophic dreams. *Psychotherapy and Psychosomatics* 27:1–7.

Ludwig, A. O. (1954). Rheumatoid arthritis. In *Recent Developments in Psychosomatic Medicine*. Philadelphia: Lippincott.

Marty, D, de M'uzan, M., and David, C. (1963). *L'investigation Psychosomatique*. Paris: Presses Universitaires de France.

Nemiah, J. (1973). Psychology and psychosomatic illness: reflections on theory and research methodology. *Psychotherapy and Psychosomatics* 22:106–111.

————— (1975). Denial revisited: reflections on psychosomatic theory. *Psychotherapy and Psychosomatics* 26:140–147.

Proust, M. (1934). *Remembrance of Things Past*. New York; Random House.

Ravenscroft, K., and Hartmann, E. (1968). *Psychophysiology* 4:396 [abstract].

Sifneos, P. (1974). A reconsideration of psychodynamic mechanisms in psychosomatic symptom formation in view of recent clinical observations. *Psychotherapy and Psychosomatics* 24:151–158.

Weiss, E. (1922). Psychoanalyse eines Falles von nervösem Asthma. *International Zeitschrift für Psychoanalyse* 8:440–445.

CHAPTER 15

PERVERSE SYMPTOMS AND THE MANIFEST DREAM OF PERVERSION

Charles W. Socarides, M.D.

During the psychoanalytic treatment of perverse patients, I have been confronted with a singular and regularly recurring phenomenon, namely, that among these patients' dreams are some that depict the same perverse acts for which they seek therapy. Upon awakening, the dreamer often pursues the apparent hallucinatory wish fulfillment of the dream, first in fantasy and then in real life, external reality becoming a setting for gratification. In the pure form of manifest perverse dream content, the perversion is pictured without interfering factors, anxieties, or frustrations; in contrast, there are the more common, impure forms in which elements of frustration and additional conflicts of various kinds are comingled. In both, the perverse content is explicit and conforms to the actual perversion in real life. In pure forms, the patient experiences little or no anxiety in the dream, and sexual pleasure is an accompanying affect. The patient often awakens considerably relieved of the overwhelming anxiety preceding sleep. Often, when these dreams are analyzed, no new information is gathered by free association with regard to their unconscious meaning; what is encountered is the diffuse anxiety that precipitated them.

In *The Interpretation of Dreams* (1900), Freud observed that a psychological theory should not be based on a single category of mental phenomena, even that of dreams, but that dreams themselves should be related to other products of mental life, especially neurotic symptoms.

Psychoanalytic theory should cast light on what dreams have in common with symptoms, as well as define the ways in which they differ from them. He repeatedly compared dreams to symptoms and noted (1909) that both often said the same thing and were in part the results of identical processes—condensation, reversal, multiple identifications, etc.—and that symptoms undergo distortion of the censorship analogous to the hallucinatory ones of dreams. Although Freud firmly asserted that "the most trustworthy method of investigating deep mental processes" was through the study of dreams (1920), there have been few subsequent investigations in the direction of understanding specific symptoms in their relation to dreams. Several notable exceptions have included Noble (1951), Lewin (1950, 1952, 1955, 1958), Katan (1960), Richardson and Moore (1963), and Frosch (1969). The relative scarcity of such reports well may be due to Freud's early shift in attention, from investigating the connection between dream and symptom to the more urgent problem of explaining the relation between symptom and anxiety.

In this paper, I present several examples of this phenomenon as occurring in various well-structured perversions,[1] describe the psychological events precipitating it, the psychic mechanisms responsible for its formation, and examine its relationship to perverse acts themselves. I am suggesting that the manifest dream of perversion, similar to the symptom, plays an integral part in maintaining the pervert's psychological equilibrium and efforts at adaptation. Understanding the manifest perverse dream enhances our knowledge of the earliest shadowy and indistinct psychic mechanisms responsible for perversion. I am further suggesting that dreams of perverse acts may well belong to Freud's (1920) *second group* of dreams, which he considered to be exceptions to the proposition that dreams are fulfillments of wishes.

From the outset, it should be noted that the hallucinatory (visual) reenactment in a manifest dream with very little or no distortion of the sexual practices carried out in waking life is not, of course, the only kind of dream reported by perverts. More common are manifest dreams of being surrounded by snakes, swept into whirlpools, enclosed in caves, etc., representing merging and fusion. Fears of the dissolution of the self-representation are often depicted in the manifest dream as fears of shooting out into space, being in an elevator whose sides are collapsing,

---

1. The phrase *well-structured perversions* is used to designate pronounced cases in which perverse development is clear and definite; the perverse acts are usually the only avenue for attainment of sexual gratification and are obligatory for the alleviation of intense anxieties.

being lost in space, becoming progressively smaller against a backdrop of darkness or afloat in a vast sea. Castration anxiety is commonly pictured by open wounds, bloody scenes of mutilation, similar to those seen in neurotics. Dreams representing negative oedipal situations are common, for example, passive sexual surrender to an overpowering masculine figure, often seen with severe anxiety or in disguise. Dreams representing severe regression embody regressive reenactment of preoedipal and oedipal fantasies, such as becoming a small infant or losing one's teeth. Dreams representing simultaneous identification with the phallic and penisless mother may be depicted by images of females with breasts appearing as elongated penises, penises growing above the vagina or on various parts of the body. Manifest content, of course, may include perverse activity in symbolic form. In general, these themes are found in all perversions, and the latent dream content can then be decoded through the technique of dream analysis and free association, as with other patients. In these dreams, the latent dream content has undergone disguise in an attempt to alleviate anxiety, even though the patient may often awaken in fright, even of nightmarish proportions. In contrast, the manifest dream of perverse activity diminishes anxiety, is easy to recall, remains in consciousness upon awakening, and commonly is followed by perverse fantasies and action. Fantasy and act may precede as well as follow the appearance of the manifest perverse dream.

THEORETICAL BACKGROUND

Historically, the explanation that symbolism disguises manifest sexual and sexually perverse content put into bold relief the fact that there was no satisfactory explanation for a dream of explicit perverse or nonperverse sexual content. In these dreams, sexual wishes and thoughts had evaded the unconscious middle operations (the dream-work), had not been barred from consciousness or from direct gratification by the ego's defenses, and invaded the manifest dream itself.

Freud commented on this vexing problem in 1925. He asked:

How can it happen . . . that this censorship, which makes difficulties over more trivial things, breaks down so completely over these manifestly immoral dreams?

The answer is not easy to come by and may perhaps not seem completely satisfying. If, in the first place one submits these dreams to interpretation, one finds that some of them have given no offence to the censorship because

au fond they have no bad meaning. They are innocent boastings of
identifications that put on a mask of pretence; *they have not been censored
because they do not tell the truth* [emphasis added]. But others of them—
and, it must be admitted, the majority—really mean what they say and have
undergone no distortion from the censorship. They are an expression of
immoral, incestuous and perverse impulses or of murderous and sadistic
lust. The dreamer reacts to many of the dreams by waking up in a fright, in
which case the situation is no longer obscure for us. The censorship has
neglected its task, this has been noticed too late, and the generation of
anxiety is a substitute for the distortion that has been omitted. In still other
instances of such dreams, even that expression of affect is absent. The
objectionable matter is carried along by the height of the sexual excitement
that has been reached during sleep, or it is viewed with the same tolerance
with which even a waking person can regard a fit of rage, an angry mood, or
the indulgence in cruel phantasies [pp. 131–132].

Freud provided two explanations. These dreams either "truly mean
what they say," in which case the dreamer may awaken in fright, the
current anxiety a substitute for the distortion that has been omitted; or
they have not had to undergo distortion because they have no "bad
meaning." Advances in our theoretical and clinical understanding of
perversions have proven that Freud's second explanation was correct on
both counts. These dreams "have no bad meaning," for in the pervert's
unconscious, it is ordinary sexual congress that is filled with guilt, anxiety,
and destructive aggression.

Glover (1960) succinctly dealt with this issue, noting that "in the
unconscious of the sexual pervert, there is a renunciation of adult sexuality
as a moral act. His regression to infantile sexuality, though by no means
guilt-free, is the lesser of two evils . . . In the sense of primitive
unconscious morality, both the neurotic and the sexual pervert are more
'moral minded' than the normal heterosexual adult" (pp. 183–184).

These dreams "do not tell the truth" because perverse acts themselves
are products of a repressive compromise (Sachs 1923). It is a solution by
division whereby one piece of infantile sexuality enters the service of
repression, that is, it helps to promote repression through displacement,
substitution, and other defense mechanisms. Pregenital pleasure is thereby carried over into the ego while the rest is repressed. The unrepressed
part is the perverse act, which is analogous to the manifest dream in that it
is disguising a more threatening latent content. Indeed, perverse symptoms (the perverse facade) might even be considered roughly analogous to
manifest dreams (Joseph 1965, Socarides 1978), so that perverse acts or
symptoms may be referred to as the "manifest perversion" and their true

meaning as the "latent content of the perversion." That perverse dreams or symptoms do not mean what they say is especially evident in those perversions with unusual or bizarre content. A vivid example is the "bug perversion" reported by Stolorow and Grand (1973). The patient would walk about until he found a woman standing alone, upon whose shoulder he would place a bug. He would inform her of this, and if she expressed shock or fright, brushed the bug off, and squashed it with her foot, he became sexually excited. He later masturbated to this image of her squashing the bug. The sexual excitement derived from an identification with a mother who spanked him and squashed flies with obvious relish. It reassured against castration anxiety: it is only a bug that is being destroyed, my penis is safe.

In *Beyond the Pleasure Principle,* Freud (1920) noted that some patients repeat in their manifest dreams what they had experienced in real life. These were dreams in which "enough is left unexplained to justify the hypothesis of a compulsion to repeat—something that seems more primitive, more elementary, more instinctual then the pleasure principle which it overrides" (p. 23). Such dreams are similar to the dreams of children, to the hallucinatory dreams occurring in toxic states of high fever, or to the dreams of traumatic neurotics and "are exception[s] to the proposition that dreams are fulfilments of wishes." They include "dreams during psychoanalysis which bring to memory the psychical traumas of childhood [and] arise . . . in obedience to the compulsion to repeat . . . what has been forgotten and repressed" (p. 32).

Freud explained:

> Thus it would seem that the function of dreams, which consists in setting aside any motives that might interrupt sleep, by fulfilling the wishes of the disturbing impulse, is not their *original* function. It would not be possible for them to perform that function until the whole of mental life had accepted the dominance of the pleasure principle. If there is a 'beyond the pleasure principle,' it is only consistent to grant that there was also a time before the purpose of dreams was the fulfilment of wishes. This would imply no denial of their later function. But if once this rule has been broken, a further question arises. May not dreams which, with a view to the psychical binding of traumatic impressions, obey the compulsion to repeat—may not such dreams occur *outside* analysis as well? And the reply can only be a decided affirmative [pp. 32–33].

It should be noted that Freud did not mention in this group of recurrent dreams those with manifest perverse content, perhaps because he did not conceive of them as representing situations from which the patient wished to escape, that is, traumatic states, but as derivatives of infantile sexuality.

In 1967 Stewart noted the occurrence in borderline cases of "overtly sexual, incestuous, sadistic or perverse dreams" and suggested that they could be better understood "if we conceive of them as modeled along the lines of the traumatic dream in the sense that they serve the original function of mastery. Because of the early points of fixation and the arrest in development, the conflicts in severely ill patients are less completely internalized than in neurotic patients and are represented in terms of the relation of self to object." Stewart cited several factors responsible for the production of these dreams: (1) the existence of an ego defect affecting the operation of the synthetic function, with the failure of free associations to cluster around the significant material; (2) the inability to master primitive fears and outbreaks of uncontrollable primitive aggression and; (3) the fear of the loss of a sense of identity. In this connection, Pulver (1978), in reviewing studies on the manifest content of dreams, commented that if the particular kind of dream reported by Stewart occurs at all frequently, it is of "real clinical importance" and "deserves further recognition" (p. 682).

My clinical material suggests that recurrent manifest perverse dreams in patients with well-structured perversions should also be included in Freud's second group of dreams, whose original purpose is "the psychical binding of traumatic impressions." These dreams are precipitated by an increasing threat to a precarious and marginal equilibrium in patients with ego deficiencies that produce uncontrollable anxiety and rage—in effect, a traumatic state. The manifest perverse dream represents a regression to a primitive mode of mastery. It brings discharge of tensions provoked by the patient's emotional crisis and ensures sleep in the face of overwhelming tension which it would otherwise be impossible to master. In analyzing such dreams, one comes up against the precipitating situation itself, a predicament from which the patient wishes to escape. It is one in which the patient's psyche is reacting with overwhelming anxiety to a disturbing change in the condition of the self, a serious depressive loss of self-esteem, or impending self-dissolution.

HOMOSEXUAL SADOMASOCHISTIC DREAMS

Patient A

The sequential appearance of a bondage sadomasochistic homosexual fantasy, leading to a sadistic homosexual dream and, upon awakening, to a homosexual sadistic fantasy and then to the enactment of a perverse act, was described by a thirty-year-old sadomasochistic homosexual actor/writer. He had just returned from a hometown, large family gathering feeling "squashed" and "masochistic." Such meetings frequently produced depressive feelings and an intensification of the need for homosexual acts. Everyone at home was both successful and heterosexual. The week before, he had experienced a severe loss of self-esteem in anticipation of this meeting, had been unable to attend his regular swimming sessions, an activity which tended to bolster his sense of body ego and masculinity, and was becoming increasingly despondent that his professional career appeared to be "going nowhere."

He related his feelings as follows: "It was being in an atmosphere of normality which made me feel abnormal and weak. I thought about X quite a lot. Everybody was having a normal sex life but me. This brings on a poor concept of myself, being there but not being myself. I feel it in my body too, like I'm empty, or like part of me is missing. If I can attach myself to a man, perhaps, I could find myself. At these times even when I'm asked to sing along with the group I cannot do it although I have a good voice. Also I realize that in the presence of my mother it's difficult for me to be a man; I lose that power. When I got home, a homosexual fantasy began with X being my lover. That helps me overcome my inadequacy. And as I start with the fantasy it becomes more and more masochistic—bondage, humiliation, being screwed in the ass, people watching. And what would I want from a man? I want him to tell me how I get through all this. It would be someone to sit by me at night, cuddle, kiss, have sex with, lie very close to, then fall asleep; like I'd like to play the female role, passive partner, where I'd be a little child and cuddle, like we could provide for each other in the real world and against it."

The patient then fell asleep and dreamt: "I was just fucking X, putting in one finger, then two, three, then four, and then my whole hand was in his anus with vaseline on it. I could see him wanting more. He was an absolute helpless mass in front of me. This aroused me."

Upon awakening, the patient masturbated to the dream images, first of X with the patient's hand in his anus, then of himself playing the passive role. After ejaculation, he went to the home of X and engaged in the sadomasochistic homosexual act as both passive and active partner in anal intercourse.

The patient usually fantasied homosexual relations some part of every day, and overt homosexual dreams of this type occurred once or twice a month. They appeared "when I have a need for homosexuality insofar as I use it for a sedative for anxiety and when I feel a desire not to do anything. In fact, most of all, when I cannot do anything and I feel paralyzed."

Patient B

The following dream of a twenty-three-year-old homosexual musician shows explicit perverse activities with very little distortion, activities which he pursued in his fantasy life every day. It expresses additional unconscious motivations such as the desire to be a female, to engage in sadomasochistic acts as a woman, to acquire the partner's penis and masculinity through incorporation, and the intensity of his overwhelming aggression. His dreams and fantasies served the function of narcissistically restoring his self-representation. Here is one of his dreams:

"In some home, and this man is there with a very long penis. He's very muscular. There's something uncouth about him. He's dark, manly, and rough. And we're in bed and I want him to fuck me and he won't. However, he has me by the penis, there's a rush of excitement. Then I think other people are coming into the room, interrupting us. Then later he's still lying in bed eating a salad. The salad is on his chest but I dump it all over his head because he wouldn't fuck me. I'm so angry. The salad turns into a jellylike substance, like sperm, I guess. Then we start kissing each other."

The patient presented the following associations: he had awakened frequently during the dream, and it appeared to take a long time; it was pleasurable on the whole except for the anger and frustration, but it culminated in a relief through kissing. He noted that Y had come over the night of the dream. He had been very attracted to Y, but he was unable to get him into bed. He became severely anxious, depressed, and had to go out "cruising" in an attempt to find another partner who would fill him up, reducing his feeling of emptiness and tension—and his dread that he might somehow "go out of control."

A MASOCHISTIC DREAM OF SPANKING

Patient C

The patient was a dignified fifty-year-old man of considerable professional achievement and social position who, since his early adolescence, had suffered from a beating fantasy and perversion (spanking perversion) which had undergone very little change over the past thirty years. In both fantasy and perversion, he dressed in young girls' clothes, baby doll pajamas whose bottom could be let down, thereby exposing his buttocks. He was Linda, a girl who never wore a bra, was never younger than fifteen years of age, and was about to be married. His sexual partner was a "Lady Gainsborough–type woman," a snob and mother to whom Linda said bad or naughty things such as curse words. The mother responded: "Now hush, you're going to get a spanking." Linda replied: "You're just looking for an excuse to tan my ass." The mother answered: "Get over my knee, but first I'll wash out your mouth with soap and water." The patient's mouth was scrubbed, both in fantasy and in reality, by a suitable willing female companion or by his wife. When Linda continued to say "naughty things," a spanking was then administered before a mirror so that the patient could view the woman's face, the slipper (or the hairbrush) with which he was being spanked, the female clothing on himself up to his abdomen, and his buttocks, which became increasingly warm, red, and painful. As he lay over the lap of his partner during the spanking, he did not attempt to touch his penis, nor did he wish to do so as he approached and reached orgasm.

The spanking perversion appeared frequently and explicitly in his manifest dream content. He dreamt: "I was with a woman in a red sweater [the color of his buttocks]. A little boy was there, and the little boy said, 'Mommy, may I have a spanking?' 'Yes, if you like. Get the hairbrush.' She got the hairbrush, pulled his pants down over him, and spanked him. 'Have you had enough?' 'Yes.' Then he went off to play. I asked her if the little boy had this before as she put her hairbrush away, and the next moment I was on top of her, excited sexually, kissing her. Watching the spanking aroused me."

Associations. The patient could say little about the meaning of his dream. The "spanking part" was part of his daily fantasy life. Almost every day it functioned to make him feel better. The dream occurred on the night he stayed at a hotel in a distant city where he was to deliver a lecture. He felt overwhelmingly sad and unhappy at being away from his wife. Performing the perverse act with her was a continual source of restoration. He experienced severe separation anxiety and panicky feelings which seemed almost to drag him from his bed toward a window from which he might be forced to leap. Intense anxiety led him to lock himself in the bathroom, writhing in agony on the floor. He sensed that he was about to "fall apart."

In most of his dream, the patient appeared as Linda, but because of the split in his ego he also dreamt of himself as a young boy. He suffered from an intense feminine identification which was not consciously acceptable in his waking life, except during the perverse acts. Exceedingly moralistic, he conceived of the genitals of both men and women as dirty, and of heterosexual intercourse as repugnant. Until later phases of the analysis, he was unable to touch his penis, even when masturbating. To him, spanking was a form of snobbery because it was practiced by the English upper classes, and in his fantasies and perversion he was a member of the aristocracy (narcissistic restoration and pathological grandiosity). Beneath the heterosexual beating fantasy and activity lay an unconscious homosexual wish to be beaten by the father and have intercourse with the father as a female. Orgasm tended to restore a sense of self-cohesiveness (Eissler 1958, Stolorow 1975, Lichtenstein 1977). The female figure was a substitute for the male, and through his unconscious homosexual wish, heavily disguised, he could incorporate the male partner's body and his penis. What usually preceded the manifest perverse dream was severe anxiety, feelings of emptiness, threats to his self-cohesion, and separation anxiety. Beneath the surface (manifest) perversion lay deeper conflicts (fear of engulfment, loss of self) representing the wish for and dread of merging with the mother in the primitive mother-child unity.

TRANSVESTITE DREAMS

Patient D

A thirty-nine-year-old professional man had practiced a transvestite perversion since the age of thirteen, when he first began to wear his mother's clothes. Although able to perform sexually on some occasions without the use of womens' underclothes, he usually found them an absolute necessity for achieving orgasm. Whenever he was unable to secure women for sexual relations, he experienced anxiety, depression, feelings of emptiness. He wore the underclothing especially when depressed, angry, upset or felt "picked on" by associates, or when he was lonely or bored. Occasionally he inserted "feminine articles" such as diaphragms, vaginal douche syringes into his anus, in order to reduce severe states of tension. Throughout the early and middle phases of the analysis, he verbalized intense oral demands, needs to suck everyone dry, especially women. They had a responsibility to provide him with things that they possessed, and they had no right to retaliate if he exploited them.

They helped him overcome feelings of separation and loneliness. The clothing was a substitute for their presence which both served erotic arousal and made him feel secure. It had a compensatory function, that of narcissistic restoration, and a warding-off function, decreasing threats to his self-esteem, relieving anxiety, and diminishing other dangers.

He frequently searched the trash baskets in his apartment house in order to find discarded women's pantyhose, put them on and masturbated. "The boredom I feel then leaves me. I want to be filled up. I feel I could get an erection if I could fill myself up with a fountain syringe . . . if I had a bra on my thighs my emptiness would be overcome; my hunger is so great, my loneliness for other people so overwhelming. I want women to cry for me; they should feed me, fill me up, and I want them to cry even after I leave them."

He was seeking revenge for the maternal deprivation and suffering he experienced during his early years: a tonsillectomy he underwent at age two, a period of institutionalization at a home for disturbed children at the age of four, which lasted for several months, and his mother's cold and unempathic attitude throughout his life.

In the following series of dreams, perverse practices appeared in undisguised form and were enacted in real life.

Dream 1. "I am in some sort of legitimate setting where wearing women's clothes is a part of a test project [superego sanction]. I'm trying on a woman's nightgown. A lot of people there. It is too small for me and won't fit. I think that there should be some regulation about the impossibility of getting a fit. It seems I want to legitimatize this fully; there ought to be some change in the rules."

Associations. "Last night I was in another city and met a woman to whom I became attracted, but I couldn't have her. Before we went to dinner, I went up to her fifteen-year-old daughter's room, looked in her drawers, found a nightgown that was too small. It was a child's nightgown like the one in the dream. It fit only over my head. I was frustrated."

Upon returning home later that evening, he was compelled to practice his transvestite perversion despite his wish to control its enactment.

Dream 2. "I am wearing women's clothing and someone is coming down the hall who might see me, a woman. I wonder how to get the clothing off without being seen."

Associations. These concerned his fear of discovery and a memory that when he told his ex-wife early in their marriage about his perversion, she had not responded; in fact, she disapproved of his perversion. On another occasion he dreamt the following.

Dream 3. "I'm supposed to be baby-sitting for somebody but I'm not there. I'm somewhere else talking, perhaps I've gone to get some women's clothes."

Associations. "Why am I choking up now? This is the dilemma: I'm there in order to be baby-sitting the way I wanted someone to be baby-sitting with me and not to feel abandoned. On the other hand, if I'm not there, someone will call and find out that I'm not doing my job of baby-sitting."

Dream 3 was precipitated by an incident in which a new girlfriend told him that she would "let him know" when she was willing to have sex with him. This greatly frustrated him, stimulating his overwhelming aggression. "But I still want to have sex with her, the feeling of being on and off. I can't see her until Saturday night. She's being cold and cynical. It's like a punishment being with her, being without her. That's not a relationship, no sex! I think of everything, about the trash basket, the garbage basket, wondering what's in there—maybe underwear. I want to go down the hall and look in there and find something. Also that night I felt I needed to call a girl in Chicago. I was terribly lonely. I am choking up with emotion now. I am thinking about being left as a child in that home—deprivation, aloneness, being without my mother, being empty, being frightened, being torn apart, like I'm losing myself. Like I might vanish like a wisp of smoke."

Manifest dreams of perversion were regularly followed by fantasies and their enactment in real life. Following one of these dreams he revealed: "It is being alone with myself that is so terrifying; and when I'm traveling alone I get very upset. It is then that I have to take women's clothing along with me. When I get anxious I feel like I'm losing myself, and also I have a *déjà vu*[2] feeling and I experience fear. I am looking out the window, I see her face for an instant, waiting for mother to come to the institution—being hungry, waiting for her, standing next to the window, screaming, trying to get out. Mommy had put me there and I'm angry. I want to get out. Angry at the crib, angry at mother. Thinking of my girlfriend now and the silence she gives me. All of my feelings of loneliness refer to previous loneliness. I'm concerned that I'll never be happy as long as I live, that I have no connection with anyone, that everyone's life is connected and normal except for mine. I want to belong

2. The patient was prone to *déjà vu* experiences when the torment of separation grew too intense. They represented a perceptual experience of returning to the mother when the ego was severely inundated by danger, through a hypercathexis of the primal love object (Pacella 1975, Mahler 1975).

to someone, like I want to belong to you. . . . I want everything from women, I want women and all the things they can give me. And every time I try to have a good time, I'm conscious of the transient nature of everything—something that is going to spoil it if I do something to foul it up. Whatever I do well is going to end up badly. What is it that I want: mother love, sense of self, sense of identity?"

The "worst" dreams were not those dealing with the manifest dream of perversion, dreams bringing relief and self-restoration, but those concerned with body-disintegration anxiety, feelings of annihilation and imminent destruction, expressed in dreams of rocket ships about to be launched with their sides missing, or finding himself hanging on the side of a building by his fingertips and fearing that he will be forced to let go. Particularly distressing were infrequent dreams of homosexuality, which the patient interpreted as a complete loss of his masculine identity and therefore a loss of the ability to secure supplies from women.

In transvestitism, he enacted the role of the phallic mother, thereby overcoming loneliness, depression, and enjoying narcissistic and oral supplies in identification with women by becoming one of them. Similarly, he enacted the role of the woman in sexual intercourse on some occasions, being penetrated with a dildo while dressed as a woman. His perversion was an enactment of his dream; the gratification experienced tended to keep in repression deeper conflicts involving separation, threat of loss of object relations, and fears of annihilation. Both dream and symptom are the end product of the same intense conflict handled in a particular manner by a deficient ego.

PRIMITIVE ROOTS OF PERVERSION DREAMS

From the case material cited, it appears that the pervert has manifest dreams of perversion when he is threatened with a further disturbance in his object relations or is confronted with a threat to his narcissistic self-image. Early impairment in ego structure has produced a defective capacity in dealing with both internal and external worlds, and his equilibrium is tenuously maintained. These patients experience severe tension, overstimulation, and threats of disintegration similar to those seen in other traumatic states in which there is a threat of disintegration of the self. The source of tension is the fear of dissolution of the self-representation, threat of imminent destructive incorporation by the mother, increasing stress on ego boundaries already severely impaired,

onslaughts against a narcissistic defensive position, and threats of erup-
tion of severe aggression endangering both self and object in the face of
the ego's inability to sufficiently neutralize aggression. Manifest perverse
dreams occur when the ego is in urgent need of reinforcement. The
hallucinatory visualization of the dream of the perversion protects and
buttresses the endangered self- and object representations during sleep, as
well as protecting sleep itself. The ego does its work in sleep by discharging panic-creating experiences which the repressive barrier has difficulty
excluding from consciousness. Otherwise, the ego might well be inundated by unbearable archaic affective perceptual experiences and feel
threatened with disintegration. Such states of severe regression are
experienced as threats of engulfment, loss of self, and fears of disintegration, and are not unusual during the psychoanalytic treatment of perversions (Socarides 1968, 1973, 1978). In these psychosis-like regressive
episodes, both the manifest dreams and perverse acts have been unable to
defend against primitive early mental contents invading the waking life,
with a resultant regressive evocation of the symbiotic phase or a fantasied
elaboration of it (Arlow 1963).

Manifest perverse dreams are similar to the "self-state" dreams:
described by Kohut (1977) in severely narcissistic patients undergoing
decompensation. In these dreams, the patient is pictured explicitly engaged in acts of extreme grandiosity or archaic exhibitionism.[3] Kohut
notes that "the very act of portraying these vicissitudes in the dream
constitutes an attempt to deal with the psychological danger by covering
frightening nameless processes with nameable visual imagery" (p. 109).
The dream does not express in visual imagery the content of drives or
wishes in an attempted solution to a conflict represented by the manifest
content, but helps the narcissist to reintegrate himself by pressing into
service primitive modes of adaptation which have proven useful and
necessary in the earliest years of life. Sexualization has played and
continues to play a major role to this end. A sexualization of narcissistic
needs promotes a discharge of narcissistic tension: seeking a penis;
incorporating the body of the male partner in homosexuality; wearing the
clothes of the opposite sex in transvestitism; the libidinization of aggression in a spanking perversion, etc., are all attempts at achieving internalization and structure formation.

3. "Self-state" dreams and perverse dreams may well be different expressions of the
same phenomenon, especially if we accept Kohut's view that it is "specific circumscribed
disturbances in the narcissistic realm which are usually the nucleus of these widespread
disorders" (1971, p. 69). However, not all perversions are accompanied by the severe
degree of narcissistic character pathology described by Kohut.

DENIAL IN PERVERSION DREAMS

A prominent mechanism involved in both manifest perverse dream and perverse symptom is denial. It occurs in response to the ego's requirement of reconciling reality with instinctual strivings and superego demands. The denying fantasy expressed in the perverse act—for example, the choice of a male partner instead of a female, dressing in female clothes contrary to anatomy, beating fantasies with multiple substitutions, displacements, changing of roles—serves the function of the ego by attempting to preserve intact the function of reality testing (Glover 1933). The patient's hallucinatory wish fulfillment in the manifest dream is one of the early expressions of the denying fantasy serving to protect the ego from overwhelming tension. Denial helps protect "the object against aggression as well as protect the ego against narcissistic mortification," and it operates "in the service of the synthetic function of the ego to resolve disturbances in the body image and sense of identity" (Moore and Rubinfine 1969, p. 33). Denial avoids painful affects around anxiety relating to threats encountered by the developing ego, involving loss of body-ego boundaries, self-concept, loss of object, loss of love, and superego disapproval. The need-satisfying object is provided by the self in transvestitism, by the willing participation of the female in the beating fantasy, by the body of the male in homosexuality, by the fetish protecting against body-disintegration anxiety in fetishism (Socarides 1960, Greenacre 1968, 1969). All relieve castration anxiety and diminish fear of loss of the mother. Gratifying experiences with a substitute object are invented in order to postpone pain, loneliness, disturbances in the sense of self, fears of separation, and the painful awarenesss of the loss of the object.

In repetition-compulsion, both asleep and awake, the pervert dramatizes the repeatedly unsuccessful attempt by the ego, both in the past and in the present, to achieve mastery of libidinal and aggressive impulses and of their archaically cathected objects. Such an ego, when faced with the task of object cathexis in the absence of suitable substitute objects and satisfactions, and in the context of threats of further impoverishment, resorts to manifest dream formation of perverse content.

PERVERSE SYMPTOMS AND PERVERSE DREAMS

In 1968, I suggested that the greatest threat to the pervert is the threat of ego dissolution or ego destruction. Salvation is achieved through the perversion, which diminishes or cancels out such threats. It should be noted that it is not the fixated erotic experience per se, the instinctual drive derivatives, that are regressively reanimated in the perversion, but rather it is the early *function* of the early experiences in "shoring up a precarious and imperiled representational world" (Stolorow et al. 1978) that is retained and regressively relied upon in the perversion in later life (Socarides 1978). To discover what is sexualized and why—that is, the specific experiences involving not only the mother and father, but other psychological factors as well—to produce a particular form of perversion, remains the ongoing task of clinical investigators in the field.

It is well known that some perverts do not enact their perversion, and therefore the perversion remains latent; or they engage in alternating forms of perverse activity, undergoing both overt and latent stages of the perversion (Socarides 1968). An ego with fewer deficiencies or subject to less stress well may resist threats to its integrity, and engagement in perverse acts does not occur, despite the appearance in the dream life of a prolific and obviously perverse content. It may well be that, in these cases, dreaming of this type may constitute a prophylactic device against the enactment of a perversion: perhaps the dream diminishes overwhelming tension states faced by an archaic ego during sleep. Commonly, however, when the patient struggles against his perversion and its enactment, he experiences emotional flooding in the form of fits of despair, crying, anxiety, often leading to suicidal preoccupation—even acts—and the fear that he is "going crazy."

Through acting out, the pervert further stabilizes his sense of self, reinforces his object relations, overcomes destructive aggression and feelings of vulnerability, and brings pleasure to an internalized self-object (Kohut 1971). The symptom represents an overcoming of his severe intrapsychic crisis by displacing and projecting the inner need and tension onto another person or object. It is a further attempt to master a traumatic internal problem through controlling the actual external object by concocting what Khan has termed "active ego-directed experimental play-action object-relations" (Khan 1965, p. 409) in which the "technique of intimacy" plays a major role. Affective release into the external world diminishes internal threats provoked by destructive aggression. Pathological internalized object relations which have led to despair and hopelessness are mitigated. The perversion is experienced as a creative and reparative act. Similarly, the absence of healthy self-esteem in relation to internal parental figures is lessened through "creating a pseudo-object relationship and mutual pleasure" (Khan). It furthermore establishes a "rudimentary mode of communication with the external object" (p. 408). The pervert, despite his attachment to the preoedipal mother, does not experience meaningful communication with either parent, and his perverse act helps break down isolation and reduces despair through contact with a real object. Because no true object relatedness is achieved through the perverse act, and no internalization of the object takes place, there is no true ego enhancement, and the perversion must be incessantly repeated. Such acting out is facilitated by: (1) deficiences in the ego, due in part to the lack of neutralized energy which has impaired the ability to control immediate responses and instinctual discharge and aggression; (2) lack of internalization of superego functions and a splitting of the superego, so that the perversion is sanctioned by the split-off part representing parental attitudes. In a primitive manner, acting out helps maintain the cohesiveness of the ego and supplies it with the opportunity to initiate reparative moves toward a real object.

The manifest perverse dream is an example of the "primitive adaptive function" (primitive goal-seeking behavior) as described by Palombo (1978). The pervert is under the control of an archaic ego whose needs must be met both in dreaming and in waking life. The adaptive function of these dreams is as important as the performance of the perverse act; both alleviate overwhelming anxiety and stabilize the sense of self. It is an attempt at mastery. The mechanisms involved—sexualization, denial, etc.—belong to an "archaic portion of the adaptive ego . . . [and are] automatisms, in the sense that they do not make use of reflective conscious thought that Freud associated with the secondary process" (Palombo 1978, p. 449).

CLINICAL APPLICATIONS

Connections made between the daytime threats to the maintenance of his psychic equilibrium, largely maintained through the practice of perversion, and their occurrence in dream life help make the patient aware of the psychic mechanisms with which he must deal and the function of his perverse activities, in the same way that analysis of the conscious and unconscious motivating factors in daily life illuminate the need for perverse acts and their function. While dreams portray aspects of his archaic ego and the class of conflict with which we have to deal, that is, an object relations conflict consisting of anxiety and guilt associated with the failure of development in the phase of self-object differentiation, a careful examination of their contents reveals healthy sectors of the patient's ego with which we can work, including elements that result from structural conflict.

Perverse symptoms are the consequence of disguise through the use of primitive mechanisms. The transformation of an ego-syntonic symptom, through the analysis of its heavy disguise and encrustations and pleasure-fulfilling functions, into ego-alien elements leads to discomfort and anxiety. This is a necessary therapeutic measure in our goal of converting the syndrome into neurotic conflict, which can then be analyzed.

Developmental deficits must be corrected in patients with perversions before we can deal therapeutically with the defensive aspects of their psychopathology in terms of the instinctual conflicts it serves to ward off. Once sufficient structuralization has taken place, one can proceed with the analysis of transference manifestations and of libidinal and aggressive conflicts. The perverse patient must be helped to develop a more stable and cohesive self-differentiation, aided in the formation of external object relations, and in the overcoming of separation anxiety and pathological early feminine identifications. While the task of therapy is to awaken the dreamer from his dream and thereby bring him to reality, a complete elimination of perverse symptoms must await the strengthening of the pervert's ego by supplying experiences that he legitimately needed but missed, before this can be successfully accomplished.

References

Arlow, J. A. (1961). Ego psychology and the study of mythology. *Journal of the American Psychoanalytic Association* 9:371–393.

———— (1963). Conflict, regression, and symptom formation. *International Journal of Psycho-Analysis* 44:12–22.

Eissler, K. (1958). Notes on the problems of technique in the psychoanalytic treatment of adolescents: with some remarks on perversion. *Psychoanalytic Study of the Child* 13:223–254.

Freud, S. (1900). The interpretation of dreams. *Standard Edition* 4:1–338 and 5:339–627.

———— (1909). Some general remarks on hysterical attacks. *Standard Edition* 9:227–234.

———— (1915–1916). Introductory lectures on psychoanalysis. *Standard Edition* 15:15–228.

———— (1920). Beyond the pleasure principle. *Standard Edition* 18:3–64.

———— (1925). Some additional notes on dream interpretation as a whole. *Standard Edition* 19:125–178.

Frosch, J. (1969). Panel report. Dreams and psychosis. *Journal of the American Psychoanalytic Association* 17:206–221.

Glover, E. (1933). The relation of perversion-formation to the development of reality-sense. *International Journal of Psycho-Analysis* 14:486–503.

—— (1960). *The Roots of Crime.* New York: International Universities Press.

Greenacre, P. (1968). Perversions: general considerations regarding their genetic and dynamic background. In *Emotional Growth,* vol. 1, pp. 307–314. New York: International Universities Press, 1971.

—— (1969). The fetish and the transitional object. In *Emotional Growth,* vol. 1, pp. 315–334. New York: International Universities Press, 1971.

Joseph, E. D. [Reporter] (1965). *Regressive ego phenomena in psychoanalysis.* In Kris Study Group, Monograph 1, pp. 68–103. New York: International Universities Press.

Katan, M. (1960). Dreams and psychosis. *International Journal of Psycho-Analysis* 41:341–351.

Khan, M. M. R. (1965). The function of intimacy and acting out in perversions. In *Sexual Behavior and the Law,* ed. R. Slovenko, pp. 397–413. Springfield, Ill.: Charles C Thomas.

Kohut, H. (1971). *The Analysis of the Self.* New York: International Universities Press.

—— (1977). *The Restoration of the Self.* New York: International Universities Press.

Lewin, B. D. (1950). *The Psychoanalysis of Elation.* New York: Norton.

—— (1952). Phobic symptoms and dream interpretation. *Psychoanalytic Quarterly* 21:295–322.

—— (1955). Clinical hints from dream studies. *Bulletin of the Menninger Clinic* 19:78–85.

—— (1958). *Dreams and the Uses of Regression.* New York: International Universities Press.

Lichtenstein, H. (1977). *The Dilemma of Human Identity.* New York: Jason Aronson.

Mahler, M. S. (1975). Discussion of Bernard L. Pacella's paper, "Early development and the *déjà vu.*" *Journal of the American Psychoanalytic Association* 23:322–326.

Moore, B. E., and Rubinfine, D. L. [Reporters] (1969). *The mechanism of denial.* In Kris Study Group, Monograph 3, pp. 3–57. New York: International Universities Press.

Noble, D. (1951). The study of dreams in schizophrenia and allied states. *American Journal of Psychiatry* 107:612–616.

Pacella, B. L. (1975). Early development and the *déjà vu. Journal of the American Psychoanalytic Association* 23:300–317.

Palombo, S. R. (1978). The adaptive function of dreams. *Psychoanalysis and Contemporary Thought* 1:443–477.

Pulver, S. E. (1978). On dreams. *Journal of the American Psychoanalytic Association* 26:673–683.

Richardson, G. A. and Moore, R. A. (1963). On the manifest dream in schizophrenia. *Journal of the American Psychoanalytic Association* 11:281–302.

Sachs, H. (1923). On the genesis of sexual perversion. *International Zeitschrift für Psychoanalyse* 9(2):172–182. Reprinted in C. W. Socarides, *Homosexuality*, trans. Hella Freud Bernays. New York: Jason Aronson, 1978.

Socarides, C. W. (1960). The development of a fetishistic perversion: the contribution of preoedipal phase conflict. *Journal of the American Psychoanalytic Association* 8:281–311.

———— (1968). *The Overt Homosexual*. New York: Grune and Stratton.

———— (1973). Sexual perversion and the fear of engulfment. *International Journal of Psychoanalytic Psychotherapy* 2:432–448.

———— (1978). *Homosexuality*. New York: Jason Aronson.

Stewart, W. (1967). Comments on the manifest content of certain types of unusual dreams. *Psychoanalytic Quarterly* 36:329–341.

Stolorow, R. D. (1975). The narcissistic function of masochism (and sadism). *International Journal of Psycho-Analysis* 56:441–448.

Stolorow, R. D., Atwood, G. E., and Ross, J. M. (1978). The representational world in psychoanalytic therapy. *International Review of Psycho-Analysis* 5:247–256.

Stolorow, R. D., and Grand, H. T. (1973). A partial analysis of a perversion involving bugs. *International Journal of Psycho-Analysis* 54:349–350.

Part III

THE DREAM IN SPECIAL
THERAPEUTIC SITUATIONS

CHAPTER 16

THE DREAM IN THE TREATMENT OF THE DISADVANTAGED

Frank M. Kline, M.D.

Current literature on dreams indicates that patients' dreams are useful to both the patient and student therapist in a low-fee teaching clinic. Fliess (1953) surveyed the analytic literature on dreams from Freud to 1950 and provides an excellent bibliography and review. Bonime (1962) thinks dreams can locate unconscious feelings and predict the course of treatment. French and Fromm (1964) describe dreams as focal conflicts. Altman (1974) regrets that dreams seem less and less interesting to psychoanalysts. Sleep physiologists say that amphetamines, alcohol, barbiturates, and tricyclics suppress dreams, and withdrawal of these substances causes nightmares. Chlorpromazine reduces dream affect. Schizophrenia and depression reduce dreaming. There is no rebound during recovery from schizophrenia, but there is during recovery from depression. Although psychotropics have obvious effects on dreaming, there is no mention of this in DiMascio and Shader (1970) or Ayd (1975). Klein and Davis (1969) note only that sleep deprivation may lead to perceptual abnormalities.

All this suggests that dreams can be used in a low-fee teaching clinic for a range of purposes. All psychiatric patients dream, and many use psychotropics. Accordingly, dreams can be used efficaciously to establish the dosage needed for therapeutically useful levels of anxiety. For example, a depressed patient should have enough medication to sleep soundly, dream little, and not be drowsy during the day. A patient on appropriate levels of phenothiazines should not have frequent or severe nightmares. Alcoholics and other substance-abusers can expect nightmares during withdrawal. Their severity can guide the withdrawal. Thus, student therapists and supervisors in low-fee clinics should be aware of the effects of chemicals on sleep and dreaming.

Dreams also provide the student therapist and supervisor with access to unstated complaints, wishes, fantasies, defenses, and transference. It is often possible to separate transference from countertransference (see cases 5, 7, and 9) through dream interpretation.

A third important use of dreams is to give the supervisor a clearer view of therapy than the trainee reports. The dream provides the supervisor with a direct communication from the patient, communication that is relatively uncluttered by the trainee's elaborations. Therapeutic stalemate, a deteriorating therapeutic alliance, an impending suicide or psychotic break, mounting unmanageable anger; anxiety, or depression can be monitored by observing sequential dreams. Increasing resistance, a desire to distance, and a wish or need for more warmth may also be revealed in dreams. The supervisor can use a patient's dream to monitor these developments, show the trainee underlying themes, and teach the practical use of dreams for treating manics, depressives, neurotics, character disorders, or good egos in temporary crisis. Dreams are as useful for work with borderline and psychotic patients as for those with better ego function.

Additionally, a patient's dream properly analyzed by a supervisor is one of the most convincing demonstrations of unconscious process and can convince students that the unconscious exists.

DREAMS TRANSCEND CULTURAL BARRIERS

Our clinic patients are multinational and multicultural. In comparing their dreams, we find that dreams are not directly related to race, culture, national origin, or social class, which suggests that basic brain programming (genetics) and the atmosphere in which humans are born, grow up, and live are quite similar. Language and minor custom may vary. Perhaps there are some minor genetic deviations, but, as demonstrated by television, cinema, plays, and dreams, there is a universal language of gestures, facial expressions, bodily movements, and dreams. Dreams seem as universal a language as art.

CLINICAL EXAMPLES

The following dreams were collected during the course of one year at a low-fee teaching clinic.

Dream of a Paranoid Schizophrenic: Case 1

"Three devils jumped out of my ear."

The patient is thirty-eight years old, Lebanese, a recent arrival in the United States, and diagnosed as having a schizophrenic reaction, paranoid type. The dream is a picturesque way of saying there is something "bad" in his ears, and he wants it out. He is using denial, splitting, and projection as defenses.

The dream tells the supervisor the patient is paranoid, probably hallucinating, and suggests some of the defense mechanisms. The patient wants to be rid of his problem and is willing to make some effort to do so. We cannot as yet directly interpret the voices as projections, but we can deal with them indirectly and use phenothiazines. More interpretive psychotherapy may be possible when anxiety decreases and there is less need for splitting and projection. The supervisor knows he should encourage the therapist to continue treatment in spite of a psychotic transference. This and subsequent dreams allowed monitoring of the dosage and indicated phenothiazines combined with psychotherapy were effective.

Homicidal Trend in a Paranoid's Dream: Case 2

"I caught my spouse in bed with the baby-sitter and poured boiling water on him. Then I drew a gun and told the baby-sitter to put her clothes on. I don't know if I killed her or not. The dream ends with me in the electric chair but before I'm executed."

The patient is a forty-one-year-old black female, married for the second time. She killed her first husband three years ago and was declared insane. Her second husband is drinking (like the first one did), and she would like to leave him but is terrified of being alone. The dream is repetitive and represents her attempt to work through guilt about murdering her first husband as well as discharging some of her anger at the present one. She is repeatedly reminding herself that if she expresses her anger directly she may wind up in the electric chair. The baby-sitter is the patient's observing ego, her superego, and the raging infant within her. She would like to kill them all, that is, get rid of the persecution of infantile demands countered by guilt and resolved by paranoia. She wants to be rid of the part that knows what is going on (observing ego).

The dream tells the therapist and supervisor that the patient is paranoid even though at the moment there may be no gross clinical evidence of psychosis. She may kill herself or her husband but at the moment neither is likely without additional provocation or stress. The therapist must reinforce her fear of punishment, discuss the problem with her husband, and help the patient to accept a more realistic view of her infantile wishes.

Both therapist and supervisor must carefully observe minor changes in this repetitive dream. For example, if the execution takes place, suicide must be most seriously considered. If, in the dream, she actually kills, homicide may be coming to the fore.

The patient is already on phenothiazines and should clearly continue. She is able to tolerate some interpretation of guilt, fear of punishment, and her reluctance to observe her psyche.

Dream Reflects Therapeutic Alliance in a Borderline: Case 3

"There is a major earthquake, and after it was over I was all right. In the second dream, security guards are looking for my parking sticker. I thought they were looking in the wrong place, but to my surprise the sticker was actually where the guards were looking, under the dash instead of on the windshield."

The patient, a thirty-year-old black female, has been in therapy for a few months. There is ambivalence in all her relationships, and she is a borderline personality. She thinks she will survive the emotional upset of therapy. To her surprise, the therapist is looking in the right place even though it seems strange. Thus, in spite of ambivalence, a therapeutic alliance is forming. She is afraid the therapist (security guard) may correct or punish but knows also he will protect her rights and is on the right track. She feels entitled to "a place to park." Even though she is depressed and feels worthless, there is a reason and place for her in life. Her right to park is hidden from her and from others. We should consider reducing the antidepressant medication since she seems committed to the therapy and is working well. There is no early morning awakening. The dreams show moderate anxiety and confidence in her physician.

Unconscious Homosexual Conflict Portrayed in Dream: Case 4

"I was looking at my mother's boyfriend's car. Mother's sweater was there. All of a sudden, the sweater was empty and fell down. Then the scene changed, and I was in the back seat having intercourse with an Oriental partner."

The patient is a twenty-eight-year-old single Caucasian male who started therapy because he was afraid of criticism, unable to start any task, and inhibited with women. His father died when he was an infant, and the patient persistently, though unconsciously, believes he killed his father. He has been in therapy for eight months. He likes his therapist, the therapist likes him, and therapy has been progressing without difficulty. The night preceding the dream he had been in bed with a girlfriend. She left the room for a minute, and he vividly felt the presence of his long dead father.

The oedipal conflict is partially resolved. The patient is able to see the mother as empty. She has nothing to give, and he no longer needs to depend on her. This makes it possible to be intimate with women. The Oriental woman suggests he is not yet comfortable with women from his own background and culture. The dream occurs in the mother's boyfriend's car, which suggests that while there is no overt oedipal rivalry, it is clearly present. Later, it will become conscious and can be expressed in words and behavior. Some confirmation of this came in the same hour. After reporting the dream, the patient suddenly remarked he was afraid the doctor might grab his crotch. Then, in a seemingly unrelated remark, he said, "I don't know why I mock gay people." He is caught among love, fear, and rivalry for and with the father and in the transference. He is afraid the therapist may castrate or love him. Homosexual concerns are preconscious. Underlying the homosexual concern is his fantasy that he killed his father. He regrets this and wants and needs to work on his relationship with the father (therapist). He confuses his ambivalent desire for father's friendship and support with homosexuality and normal male rivalry with murder, which needs to be resolved. The patient does not need medication. There is a solid cooperative working relationship, and anxiety is decreasing and well within manageable levels.

Negative Transference in Dream of a Homosexual: Case 5

"I am with a group of homosexuals in a long corridor or maze with a game room at the end. Mother and some female attendants are there, too. The female attendants are constantly in the way. They are fumbling types. I try to correct them so they will not mess things up but can't. My mother is terribly entertaining to the others, but not to me. My friends are gathered around her, and I wander along the walls with the clumsy female attendants. I feel very tired and want to go home, but mother won't let me. Then I walk to the car with a package. I think it is liquor. It drops and breaks. The back of the car is full of packages, maybe liquor. There are two gypsy-type women on the sidewalk beside the car. One older, one young, pretty and flirtatious. I look into the car again and think maybe the containers are full of semen, not liquor. The flirtatious young gypsy picks up a bottle and puts it in her dress. I try to get it back. The older woman says, 'Leave her alone.' She grabs the younger one's baby and swings it at my head. I jump back. She puts the kid down. Then she comes at me with a hat pin. Next thing I know I am home, and there are no packages."

The patient is a forty-one-year-old Jewish-Protestant Caucasian homosexual. The dream occurred early in treatment and, as early dreams often do, clearly reveals dynamics and future transference.

The dream shows that the mother's narcissism interfered with the patient's development. She pushed him into the background, first as a man, then even as a clumsy "woman." The mother was two-faced, charming to others while ignoring the patient's needs and wishes and interfering with his interest in young women. He cannot relate to them without feeling he has lost something. His mother attacks him every time he tries. First, she uses his infantile needs against him; if that fails, she needles him viciously. Mother and all other women are seen as depriving and interfering. They take things and give nothing back.

We expect the patient to see the therapist as an interfering, depriving person, someone trying to steal something vital and precious. The patient thinks that if he tries to keep what is his or get back what belongs to him, the therapist will attack him in a vicious way. He may be afraid to accept anything, including interpretations. In the patient's fantasy, the therapist combines images of a baby, a young flirtatious woman, an old vicious withholding woman, a clumsy woman, and a homosexual. As the anticipated negative transference develops, the supervisor can comfortably assume the resident has not contributed to this. By early prediction, the supervisor can give the resident a convincing demonstration of transference, the unconscious, and the utility of dreams. The anxiety level in the dream is mild, indicating that the patient can be treated with little or no medication. Active interpretation is possible.

Dream Reveals Punitive Superego in a Tubercular Vietnamese: Case 6

"I was back in the Army fighting. I saw my father look very stern."
The dreamer is a thirty-one-year-old Vietnamese, recently arrived in

the United States. Unable to sleep, he is tired and without energy. There has been a history of tuberculosis, the first episode in 1964, another in 1972; he had a nervous breakdown after the second episode. Two months before the dream he coughed blood. After he knew he had tuberculosis again, he felt good, then suddenly became depressed. His doctor advised him to stop work even though he is the sole support of a large family. He is usually energetic, nervous, and active. Now he feels constantly tired and irritable—every little thing upsets him. Almost in passing, and after he reported the dream, he commented that there was much injustice in Vietnam. The dream was reported in the first week of treatment.

The patient is fighting hard against a life-threatening situation. His stern conscience tells him he must work. The dream suggests that the patient, because of his excessive sense of duty, may be working too hard and not resting enough. He is probably driving himself harder than he should. The therapist must help the patient to realistically appraise the amount of rest necessary for cure. The family should understand and support proper medical care.

The supervisor should recognize this is a realistic problem and help the trainee therapist keep that firmly in mind. The student should not waste time looking for fancy dynamics, nor should energy be wasted on elaborate but unnecessary interpretations. A brief explanation to the patient and his family may resolve the depression. If not, antidepressants and supportive therapy are indicated. It may help to contact a welfare agency and see to it that the patient and his family are provided for. His stern conscience may prevent him from accepting available help. In short, this is a well-integrated patient under serious and realistic stress. Even if there were serious pathology, it should wait for "crisis resolution."

Dream Exposes Impending Psychosis: Case 7

The following is a recurrent dream: "I'm floating in a black sea, bouncing up and down. Suddenly, there is a long tunnel. I march down into the tunnel and wake up. The dream terrifies me."

The patient, thirty years old, a married male, employed as a professional entertainer, and African-born, has been in the United States for a few months. He sought treatment because of overwhelming anxiety, fear of imminent death, and insomnia. When he was fifteen he tried amphetamines and had an acute psychosis. He had a second acute psychosis when he smoked marijuana. A friend treated his disorder by putting black powder on hot coals and forcing the patient to inhale the fumes. To concentrate the smoke, the friend placed a small, tentlike cover over the patient and the coals, which resulted in panic. The patient imagined he was in hell, and subsequently he stopped using all mood-changing chemicals. Associations to the dream were the death of a younger sibling, whom he misses, and his father not coming home. The father, found confused and wandering the streets, had been put into a hospital. He returned home but never regained his health and died fourteen months later when the patient was thirteen. The patient's nightmares started shortly after his father's death.

Treatment with chlordiazepoxide, 25 mg three times a day, alleviated most of his symptoms. He had been in treatment for seven months and did well in therapy as long as he received chlordiazepoxide and supportive psychotherapy. After more intensive psychotherapy began, anxiety increased, and the patient left therapy.

The dream and associations suggest a more serious diagnosis than the student therapist's working diagnosis (acute anxiety reaction with psychophysiological features). The therapist's interpretations were evoking ominous anxiety. The patient's increased anxiety indicated that the therapist should rely more on medication and less on interpretation. Any interpretation should have aimed at his fear of abandonment; his wish to join the father in death may be interpreted after fear of abandonment is resolved. The therapist clearly missed the point. He interpreted oedipal conflict in a man struggling with unbearable preoedipal anxiety. It is not surprising that the patient quit therapy.

Dream Shows Neurotic Helplessness and Good Therapeutic Alliance: Case 8

"I was with a man at a New Year's Eve party. He asked me to dance. I gave him the phoney excuse that I had to take care of my baby. Then, I was afraid no one else would ever ask me to dance, so I told him I could dance after all."

The same night the patient had a second dream. "I was traveling somewhere and realized I could take a shorter way home, but it didn't matter much. Next time I would get it right."

"In a third dream, my boyfriend Mike appeared as a helpless drunken old man. I had to take care of him. Then, I left the room for a moment. When I came back, he was gone. I was surprised."

The patient has been unsuccessful financially and personally. She runs away from male relationships. She is afraid she will get hurt. She acts helpless and then feels pushed around when others try to direct her. She is afraid she will hurt or disappoint the people she is close to.

The three dreams recounted above were reported after six months of treatment and after a date with Bill, a man she admired. She arranged to bring several friends along on the date which she felt spoiled the evening for everyone.

In the first dream one can see that her constant babying of herself prevents a relationship with men, although she realizes that she can arrange things so that her internal baby does not interfere. This is a hopeful sign. The second dream shows she unconsciously knows that she is unnecessarily delaying her maturation. She is learning and will be able to be more direct and efficient. The last dream suggests that she no longer feels that she must limit her relationships to inadequate boyfriends who have to be taken care of.

There is no need for medication. The therapeutic alliance is solid and she is working on central problems and beginning to resolve them. The supervisor can comfortably relax and let the student therapist work. There is nothing he has to do except indicate that therapy is proceeding satisfactorily and point out the dynamics suggested by the dreams.

Resistance in Dream of a Depressive: Case 9

"I was taking subways and buses to therapy. Then, I'm with two friends driving. The car breaks down, and the three of us are too tired or too drunk to go on. We abandon the car in the middle of the highway, find a farm house, and crash [sleep]." The scene changes. The patient is alone, desperately trying to get a subway to therapy. When she gets to therapy, she finds two therapists and innumerable obstacles and complications.

This is a twenty-six-year-old single Caucasian female. She lives alone and is unemployed, living on unemployment insurance. She came to Los Angeles to be an actress. She is trying to be independent of her parents and has been in therapy four months, twice a week. She had one year of private therapy in New York with a male analyst, for which her parents paid.

The dream indicates a tolerable working alliance and an ambivalent transference—there is a mixture of dependency and independence. The dominant theme is resistance, avoidance of feeling, and constraint. The supervisor must note the resistance and keep in mind that the therapist may be avoiding as much as the patient. Both need to be aware that there are elaborate and complex maneuvers which prevent effective therapy. All interpretations must wait until the resistance is dealt with. There is no indication for medication.

Prognostic Features in Dream of an Obsessional: Case 10

"I got into an argument with someone. It was rather vague. I couldn't tell who it was. I said a lot of angry things and woke up feeling great."

The dreamer is a twenty-year-old, postgraduate student. He has a severe, punishing superego and an obsessional personality. His father is a successful, unemotional, and overly conscientious physician. The father had a serious psychotic depression a few years before the patient started therapy. The patient has been in treatment several months for "lack of relationships, difficulty dating, and the recent death of an old male friend." He was recently rejected by two girls. Immediately preceding the dream, the doctor cancelled two sessions.

Although this man is highly successful and has excellent ego function in most areas, his dream is as bare, direct, and as sparse as that of the schizophrenic Lebanese (Case 1). Dream impoverishment is typical of some obsessionals. Also typical is an argument with a vague, unidentifiable figure. It is interesting that the dream is reported in past tense. This indicates emotional distancing. Two things suggest a good prognosis. First, the patient dreams about getting into an argument even though the person is vague. Second, he wakes up feeling great, suggesting that he is breaking free of his father's pattern of inhibition and depression. The patient feels comfortable enough to report aggressive dreams and fantasies and no longer feels that he must uncomplainingly accept hard work and isolation. Even though there is sparse emotion, work should continue. In this particular case, the student therapist was discouraged by the patient's apparent lack of progress. The dream shows that the patient is forming an alliance and making progress. This makes it reasonable to continue treatment. The supervisor should encourage the student to continue the work. There is no indication for medication.

TERMINATION DREAMS

Most of the patients in our clinic disappear before a "proper" termination occurs. Some stop treatment unilaterally. Some stop and never return when the student therapist leaves the clinic. Some achieve whatever limited goals they had in mind and leave before they reach the therapist's idea of a proper ending. There were many dreams of anxious separation, but no "termination dreams" during the year I collected these dreams. Cavenar and Nash (1976) discuss dreams as signals for termination. They are convinced these dreams make their appearance before termination is discussed by analyst or analysand, but caution that dreams alone cannot indicate a termination. However, if structural changes have taken place, ego functioning is improving, and transference is resolved, termination dreams will appear. Cavenar and Nash are convinced that termination dreams indicate symptoms *will not* recur during the termination phase. Obviously, the authors cannot statistically prove these dreams are valid indicators of termination but the examples they give are convincing.

SUMMARY

Dreams are useful and should be used in low-fee teaching clinics. The supervisor should encourage the student therapist to seek and report patients' dreams. Dreams can help the student therapist and supervisor monitor impending psychosis, increasing risk of homicide or suicide, the need for medication, unspoken criticism of therapy and therapist, or the disintegration of the therapeutic alliance. Students and supervisors can see dynamics, defense mechanisms, and the balance of psychic forces.

Dreams can help the therapist decide whether or not he should deal with a realistic problem, interpret dynamics, or start or modify medication. They can guide the type and rate of therapy. They can predict acting out and allow monitoring and control of a working level of anxiety in therapy. Dreams are the most effective clinical evidence of the unconscious and its effect on behavior and beliefs. Properly used, dream interpretation can convince students the unconscious exists.

References

Altman, L. L. (1974). *The Dream in Psychoanalysis,* rev. ed. New York: International University Press.
Ayd, F. J. (1975). *Rational Psychopharmacology and the Right to Treatment.* Baltimore: Waverly Press.
Bonime, W. [with Florence Bonime] (1962). *The Clinical Use of Dreams.* New York: Basic Books.
Cavenar, J. O., Jr., and Nash, J. L. (1976). The dream as a signal for termination. *Journal of the American Psychoanalytic Association* 24:425–436.
DiMascio, A., and Shader, R. (1970). *Clinical Handbook of Psychopharmacology.* New York: Jason Aronson.
Fliess, R. (1953). *The Revival of Interest in the Dream.* New York: International University Press.

French, T. M., and Fromm, E. (1964). *Dream Interpretation: A New Approach.* New York: Basic Books.

Kales, A. (1969). *Sleep Physiology and Pathology: A Symposium.* Philadelphia: Lippincott.

Klein, D. F., and Davis, J. M. (1969). *Diagnosis and Drug Treatment of Psychiatric Disorders.* Baltimore: Williams and Wilkins.

CHAPTER 17

THE DREAM IN TRAUMATIC
STATES

Harold Levitan, M.D.

FAILURE OF WISH-FULFILLMENT FUNCTION IN
CATASTROPHIC DREAMS

The dreams of traumatic neurosis served as an important stimulus to
Freud's thinking. Since he could not explain the recurrence of traumatic
events in them by means of his theory of the wish fulfilling function of the
dream, he was forced to seek a new solution. The principle of the
repetition compulsion was his first attempt at a new solution (Freud
1920). He conceptualized the repetition compulsion as a primitive quasi-
instinctual force which was somehow capable, by means of repetition of
the traumatic event, of binding the excess energy originally generated by
the event within the mental apparatus. However, he did not remain
satisfied for long with the principle of the repetition compulsion as an
explanation for the recurrence of traumatic events in dreams. In his
discussion of traumatic dreams in the *New Introductory Lectures* (1933)
he omitted to mention it. He reverted instead to his old theory of the wish
fulfilling function of the dream, but at this time he referred to it in the
negative, in the sense that the recurrence of traumatic events in dreams
indicated a failure of wish fulfillment. As he put it (Freud 1933, p. 29):
"Unconscious fixation to a trauma seems to be foremost among [the]
obstacles to the function of dreaming. ... [The] dream-work ... would like
to transform the memory-traces of the traumatic event into the fulfillment of a wish," but cannot succeed in doing so.

It is important to stress that there is a vast difference between a concept such as the repetition compulsion, which attempts to account for psychopathological phenomena as the result of the operation of a function, and a concept which attempts to account for psychopathological phenomena as the result of the failure of a function. The former concept implies activity on the part of the mental apparatus while the latter concept implies passivity. The concept that failure of a function might lead to psychopathological phenomena is a novel one for psychoanalysts who are accustomed to view the development of psychopathological phenomena solely as the result of an active compromise between the agencies of the mind.

It is interesting to note in regard to this last point that attempts to explain the recurrence of traumatic events in dreams as the result of a wish fulfilling mechanism which is successful are still very much in evidence. Schur (1966), focusing on the wishes of the patient's ego rather than of his id, suggested that the patient's ego wishes to undo the trauma. The repetition of the trauma in endless variations in his dreams is, according to this hypothesis, a necessary step in the process of undoing it. Stein (1965) likewise focused on the wishes of the patient's ego rather than his id. However, he ingeniously transferred the locus of the wish from the dream itself to the post-dream waking state. He suggests that the patient incorporates the traumatic event into the dream so that he can wake up and state: "It was unreal, it did not really happen, it was just a dream!"

In this paper I will present several examples of post-traumatic dreams which bear out Freud's concept that in this type of dream the dream has failed to carry out its function. The dreams are incredibly catastrophic. The action in the manifest content of each of them progressed until total destruction of the dreamer's body had occurred. Indeed, it is clear that the failure on the part of the mental apparatus in these examples included not only the failure to fulfill wishes as was suggested by Freud, but also the failure to protect the organism from the effect of the fully realized recurrence of the trauma. The presence of the fully realized trauma in the dreams is important as regards our theory of dreams. Consideration of this phenomenon will enable me to formulate a fresh viewpoint on the nature of the post-traumatic dream.

RARITY OF CATASTROPHIC DREAMS

Dreams of this type are rare or at least are rarely reported. Kardiner (1932) is the only author besides myself (Levitan 1967, 1976–1977) who has reported them. It is significant that Freud never encountered a dream of this type. They provide data which are at variance with his clinical experience which shaped his views regarding the factors responsible for the creation of the traumatic neurosis. He dismissed the idea that the traumatic neurosis could arise as a direct result of the fear of death because, in his experience, "The unconscious seems to contain nothing that could give any content to our concept of the annihilation of life . . . " as opposed, for example, to castration, which "can be pictured on the basis of the daily experience of the faeces being separated from the body or on the basis of losing the mother's breast at weaning. But nothing resembling death can ever have been experienced; or if it has, as in fainting, it has left no observable traces behind" (Freud 1926, pp. 129–130).

WAKING LIFE TRAUMA REPRESENTED IN CATASTROPHIC DREAMS

It is evident that only a specific type of event in waking life can give rise to the experience which occurs in these dreams. The event must cause the registration in the mind of an experience in which the body is destroyed, and yet at the same time it must not destroy the actual body. In two of the cases I was able to identify the original event as a grand mal seizure which had occurred on the day before the dream. In each of the other three cases I was able to identify, albeit with less confidence, a more remote reality event which fit the above criteria.

Grand Mal Seizure: Case 1

Mrs. M, a thirty-five-year-old woman, had the following dream while hospitalized on the medical ward for a flare-up of chronic dermatomyositis: "President Nixon is going to have me shot from a cannon because it is the only way he can get rid of me. I am placed in the cannon and I am shot out. I *explode into a thousand pieces like the atomic bomb.*"

She awakened in the morning after the dream in an acute catatonic state which lasted one month. She was unable to give any associations to the dream. However, on reviewing her hospital chart, I noticed that on the day preceding the dream she had had a grand mal seizure which she did not remember.

Grand Mal Seizure: Case 2

Mrs. G, a thirty-seven-year-old woman with temporal lobe epilepsy documented by EEG, had the following dream after having had a grand mal seizure the previous day: "Someone dragged me to the Empire State building. They took me to the top and threw me down. *I splattered into pieces* at the bottom. I was dead and I was looking at the pieces. I woke up" She noted that on the day following the dream she felt very depersonalized. She was especially aware of a sense that her body did not belong to her. Her whole life appeared to her to be a waking dream. Sometimes she thought she was one of the characters on the TV screen looking out at the family.

She was unable to give any associations to the dream, and she did not herself link the dream with the seizures. She had been told that she has seizures, but like the previous patient she could not remember the actual experience while having a seizure.

This dream is identical to the dream reported by Kardiner's patient, who also had a history of convulsions. In order to avoid confusion on this issue of convulsions, it is necessary to point out that the body-shattering experience reported in these dreams definitely does not reflect an ongoing convulsion. It represents rather the memory of the convulsion. An ongoing convulsion obliterates consciousness in dreams just as it does in waking life.

Falling in Infancy: Case 3

Mrs. R, a twenty-year-old married woman, reported the following dream during a period of intense marital upset: "I am climbing the side of a mountain in the company of my husband and mother. I call out: 'Be careful because the rocks are slippery!' Then I lose my footing and fall into space. I am horrified and screaming all the way down. I see the bottom and hit with a thud, and my body *splatters in several directions*. I feel foggy and light-headed as if walking on air but I do not awaken."

In the morning she continued to feel foggy and light-headed just as she did in the dream. She also had many other feelings associated with the depersonalization syndrome including a sense of being "out of it" and a particularly annoying awareness of her body, "as though it was moving in slow motion."

Though she herself was unable to provide a conscious memory of a prior experience which could have been the template for the fall and the splattering, I was able to elicit data regarding a particular childhood experience which seemed to fit the criteria I have specified. When she was an infant, her sadistic father regularly played a game of tossing her high into the air and then catching her at the last minute. Presumably the impact of the landing which occurred at a time of life before the body image was fully consolidated produced the experience of being shattered which is reproduced in the dream. She had heard about this game which her father played with her, but, as noted above, she was unable to remember her experience of it.

Another interesting feature of this case relates to the long period of time between the presumed original traumatic event and its reappearance in the dream. The memory of the childhood experience seemed to have been evoked by a current traumatic event in her new marriage—her husband's threat to leave her. Her associations to the dream indicated that the memory of the experience of the fall and the splattering epitomized for her the dreadful fate she anticipated if her husband carried through on his threat. Apparently the ancient traumatic experience remained in repression like a time bomb until just the right chain of circumstances enabled it to emerge in the dream.

Abortion: Case 4

Mrs. M was a thirty-year-old woman being treated for frigidity and associated marital problems at the time she reported the following dream: "I see a group of Catholic boys coming towards me with dynamite. I am apprehensive . . . they throw the dynamite at me, and it explodes. I *disintegrate into a thousand pieces."* She awoke the morning after this dream with symptoms of depersonalization including a persistent feeling of dreaminess and a sense as if the world were not real.

She associated to this dream an abortion under general anaesthesia which she had undergone some ten years earlier. She remembered nothing of the experience of the operation after the anaesthetic mask was placed on her face. I am making the assumption, partly on the basis of her own associations but also because the surgical experience fits the specified criteria, that the portion of the dream in which her body disintegrates is a reenactment of her bodily experience during the operation which was recorded in a layer of her mind while it was going on. It is possible that the operation was performed under insufficient anaesthesia.

In these last two patients the clues which serve to identify the original event which is repeated in the dream are slight. However, it is important to note that even if I am not correct in my designation of the original event, the original event must have been of a similar nature which conforms to the specified criteria. Bodily events of the type which occurred in these dreams cannot be created afresh; they can only be reproduced.

In this case, as in the previous case, a long period of time elapsed between the occurrence of the presumed original traumatic event and its reappearance in the dream. Mrs. M's frigidity had begun following the abortion about which she felt extremely guilty. On the day prior to the dream, her husband had inflicted a fresh trauma upon her when he became especially abusive regarding the abortion which had occurred before their marriage. Her associations to the dream indicated that the death by explosion epitomized for her the punishment she felt she deserved. She is a devout Catholic and placed special emphasis on the fact that the boys in the dream who threw the dynamite were Catholic.

Third Degree Burns in Early Childhood: Case 5

Miss L, a twenty-three-year-old college student in intensive psychotherapy, reported the following dream early in her therapy. At the time she was involved in a series of bitter quarrels with her father.

"An old man [presumably father] with a stick walks by me. He hits me on the back of my head with the stick ... I become very angry and broke the end of the stick. . . . Then he became more angry than ever and started screaming at me . . . I ran and hid in the doorway of a building. . . . After a while I went outside on the sidewalk. . . . The man was there again. . . . He was exuding hate . . . I could feel the rush of hate from him. . . . It was like a bazooka . . . I felt myself vibrating inside. . . . Suddenly there occurred a flash of light . . . I am *exploded into a thousand bits.*"

She awoke in the morning in a very depersonalized state. Everything seemed unreal to her. She had a sense of being separated from the world by a layer of invisible glass. Her extremities also felt numb.

She immediately related the dream to a traumatic experience which had occurred when she was age one and a half. She had been standing in a bath tub talking to her mother who was doing the wash. Suddenly the pipe between the tub and the washing machine unfastened, releasing a huge jet of scalding water over her. She remembered only a flash of light before losing consciousness. She suffered third degree burns on the chest and shoulders which caused her to be hospitalized for several weeks.

The dream quoted above contained the full denouement which was woven into the action as part of a coherent narrative. In other dreams the memory of the traumatic moment occurred as an isolated experience, for example: "I am turning into a beam of white intense burning light. . . ."

In still other dreams various fragments of the traumatic experience which preceded the experience of total bodily destruction such as the perception of the flashing light, the sense of being paralyzed, and the sensation of being burned occurred as part of the narrative. For example: "I am facing a young boy. . . . His eyes are brilliant. . . . They emit *flashes of burning light* . . . I am *paralyzed* by the flash. . . . He comes close and puts his mouth over mine . . . I am overcome by passion. . . ." Or: "I am making love with my sister. . . . A feeling of pleasure is spreading in the dream . . . I suddenly feel her mouth wide open against my throat. . . . *Boiling saliva* is pouring from her throat onto my neck. . . . It's *burning* me!"

These last two dreams are especially interesting because sexual passion rather than hate is the dominant feeling in them. The fact that these dreams of passion contain fragments of the traumatic experience indicates the sharp ambivalence which lay behind her sexuality.

IMPAIRED EGO FUNCTION DURING TRAUMA

Freud (1920) has pointed out that preparedness for anxiety via hypercathexis of the receptor systems constitutes the last line of defense against stimuli entering the mental systems. It is important to note in this regard that in all five instances the patient was unable to perceive or comprehend the overwhelming stimulation at the moment the trauma occurred in real life. In the two patients with grand mal seizures the neurological event did not come within the ken of the ego's defensive functions which operate in the psychological realm. In Case 3 the ego functions of the infant were not sufficiently developed to enable her to understand the nature of the stimulation. In Case 4 the ego functions had been abolished by the anaesthesia. In Case 5 the fact that the patient had been taken off guard precluded any possibility of her grasping the nature of the stimulation.

Indeed, I did not feel it was necessary to include more detailed data on the past history or personality of these five patients because the essential factor which brought about their original powerlessness to respond to the real-life trauma seemed so obviously to be the temporary and natural state of the ego enforced by the cluster of circumstances at the moment of trauma. In other words, it seems to be the nature and timing of the trauma which thereby encountered no stimulus barrier rather than the personality upon which it impinged which was significant.

THE REINTEGRATIVE FUNCTION OF CATASTROPHIC DREAMS

The real life experience in the first four cases was unremembered and probably unrememberable in its original form due to the particular circumstances of the event which, as just mentioned, caused the nonparticipation of the ego at the instant it occurred. The patient who recalled consciously a flashing light from the moment of trauma (Case 5) was unable to recall the actual bodily experience accompanying it. Because of this nonparticipation of the ego, various functions including those involved in perception, organization, and registration of sensory impressions were not fully available. However, since the manifest content of each of the dreams does contain the shattering experience, we can assume that the portion of the original experience directly affecting the body image had been recorded as a sensory impression at some basic level in the mind by a process which did not require the participation of the waking ego. The manifest content of each of the dreams also indicates that the ego present during the dream had been able to weave the earlier unmastered sensory impressions, which are the dream's latent content, together with memories and thoughts already present in the mind to form a coherent psychological experience containing recognizable images. The creation of a coherent psychological experience in this fashion constitutes an important stage which is preliminary to the stage of actual defense because it serves to bring the trauma to the body within range of the ego's defense mechanisms, which cannot operate at the more or less neurological and imageless level of the unmastered sensory impressions. Ferenczi (1934) who had been impressed by the discrepancy in certain cases of traumatic neurosis between the amnesia for the traumatic event in the daytime and the recurrence of the traumatic event in dreams was the first to suggest that the dreams following a trauma provide a means whereby the trauma can gain psychological representation. He attributed the daytime amnesia to the powerful effects of the unexpected and overwhelming shock which acts as if it were an anaesthetic insofar as it inhibits the higher levels of the mind which are required to create imagery. He gave several examples of post-traumatic dreams which were blank presumably because the dream ego in them, in contrast to our examples, had failed in its task of translating the imageless trauma into imagery.

However, despite this important first step involving the creation of a coherent psychological experience, it is evident in all five instances that the dreaming ego could not muster sufficient resources either to modify the trauma or to awaken the sleeper prior to the denouement. The restricted constellation of functions available to the ego in the dream seems to reflect the restricted constellation of functions which had been available to the ego at the instant of the trauma in waking life. Indeed, the powerless ego of the dream may have been carried over in wholesale fashion into the dream from waking life as a part of the total representation of the traumatic event. It is possible that these post-traumatic dreams containing unmodified trauma are examples of an early stage in the process of defense against the trauma and that more successful defense occurs during later nights when in the course of many repetitions of the dream, ego functions which belong to the current ego state emerge to take the place of the functions which had been missing at the instant of trauma and in the early dreams.

It is important to note that no trace of an anxiety response is present in the dream of either of the patients with grand mal seizures. Since anxiety is the stimulus which sets in motion defensive operations in dreams as in waking life, it is completely understandable that, under conditions of its absence, the trauma is played out to its denouement. However, in the dreams of three patients (Cases 3, 4, and 5) an adequate anxiety response is discernible. In the dream of the patient in Case 5 the dreamer is initially so frightened that she runs away to hide. In the dream in Case 4 the dreamer notes that she is apprehensive as the boys carrying dynamite approach her. In Case 3 the dreamer calls out, "Be careful!" and she is aware of being "horrified" as she is falling. In these instances it is necessary to assume that even though an adequate anxiety response was present other ego functions necessary for the production of successful defensive maneuvers were not present. It is especially puzzling that these dreamers were not able to awaken prior to the denouement despite the adequate anxiety response. Apparently, even the ability to awaken which we tend to take so much for granted requires the presence of certain ego functions. The especially long period of time which elapsed in the last two cases between the occurrence of the trauma in real life and its recurrence in dreams is of great theoretical interest. Evidently, it is true that once a quantity of traumatic stimulation has slipped by the stimulus barrier it is ever after available for revivification under the proper circumstances. Freud (1926) and Rank (1929), without particular reference to dreams, had speculated about the possibility that the experience of the trauma of birth is retained in the unconscious and is available throughout life as the template for the anxiety reaction. The reoccurrence of the trauma in these instances, especially in Case 3 in which the presumed real-life trauma occurred in earliest infancy, tends to support their view.

DISSOCIATIVE RESPONSES TO CATASTROPHIC DREAMS

These dreams, involving total destruction of the body image, appear to have an effect which lasts into the next day. It is surely no coincidence that four of the patients awakened after the dream in a depersonalized state, and the fifth in a catatonic state. It is important to stress in this regard that the sequence of events reported in these dreams represent failure of the ego's defensive processes. I have suggested elsewhere (Levitan 1967, 1968, 1969, 1970, 1972, 1976–1977) that when awakening has failed to occur at a moment of intolerable trauma in a dream, an alternate response involving sudden regression into deeper sleep may take its place. This regression into deeper sleep seems to be a last ditch protective measure which is set in motion automatically when the body is threatened. Under these circumstances the dissociation between body and mind which is characteristic of the dreaming state is apparently carried over into waking life. This maintained condition of the dissociation between body and mind which is actually a state of partial nonawakening accounts well for the symptoms of depersonalization, including the splitting of the sense of self into an observing and a participating portion, the change in quality of percepts toward the unreal, and the sense of alienation of body parts.

CATASTROPHIC DREAMS AS HISTORICAL EVENTS

Freud considered the manifest dream to be merely a facade: "It is . . . like a piece of brecchia, composed of various fragments of rock held together by a binding medium" (Freud 1915–1916). Accordingly he focused his attention on the latent dream thoughts. However, these dreams, containing the full enactment of a traumatic experience which themselves produce the effect of a fresh traumatic experience, compel us to view manifest dreams, at least traumatic dreams, as historical events in their own right. It is important to remember that the pathogenic potential of traumatic events in dreams is enhanced by the fact that, in contrast to traumatic events in real life, traumatic events in dreams tend to be repetitive. It is possible to speculate that the pathogenic effect of a traumatic event lies not only in the original occurrence of the event but also in its recurrence in repetitive dreams.

References

Ferenczi, S. (1934). Gedanken uber das Trauma. *International Zeitschrift für Psychoanalyse* 20:5–12.

Freud, S. (1900). The interpretation of dreams. *Standard Edition* 4:1–338 and 5:339–627.

—— (1915–1916). Introductory lectures on psychoanalysis. *Standard Edition* 15:15–228.

—— (1920). Beyond the pleasure principle. *Standard Edition* 18:7–64.

—— (1926). Inhibitions, symptoms and anxiety. *Standard Edition* 20:77–175.

—— (1933). New introductory lectures on psycho-analysis. *Standard Edition* 22:3–182.

Kardiner, A. (1932). The bio-analysis of the epileptic reaction. *Psychoanalytic Quarterly* 1:375–483.

Levitan, H. (1967). Depersonalization and the dream. *Psychoanalytic Quarterly* 36:151–171.

—— (1968). The turn to mania. *Psychoanalytic Quarterly* 37:55–62.

—— (1969). The depersonalization process. *Psychoanalytic Quarterly* 38:97–109.

—— (1970). The depersonalization process. II. *Psychoanalytic Quarterly* 39:449–470.

—— (1972). Dreams preceding hypomania. *International Journal of Psychoanalytic Psychotherapy* 1:50–61.

—— (1976–1977). The significance of certain catastrophic dreams. *Psychotherapy and Psychosomatics* 27:1–7.

Rank, O. (1929). *The Trauma of Birth.* New York: Robert Brunner, 1952.

Schur, M. (1966). *The Id and the Regulatory Principles of Mental Functioning.* New York: International Universities Press.

Stein, M. (1965). States of consciousness in the analytic situation: including a note on the traumatic dream. In *Drives, Affects, Behavior,* vol. 2, ed. Max Schur, pp. 60–86. New York: International Universities Press.

CHAPTER 18

THE DREAM IN THE SUICIDAL SITUATION

Robert E. Litman, M.D.

People rarely commit suicide as an impulsive, unpremeditated act. Usually, the idea of suicide is first considered as a potential avenue of escape from mental pain which is felt to be intolerable. Initially, the suicide idea is alien and frightening. Other solutions to the mental pain are sought and attempted. When other alternatives fail, the suicide option becomes more attractive. Suicide is rehearsed in fantasy and reality. A weapon is selected or poison is collected, and a specific suicide plan is evolved. The person then enters in what I have called the "suicide zone" and the psychotherapist is involved in a "suicidal situation."

There are numerous conscious and unconscious motives and determinants for suicide. Any one suicide usually results from a combination of several factors. In addition to feeling hopeless and wishing to escape, suicidal persons often express the following: (1) a wish to join someone who is dead—more profoundly, an erotic desire to fuse with death; (2) self-punishment, expiation, and guilty atonement; (3) anger, rage, plans for revenge through destruction; (4) fantasies of rescue and rebirth.

In my experience, the dreams of suicidal people have in common certain basic themes, with variations among individuals according to their unique symbols and patterns of communication. The basic themes include death and dead persons; destruction of self, other people, and symbols of other people; and being trapped and struggling unsuccessfully. When the suicide plan has matured, the final decision is often signaled by peaceful dreams of taking leave.

DREAMS OF STRUGGLE AND RESIGNATION

Case 1. A fifty-year-old male lawyer was referred to psychotherapy because of depression, sleep disorder, inability to concentrate, deep pessimism, and suicidal preoccupation. He described recurring, frightening dreams, starting in childhood, often with the content that he was being gored by an animal. His first dream was the following: "There lay a piece of meat, laid out and revealed. Somehow I felt that piece of meat was me." A second dream: "This dream is similar to many others I have had. I was inside a walled building. There was a gate with the door ajar. I felt anxious, I stepped out and slammed the door shut and started away. Then I became frightened and tried to get back." The dreams indicated low self-esteem, indecision, and preoccupation with escaping from the treatment and from his life style, but he was not yet suicidal.

The patient has risen a long way from humble beginnings through hard work and some good fortune, but his high achievement aspirations were not fully realized, partly because of an intense conflict between the achievement aspirations and his dependency needs. His alcohol intake was excessive. Gradually, it became clear that he was rather poorly regarded in his profession, and his firm had indicated that he would never become a full partner. Most of the time, he was angry and dissatisfied with his work and with his home life. It became obvious that his situation at work and in his marriage was untenable and he needed to reorganize both these aspects of his life, but he felt incompetent to take action in either regard, although he made many attempts. With each failure, he became more convinced that the only solution for him was suicide, and it was only a matter of time. He dreamed he fell into a lake full of terrible rough waves and became exhausted and drowned. In other dreams, "There were things on the roof. The whole house was falling apart. The whole thing collapsed." "I was standing in the middle of dead bodies. Was I responsible?" Various treatment efforts, including antidepressant drugs and brief stays in psychiatric hospitals, were only temporarily helpful. Earlier, he had done service work in a small, rural community in a foreign country, and he came to dwell upon this experience as the one ideal time in his life. As he became more certain of his decision to kill himself, he began to dream regularly of returning to that community, with a feeling of peace and resolution.

In retrospect, I believe I underestimated the importance of alcohol in this patient. Later, I learned that the combination of depression and alcoholism carries an extremely high suicide risk, but the alcoholism has to be dealt with first, before a successful impact can be made on the basic depression and the suicidal plans (Litman and Wold 1976). Alcoholism and drug abuse provide alternatives to suicide but usually lead the person back to the suicide option, eventually. When this patient was making plans for suicide, his dreams were replete with symbols of the destruction of himself, other people, his home. Before that, he felt trapped, partly because of his superego need to conform, and partly because of his dependency need to be taken care of, and he could never open the door and walk out and stay away, except through achieving the self-destruction that was symbolized in his dreams.

Case 2. A research professor felt himself to be lacking in ambition and in talent and wondered seriously if he should not change his profession. He felt that he had gained his status through politics rather than ability. There had been one previous episode of depression which had been resolved by a temporary leave of absence from work. On a current, important project, he felt that he was not doing satisfactory work, and began to talk about ending it all by committing suicide. He was transferred to a different section where he still felt out of place and continued to have symptoms of sleeplessness, inability to concentrate and feelings of self-depreciation. Friends planned a party in honor of his fortieth birthday. The night before, he lay in bed restlessly, wondering what to do with his life. Finally sleeping, he dreamed of a large black cube which lay in his way as he tried to walk along a path, and no matter how hard he tried to move, the cube moved with him so that he could not proceed. Finally, he gave up and merged with the black cube. The dream feeling was one of resignation and peace. That day, he went to the party but was unable to face his colleagues, and instead, he abruptly left the parking lot, drove to a nearby motel, wrenched the gas pipe loose from the heater, and after writing several farewell notes, he laid on the floor by the gas jet, prepared to die. When he was found twenty-four hours later, he was still alive, but there was moderate, irreversible brain damage. The cube represented his feelings of frustration and being trapped and his inability to assert himself further. The specific personal symbolism of the large black cube had to do, in part, with the type of work he did and his modes of thought. The black cube reminded him of "entropy, black holes, no form, no matter, null and void." Giving up and merging with the cube symbolized the end of his efforts to cope and his acceptance of death.

Case 3. A seventy-year-old woman had suffered from cyclic depressions for forty years, and had made several suicide attempts. She had been treated with electric shock treatment and with antidepressant drugs, each time with only temporary success. She reported two types of dreams. Sometimes, she dreamed of being alone and abandoned. Other times, her dreams were filled with disasters: frightening earthquakes, floods, and high winds. She stated that when she was depressed, she longed for death, but tried to stay alive because her children would be hurt by her suicide. She finally did complete suicide by drowning herself around 4:00 AM in her daughter's swimming pool. The next day, I received a note from her in the mail stating that she had made the decision to drown herself and felt a great relief, together with peaceful and pleasant dreams.

During the stage of ambivalence about suicide, she had disturbing dreams in which she tried to cope with feeling alone, and with intense destructive emotions which were very frightening. The decision for suicide was associated with relief from the conflict and fear.

Case 4. A thirty-three-year-old male surgeon had become addicted to narcotics. He was married, had children, was successful in his practice, but he felt desperate, lonely, and insecure, and had become accustomed to starting his day by giving himself a shot of Demerol. In his first reported dream, he was trying to catch a train but missed it and was caught in a labyrinth. His associations indicated that it was hard for him to understand psychotherapy, that he felt trapped in his marriage and didn't know where he was going.

Efforts were made to get him off narcotics. He tried antidepressant and antipsychotic medicines. He still continued to practice surgery. He had dreams of a great explosion in which many people were injured and killed. He was then hospitalized. For a while, he felt better and reported a long elaborate dream in which he went to the land of a primitive tribe of people who knew nothing of money. Their only crop was opium and they consumed it all. Gradually, during this detailed dream in which he became the possessor of all the opium, violence broke out and he had to shoot people; there were injuries in the dream, and he felt that as a doctor, he should have been able to do something about the injuries, but he couldn't. Two days later, still in the hospital, he had a long dream about being a military surgeon in Vietnam. Everything in this dream was frustrating. He felt trapped and helpless. After leaving the hospital, he continued to have dreams of battles, rocket ships, and death.

He was put on probation for narcotics violations, separated from his wife, had another long stay in the hospital. He dreamed about antimissile defenses in Canada, all having failed and the country being bombed. Another dream about three people in an apartment: "I shot them but nothing happened." He felt that his life was wasted, dreamed frequently of opium and escaping into opium, finally died of an intentional overdose of narcotics.

He was driven towards achievement in a difficult profession but he always felt embattled in a struggle, so that his daily life produced intolerable tension and psychosomatic symptoms. These issues were symbolized in his dreams as being trapped and through violent explosions and injuries. His alternative was escape through narcotics, and in his dreams, opium came to symbolize the more permanent narcosis of extended sleep and death. The dreams also represent in their manifest content the unbridgeable gap between aggressive actions and passive dependency.

DREAMS AS SOLUTION TO A LIFE CRISIS

Case 5. An eighteen-year-old woman attempted suicide by driving her car over a cliff. The car was totally wrecked and she escaped with bruises, black eyes, and a broken shoulder. She said that the car wreck was deliberate. "I dreamed the night before that I drove the car over that particular cliff and it killed me." She felt that she could no longer tolerate living, because she was overweight, disliked her own personality, and felt totally estranged from her mother and her whole family. This dream illustrates that under certain circumstances, for instance in a suicidal crisis, the manifest content of the dream expresses what the person has in mind with very little disguise. Her dream offers suicide in a particular manner as the proposed solution to a life crisis.

Case 6. A married woman felt depressed and estranged from her husband. She dreamed there was a woman who was swimming in the ocean and became very tired. Then a bottomless hole opened up and she started to fall in. "I knew she would fall in. I saw her sinking slowly and disappearing." The next day, she cut her wrists and was taken to an emergency hospital where the injuries were repaired. That night, she dreamed that she was going through customs and a man blocked the gate, asking for her passport and would not let her through. In her first dream after entering therapy, she dreamed about someone who had died. This patient was regarded as suicidal, and was treated with antidepressant drugs, individual therapy, and marital conjoint therapy. Many months later, her husband decided that the marriage was hopeless. When he left, the patient committed suicide. The early dreams in therapy give a vivid representation of her sense of depersonalization and estrangement and her dependency on her husband or some other person to validate her passport to live or die.

EROTICISM AND GUILT IN DREAMS

Case 7. A professional woman in her forties had some somatic complaints, was terrified of growing old, and she felt trapped and all alone. "I could scream, where is everybody?" She dreamed she was on a rubber conveyor belt in a factory. Everything was black and jiggling. Voices chanting, "Come, come in this beautiful world," there was "loud, taunting Greek chorus thundering." The belt was going faster and faster, and she had a certainty that at the end of the belt it would convey her into a pit. She felt this with terror and woke up struggling. She had been helpless and terrified. In another dream, she was "into a river, chest-high, very dark and muddy, crocodiles with open mouths. Desperate to get away, but no way out." In another dream, "I was tortured in a POW camp, then liberated and then interrogated. I jumped over a cliff with my lover to escape from the police and broke both my legs." Another dream: "I was in a hospital on a ward, but in someone else's bed. They found me, I apologized. There was a great monster of a man with a bottle of pills for an overdose. I felt, they can't help me here." She thinks of death as delicious oblivion.

The patient has had active erotic fantasies for which she feels a tremendous amount of guilt. She punishes herself with waking fantasies of being cast out of her home and dying alone, and with dreams of being tortured. In her dreams, death has an erotic fulfillment aspect; there are mixtures of guilt and anger, and images of being trapped and struggling unsuccessfully.

Case 8. A forty-year-old woman became depressed after the unexpected death of her husband from cancer. She made efforts to form relationships with other men, had several love affairs, and when all of these failed, she made a serious suicide attempt with pills and was hospitalized. She said she felt a great deal of guilt over her love affairs and feels that the bible is probably right, a person should be killed for committing fornication. The principal themes of her therapy came to be guilt expiation, and atonement for her intense dependent and erotic needs. She had always been an extremely dependent person and, in fact, would prefer to have her life style, her sexual experiences, and her death ordered by someone else. The men she loved were strong but depreciated because of some physical or emotional handicap. During her therapy, there were periods of improvement, but also many negative therapeutic reactions and more than one suicide attempt. The therapist learned to predict the onset of a suicidal situation from her dreams, which would express erotic death wishes. Here is a typical example.

"In this dream, there were a lot of us, mostly mothers with children, some old grandmothers. We were on a plain going toward the horizon in a group of wagons. A big Negro is in charge of the train. He is my lover. I love him a great deal, and he really loves me too. It's terrible to love a Negro because the marriage would probably be doomed by social pressure and the children won't belong anywhere, like me. But it doesn't really matter because this is the end of the world, and we are going towards the sunset. Then I am pursuing a man who has done something wrong. If he catches me he will kill me, but I must find him. I go into a dark hallway. People tell me not to. The man puts a pale blue silk scarf around my neck. I don't make a sound, but I am terrified. This is really the end."

After such a dream, the therapist would interpret her dependent and erotic feelings together with her guilt. For example, the therapist would say approximately the following: "This is another example of your pattern. Last week you were feeling stronger, more independent, needed me less. Now you feel distanced from me, with too much expected of you, and are starting to panic. You feel guilty about wanting to hang on to me so you pay for love with your life. You want to feel overwhelmed with care and protection, smothered with kindness, killed with love. I want to reassure you that the therapy relationship is secure even when you feel stronger and more assertive. If we don't work it through now, you will feel like killing yourself tonight."

Case 9. A fifty-year-old woman had attempted suicide several times before, always in reaction to the breakup of a love affair. She was childless, married to a businessman who did not seem to know or understand her, and ignored her constant involvements with other men. These relationships which lasted from several hours to several years had provided her with an identity, and with her reason for living. She felt that her beauty was fading, that men were harder to attract and did not admire her so much or as intensely, and that she was not getting the attention she had formerly received. Efforts to develop a career or other interests were tried but she did not feel them to be rewarding. Probably, the precipitating event for her final suicide attempt was the vacation of her therapist. She waited for him to return, and in her next therapy hour, reported the following dream: "I was walking down a street with my brother and we said goodbye to each other. I turned and walked off the road into a beautiful meadow with flowers and sunshine, peaceful and lovely. He, on the other hand, walked on into a dirty, dark, dangerous alley filled with garbage and filth."

Her brother was the only person with whom she had a consistently supportive relationship, and in the dream, she was bidding goodbye to him and to the therapist. The dream's symbolism of the dirty, dark, dangerous alley indicates her low estimation of the world she plans to leave, and the beautiful meadow symbolizes her wish to be reborn into a different life style, possibly to regain her youth. Both the patient and the therapist interpreted the dream as expressing her intention to commit suicide, but the therapist did not anticipate that it would be so immediate. She died of an overdose of sleeping pills the next day.

USE OF DREAMS IN TREATMENT

Case 10. A twenty-seven-year-old mechanical engineer was being treated for a mood and thought disorder with tranquilizers and anti-depressants, and being seen for evaluation of the drug treatment once every two weeks or once every month. The patient was diagnosed as borderline schizophrenic with low self-esteem and much self-criticism. Because he was sensitive to slight rejections, he avoided social contacts and lived in social isolation, but the psychiatrist felt that the patient was doing well to work successfully and stay out of interpersonal trouble. It was a dream which first alerted the doctor to a well-developed suicidal plan.

Unexpectedly, the patient volunteered the following, "Last night I had a vivid dream. In my dream, there were two of me sitting in my jeep parked at Lookout Point in Bouqet Canyon. I was in the driver's seat holding a gold-plated gun to my head. Then the passenger (who was also me) put his hand on the gun and pulled the trigger spattering stuff all over. The one in the driver's seat said, 'Oh no!'"

Associations were to his major hobby, which is driving a four-wheel drive vehicle in the mountains and deserts. Several times he had stopped his jeep at the dream scene, a high precipice, and rehearsed the fantasy of releasing the brake and shooting himself as he went over the precipice. The effect of the dream was to mobilize the therapist to realize that occasional interviews, together with tranquilizing and antidepressant medication, were insufficient for this patient, that he needed much more human contact. The patient was given more frequent individual therapy appointments, plus group therapy, which resulted, eventually, in considerable improvement in his social adjustment and in his self-esteem.

Case 11. A thirty-five-year-old woman, who was in psychoanalysis when she and her husband separated, made a suicide attempt with sleeping pills. After this, the analyst obtained regular supervision from me. We noted that the patient was terrified when her dependency attachments were threatened. There were rapid shifts of emotion with murderous anger, then guilt, then detachment, then more anxiety. At times of conflict when she was on the verge of some impulsive self-destructive act, her dreams became violent and masochistic. "I was in surgery. Someone cut into my neck with a knife, and a flap opened up." Her estranged husband is a surgeon. She feels the divorce is cutting her open.

The mood swings became more severe. She dreamed, "My husband's grandmother was dying in a beautiful room. She looks better but she's really dying. We need to put her out of her misery, but how? Someone tells me this thin needle will do it, she won't feel a thing and it will all be over." Associations indicated the patient wanted to die and feels suicidal.

At this point, the analyst became extremely concerned, and decided to transfer the patient to a psychotherapist who also had experience with psychopharmacology. The patient was given a tricyclic antidepressant, the frequency of interviews was reduced and the therapy was much more supportive. She tried lithium carbonate medication, but stopped because of side effects. The theme of the psychotherapy became "What am I alone, without a man?" In her dreams, she began to see herself with other men. There was much emphasis on successfully caring for herself and her children. She began to work at a new job, made new friends, accepted the divorce as final.

Then her husband rejected the completed divorce settlement and talked of reconciliation. Again, her hopes and expectations were alternately raised and shattered in a renewal of their destructive interaction. In her therapy, she was frantic with helpless rage. "I dreamed all night I was sticking a knife in him. Also, there was a cat tearing everything to pieces. I was trying to restrain it. I'm sure the cat was me, I'm afraid of my own anger." The dream was interpreted to remind the patient that she was regressing into feelings of helplessness, vulnerability and great anger, and there was a danger that she might turn that anger on herself in another suicide attempt. Therefore, it was important to distance herself from the source of the painful feelings. She followed the advice to allow the lawyers to negotiate for her while she took a vacation. Later, she returned feeling in control of herself and the situation.

Case 12. A thirty-five-year-old white male, a salesman, who had made a suicide attempt in the past, requested treatment because of chronic, depressed feelings and recurrent suicidal ideas. Although he had many brief sexual encounters, he was a lonely man who had no close relationships with either sex. He was moderately successful in his business, but was afraid to take risks.

In the early stages of this case, the patient was given antidepressant drugs and he had a trial of lithium carbonate medication. After that, for several years, the anlayst had confidence in his ability to understand the patient and the patient's dreams sufficiently to interpret suicidal trends, and the patient was treated without drugs.

About six months after starting treatment, he began to live with a woman. Four or five months into this more intimate life style, it became apparent that he would have to make adjustments to change his self-centered attitudes. He became depressed, and the following dreams were associated with the depression: "I dreamed I was having brain surgery which was necessary for everybody, to transform kids into adults." His association was that the treatment was a sort of lobotomy. He thought he was being brainwashed by the analyst and that the love affair was castrating him. There were a series of subsequent dreams: "I dreamed my mother was beating my brother while I was in the shower. He was yelling and I couldn't stand it. I decided that I would have to kill her." "I was afraid I might have killed someone with a hammer that I dropped on some people from a height, but the police decided that the people had killed themselves." "I was frightened that a teacher had injected me with something." "I was robbing a bank with a bearded old man, we both had machine guns." His associations were hatred of mother and all women, suspicion and distrust of men. He didn't want to give anything to anybody. He felt that he was deprived as a child, and he was out to rob, and, if necessary, to steal to get back what he deserved. He had extremely ambivalent feelings towards the analyst and towards his housemate. After several more months, he asked her to leave. During this time, he was depressed with a few thoughts of suicide, but was not seriously suicidal.

During the next year, he began to dwell at great length on his father as a failure, as a loser, with great anger and with the feeling that there was no use going on, he was doomed to fail like his father, and he might as well kill himself and get it over with. He reported, "I woke up around 3:00 AM from a dream I had murdered someone. I felt I had to commit suicide. I felt hopeless, helpless, way down." In his dreams, he met his (dead) father who tried to sell him a used car. "What you see is what you get." He bought the old car, the brakes failed, he smashed into a concrete storefront, and he thought, "My father was found dead in a toilet." At this time, he was seriously suicidal. Interpretations of his fear of injuring the analyst and of being rejected and being abandoned helped him to hold onto the analyst as someone who was strong enough to help him. Repeatedly, in dreams, he returned to the ghetto where he was reared. "I was trying to collect rent. Some guys were following me. They had guns and they were out to get me." His associations repeated the themes of punishment for fantasies of stolen wealth and power. In his dreams, he was stabbed by assassins and dogs bit him; he was kidnapped and held hostage. He began to get some insight into the relationship between his (unconscious) omnipotent requirements of life and his frequent feeling of dissatisfaction with life. While he was still suicidal, he dreamed he was back in the ghetto. A beautiful girl was being threatened by a gang. He tried to rescue her like John Garfield in an old movie and everyone turned on him. Someone killed him, and he thought to himself, "That's the way I want to go, like a hero."

To compensate for his disappointment in his parents, he had developed narcissistic fantasies of great wealth and power. Real life, by comparison, offered meager rewards. The suicidal ideas expressed not only his despair at being trapped in the ghetto, but also a fantasy of being reborn and redeemed as a hero. With insight and working through, he could assert himself to obtain and enjoy ordinary rewards, his self-esteem improved, and the suicidal ideas were put aside.

SUICIDAL DREAMS VERSUS NEED FOR CHANGE

I must emphasize that dreams of death and destruction do not always, necessarily, or even usually, indicate suicidal situations. A psychiatrist dreamed, "My sister died." His first association involved a cousin who shot herself. He was not suicidal, but he was in the process of recognizing that he was immobilized in an untenable working situation which he had to change. The dream symbolized change and rebirth. A woman's dream of being dead, lying in a coffin, referred to her sexuality in her marriage without implying that she was suicidal.

Gutheil (1948) illustrated his paper on dreams and suicide with clinical experiences very similar to mine. His suicidal patients dreamed of persons now dead, found their road blocked, felt pessimism in the dreams, were accused of crimes, tried to run away frantically, and found themselves lost in a maze of rooms and corridors like a labyrinth. Gutheil distinguished suicidal dreams from dreams in which death symbolized something else, for instance, the end of a relationship or a fear of impotence.

According to Mintz (1968) clinical experience suggests that certain tentative hints concerning increased suicidal danger may be drawn from the manifest content of the dream. When death or suicide is viewed, either consciously or unconsciously, as revealed by dream or fantasy material as an idyllic, satisfying, or fulfilling solution to chronic conflicts and unhappiness, the danger of suicide is increased. Also, when the manifest content of the dream becomes increasingly violent and destructive, or replete with themes of dying and death or the affective component of the dreams increasingly depressive or anxious, or the expressed attitude one of giving up or surrendering, the suicidal risk is often greater.

SUICIDE AND DEPRESSION

The dreams of suicidal persons are not identical with the dreams of depressed persons, although there may be considerable overlapping, since many suicidal people are also depressed. According to Beck and Ward (1961) dreams of depressed persons are characterized by the following themes: being deprived, disappointed, mistreated; being thwarted, exploited, disgraced; being rejected and abandoned; being blamed or criticized, ridiculed; being punished or injured; being lost or losing. Dreams of death, of violence, giving up, and of peaceful departure are suggestive of a suicidal trend.

In this context, I agree with Sandler and Joffe (1959) who conceptualized mental pain as a psychobiological reaction which signals the loss or threat of loss of a desired state of well being. Mental pain is not synonomous with depression. It is only when coping attempts fail, resulting in feelings of resigned helplessness, that a depressive reaction is said to have occurred. It is quite possible for an individual to go directly from mental pain to suicide without going through a recognizable depressive reaction. For example, the path to suicide might be by way of alcoholism.

DREAM REPORTS

In a psychoanalytically oriented review of books on suicide, Warren (1976) stated that although there has been a remarkable increase of interest in the topic of suicide, one is struck by the scarcity of articles presenting psychoanalytic points of view, clinical or theoretical. The literature has few reports of longitudinal psychoanalytical studies in contrast to the numerous articles on crisis intervention, and sociological and statistical studies.

A notable exception is Binswanger's (1958) detailed report on the case of Ellen West. This patient had extensive psychiatric treatment in and out of hospitals, and she had consultations with the leading psychiatrists of her time and place. It was decided that she could not be reasonably detained in the hospital, although there was a very strong probability that she would commit suicide. At the time of her discharge from the hospital, a month before she died of an overdose, she reported, "I dreamed something wonderful: war had broken out, I was to go into the field. I said goodbye to everyone with the joyous expectation that I was soon to die. I am glad that before the end I can eat everything; I've eaten a large piece of mocha cake." (Anorexia was an important part of her symptomatology.) In other dreams, she feels sick and asks her husband to get a revolver and shoot them both; in another dream, she jumps into the ocean; and in another dream, she wants to set herself on fire.

The writer and poet, A. Alvarez, described (1970) his own dream at a time when he was still suicidal after a suicide attempt with pills.

> On Friday night I had a terrible dream. I was dancing a savage, stamping dance with my wife, full of anger and mutual threat. Gradually the movements became more and more frenzied, until every nerve and muscle in my body was stretched taut and vibrating, as though on some fierce, ungoverned electrical machine which, fraction by fraction, was pulling me apart. When I awoke, I was wet with sweat, my teeth were chattering as if I were freezing. I dozed off almost at once and again went through a similar dream: this time I was being hunted down; when the creature, whatever it was, caught me, it shook me as a dog shakes a rat, and once again every joint and nerve and muscle seemed to be rattling apart. At last, I came awake completely and lay staring at the curtains. I was wide-eyed and shuddering with fear. I felt I had tasted in my dreams the death which had been denied me in my coma. My wife was sleeping in the same bed with me, yet, she was utterly beyond my reach, I lay there for a long time, sweating and trembling. I have never felt so lonely [p. 278].

In my opinion, there are three reasons for the infrequency of psycho-analytic or dream oriented case reports on suicide. First, committed or completed suicide occurs infrequently. Second, every suicide remains ultimately something of a mystery, the psychology never fully understood.

Third, suicides of patients are painful for therapists, something they prefer to forget (Litman 1965).

Concerning frequency, for most psychiatrists and psychoanalysts, the actual suicide of a patient while in treatment or within a few months after terminating, is a rare event, occurring only once or twice in a career. On the other hand, "suicidal situations," defined as situations in which a patient has serious ideas of suicide, communicates an intention, or commits an act of self-destruction such as attempted suicide—all of these suicidal behaviors in aggregate are probably a hundred times as frequent as committed suicides. Thus, suicidal situations as special problems during treatment can be expected to occur from time to time in every psycho-therapist's practice.

Concerning the mystery, a comprehensive overview of the multiple determinants of suicide was offered by Kubie (1964). He discerned a multiplicity of interacting, often contradictory goals, purposes, fantasies, causes, and intentions. He doubted whether we could gather so many threads into any single cohesive pattern of motivation, affect, conflict, needs, impulse, symbols, and warnings. Kubie suggested that studies of the dreams of those who have attempted suicide might furnish important clues.

DREAM EXPERIMENTS

An experimental effort to explore the psychodynamics of suicide through dreams was made by Hendin (1963). Hendin gave hypnotic instruction to persons who survived a suicide attempt to have a dream corresponding to how they felt before the attempt, which might explain their motives. A number of patients did produce dreams, which Hendin interpreted. There were, for example, dreams of retaliatory abandonment, reunion through death, death as rebirth, and death as self-punishment.

One patient had made three suicide attempts, scattered over a period of some twenty to twenty-five years, each one in relationship to an unhappy love affair. Her dream was, "I was living in an apartment in Baltimore that I lived in twenty-five years ago. There were a lot of people around telling me to put on a beautiful wedding dress that was hanging on the wall, and I would not put it on." Her associations were to the first really great love of her life, which had ended painfully. In the dream, the wedding dress looked more like a shroud than like a wedding dress. Reunion with this first love was to be achieved, apparently, only through her death. In the dream, she was struggling with the fantasy of death. Another example was provided by an unemployed, middle-aged man who dreamed, "An atom bomb was falling. . . . I was in hell and about to be burned." According to Hendin, suicide for him was an act of atonement, and death a punishment he deserved for his anger and his useless life.

With a more objective research orientation, Raphling (1970) compared the dreams of persons who attempted suicide with the dreams of acutely disturbed, nonsuicidal psychiatric patients. Various aspects of manifest content were rated, and specific differences in the thematic content were found. The themes of death and destructive or violent hostility were present in dreams of suicidal patients to a significantly greater extent than in the dreams of the comparison group. Examples of dreams of suicidal patients included a dream about a dead aunt. "I was crying in the dream. I felt she had come back, that she hadn't died." Another patient reported, "I dreamed someone was drowning." Another example, "There was this man who was insane, who was trying to kill me. Every place I ran, he was trapping me."

Hendin (1975) has continued to focus on dreams in his recent investigations of college student suicides. In summary, Hendin feels that a whole generation of students have been "growing up dead." By this he means they are out of touch with their feelings, playing it cool, avoiding emotional involvement, and often unable to deal with mental pain except by numbness, drugs, depression, and suicide. The dreams reveal what the students cannot feel. For example, Hendin reports that before a suicide attempt, a young woman, Maria, dreamed of a dead cat suspended by its hind paws from a clothesline. The cat was herself. Another young woman, Cathy, had no idea why she had made a suicide attempt after a party. A dream provides the clue: "Cathy was in the car with Ray, who was driving fast to elude a man who was pursuing them. They had to abandon their car because they had a flat and they started running. The man caught up with them and shot Cathy dead." Associations revealed that Cathy had ample grounds to be angry at Ray, who has caused her much pain. Another example: the night Bill overdosed with sleeping pills, he dreamed of a teacher who represented his mother. He felt he must die young because she did.

APPEAL FUNCTION OF DREAMS

Of special importance for psychotherapists is the fact that suicidal behaviors function as "appeals." Imbedded in every suicidal situation is a fantasy of being rescued (Jensen and Petty 1958). Unfortunately, often the designated rescuers do not respond to the appeal communications. The communications may be misperceived or denied by the designated rescuers, or the rescuers themselves may be exhausted and unable to respond. Dreams of the "significant others," who might be spouse, friend, or therapist, reveal some of the elements of the immobilization reaction (Litman 1964).

For example, Mrs. A called the Suicide Prevention Center regarding her husband who had been unable to work, constantly taking sleeping pills, and talking of death and suicide. She said, "Last night, I had a horrible dream . . . that I or my husband was dead, or both of us were dead, by hanging. . . . I was confused—couldn't tell which of us was which, or which of us was dead, and who had killed us or if we had killed each other." Both husband and wife had become depressed and helpless. She rejected the urgent recommendation for immediate consultation and possible hospitalization for her husband. That day, he killed himself. Later, I talked with the wife as part of bereavement counseling interviews. I was impressed by the strong identification with her husband, the intense mutual dependency, and the unwillingness to accept any interruption in the relationship.

Sometimes, with suicidal patients, especially when they are relatively young, attractive, and intelligent and endowed with wealth or talent, therapists become closely involved with the patient they are attempting to rescue, and there are intense countertransference problems. One signal of a countertransference crisis is a dream by the therapist of the patient. Such a dream suggests the need for consultation on the case, and probably, some change in the therapeutic plan.

SUMMARY

The latent contents of the dreams of suicidal persons include multiple interacting, often contradictory, elements such as goals, purposes, fantasies, memories, motivations, affects, conflicts, and warnings. In addition, the manifest contents of the dreams of suicidal persons have in common certain basic themes, with variations among individuals according to their unique symbols and patterns of communications. These basic themes include the following: death and dead persons; destruction of self and other persons; images of being trapped and struggling unsuccessfully. When the suicide plan has matured, the final decision is often signaled by peaceful dreams of taking leave.

References

Alvarez, A. (1970). *The Savage God.* New York: Random House.

Beck, A. T., and Ward, C. H. (1961). Dreams of depressed patients. *Archives of General Psychiatry* 5:462–467.

Binswanger, L. (1958). The case of Ellen West. In *Existence,* ed. R. May. New York: Basic Books.

Gutheil, E. A. (1948). Dreams and suicide. *American Journal of Psychiatry* 2:283–294.

Hendin, H. (1963). The psychodynamics of suicide. *Journal of Nervous and Mental Disorders* 136:236–244.

―――― (1975). *The Age of Sensation.* New York: Norton.

Jensen, V. W. and Petty, T. A. (1958). Fantasy of being rescued in suicide. *Psychoanalytic Quarterly* 27:327–339.

Kubie, L. S. (1967). Multiple determinants of suicide. *Journal of Nervous and Mental Disease* 138:3–8, 1964. Revised and reprinted in *Essays in Self-Destruction,* ed. E. S. Shneidman. New York: Jason Aronson.

Litman, R. E. (1964). Immobilization response to suicidal behavior. *Archives of General Psychiatry* 11:282–285.

―――― (1965). When patients commit suicide. *American Journal of Psychotherapy* 19:570–576.

Litman, R. E., and Wold, C. I. (1967). Beyond crisis intervention. In *Suicidology: Contemporary Developments,* ed. E. S. Shneidman. New York: Grune and Stratton.

Mintz, R. S. (1968). Psychotherapy of the suicidal patient. In *Suicidal Behaviors,* ed. H. Resnik, pp. 271–296. Boston: Little, Brown.

Raphling, D. L. (1970). Dreams and suicide attempts. *Journal of Nervous and Mental Disease* 151(6):404–410.

Sandler, J., and Joffe, W. G. (1959). Toward a basic psychoanalytic model. *International Journal of Psycho-Analysis* 50:79–90.

Warren, M. (1976). On suicide. *Journal of the American Psychoanalytic Association* 24:199–234.

CHAPTER 19

NIGHTMARES

Claude T. H. Friedmann, M.D.

A journey into the nightmare is both a journey into the occult and a short sojourn through the history of psychiatry. It is, in addition, a trip into modern neurological science. Perhaps no other area of study focuses so acutely on our past and future, as regards mysterious and frightening mental disturbances. It serves as a reminder that it is only in the last few decades that emotional illness has emerged from the medieval shrouds of sorcery and spirits into the more rational concepts of the unconscious and dopamine. It further serves as a sobering lesson to those of us who have lost sight of our supernatural and irrational collective past, a fitting reminder that our scientific advances are but a few steps away from the ghosts, devils, religiosity, and parapsychology which permeate the various subcultures and strata of our diverse society.

LINGUISTIC HISTORY OF THE NIGHTMARE

The interconnection of past to present, occult to scientific, is particularly well illustrated in the vocabulary we will use in this chapter. To begin with, let's take the word "nightmare" itself. This noun is derived from both the French *couchmar* and the German *nachtmar*. A "mar" is a "devil." If you are French, you talk about the "pressing devil" which is couched upon your chest; if German, about the "night devil." At any rate, when we say the word "nightmare," we may mean many things, but we imply that a devil has come upon us while asleep.

Another term is *pavor nocturnus*. "Pavor" is Latin for "terror." We speak then of nocturnal terror. Some authors have used it as a synonym for nightmare, while others reserve it for deep sleep (stage 3–4) phenomena only, preferring to call the "bad dream" that occurs during rapid eye movement (REM) sleep a "nightmare." To add to the confusion, and really jazz up the parapsychological end of things, we have the peculiar terms "incubus attack" and "succubus attack." An incubus is a spirit or demon who "lies upon" sleeping women for the purpose of sexual intercourse. A succubus "lies under" sleeping men for the same purpose. Some nightmares, most especially stage 3 or 4 night terrors, are sometimes termed incubus attacks (Broughton 1970). In addition, night terrors are related to enuresis, somnambulism, and sleep talking (Broughton 1968). To round things out, nightmares are often a symptom within a constellation of severe diurnal psychopathology.

Broughton (1968), Fisher (1974), and others have begun to bring both the light of science and the order of classification to this murky semantics. Before summarizing their findings, however, let me say a bit more about the symptoms. It is probably no coincidence that medieval concepts, demons, devils, and *pavor* have found their way into the vocabulary of nocturnal sleep disturbances. One can hardly imagine a more terrifying event in the life of a "normal" human being than the nightmare. Fast asleep, all ego defenses down, there suddenly emerges into one's consciousness an irrational, hallucinated, emotional episode, often so frightening as to awaken the sleeper, who may well find himself in a cold sweat, his hands trembling and his breath short and labored—the nighttime equivalent, as Freud (1895) put it, of the anxiety attack.

Jones (1910) wrote of a triad: (1) dread, (2) weight on the chest, (3) paralysis. Both he, Freud, and others of their school spoke of the oedipal and psychosexual conflicts which they considered the root cause of such difficulties. Yet some (Fisher 1974) today see Freud and Jones as probably dealing with REM-sleep "bad dreams" and not with true night terrors, or at least as not clearly differentiating between them. As terrifying as the REM nightmare is (and, I suspect, we've all had them), the true "night terror" is even more frightening.

DIFFERENCES BETWEEN NIGHTMARE AND NIGHT TERROR

Keith (1975) reviews the salient differential points which separate the REM "nightmare" or "bad dream" from the stage 3–4 "night terror." In so doing, he points us further along the trail blazed by the analysts: out of the Middle Ages and into the age of science. He also gets us into a position to understand Fisher and Broughton, which will prepare us for trying to understand our case study. A night terror, *pavor nocturnus,* possesses, according to Keith, the following features. It usually occurs during stage 4 (deep) sleep, with arousal to an awake, alpha pattern in the EEG. There is pronounced autonomic activity during the attack (fast pulse, perspiration, rapid breathing); there is also pronounced physical activity (thrashing, somnambulism). Verbalizations almost always signal the onset, and there is often loud screaming. The content of the dream, if recalled, is terrifying, violent, aggressive, and of a singular nature as to the thought or emotion. The patient is confused, disoriented, and amnesic if awakened.

In contrast, the "bad dream" or "common nightmare," called by Keith the "anxiety dream," occurs during REM sleep, with only minor autonomic changes, decreased muscle tone, little physical movement, only occasional verbalizations, little screaming, and elaborate, vivid mental content. If awakened from a REM anxiety dream, the dreamer is easily calmed and quickly lucid. The memory for content is much greater in the REM "nightmare" than the night terror.

NEUROPHYSIOLOGIC MECHANISM IN NIGHT TERROR

Broughton (1968) has demonstrated that the night terror of adults and children, as well as somnambulism and nocturnal enuresis, all involve a specific neurophysiologic mechanism, namely, a sudden change in the mental state from that of deep sleep (slow-wave EEG pattern) to an arousal pattern (alpha-wave EEG). Thus, although the person is physically asleep, the brain is in a "dissociated" state of arousal. This "arousal" state is normal to all of us and occurs at regular cycles throughout the night in each and every one of us. It is in parallel with this state, interestingly enough, that virtually all night terrors occur. Why some people have night terrors, enuresis, or sleep-walking during these periods of arousal is a question we will address, albeit gingerly, later on in this chapter.

From here on, the term *nightmare* will refer to all the phenomena heretofore described (i.e., anxiety dreams, night terrors, etc.). The term *REM nightmare* will refer specifically to anxiety dreams, as opposed to night terrors.

We have just briefly traced the nightmare through its metaphysical, analytic, and scientific history and paved the way for the study of a most unusual case. Although most problems with nightmares occur in children, the adult is far from immune. Our patient, an adult, suffered from nightmares for twenty years. As we unfold her tale, we should try to answer the following questions: (1) Did she suffer from anxiety dreams or *pavor nocturnus?* (2) What is her psychiatric diagnosis? (3) What dynamics could explain her problems? (4) Are we dealing with a neurophysiologic difficulty, a psychogenic illness, or a combination of both? (5) Was her treatment optimal? Without, then, further ado, the case of Miss T.

NIGHT TERROR: A CASE HISTORY

When one combines intelligence, energy, and perfectionistic traits with a degree in psychology, suicide attempts, self-mutilation, and theatricity, one has the ingredients for a most complicated and fascinating therapeutic encounter. If, in addition, one adds a history of terrifying but unrecollected dreams since a rape at age eleven, one has the ingredients for a chapter in this book. If that's not enough, there's one more thing: the patient is a crack shot, and threats of violence are never very far away.

When I first met Miss T, she was sitting tensely in a chair in my office. Her legs were crossed and she was hunched forward. She stared at me with small, dark, angry eyes. Then she began to cry. She was thin. I thought at times that I was speaking to a small child. A ten year old? Yet she was thirty-one. She pleaded for my help, then kicked me in the shins. Then she cried again and apologized. Her history, given in obsessional detail, was thus wrapped in a shroud of overt, demonstrative emotion. Schizophrenia? Hysteria? Obsessive-compulsive disorder? I had, at that moment, no idea whatsoever.

What she recounted went more or less like this. She'd been "falling apart" for two years, out of work for one, and in "very bad shape" for eight weeks. Her symptoms included nervousness, insomnia, weight loss, decreased appetite, and "nightmares." In addition, she occasionally hallucinated voices. Sometimes she impulsively and uncontrollably broke objects in her room, bones in her body, or bruised her extremities. She had abused Placidyl on and off for two years, but had stopped a month before we met. She was afraid she might kill herself—she'd tried a year ago. She was even more concerned about killing someone else, most particularly the uncle with whom she lived. Guns and she were by no means strangers.

There was little doubt that she required hospitalization, and she was admitted to the Inpatient Service at the UCLA Neuropsychiatric Institute, where I helped care for her for two months. Over time, as we talked, the rest of her story unfolded. We also became friends. I didn't get kicked again. But sex, guns and violence—especially violence against men—were constant topics.

The patient was the only daughter of a rather soft-spoken, homespun, "unliberated" mother, and a hard-nosed, chauvinistic, rustic father. Indeed, "rustic" is a good term with which to describe the entire family: almost like a page out of your favorite Western. Daughters in this family were not of value: Miss T was to have been like her older and younger siblings, a son. Her father never forgave her for it. She hated him in turn, and he was to become the focus of many of our talks. Her mother never came up, until we began to have family sessions. Miss T tried very hard to be a son: she was a tomboy, got a master's degree, learned to shoot guns, wore her hair short, talked tough, and never backed away from a fight. But when we talked, and she turned inside out, I saw a very frightened little girl.

When she was about eleven, she babysat regularly for a family next door to her home. The child's father, "Larry," came in one night and raped her. He threatened to kill her younger brother, Tom, if she told anyone. Until she told me, she had lived with this hellish memory and agonizing fear, without sharing them with a soul. For twenty years the trauma was, literally, locked up inside her. It became, as it were, her personal "devil," her *nachtmar*. From that day forward the nightmares, hallucinations, and physical destruction began.

With varying frequency, over the subsequent twenty years she experienced the following: she awakens suddenly in extreme confusion and terror, often screaming, often crying for help. Then she may get intensely angry, get out of bed, and break something in her room. Once in a while the object of her rage becomes herself, and she has banged her arms and legs against the wall, kicked herself, hit herself with a hammer, and once even broken her own knee. She told me that her uncle, with whom she'd lived since age eighteen is roused by her screams. If he is able to awaken her quickly enough, the destructive behavior is aborted. Usually this is done by holding her down on the bed until she is fully awake. Her uncle has informed her that she will often scream his name aloud, or the name "Larry." She, however, never remembers a single thing. In fact, she has never recalled a single dream in her entire life—as far back as she can remember. Whatever it is that rouses and terrifies her is completely unknown to her. Ghost? Devil? Suppressed unconscious drives? Incubus? I was fascinated, but baffled.

I was even more baffled when she told me that, despite her constant "nightmares," repetitive self-mutilation, and a very lethal suicide attempt, she had never had any psychiatric care, even though she herself was a psychologist! And, what's more, her family thought she was a very normal girl! Or, at least, that's what they told her. I began to harbor the desire to meet this extraordinary family. I was not to be disappointed—colorful, to say the least, they were.

But before we go into that, let's complete the history. First off, this lady had strengths. Despite her handicaps, she obtained both an M.S. and an M.A. in psychology and counseling. She actually worked for a couple of years as a school counselor until, in April of 1970, she "overidentified" with a junior high student who, like her, had a hostile father, problems with boys, and was called "ugly" and "no good" by her peers. Our patient became extremely anxious and actually fainted upon hearing the pupil's woes. She abruptly quit her job and, after a respite, became a teacher. She didn't like teaching, so quickly left that for a job in a bank which she held for about twelve months. About a year and a half before admission (halfway through the bank job), she fell in love with "George." Six months later they became engaged. Her family organized a large engagement party for them, but George never showed up. Six days later she loaded her shotgun, called him up, and asked him over to her house. He arrived to find her comatose from twelve capsules of Placidyl, the loaded gun at her side. She never saw him again, and, as she put it, "Everything has gone downhill since then." This was thirteen months before admission. Thirty days later she quit her bank job; she hadn't worked since.

About three months before I met her, she began to hear voices. This was not a new phenomenon for her—she'd suffered from such things on and off since the rape. Always terrified by the voices, she nonetheless knew that they were a figment of her own imagination. They always consisted of men arguing: her uncle, father, brothers, Larry, George, and Andy.

Oh, yes, Andy. Andy was the man who finally got Miss T into treatment. He was a very effeminate, quiet, shy young man—a fitting contrast to this outwardly masculine woman. They had met at a skeet shoot, and he'd been impressed when she hit forty-nine out of fifty targets. (A fact which, I must admit, I also found impressive. My supervisor, who'd recently been shot at by one of his own patients, virtually panicked!) As Andy pressed his suit, she became nervous and hostile. He thought an encounter group might help them. When Miss T physically asaulted the group leader, Andy suggested UCLA. Two weeks later she was at my door. Andy never deserted her, but she eventually was to outgrow him. Yet she would forever be in his debt.

In the story of the rest of her past the true excitement of her case unfolds and the puzzling facts of her nightmares are revealed. Miss T was born and raised in the Los Angeles area. At age eighteen, she and her father had a severe disagreement. He felt college was wasted on females. She wanted to go. So she left home and moved a block away to the home of her bachelor Uncle Clyde, her father's brother. There she stayed until her hospitalization. Her two brothers eventually married, but, of course, she did not. She loved and idolized her younger brother but loathed the older one. She had never used alcohol, but, as stated above, had abused Placidyl. Physically, she always had been in good health and had never required medications.

So, on November 19, 1973, we began to unravel the intriguing mystery of Miss T: her terrifying, repetitive dreams, her poor sexual identity, her self-destructive impulses, auditory hallucinations, and suicidal thoughts. Although we never totally clarified the diagnosis, or, for that matter, the nature of her nightmares, we effected a very fine therapeutic result. What will follow is a description of her hospital course, with a special emphasis on her nightmares.

Nightmares and Hallucinations During Hospitalization

We can follow her hospital course using three threads: her nightmares and hallucinations, her medications, and her family sessions. All three intertwine, and the result is an intriguing pattern, a pattern which comes into increasing focus over time, but not without accruing a deeper texture of mystery.

We began systematically observing Miss T's nightmares shortly after her admission. She had at least one of them every night until December 21. We would be apprised of her "devil" by loud shrieks of panic, then come upon her thrashing wildly in her bed, her legs and arms rattling the side rails as she banged against them. Her fists were usually clenched, her face frozen in fear, and her eyes open. On December 6 she screamed, "Don't hit her." On December 7 she sobbed, "It is gone, it is gone!" On December 10, after a leave from the ward, during which Andy and she tried having intercourse, her night outcry was: "Larry says he'll kill them all!" The next night she yelled, "I'll kill him!" On December 14 she screamed, "Dr. Friedmann promised *he* wouldn't be here." After being awakened by the nurses, she couldn't recall who "he" was. After each nightmare, which would last from two to five minutes, she would either fall back to sleep, or, if the nurses were alarmed by the violence of her thrashing, be awakened by them. She could never remember the dream and often was reported confused and disoriented during the first minute or two after waking up.

Her *nachtmar* would begin fifteen to twenty-five minutes after falling asleep, last two to five minutes, and always be accompanied by loud screaming, talking, and much sweating and physical activity. Yet, her pulse was never recorded as greater than ninety beats per minute. When she awoke, she was unable, for a brief period, to recognize the people around her, and she often talked incoherently. About five minutes later she would fall back to sleep, exhausted, and only occasionally be bothered by a second terror in a given night. On December 17 she awakened screaming, "Larry is trying to kill Dr. Freidmann." On December 20 she yelled, "Clyde, don't." On December 21, I had one of the most extraordinary experiences of my life. And Miss T, after that, never had another nightmare.

I was "on call" and had prearranged for a videotape machine to be placed in the patient's room. She had consented to have a nightmare recorded. The nurses were instructed to phone me when it began and to turn on the machine. Around 1:00 AM I came rushing in and observed Miss T thrashing about and screaming, "Clyde, Clyde!" She then sat bolt upright in bed and opened her eyes. "Larry's gonna kill you!" But she wasn't talking to me. She looked right past me into space. I decided, on a hunch, to talk to her. "Miss T," I said, "it's Dr. F. Can you hear me?" "Who?" she whimpered. "Dr. F. You're having a dream. Tell me about it." "They're all here. Larry's gonna kill Clyde. He told me not to tell. Now he's gonna kill my brother, and you, and everyone." "Where is Larry?" "Right here in the room. Can't you see him?" "No." "He's right here." "It's only a dream. No one is here but me."

We went on like that for a good twenty minutes. Then she laid down and went to sleep. The next day we viewed the tape together. "Who's that woman?" she exclaimed. "That's not me!!"

As I said, she never had a nightmare again. In fact, she began to have, for the first time in her life, pleasant and recalled dreams! Several people viewed the tape with me. None of us was ever certain whether she was awake during it or in an altered state of consciousness.

Medications During Hospitalization

Let's go back, briefly, to December 10. That was the day Andy and she attempted sexual intercourse. She had taken off all of her clothes and laid back on his bed. But when he disrobed she literally froze in panic and couldn't move. After several attempts to mollify her, Andy gave up, dressed, and left the room. From that moment on, her auditory hallucinations became loud and constant. They consisted of the same personages who appeared during her recorded nightmare: Larry, George, Andy, Clyde, her father, and her brothers, arguing and yelling at each other, at her, and at me. Larry would often threaten to kill her, me, or us all. Subsequent to the videotaped dream, her voices reached a crescendo. It almost seemed as though her unconscious night terrors had become conscious, daytime hallucinations. We increased her thiothixene to 35 mg/day on December 22, and within a week the hallucinations were gone.

Miss T had been given thiothixene since December 14, in an attempt to quiet her auditory hallucinations and to diminish her daytime anxiety. In addition, she'd been taking diazepam since November 21. The diazepam was taken 10 mg at bedtime from that date until her discharge. The thiothixene was increased steadily from 5 mg b.i.d. on December 14 to 35 mg q.d. on December 22. When she was discharged on January 18, her regimen was 35 mg/day of thiothixene and 10 mg of diazepam at bedtime.

Family Sessions During Hospitalizations

Meanwhile, we'd been conducting the usual individual and group therapies customary to inpatient milieus, and, in addition, family therapy. Without going into all the details, we can sketch a few outstanding moments. On December 3, during the second family session, she informed her parents and uncle that she'd been raped at age eleven. Her father wept openly and hugged her, her uncle declared he'd "get Larry," and the mother almost collapsed. This was truly a noncommunicative family: silent mother, angry father, and loving uncle. Only Miss T seemed capable of talking about her feelings, at first. But after the "secret" was divulged, they all opened up. By the eighth session we were all "friends," although there was still much ambivalence in the father as to whether psychiatry had anything of value to offer. Her trust in me and the ward seemed to transcend her family's pathology, and they slowly overcame their last doubts when Uncle Clyde reported three consecutive nights without a nightmare during a weekend pass. By the time Miss T left the ward, they were all "eternally grateful."

The one sad note was for Andy. Miss T "broke up" with him on December 26. She felt all he wanted of her was "a sick patient to help," and "now that I'm healthier, he doesn't seem as excited by me anymore." Miss T was truly growing up. She was discharged on January 18, 1974, to the Day Treatment Service of our hospital, where she remained for three months before being transferred to weekly outpatient group therapy with a private therapist. She required ever-decreasing dosages of thiothixene, got a job and a boyfriend, and seemed to be making profound strides in other areas when last I heard from her, about nine months after she had left the ward.

I still puzzle over her to this day.

Differential Diagnosis

With the exception of the autonomic phenomena, our patient clearly displays the signs and symptoms of *pavor nocturnus*. The timing (first third of the night), length of episode (two to five minutes), onset with a scream, violent content, sleep talking, severe terror, lack of recall, thrashing, somnambulism, and disorientation on waking are all classical features of the stage 4 night terror. Yet the nursing staff never recorded tachycardia or hyperpnea, which are usual features of this type of nightmare. One must, I think, assume that the nurses came upon our patient too late in the process of the attack, after the pulse rate and breathing had returned to normal. After all, our ward was not a sleep lab, and staff didn't come to her until after she began to scream. We tried several times to record a sleep EEG, but Miss T never was able to fall asleep with the electrodes in place: she was too anxious to do so, and a recording was never made.

Some of the staff speculated that Miss T suffered from the anxiety dream, or REM nightmare, and others felt that her nightmares were really a theatrical feature of an hysterical personality, somehow "put on," or at least part of her hysterical neurosis. The former speculation is quickly ruled out by a second look at Keith's (1975) summary (see above). The latter is a bit harder to dismiss.

Miss T was a very histrionic, neurotic woman, with severe sexual conflicts, amnesic episodes, a great need for love and attention, labile affect, and auditory hallucinations. To assume, however, her severe terrors of twenty years' duration to be a "put on" might be a bit farfetched, especially since she fits so nicely into a classical entity. And remember, night terrors don't usually exist in isolation. As with so many others, Miss T's night terrors were not an isolated mental phenomenon in an otherwise normal personality. Flenenbaum (1976) states that the incidence of night terrors in children is roughly 3–4 percent; the incidence in adults is less. Keith (1975) notes that adult patients like Miss T, who have frequent night terrors, are generally neurotic and anxious during the day. Put another way: most adult patients who suffer from night terrors also have daytime psychopathology. Most hysterics, borderlines, schizophrenics, and so on, do not, in contrast, suffer from night terrors. She may have been severely neurotic or even psychotic, if you wish, but she also was afflicted with night terrors.

As to her overall psychiatric diagnosis, her chart reads like a summary of the DSM II. Two observers called her "schizophrenic," two others "hysterical neurosis, dissociative type," another "obsessive-compulsive neurosis," and still another "anxiety neurosis with depression." An argument could easily be made for all of these, and many an hour was spent around the table debating the merits of each classification. We tried to resolve the question with some psychological tests: the Wechsler Adult Intelligence Scale, Rorschach, and Draw-A-Person Test were given. But Miss T became acutely anxious during the testing and literally threw the materials at the psychologist while storming out of the assessment lab. Although she finally was able to return and finish them, the results were certainly contaminated. In any event, her full scale IQ came to 115, verbal IQ 123, and performance IQ 102. The "readout" was: "Anxious, intellec-tualizing, paranoid, hallucinatory, poor sexual identity." Beyond that, nobody's neck was stuck out.

I suspect that by today's light and the retrospectoscope she would be called "borderline." Her poor self-identity, constant anger, transient psychoticlike symptoms, suicidal and homicidal ideation, labile affect, difficulty with relationships and separations, and so on, clearly fall within the concept of "borderline" as summarized by Grinker et al. (1968). At the time, we treated her as an hysterical neurotic with obsessional traits, steering clear of any psychotic diagnosis, and thus, at least giving her the benefit of the therapist's positive expectation for change and recovery, an important factor in any healing process (Freidmann et al. 1978, Frank 1973).

Since the purpose of this chapter is a discussion of the nightmare, let's leave the issue of diagnosis and dive into the muddy waters of theory and therapy. Although I suspect all the mud will not settle as we proceed, some of the water, at least, may become potable. Melitta Sperling (1958) has suggested that the night terror can be split into two types: Type I, with hypermotility, psychoticlike behavior during the attack, and retrograde amnesia; and Type II, the post-traumatic night terror. In Type II the nightmare is a repetition of the trauma, and she speculates that the waking up from the nightmare is a way of mastering the trauma. Type I she sees as merging with such states as petit mal, fugue, and frank psychosis in children. The onset is early and insidious, the parents are often overtly sexually seductive to the child, and the prognosis is often poor. Our patient would seem to be a Sperling Type II, but she also has some Type I characteristics (psychoticlike states, fugue states). Perhaps, then, the distinction between Type I and II *pavor nocturnus* is somewhat of an artifact, or, at least, worthy of rethinking.

OLD WIVES' TALES ABOUT NIGHT TERROR

What is, frankly, the most fun for me at this point—and, perhaps, the most enjoyable aspect of psychiatry as a whole—is the chance to continue along the paths of the various theoretical speculations regarding night terrors. What makes the job baffling is the fact that each of the three major theoretical frameworks—the parapsychological, the analytic, and the neurobiological—can explain some or all of Miss T's affliction. But, before we do that, let's dismiss a few old wives' tales. Large adenoids or tonsils resulting in anoxia due to partial apnea, heavy meals and indigestion, and the telling of ghost stories are a sample of these, according to Stern (1915).

An incubus, as you recall, is a male demon who has intercourse with sleeping women. If I were a believer in the occult, I could easily convince myself that Miss T was being raped nightly by such a ghost or spirit. The contents of some of her outcries, the belief that Larry was with her and ready to attack all other men, would be "data" I could use to support my point. Since I am a physician and scientist, my inclination is to dismiss these speculations with the same swiftness as the "wives' tales" outlined above. But, then, I am a rather firm disciple of the Age of Reason.

THEORETICAL EXPLANATIONS
FOR NIGHT TERROR

The Freudian and neo-Freudian notions of trauma, repetition of trauma in the hope of mastery (Sperling 1958), oedipal conflicts and repressed sexual impulses, as well as Jones's (1910) notion of intense psychosexual conflict and Klein's (1932) notion of the child's aggression against the oedipal mother, all have a ring of truth to them. In Miss T we find a woman raised to be a man, a woman who hungered for her father's love and esteem and learned to despise herself and her mother, who was raped at age eleven and whose incestuous impulses must have been roused by that event. She lived with her own uncle as a combination "wife" (she did all his housework) and "child" (he controlled her at night and "fathered" her), and she was never able to achieve physical or emotional intimacy with men. Her *nachtmar* and daytime hallucinations recapitulated the intense conflicts: Larry was both her attacker and lover, her "men" constantly fought over her, her "voices" toyed with death for herself, her father, her brother, and her doctor. Clearly, the trauma of her rape, placed within the context of her family and her oedipal conflicts, could easily pave the road to her subsequent psychopathology.

But, according to Keith (1975), Fisher (1974), and Broughton (1968), there is still another necessary element before the crucible can give rise to night terrors. That element is what they term the *Disorder of Arousal*. Briefly put, there occur during each sleep cycle periods of arousal from deep (stages 3–4) sleep to an alpha (awake) EEG pattern. For most of us, these brief periods are without problem. Some people, however, do not fare so well: they have enuresis, somnambulism, or night terrors during these periods of arousal. Broughton (1968) has found that those individuals who do have these disorders are generally "hyperactive" physiologically during the entire night, and the arousal period merely pushes them "over the edge" clinically. That is, enuretic children have an increased number and depth of bladder contractions during sleep as opposed to normals; people with night terrors have increased cardiorespiratory rates throughout the night. The night terror, then, could be the "cart," not the "horse": the feeling of terror could come out of a "void" occurring in a person with an abnormality of the neurological or cardiorespiratory system. When the pulse and respiration are pushed to a super-rapid rate during the alpha arousal periods, a subjective feeling of terror might occur. The nightmare itself, the mental content, could be the "cart," that is, it would be "filled in" later as an attempt to explain the phenomenon to the victim's conscious or unconscious mind. That is, rather than having sexual conflict, and so on, as the root cause of the nightmare, the neurophysiology could trigger the terror, which in turn, as an afterthought, gives rise to mental content.

As a rule, I try to steer clear of chicken-and-egg arguments until all the evidence is in. To date, so far as I can tell, the jury is still out. Did Miss T's night terrors stem from her conflicts and trauma, her terror being the result of her repressed past intruding into the unguarded ego of deep sleep? Or did the physiological correlates of an abnormal arousal state during stage 4 sleep give rise to the physical equivalent of terror, a feeling so close to that felt during her rape at age eleven that, in her mind, the two became eventually coupled? I don't know.

THE ECLECTIC TREATMENT APPROACH

Finally, why did she get better? Was it the videotape? The family therapy? The ward milieu? Group therapy? Individual therapy? Medications? Or, as Fred Silvers and I (1977) postulated in a paper about the multimodal treatment of an obsessive-compulsive inpatient, a synergistic combination of all of these? Fisher et al. (1973) have demonstrated that diazepam in doses from 5-20 mg/day reduces stage 3–4 sleep, as well as the incidence of night terrors. They note, however, that the nightmares may go away without the stage 3–4 reduction, and, vice versa, the nightmares may remain even if the stages are completely obliterated. Miss T had been on 10 mg q.h.s. of diazepam for about thirty days when her nightmares ended. Was it cause and effect? Or a synergy? We felt at the time that the videotape replay of her night terror was the key, but maybe not. On the other hand, her night terrors did not decrease slowly over time, but dropped out suddenly, and we did not push the diazepam to the hilt. Which is to say, we don't know for sure.

In addition, there were many dramatic moments during her family therapy, such as the one when she admitted her rape to her parents. She also learned to relate to peers better, to me as a therapist, and to men in general.

I guess, to sum it all up, she and we were just plain lucky. Or were we? If we look at it another way, since ghosts, conflicts, and synapses all seem theoretically reasonable causes of night terrors, by hitting at all three areas (via videotape "exorcisms," analyticlike therapies, and medications), plus throwing in a few nonspecific and adjunctive therapeutic modalities, we both hedged our bets and attacked at all possible levels. Eclecticism may be, after all, a viable answer to the mystifying and fascinating phenomenon known as the night terror.

References

Broughton, R. J. (1968). Sleep disorders: disorders of arousal? *Science* 159:1070–1078.

————— (1970). The incubus attack. In *Sleep and Dreaming,* ed. E. Hartmann, pp. 188–192. Boston: Little, Brown.

Fisher, C. (1974). A psychophysiological study of nightmares and night terrors: II. Mental content and recall of stage 4 night terrors. *Journal of Nervous and Mental Disease* 158:174–188.

Fisher, C., Kahn, E., Edwards, A., and Davis, D. M. (1973). A psychophysiological study of nightmares and night terrors: the suppression of state 4 night terrors with diazepam. *Archives of General Psychiatry* 28:252–259.

Flenenbaum, A. (1976). Pavor nocturnus: a complication of single daily tricyclic or neuroleptic dosage. *American Journal of Psychiatry* 133:570–572.

Frank, J. D. (1973). *Persuasion and Healing: A Comparative Study of Psychotherapy.* Baltimore: Johns Hopkins University Press.

Freidmann, C. T. H., and Silvers, F. M. (1977). A multimodality approach to the treatment of obsessive-compulsive disorder. *American Journal of Psychotherapy* 31:456–465.

Friedmann, C. T. H., Procci, W. R., and Fenn, A. (1978). The role of expectation in outcome for psychotic patients. *American Journal of Psychotherapy* (in Press).

Freud, S. (1895). On the grounds for detaching a particular syndrome from neurasthenia under the description 'anxiety neurosis.' *Standard Edition* 3:87–117.

————— (1900). The interpretation of dreams, *Standard Edition* 4:1–338 and 5:339–627.

Grinker, R. R., Werble, B., and Drye, R. (1968). *The Borderline Syndrome: A Behavioral Study of Ego Functions.* New York: Basic Books.

Jones, E. (1910). On the nightmare. *American Journal of Insanity* 66:383–417.

Keith, P. R. (1975). Night terrors: a review of psychology, neurophysiology, and therapy. *Journal of the American Academy of Child Psychiatry* 14:477–489.

Klein, M. (1932). *The Psychoanalysis of Children.* London: Hogarth Press.

Sperling, M. (1958). Pavor nocturnus. *Journal of the American Psychoanalytic Association* 6:79–94.

Stern, A. (1915). Night terrors: etiology and therapy. *New York Medical Journal* 101:951–952.

Part IV

THE DREAM IN
THE VARIOUS
PSYCHOTHERAPEUTIC
MODALITIES

CHAPTER 20

THE DREAM IN PSYCHOANALYSIS

Samuel Eisenstein, M.D.

The birth of psychoanalysis and the discovery of the meaning of dreams occurred about eighty years ago, when Freud (1900) published *The Interpretation of Dreams*. Initially, dream interpretation was seen not only as the main avenue to the unconscious, but also as the most useful tool of psychoanalytic technique.

As psychoanalysis has developed, from its early to its current varied theoretical conceptions, so have approaches to the dream. At present, some analysts still consider the dream the most important technical resource for treatment. Others consider the dream no more important than any other manifestation of the patient's unconscious. This latter view of the dream may be due to: (1) the development of ego psychology, (2) emergence of new views on narcissism, and (3) other formulations which have drained interest away from the id and toward the ego and the self.

One must also include the research on sleep and dreaming, which has added a neurophysiological dimension to the previous purely psychological concept of the dream. Some have used these new laboratory researches on the dream as evidence that the dream belongs in the realm of psychobiology and has no claim to be the "royal road to the unconscious." Others see these new researches as a neurophysiological confirmation of Freud's theory of the dream, namely, that the dream is a "regressive phenomenon which returns us to primitive states in infancy" (Altman 1969).

DREAM WISHES AND INSTINCTUAL DRIVES

The idea probably accepted by many analysts is that dream content is the product of an unconscious wish which in turn is derived from an instinctual drive. Nevertheless, there are other views which regard the dream as an expression of the ego which tries, via the dream, to resolve conflictual wishes and longings and to adapt them to immediate reality. Franz Alexander (1930) stated that "not only repressed wishes but also the socially adjusted part of the personality, that is, our normal feelings, are able to produce dreams which are in a larger sense wish fulfillments, although not fulfillments of asocial repressed wishes, but of the claims of conscience. Guilt feelings or the sense of duty disturbs the sleep as well as any genuine wish." Freud viewed the dream as an attempt to protect sleep by the aid of hallucinatory processes which are suitable to relieve disturbing tensions. Alexander, however, felt one has to consider that these tensions may also have their source in organic stimuli, unfulfilled or repressed genuine wishes, as well as claims of conscience.

The existence of symbolism is almost universally accepted, although the meanings of symbolism may be variously interpreted. One of Freud's earliest contributions to the understanding of the dream was his view that the remembered dream is only the manifest expression of the dream and that interpretation of the dream requires the patient's free associations. These associations reach to the latent content of the dream, and the real meaning of the dream is thereby uncovered.

DREAMS AND THE STRUCTURAL THEORY

The most important change in the theory of dreams took place when Freud developed the structural theory. Until the structural theory, the dream was thought to represent a conflict between the conscious and the unconscious. This concept had its flaws, and the introduction of the concept of id, ego, and superego helped eliminate some basic contradictions. The dream could now be seen as the result of conflict involving the above mentioned structures. In the structural theory, the id contains the sexual and aggressive impulses which are represented as wishes. These wishes find their expression through the dream. The ego attempts to curb these wishes when they conflict with the dictates of the superego and the restrictions imposed by reality. However, as Altman (1969) points out, the dream represents not only the conflict between the structures of the mental apparatus, it also represents the conflict between the "contending views within each one of them."

Since the introduction of the structural theory, the dream has been seen as the end result of conflict between opposing forces and the compromise reached between these forces. The structural theory also helped resolve whatever contradiction existed between the idea of wish fulfillment and unpleasant affect in dreams. Altman (1969) points out that the concept of a division of the mental apparatus into id, ego, and superego, resolves these discrepancies, and it is the conflict between the functions of the different structures that brings out unpleasant affects in the dream. The introduction of structural theory added another important element to the use of the dream in analysis, by creating an increased realization of the important role of the dream in the analysis of the transference.

A debate has been going on between those who agreed with Freud that the dream represents an expression of drives and wishes originating in infancy which are reactivated in the analysis, and those who claim the dream to be an expression of the ego without much participation of the id. Freud himself contributed to the concept that some dreams represent an attempt at mastery of past or recent traumatic events. Erikson (1954) eloquently demonstrated that dreams can perform many functions: "Dreams not only fulfill naked wishes of sexual license, of unlimited dominance and of unrestricted destructiveness, they also lift the dreamer's isolation, appease his conscience, and preserve his identity, each in specific and instructive ways."

Here it should be added that some analytic writers on the dream, such as Leon Altman (1969) and Ralph Greenson (1970), take the view that if the dream has come to be regarded of little importance by some analysts, this is because they were educated under the influence of ego psychology, and have not had enough experience with their own dreams to be very interested in their patients's dreams. This assertion should be verified; a survey by the American Psychoanalytic Association on the present role of the dream in psychoanalysis is long overdue. Such a survey should ascertain the age and the year of graduation of respondents.

DREAM PHYSIOLOGY AND PSYCHOANALYSIS

The recent research on sleep and dreaming seems to have come near to Freud's original hopes that his psychology could eventually be based on neurophysiology. These recent discoveries, described by C. Fisher (1965), confirm the psychoanalytic view that dreaming is a universal phenomenon. Many researchers established the existence of a dream-sleep cycle, characterized by periods of dreaming and nondreaming (REM and NREM) sleep. REM indicates rapid eye movement, a phenomenon noticed in almost all those studied during sleep. REM is always present during dream periods and occurs only during stage I of the EEG. Psychoanalysts doing sleep and dream research generally agree that nonrecallers of dreams are afflicted with more unconscious anxiety than dream recallers, and nonrecallers make more use of repression in their dreams. Studies of subjects deprived of dreaming showed significant behavioral disturbances, and at the first opportunity, these subjects tried to make up for their previous dream deprivation by experiencing increased dream sleep.

Fisher discusses the psychoanalytic implications of these new findings and is impressed by how well "Freud's theory of dreaming can include many of the new recent findings." However, he thinks that some changes in the theory may be required. Fisher postulates that an important change would involve Freud's view that the function of the dream is to release instinctual drive energies and also to protect sleep. Fisher instead proposes the following view: "when the dream work is successful, and the binding of anxiety through an attempt at wish fulfillment is accomplished, sleep will be preserved." Successful dream work would appear to be the real "guardian of sleep," and the preservation of sleep is not a purpose of the dream. The new researchers show that a physiologic need for dreaming is present in the organism from birth. Thus, according to Fisher, physiology precedes psychology. However, he adds that during early childhood development, physiological mechanisms are taken over by psychobiological mechanisms, and instinctual drive discharge takes place through hallucinatory wish fulfillment. What this implies is that Freud's view on the purpose of dreaming can easily be adapted to the new empirical findings. The Freud of the early "Project for a Scientific Psychology" would have had little difficulty accepting this view. On the contrary, he would have welcomed it.

Richard M. Jones (1965) is critical of the wish-fulfillment theory, the infantile wish concept, and the statement that "in the case of adults the wish originated from the unconscious, and in the case of children, an unrepressed wish from waking life" (Freud 1900). He thinks that Freud's efforts to construct both a method of dream interpretation and a psychology of dreaming may have led in "dream psychology to reifying the interpretive concept of 'latent content' and to overgeneralizing the interpretive principle of 'dream distortion,' and in dream interpretation to misapplying the wish-fulfillment hypothesis."

CHANGING ROLE OF THE DREAM

In order to view the position of the dream in present-day psycho-analysis, one has first to accept the view that there is now no general agreement about the role of the dream. A comprehensive survey took place at the Twenty-ninth International Psychoanalytic Congress in London in 1975. In that survey, Harold Blum (1976) stresses the impor-tance of the dream as a "link in the chain of associations and a source for further associations which help to retrieve the latent meaning of the dream and other communications." Blum adds that "the dream is not only a normal regression, but a psychic state which may be especially illustra-tive of unconscious personality organization, fantasy and conflicts." Blum addresses himself to those who claim that the dream may be a source of creativity by stating that "dreaming is not a mature creative process, but may be a source and a spur to creativity." Blum placed the dream within the framework of ego psychology.

M. Masud R. Khan (1976) succinctly stated the prevailing view of the changes that have taken place in dreams in modern psychoanalysis. He says, "the dream still provides us with the most condensed, vivid and complex specimens of the conflictual, intrapsychic, intersystemic, as well as the interpersonal experience in any given individual. Furthermore, one has to admit that though our clinical usage of dreams has changed, our understanding of dreams is not significantly more than where Freud left it." Khan adds his own views about the "good" and "bad" dream. The good dream is the result of intrapsychic functions and ego capacities, that is, ability to maintain sleep and to check on primary process impulses, and to maintain an harmonious balance of day residues in order to weave the latent content into the dream itself. Khan avers that the bad dream fails in these attempts.

He then offers the idea of a "dream space," an area in which new experiences are brought forward to be accepted or rejected. How a patient uses the "dream space" determines whether a "good dream" will take place or whether the dream will fail. Khan then proceeds to develop the concept of the "dreaming experience" which he defines as a distinct psychic event not similar to the remembered dream, but rather "an entirety that actualizes the self in an unknowable way." Khan thinks that the dreaming experience influences the behavior of the individual even though it cannot be cognitively recognized or verbally expressed. The dreaming experience is not symbolic but is the result of the work of the primary process. The manifest content of the dream is an entity in itself and not just a disguised expression of the latent content.

In the dialogue, reported by Curtis and Sachs (1976) at the London Congress, Marion Milner stresses the importance of the "self" in the dream and quotes Ernest Jones' use of the term, as among things which are symbolized in the dream. Milner suggests: "It is both the drive to know the self as well as not to know the self, and not just bits of the self, but the wholeness of the self. Thus, the dream itself can be a mirror of what one is." Donald Meltzer expresses the Kleinian concept of a space inside the child's body and the mother's body. He perceives a space where psychic reality is present and where meaning is created. By participating in the patient's dreaming experience, the analyst may be able to instill new significance into the work with the patient. The dream, according to Meltzer, is an experience unto itself.

Otto Kernberg, in the same discussion (Curtis and Sachs 1976), says that clinical evidence suggests that patients experience affects differently according to their pathology. For example, in patients with some disturbance in object relations there is an increased tendency to experience something akin to persecutory anxiety in their dreams, and in even more disorganized patients terrifying experiences of emptiness and space which have lost human meaning may occur. It is well known that the term "emptiness" takes on different meanings when applied to experience of the schizoid as opposed to the depressed patient.

Angel Garma (quoted in Plata-Mujica 1976) believes that unresolved conflicts which require symbolization are both inherited and acquired experiences, woven around the day's residue. This introduction of inherited conflicts is not acceptable to most analysts. However, Garma's view that the dream is a misleading effort to resolve conflicts and traumatic situations is generally accepted. Therefore, according to this view, wish fulfillment, as seen by Freud, is not the major force behind the dream, but another attempt by the dreamer to overcome anxiety due to unresolved conflict.

Ernest Hartmann (1976) stresses the importance of the modern study of dreams and dream physiology as a new contribution to the biological foundation of the mental apparatus. He expresses the view that since there is some similarity between dream formation and the waking life of the schizophrenic, there is some hope that understanding the biology of dreaming might one day lead to increased knowledge of the biology of schizophrenia. For example, he cites promising work being conducted on the role of norepinephrine as it relates to schizophrenia.

KOHUT, THE SELF, AND THE DREAM

H. Kohut (1977) in his book, *The Restoration of the Self,* sees the existence of two types of dreams, "those expressing verbalizable latent contents (drive wishes, conflicts, and attempted conflict solutions), and those attempting, with the aid of verbalizable dream-imagery, to bind the nonverbal tensions of traumatic states (the dread of overstimulation, or of the disintegration of the self [psychosis]). Dreams of this second type portray the dreamer's dread vis-à-vis some uncontrollable tension-increase or his dread of the dissolution of the self. The very act of portraying these vicissitudes in the dream constitutes an attempt to deal with the psychological danger by covering frightening nameless processes with namable visual imagery." Kohut continues: "It is the analyst's task, with regard to the first type of dream, to follow the patient's free associations into the depth of the psyche until the formerly unconscious meaning has been uncovered. In the second type of dream, however, free associations do not lead to unconscious hidden layers of the mind; at best they provide us with further imagery which remains on the same level as the manifest content of the dream. The scrutiny of the manifest content of the dream and of the associative elaborations of the manifest content will then allow us to recognize that the healthy sectors of the patient's psyche are reacting with anxiety to a disturbing change in the condition of the self—manic overstimulation or a serious depressive drop in self-esteem—or to the threat of dissolution of the self. I call these dreams *'self-state dreams. . . . '*"

Kohut views these dreams as being similar to dreams of children and dreams of traumatic neuroses mentioned by Freud, and to the hallucinatory dreams occurring under the influence of toxic conditions of high fever. He does, of course, acknowledge the other type of dream that conforms to the structural view of conflict. He states that this latter type of dream can be analyzed with the help of free association which will uncover unconscious wishes and drives.

EMPHASIS ON MANIFEST CONTENT

There are those who, echoing Jung, stress the importance of constructive forces in the dream. Distortion and censorship are not too important.
Others see the dream more in the context of ego psychology and the dream
as an attempt to reconcile conflicting needs. The unconscious takes a
secondary role in the drama of the dream. Still others regard the dream as
an attempt to relieve the difficult problems of living. Some therapists,
who believe that man's personality is not influenced by instinctual
impulses and defenses against them, consider the dream and its symbolism as specific for the individual dreamer and for his own life experiences.
In all of these views, one can notice a departure from Freud's view of the
unconscious and the reduction of its role in dream formation and dream
symbolism.

GREENSON AND THE CLASSICAL VIEW

Some analysts stress the importance of the manifest content of the
dream at the expense of the latent content; others, while still recognizing
the cardinal role of the latent content, elevate the manifest content to
equal importance.

At this point, one should ask whether Freud's insistence on the central
role of wish fulfillment in the dream retains its primacy. After all, Freud
built his psychology of the dream around this concept. One can safely
deduce from the literature on dreams and from symposia and papers read
at psychoanalytic meetings that most analysts still subscribe to this view.
The same can be stated for Freud's view that "the interpretation of dreams
is the royal road to a knowledge of the unconscious activities of the mind"
(Freud 1900).

This classical position is well espoused by Ralph Greenson (1970) who
accepts the new findings in dream research and finds a place for such
findings among established concepts of the psychology of the dream. He
adds to these views Freud's statement that the dream is the guardian of
sleep and that sleep is necessary to protect the need to dream. The
regression from conscious ego activity and the function of the superego as
the censor of dreams is stressed by Greenson. The dream clearly reveals
the different situations in which the activities of the id, the repressed, the
unconscious ego and superego and some ego functions are present. To
this, Greenson adds that the dream offers open access to dynamic, genetic,

and economic information of great importance. No other clinical material leads to affects and drives as the dream does. He refers to the views of Freud and Lewin that the dream has a close relationship to childhood memories since both use pictorial representations. He quotes Kris who mentions the "good analytic hour," the one in which dreams are present and repressed memories are recovered. He states that the dream is the freest of free associations. Patients will more readily recognize the dream as "their own" creation, rather than accept slips of the tongue or acting out as products of their unconscious and regressed mental life.

Greenson warns about the risks of interpreting the manifest content of a dream on the basis of the analyst's theoretical persuasions. He believes that the dream is "the royal road to a knowledge of unconscious activities for both the patient and the analyst, provided the psychoanalyst is not seduced into narrow bypaths and dead end streets by technical or theoretical prejudices." A quotation from Freud's *New Introductory Lectures on Psycho-Analysis* (1933), concludes Greenson's paper: "Whenever I began to have doubts of the correctness of my wavering conclusions, the successful transformations of a senseless and muddled dream into a logical and intelligible mental process in the dreamer would renew my confidence of being on the right track."

Most analysts accept and use the basic features of the dream work: condensation, displacement, symbolism, and secondary revision. Thus, Greenson's work needs special attention precisely because it represents the views on dreams held by the majority of analysts whose views constitute the mainstream of psychoanalytic thinking today.

In the beginning, analysts eagerly employed the technique of dream analysis as the most important aspect of analysis. Much early work in analysis consisted of interpretation of dreams. Freud (1911) cautioned that dream interpretation should not be pursued in analytic treatment as an art for its own sake, but that it should be utilized in the treatment. By this, he implied that we should not use the dream as the main method of analyzing a patient's unconscious life. The dream has maintained its cardinal place in analysis, but it shares importance with the transference, free association, and the real world in which the patient lives.

HAS THE UNCONSCIOUS CHANGED?

At this point, it is appropriate to ask whether much hasn't changed in eighty years. Probably not much has changed with respect to the psychology of the dream itself. Certainly, there have been important contributions from many sources, but Freud did such gigantic work that his basic formulations have resisted the test of time. However, if the unconscious and one of its major manifestations, the dream, have not changed much, perhaps the dreamer, and certainly the world he lives in, have changed.

Have not the great convulsions during and after World War II brought new realignments in man's conscious life and possibly in his unconscious life? Why is the dream questioned today more than in the past? Has Freud's discovery been bypassed by new research? Has psychobiological research finally given us the answer so long expected by so many, Freud included? (I refer to the answer that Freud thought would come from the "test tube.") Or has something else changed that affects the unconscious mind and its most important manifestation, the dream?

The Freudian dream was born, like psychoanalysis, in the Victorian era and inevitably expressed conflicts of that era. Eighty years later, if the unconscious has not changed, certainly the kind of unconscious wishes which are repressed have radically changed. "Sexual liberation" is the expression of this change. Enormous differences between men's and women's attitudes toward sex existed in Freud's times. The attitudes toward sex among the young women and men of today are not so different from one another as they were in the past. A blurring of the boundaries has taken place. Whether for better or worse, young people today have less need to repress their sexual impulses. The dream of the young man or woman who brings a sexual partner to the parental home to sleep with under the parental roof will be different from the dreams of the parents and grandparents. In our work with patients, this is quite evident. It is much easier for people to talk about sexual fantasies today than it was in Freud's time. Women were particularly inhibited in the past. This does not imply that there is no strain or that guilt feelings have disappeared. The millenium has not arrived; it only means that today fewer people blush when talking about their sexual life. It takes much less effort today to reduce resistance when working with sexual problems presented by patients. What is true for patients is true for people in general. Magazines that sell millions of copies demonstrate that what one formerly had to dream about or indulge through fantasies is today served in glossy, colorful pages, available to anyone of any sex or age.

Has the unconscious changed? No, but what used to be repressed and made unconscious is now available to the ego and is uncensored. As long as we considered wishes from the basic drives unacceptable, dreaming was for most people one of the only ways that their drives could find discharge.

However, with the great changes in our views on sexuality, much that was only dreamed about has become available for expression in real life. Infantile sexuality, considered in adults to be perverse, has become part of sexual experimentation for many. This acceptance of sexuality has permeated all parts of the population. It is not uncommon for an analyst to hear a woman patient open up a session with a dream line, "I was sucking my friend's penis." Could anyone imagine Emily von N or Elisabeth von R bringing such a dream to Freud? Not even many of us would have heard patients express their sexual fantasies with such freedom ten or twenty years ago. Of course, there are patients who still repress such impulses and who feel guilty about such fantasies, but people are much freer than in the past.

This freedom also extends to waking life, and is not present only in dreams. Nude meetings, nude bathing, group sex, are extensively experimented with. For many people, cross-sexual involvement takes place with much less anxiety than one would have expected in the past. A young woman deeply disappointed in her relationship to her husband and to men in general, at first dreamed that she made love to a woman. Then she decided to fulfill that wish and proceeded to make love to and be loved by a woman. She reported in analysis that she didn't find the experience particularly satisfying and that she could take it or leave it. She did not become a homosexual, but the striking fact was how little anxiety, if any, was present. A man in analysis decided to join a group that swapped wives. He and his wife did this with another couple and he reported that it wasn't what he had expected. He added, "Is this supposed to be acting out one's homosexual fantasies towards the male friend?" This episode also was noteworthy for its lack of anxiety. One could say that many patients no longer are compelled to blush over their sexual activities.

Does this imply that the id drives have become more acceptable to the ego and the superego, following the concepts of the structural theory? Probably not. What has definitely changed is reality, the most important factor that the ego has to consider in its attempts at regulating the id impulses. Reality has changed considerably. For many people, there is no longer restriction of wishes and fantasies that originate in the id. The language has changed, and words that were rarely used in the past have become part of daily conversation. Our culture has changed to the extent that nudity in plays and films has become acceptable. Today's oedipus does not run the risk of blindness. Dreams clearly reflect this change. Symbolism is gradually adapting to this change. Much that used to be elaborated by the dream can now appear overtly in the manifest content, which may explain why some analysts take particular interest in the manifest sexual dream (Natterson and Gordon 1977).

Change brought about in recent years has not only affected the sexual drives, but also the aggressive drives. Here, too, we have witnessed changes that were inconceivable before the second world war. When Freud wrote about the biological condition of man and the difficulties man meets in civilized life to control or sublimate his basic drives, and the price man pays for being civilized, he considered aggressive as well as sexual drives. I regard the beginning of World War II as the nodal moment because then began an unleashing of aggression unprecedented in history. Civilized and sublimated behavior, gradually and painfully achieved in previous centuries, was massively eroded. Controlled aggression was finally "liberated" during the war. A return from the repressed was encouraged and condoned. A highly educated German officer, when interrogated at one of the war crimes trials after World War II on his participation in atrocities (nothing in his background predicted such behavior), answered, "I don't know, everybody was doing it."

As one would expect, though, the end of the war did not return the flood of aggression to its prewar channels. Modern man, witness that aggressive drives could be released from repression, found himself tempt- ed to continue what was initiated during the war. *The return of the repressed is contagious.* Freud's most pessimistic views of man have been confirmed on countless occasions. The Vietnam War gave us another example of how aggression can be "liberated." Contemporary man toler- ates aggression both as a means of entertainment and as a part of modern life. Destructive aggressive acts are taking place all over the world, in the less developed countries as well as in the highly developed and "civilized" countries of the West. The soft voice of the intellect has become more distant. However, most societies do not look on the free expression of aggressive drives with the same indulgence as they view sex. This is understandable. Aggression threatens the essence of civilization and efforts are continuously being made to return it to the repressed from which it emerged. If this is not successful, society threatens to visit on the aggressor the reprisals of the superego. This is somewhat different from what occurs in the expression of the sexual drive. Having released for a while their control over the aggressive drives, the ego and the superego are now attempting, under the threat of extinction by those drives, to limit their free expression. This is reflected in dreams in which we encounter far fewer aggressive drives that pass the limits of the ego as freely as do the sexual drives. Whether this will be successful is difficult to tell. The danger of nuclear holocaust and destruction of the civilization as we know it is always a threat hanging over mankind. It seems that man can adapt more safely and easily to lifting repressions associated with sexual rather than to aggressive drives. Sexual liberation may be progress; the liberation of aggression threatens man's survival.

References

Alexander, F. (1930). About dreams with unpleasant content. *Psychoanalytic Quarterly* 4:447–452.

Altman, L. (1969). *The Dream in Psychoanalysis*. New York: International Universities Press.

Blum, H. P. (1976). Changing use of dreams in psychoanalytic practice: dreams and free associations. *International Journal of Psycho-Analysis* 57:315–324.

Curtis, H. C., and Sachs, D. M. (1976). Dialogue on 'The changing use of dreams in psychoanalytic practice." *International Journal of Psycho-Analysis* 57:343–354.

Erikson, E. (1954). The dream specimen of psychoanalysis. *Journal of the American Psychoanalytic Association* 2:5–56.

Fisher, C. (1965). Psychoanalytic implications of recent research on sleep and dreaming. *Journal of the American Psychoanalytic Association* 13:197–303.

Freud, S. (1900). The interpretation of dreams. *Standard Edition* 4:1–338 and 5:339–627.

——— (1911). Papers on technique. The handling of dream-interpretation in psycho-analysis. *Standard Edition* 12:89–96.

——— (1933). New introductory lectures on psycho-analysis. *Standard Edition* 22:3–182.

Greenson, R. (1970). The exceptional position of the dream in psychoanalytic practice. *Psychoanalytic Quarterly* 39:519–549.

Hartmann, E. (1976). Discussion of "The changing use of dreams in psychoanalytic practice": the dream as a "royal road" to the biology of the mental apparatus. *International Journal of Psycho-Analysis* 57:331–334.

Jones. R. M. (1965). Dream interpretation and the psychology of dreaming. *Journal of the American Psychoanalytic Association* 13:304–319.

Khan, M. M. R. (1976). The changing use of dreams in psychoanalytic practice: In search of the dreaming experience. *International Journal of Psycho-Analysis* 57:325.

Kohut, H. (1977). *The Restoration of the Self*. New York: International Universities Press.

Natterson, J., and Gordon, B. (1977). *The Sexual Dream*. New York: Crown Publishers.

Plata-Mujica, C. (1976). Discussion of "The changing use of dreams in psychoanalytic practice." *International Journal of Psycho-Analysis* 57:335–341.

CHAPTER 21

THE DREAM IN
PSYCHOTHERAPY

Robert Langs, M.D.

DREAMS AND EFFECTIVE PSYCHOTHERAPY

Freud illuminated the structure and function of neuroses through his insights into dreaming (Freud 1900). As dreams are a special form of communication, they possess distinctive features. Yet they have qualities that are shared with other means of expression—memory, thought, narrative, action, and the like.

Dreams embody nonneurotic expression and yet typify a communicative mode of the neuroses as well. This mode, characterized by a predominance of primary process mechanisms, I have termed derivative, convoluted communication (Langs 1978b). The clinical study of dreams, then, provides an opportunity for understanding the basics of the listening process (Langs 1978b), and has implications for interpretive interventions and efforts to manage the framework (ground rules) of the therapeutic situation.

The present study of dreams in psychotherapy, then, is a way to consider effective psychotherapeutic practice. While the therapist should respond somewhat differently to dreams because they have certain special qualities, he should utilize the same basic principles of technique, because dreams are merely one among many means of communicating the unconscious fantasies, memories, introjects, and perceptions on which neuroses are founded, sustained, and modified.

I will develop my discussion (1) by providing a framework for my exploration of dreams, which includes an outline of the main features of the therapeutic interaction (see also, Langs 1973, 1974, 1976a,b, 1978b,c,d); (2) by discussing two principles for interpreting dreams in psychotherapy; (3) by describing some relatively unexplored aspects of dreams in psychotherapy; and (4) by presenting two case vignettes with relevant commentary and theoretical points stimulated by the content of the vignettes.

DREAMS AND THE BIPERSONAL FIELD IN PSYCHOTHERAPY

Psychoanalytically oriented insight psychotherapy is adaptational and interactional. The treatment situation is a bipersonal field with boundaries and a frame, with the patient and the therapist at opposite poles (for details, see Langs 1976a,b, 1978b,c,d), and is defined by a set of ground rules, implicit and explicit, which give this relationship its special communicative and potentially therapeutic qualities (Langs 1975b).

This unique situation is created by the patient's free associations and the therapist's capacities to establish and manage the framework and to develop verbal interventions geared toward interpretations. Basic to the process of cure are: (a) the patient's experience of an adequate therapeutic hold; (b) the therapist's ability to contain and metabolize the patient's projective identifications so as to process them toward cognitive understanding; (c) the specific cognitive insights, conflict resolution, and adaptive resources derived from the therapist's valid interpretations and reconstructions; and (d) the positive introjective identifications that accrue to the patient from a therapeutic interaction with a therapist who is effective in each of these spheres (for details, see Langs 1976a,b, 1978d).

Within the bipersonal field, the unfolding interaction is spiraling, the therapist and the patient each responding adaptively to the other's communications. The patient's communications are prompted by intrapsychically significant adaptive contexts, almost all of which pertain to the therapeutic relationship. He responds with derivative communications that contain his unconscious fantasies, memories, introjects, and perceptions (Langs 1972, 1973, 1976a, 1978b).

MANIFEST CONTENTS AND TYPE ONE AND TYPE TWO DERIVATIVES

Patient material is organized in three ways (Langs 1978b,c,d): *manifest contents,* surface phenomena without meaning for the neurosis;

Type One derivatives, readily available inferences from the manifest content, providing ill-defined clues to unconscious processes and contents; and *Type Two derivatives,* inferences organized around a specific adaptive context, which yield dynamic meaning and foster definitive interpretive interventions.

THREE TYPES OF COMMUNICATIVE FIELD

There are three basic types of communicative bipersonal fields in psychotherapy. The *Type A field* has a well-defined frame in which illusion, play, transitional space, and symbolic communication are characteristic. It involves a patient communicating through Type Two derivatives whose resistances can ultimately be interpreted on that basis. It fosters the symbolic interpretation of specific unconscious fantasies, memories, introjects, and perceptions, and their genetic underpinnings.

The *Type B field* is characterized by projective identification and action-discharge. Nonsymbolic communications discharge psychic tension and place contents and mechanisms into the object. This communicative field develops when the framework is modified or when either party uses projective identification. The therapist must introject the patient's projective identifications, metabolize and detoxify them through cognitive understanding and interpretation, and thereby return contents and mechanism in a less toxic form.

In the *Type C field,* action and language destroy the interpersonal links between the patient and the therapist, and erect barriers which seal off their inner chaos. Nonmeaning, lies, destruction of therapeutic linkage between patient and therapist, are characteristic. Patients ruminate about insignificant events (the so-called *Type C narrator;* Langs 1978b,c), or allude to meaningful adaptive contexts without producing useful Type Two derivatives. These patients, on occasion, will communicate isolated metaphors of the Type C field and mode, which must be interpreted. A therapist who contributes to this communicative field uses the psychoanalytic cliche, intending to provide meaning, but instead expresses needs to destroy true meaning and relatedness with the patient (for further details, see Langs 1978c)

It is also essential that psychotherapy take place within a well-defined field and frame and include the fundamental rule of free association. The couch may or may not be used. And it entails an attitude of containing, metabolizing, managing the frame, and interpreting on the therapist's part (for details, see especially Langs 1973, 1974, 1976a,b, 1978b,c).

PRINCIPLES OF EMPLOYING DREAMS IN PSYCHOTHERAPY

The literature on dreams in psychotherapy is relatively sparse. The prevailing view about dreams in psychotherapy is as follows. Dreams are less significant in therapy than in analysis. Meaningful associations and time for study of dreams are scant. This view holds that the therapist must work essentially with the manifest content. Sometimes, dreams are in a subordinate role. And the therapeutic relationship is secondary to outside relationships. Therefore, dreams are not used in therapy to analyze the therapeutic relationship, mistakenly alluded to as "the transference" or "transference neurosis" (see below, and Langs 1976a,b, 1978b). This viewpoint sees psychotherapy as different from psychoanalysis in that a so-called transference neurosis or analyzable transference constellation does not emerge in psychotherapy (see Langs 1976c, chapter 18).

My observations do not support this view. Every communication from the patient in psychotherapy alludes to his relationship with the therapist, in terms of transference and nontransference—pathological unconscious fantasies, memories and introjects on the one hand, and nondistorted unconscious perceptions and introjects on the other. The manifest content of the patient's associations may refer to aspects of the therapeutic relationship, or to outside interactions. But on an unconscious level, there is a consistent thread that relates the material to the therapeutic interaction. Interpretation of this interaction is the crux of therapeutic work, requiring consistent monitoring of the patient's material in this regard.

These findings are pertinent to two clinical principles of dreams in psychotherapy:

1. It is possible to make full use of dreams in psychotherapy.

Dreams have special communicative qualities which are potentially available in all other forms of material. Dreams may be reported primarily in the service of either resistances or the communication of core unconscious fantasies, memories, and introjects. The report of a dream can imply that the patient is prepared to communicate in some meaningful manner. No special variation in technique is necessary when listening to a dream (for a full discussion of the listening process, see Langs 1978b). There is a full range of possibilities in listening to, processing, and interpreting dreams in psychotherapy.

There may be limitations in the degree to which a dream can be interpreted in psychotherapy as compared to psychoanalysis. These derive from the infrequency of the sessions and the face-to-face mode. However, the therapeutic setting is only one of a number of variables that influence the analytic work with dream material. Other factors include the personality of the patient, his psychopathology, qualities in his dream report, and his ability to associate and work with dreams; the day residue or precipitant of the dream; and a wide range of factors within the therapist, involving countertransference and noncountertransference capacities. Some of these elements may enhance the work with dreams, while others are restrictive. The goal should be to work as meaningfully with dreams as one would with any other material, and to adhere to an essentially in-depth interpretive effort.

2. In responding to a dream, the fundamentals of the listening process should be consistently applied.

Most of the detailed efforts made by Freud (1900, 1905) in developing the listening process unfolded through his investigations of dreams. Because of this, and partly because dreams are definable and meaning-laden communications, much psychoanalytic understanding of listening and formulating has been developed through models based on the analysis of dreams.

Freud (1900) himself discovered the basic interaction between reality and fantasy in his study of the relationship between the day residue and the dream—more precisely, the external stimulus and the intrapsychic response. This basic adaptive model is essential to our understanding of neuroses to this day and far from fully appreciated.

In a way, it is unfortunate that Freud discovered the dream and its latent content first, and the day residue second. This occurred largely because his focus was on the intrapsychic aspects of psychopathology, more than on the interplay between reality and fantasy. If his theory of dream formation and analysis had established the day residue as its cornerstone, considerable misunderstanding might well have been avoided.

This confusion stems from starting with the manifest dream content, and tracing from there the day residue in one direction and the intrapsychic latent content in the other. However, a delineation of unconscious meanings and functions that begins with the external precipitant permits greater conceptual clarity and facilitates recognition that the basics of the listening process as applied to all other material from the patient are comparable to those which are used with dreams.

A dream is prompted by some reality stimulant or day residue (Freud 1900, Langs 1971). These adaptive contexts have manifest and latent content. In psychotherapy, these latter are usually pertinent to the therapeutic interaction. The dream is an adaptive effort and constitutes a working over, directly and indirectly, of the conscious and unconscious implications of the day residue.

The manifest dream is a direct and linear communication. Still, the dream may reveal a variety of Type Two derivatives—latent content— that involve convoluted, neurotic communication when the dream and the associations to the dream, with the day residue (adaptive context) as their nodal point, producing unconscious meanings. Without knowledge of the adaptive context, the therapist is restricted to readily available inferences, his understanding of symbols, and to the monitoring processes to be described below—the level of Type One derivatives.

The essential steps in the listening process are as follows (Langs 1978b): taking in freely and without organization; searching for the specific adaptive context for all of the material, including the dream; applying the abstracting-particularizing process to the ongoing material by identifying first-order manifest themes, generating meaningful abstractions, deriving specific second-order themes; monitoring the material in terms of the therapeutic interaction and the me/not-me interface; deriving a series of Type One derivatives in the absence of an adaptive context, while generating a series of Type Two derivatives in the presence of the primary adaptive task; and finally, evaluating all derivatives for mixtures of reality and fantasy, distortion and nondistortion, transference and nontransference.

This approach permits the processing of all of the material from the patient, for both unconscious fantasies and unconscious perceptions, and for significant defenses-resistances and contents. The primary process mechanisms first described by Freud (1900) as the means through which the latent content of a dream is transformed into the manifest content— condensation, displacement, symbolization, and considerations of representability—allude more broadly to all of the ego's unconscious defenses and cognitive capacities as they are brought into play in response to a significant adaptive stimulus and in the generation of a manifest dream.

As one is able to broaden the listening process itself, one recognizes that the dream-associational network is rich in derivative communication, and lends itself in psychotherapy to an extensive application of a basic interpretive approach. Therapeutic efforts of this kind offer the patient the best opportunity for insightful, adaptive inner change and symptom relief.

In the course of recent research into the bipersonal field, a number of insights relevant to dreams have unfolded. Here are those that have been most validated and seem most important to clinical practice.

DIFFERENCES IN DREAM REPORTS IN TYPE A, B, AND C FIELDS

In each type of communicative field, there are important differences in the ways in which patients report and associate to dreams, and in the techniques required for their processing and interpretation.

The role and function of dreams in each of the three types of communicative bipersonal field described above shed light on individual styles of dream reporting and associating. The prevailing present-day, general conception of dream communication and analysis applies only to the Type A field. Patients who use the Type A communicative mode tend to report dreams frequently. Typically, associations reveal the day residue and its unconscious links to the therapeutic interaction. Associations may be directly linked to a dream element (direct associations), or may be unrelated to the manifest elements, but nonetheless contain latent meanings when organized around the adaptive context (indirect associations). While both kinds of associations may serve the ego's defenses and be used as resistances, the day residue–manifest dream associational network will tend to reveal the unconscious meanings of these resistances. At other times, this network permits the interpretation of specific, meaningful, pathology-related unconscious fantasies, memories, introjects, and perceptions.

While the day residue–manifest dream associational network may not yield analyzable latent meaning in a particular session, Type A patients will soon shift to communicative constellations, with or without dreams, that are interpretable. For these patients, dreams represent and symbolize their inner mental world in a manner that lends itself to interpretation through the development of Type Two derivatives that can be organized around an immediate adaptive context. The latter tend to involve the therapeutic interaction. Eventually, the adaptive response can be traced out to its genetic antecedents—whether primarily in the sphere of transference or of nontransference. These patients utilize the therapeutic situation and their own communications, including dreams, as a means of conveying illusion and in an effort to generate cognitive understanding. In all, then, they meet the usual criteria for dream communication and its analysis.

In the Type B field, dreams are utilized as a means of projective identification and action-discharge (Bion 1977, Segal 1977). These patients utilize their dreams and communications to discharge and to place disturbing inner contents and defenses, and occasionally good contents, into the therapist for processing, for proxy evocations (Wangh 1962), and to manage such mental products outside of themselves. At times, dreams are also used as a vehicle for disturbing or disrupting the functioning of the therapist.

Type B patients report relatively few dreams as compared to Type A patients. Their dreams are often fragmented, quite blatant or primitive, and are responded to with intense aversion. The Type B patient will characteristically isolate his dreams or report them in rather divergent fragments. The day residue is often unclear. When available, it is difficult to relate the dream associational material to the adaptive context. Nonetheless, at times, the recognition of the dream stimulus does permit a better appreciation and metabolism of the prevailing projective identifications.

Type B patients produce few direct associations. When reported, their associations are largely an effort to read some meaning or inference from the surface of the dream. These associations tend to be highly defensive rather than dynamically meaningful. The indirect associations tend to be unrelated to the day residue–dream network. The result is a relatively fragmented associational network, difficult to contain, metabolize, and interpret.

The Type B patient has little interest in deriving understanding from the dream network, as he concentrates his efforts on projective identification and discharge. When the therapist interprets these dreams and associations, even in terms of a particular adaptive context, without alluding to their use for projective identification, these interpretations are only rarely validated (see Langs 1976b, 1978b). The focus on meaning is experienced by the patient as a failure in containing and metabolizing, and the erroneous intervention often constitutes a projective counteridentification (Grinberg 1962)—the unconscious reprojection into the patient of poorly metabolized contents and mechanisms.

A more valid intervention is derived from the introjective identification and containing of the patient's projective identifications and efforts at discharge, working them over in light of the associational material, identifying both the adaptive context and the threads of cognitive communication, and processing all of these inputs toward a cognitive interpretation of the projective function of this particular type of dream communication. It is quite crucial for the therapist to validate the impressions derived on this basis through his own subsequent subjective experiences, and especially through the patient's cognitive material (see Langs 1976a, 1978b,c,d).

The patient in a Type C communicative field seldom reports dreams. Those that are reported tend to be limited and realistic. A significant adaptive context is seldom available, and associations are sparse. The day residue–manifest dream associational matrix is filled with gaps, and lacks depth and meaning. The dream serves as an opaque barrier to therapeutic relatedness and to underlying catastrophic truths which exist within the patient, and sometimes, within the therapist and therapeutic interaction.

In a Type C field, the therapist may be confronted with another extreme: detailed dreams, without a clear-cut significant adaptive context or with so many particulars that it is not feasible to derive unconscious meanings from the patient's communications. Such patients might be termed "Type C dream narrators." They utilize extensive associations as barriers and as a means of breaking meaningful ties between themselves and their therapists. These patients often associate in terms of Type One derivatives, repeatedly suggesting implicit and often obvious meanings for the many dream elements reported. They treat their dreams like detached observers attempting to intellectually read off implied meanings based on the manifest content. As a result, the day residue–dream associational matrix is highly intellectualized, detailed, and lacking in clear meaning.

Unconsciously, this mode of communication is an attack upon the therapist's listening and integrating capacities. To the extent that there are qualities of projective identification in the Type C communicative mode, the barren communicator generates "a negative projective identification" (Langs 1978c)—a destructive void. The Type C narrator may also overtax the therapist's containing capacities to the point of destruction and denudation (Bion 1962).

In the midst of all this, the Type C patient will, from time to time, communicate metaphors of a Type C field. These may be isolated dream images related to walls and barriers, to voids and vacuums, to impenetrable barriers, to the destruction of relatedness, and to lies and falsifications. These metaphors must be interpreted to these patients, either as Type One derivatives or, when feasible, as Type Two derivatives around a specific adaptive context that has evoked the Type C defensiveness (Langs 1978b,c). The material usually does not permit an analysis of the underlying fantasies, memories, introjects, and perceptions. However, such interventions are often followed by a reduction of the Type C barriers, and some of the underlying chaos emerges in derivative form and is momentarily analyzable.

Efforts to interpret the contents of dream communications from Type C patients are met with nonvalidation. They convey the therapist's failure to understand the essential function of the patient's associations and reveal the therapist's need to find meaning in the midst of its essential absence. Technically, such interventions also represent a failure to deal with communicative modes before other resistances and contents, a variation on the principle of interpreting resistances before core unconscious fantasies and memories.

WHAT DREAMS REVEAL ABOUT THERAPIST AND FRAME

The day residue–manifest dream associational network is an important source of information about the therapeutic relationship. This network reveals the state of the patient's transference responses to the therapist. In addition, it contains unconscious perceptions and essentially valid introjects derived from that relationship and provides insights into the framework and the communicative properties of the bipersonal field (Langs 1976a, 1978c).

The patient's relationship with the therapist is viewed as having transference and nontransference elements, and the transference component is seen essentially in terms of unconscious fantasies, memories, introjects, and interactional mechanisms; it is viewed adaptively as being evoked by some aspect of the current therapeutic interaction which prompts a distorted, albeit adaptive, response in the patient.

Dreams are, of course, often among the most analyzable of these adaptive reactions. Their implications can be interpreted if the therapist identifies the specific adaptive context within the therapeutic relationship, often in the form of unconscious implications conveyed in his interventions—and traces, through the manifest dream and associations, the distorted unconscious meanings, perceptions, and pathological defenses with which the patient has responded. In addition, interpretation of the genetic aspects is necessary for a complete intervention. This characterization of therapeutic work with dreams implies a Type A field, the relative absence of countertransference-based inputs from the therapist, and a predominance of the patient's pathological reactions.

Often, however, the actual therapeutic situation is considerably different than implied in this first model. A very crucial aspect of the therapeutic relationship, in which dreams are vital means of communication, is often overlooked: the primarily nontransference sphere—the patient's valid unconscious perceptions of, and reactions to, the therapist, and the resultant introjects. While such responses have a valid core, they may be extended subsequently into pathological fantasies, thereby reaching into the realm of transference.

It is essential to recognize the nondistorted aspects of these responses, since they involve major sectors of healthy and adaptive functioning in the patient, and even unconscious curative efforts on the therapist's behalf (Searles 1975, Langs 1975a, 1976a). The day residue–manifest dream associational network will, as a rule, contain the relevant unconscious perceptions and introjects in the form of Type Two derivatives when organized around a specific adaptive context. On this basis, we might rephrase and extend Freud's (1900) well-known dictum, that dreams are the royal road to the unconscious: not only are they a royal approach to transference, but also to nontransference—and to countertransference and noncountertransference as well.

The dream network also bears strong commentary on the ground rules or framework. Situations with any degree of deviation emanating from either the patient or therapist serve as a crucial adaptive context and day residue for a patient's dream (see especially Langs 1975b, 1976a). The dream-associational response is imbued with unconscious perceptions and introjects of the unconscious implications of the therapist's deviation, to which the former may add distorting elements. Organized as Type Two derivatives around the adaptive context of the alteration in the framework, the dream network serves as the vehicle for insights, and further, as a guide to the necessary rectification of the frame (Langs 1975b, 1976a,b, 1978a). Interestingly, it is characteristic of patients with all three communicative styles to respond in the Type A mode, often through meaningful dream networks, to unneeded alterations in the framework.

It is especially important, then, for the listener to monitor all of the material from the patient in a session in which a dream has been reported in terms of the therapeutic relationship and along the me/not-me interface—as referring simultaneously to both the patient and the therapist (Langs 1978b). When the day residue and adaptive context are known, the monitoring can take place through Type Two derivatives referring to both participants, can be tested for elements of distortion and nondistortion, and can generate important interpretations keyed to the therapeutic relationship—transference and nontransference. A similar process in the specific context of an alteration in the framework will lead to both the necessary rectification of the frame and the interpretations of the relevant unconscious fantasies, memories, and perceptions. In clinical practice, much therapeutic work is carried out along these lines.

THERAPIST INFLUENCE ON DREAM REPORTS AND CONTENTS

There is a multileveled interplay between the patient's dreams and the analyst's essentially valid, noncountertransference-based functioning and the effects of his countertransference-based inputs as well.

Both the therapist's assets and sensitivities, and his unresolved residuals of psychopathology and countertransference, influence the quantity and analyzability of his patient's dreams. A Type A therapist, able to hold the patient, contain his projective identifications, and interpret his communications, will create an excellent field for symbolic and illusory communication. Patients are likely to report dreams, and to do so through a Type A communicative mode. With a Type A therapist, Type B and Type C patients may experience the adequate containing, metabolizing, and cognitive interpretations of the actual functions of their dream reports, and will tend to describe more frequent analyzable dreams.

A Type B therapist has difficulty containing and metabolizing toward cognitive understanding his patient's symbolic dreams and those dreams used for projective identification, or which are part of a Type C barrier. He tends to experience dream communications as disturbing projective identifications into himself, and is likely to have considerable difficulty in working cognitively with the day residue–manifest dream associational network. These problems generate unconscious pressures on his patients to either not remember and report their dreams, or to utilize dreams for pathological projective identification and discharge.

The Type C therapist will be unable to meaningfully interpret his patient's dreams, will have little capacity to contain and metabolize those dreams that are utilized for projective identification, and will drain the dream network of vital meaning. He will use clichéd interventions as a means of creating major barriers against inner mental contents and true relatedness, and falsifications designed to seal off his own underlying chaos, as well as that of the patient. His patients seldom dream and restrict their associations to such dreams, tending to use dream material for Type C barriers.

The patient's report of a dream, and the associational matrix within which it is embedded, then, is an interactional product, influenced by patient and therapist factors stemming from their respective mental lives and shared relationship. The extent to which dreams are involved in resistance and communicate Type Two derivatives related to the unconscious dimensions of the patient's psychopathology—and that of the therapist—are also under constant interactional pressure. Resistances to dream reporting, use of dream networks for resistance, and other problems of dream usage, require study of the role of both therapist and patient. As Little (1951) pointed out, the patient is a mirror for the therapist. The patient is also a container for the therapist's projective identifications and unconscious communications. These unconscious inputs generate introjects with valid sensitivities, whatever the additional distortions. Patients react by attempting to exploit these introjects for the maintenance of their neurosis, while engaging in unconscious efforts designed to cure the introject and the therapist (Searles 1965, 1975, Langs 1976a,b).

A dream-associational network is a frequent response to a countertransference-based intervention and is a greatly overlooked communication and resource. The therapist who is alert to his unconscious countertransference fantasies and interactional mechanisms can learn much about himself from the patient's dreams. These dreams are filled with Type Two derivatives pertinent to unconscious perceptions and introjections of the therapist and his pathology, and can be understood and implicitly interpreted on that basis. It is here that monitoring the patient's material along the me/not-me interface for self and object representations, and for communications related to the inner mental world of both participants, takes on its clearest meaning. While Freud (1900) noted that every figure in a dream is a representation of the dreamer, it can now be added that every figure in a dream (and in a dream-associational network) is a representation of both the patient and therapist—the "me" and the "not me," as stated from the patient's vantage point (Langs 1978c).

In response to the influence of the therapist's countertransference-based interventions, patients will often have "curative dreams" (Langs 1976a). These are unconscious efforts, through a dream-associational matrix, to alert the therapist to the presence of a disturbance, to the need to rectify a damaged frame, and to a need to modify a countertransference difficulty. The associational matrix will pinpoint the nature of the therapist's disturbed communications, and will reflect unconscious interpretations (Little 1951, Langs 1976a,b), using the patient's unconscious experience and his curative wishes toward the therapist. These efforts may extend into transference distortions, but much is valid and should be interpreted as such.

Soundly interpreted, the patient's dream-associational network will reflect constructive and ego enhancing unconscious perceptions and introjects. In all, then, the dream-associational network is an important means of detecting and resolving countertransferences.

WRITTEN DREAMS

Blum's findings and literature review (Blum 1968) suggest that written dreams serve both resistance and communication. I find that writing dreams is an attempt to modify the framework of the bipersonal field. This diminishes the Type A communicative mode, and increases either a Type B or Type C communication.

The written dream is a modification of the fundamental rule of free association. It alters the framework and increases framework or misalliance cure (Langs 1975a, 1976b). It is primarily a resistance, in terms of the alteration in communicative mode. Writing a dream can be used as a means of action and discharge, fostering the use of the dream as a projective identification—the Type B mode. It is an effort to gain distance from the dream and the chaotic world within patient or therapist, and thus it is Type C barrier, transforming the alive and threatening dream experience into a dead and empty psychological cliché.

The functions of this communicative mode must be interpreted and the mode itself modified, before the contents of the dream can be analyzed. The latter cannot be dealt with under the conditions of a written dream. Often such dreams contain some representation of the action-discharge Type B communicative mode or of the Type C barrier, and it is here that the interpretive work must be concentrated.

CLINICAL VIGNETTES

I will now offer material from supervision of psychotherapy. I will focus on therapeutic understanding and the approach to dreams. There will also be comments on the techniques involved in working with dreams.

Miss A

Session 1. Miss A was a young woman in twice-weekly psychotherapy for depression and difficulty in relating to men. At this point in therapy, she had started dating a seductive man. Indirect links to the patient's unconscious perceptions of the therapist were evident, as well as some transference distortion of these perceptions. The therapist had difficulty understanding the material. He had attempted to link the patient's sexual anxieties to himself, did this with confusion, and quickly shifted to comments about the patient's surface feelings and fantasies about the boyfriend.

Session 2. In the following session, the patient stated that just when things seemed to be under control, something terrible had happened. Her fears of trains had intensified in recent days, based on a fear of riding in dilapidated instead of modern commuter cars. She wished to avoid people. She described how she stood up to her boss, thus getting, and doing well on, an important editorial assignment. Yet she felt bad, different, stigmatized, and defeated. She wanted to go home, where she lived with her parents and a sister, to sleep and withdraw. A man had seen her bypass her commuter train on her way home, just prior to the session, and she felt that he must have thought she was absurd.

The therapist reminded her that in the previous session she had brought up sexual issues regarding her new boyfriend. He added that in his comment to her, he had been uncertain as to whether the sexual matters concerned him or the boyfriend. He linked this confusion to the patient, saying that she felt good in some respects, and yet badly, absurd, and in need to avoid others. He suggested that her fear of the man who watched her bypass the train implied that she felt that if she brought her sexual feelings toward the therapist into the session, he would laugh at her. The patient responded that she did not feel that the therapist had vacillated in the previous session, and that she had left feeling helped and good. For now, she didn't feel like talking about closeness and spoke again about wanting to go home in order to retreat into bed.

Session 3. In the following hour, the patient described more fear of old trains. Her boyfriend had arranged that they visit friends, without telling her. She had asserted that she wished he had told her; he expressed surprise at her being upset. She wondered why he judged her by himself, and then described visiting a couple with two little children. The patient felt panicky, unable to love anyone, and sad; and she asked the therapist what she should do. She disparaged herself and felt there was something missing inside of her.

She then described a nightmare: she was going into her old apartment house, chased by a gang of boys. She got to her apartment, but her mother wasn't there. She was just able to open the door and woke up with a persistent image of running and having to lock the door.

This was a repetitive dream, and one that she had not dreamed in some time. She spoke again of feeling incapable and empty, but wanting a man. She thought of an earlier boyfriend with a violent temper and of how she could not contemplate marrying him.

The therapist said that the patient was being chased in the dream, and was locking the doors; she also was talking of feeling empty and unable to love. He recalled that in the previous session, he had brought up their earlier discussion of her sexual feelings, and he suggested that her dream and association was an attempt to avoid that material—a reflection of her wish to feel nothing and to lock the doors. The patient responded that she thought again of nothingness, and of drowning in oneness. When she fell silent, the therapist alluded to the couple and their two children, and asked what images came to mind. The patient said that she knew the couple, thought they were depressed, and now discovered that they weren't. She wondered how they managed to support two children, even though they both were working.

The therapist spoke of the couple and their two children; he suggested that in some way they were connected to the patient's mother and father, indicating that her misperceptions of the couple's boredom and coldness fit in with her perception of her parents. The patient saw this as a marvelous intervention, because after all, how could she ever think of escaping her parents. The apple doesn't fall far from the tree. Still, she felt depressed and unable to love, and she suggested that her parents had destroyed her ability to love and to hope.

This therapist had countertransference anxieties and fantasies when the patient introduced sexual experiences and fantasies. These underlying problems are reflected in his premature interventions in that area. Thus, in Session 2, the therapist introduced his previous intervention and the patient's sexual material without related derivatives from the patient in that particular hour. His own fantasies and associations led him to suggest that the patient's discomfort about the man who saw her bypass the train contained a conscious or unconscious concern that the therapist would deride her if she mentioned her sexual feelings toward him. The therapist's initial intervention is like a pathological projective identification into the patient of his own sexual fantasies and anxieties, and indicates his use of repressive and fragmenting defenses.

The patient's response was ruminative and not validating, and characterized by a sense of denial. She seems to have had little wish to contain the projective identification from the therapist, and described a reluctance to talk about the issue of closeness; instead, she ruminated and thought of retreating.

The portion of the next session that precedes the dream can best be formulated for the moment in terms of the adaptive context of the therapist's interventions in the previous hour. The material has qualities of what I have termed a "transversal communication" (Langs 1978b), in that it contains a condensation of both valid unconscious perceptions and neurotic distortions. In essence, in the adaptive context of the therapist's interventions, the material regarding the patient's boyfriend and the couple with two children suggests an unconscious perception of the therapist as controlling and provocative, and as judging the patient in terms of himself rather than in the light of her own needs and communications. Along the me/not-me interface, the patient's anxieties about having children and her feelings that something is missing within herself refer on one level to her own sexual conflicts and fantasies. On another level, however, this material conveys a perception of similar problems in the therapist, whom the patient is suggesting tends to intervene in a penetrating and impregnating manner, largely out of a fear of silences and a need to fill his own inner emptiness.

In the sequence of the patient's associations, the dream of being chased appears after the patient had spoken about her date and her fear of having children.

The usual approach to a session in which a dream appears is as follows: the patient is implying that the dream was prompted by her date and by some thoughts regarding her fears of having a baby. While the manifest content of the dream has to do with being chased by a gang of boys, the latent content as developed from these associations would be seen to suggest that the patient feels threatened by her new boyfriend, endangered by his sexual overtures, and in dread of impregnation. She wishes to find protection from her mother, who is unavailable. She tries instead to lock the door, and thereby shut out her boyfriend. The patient then mentioned that this is a repetitive dream and spoke of feeling empty, wanting a man, wishing to marry, but not having a suitable suitor. These associations would be taken to suggest that the dream is an effort to deal with repetitive conflicts and anxieties about dating and about her fear of men.

In the terms presented in this paper and in my work on the listening

process (Langs 1978b), these formulations are based on relatively undisguised and direct associations, and on an adaptive context outside of the
therapeutic relationship which in no way specifically illuminates the
nature of the patient's intrapsychic conflicts and pathological unconscious
fantasies, memories, and introjects.

For example, the patient is suggesting that her boyfriend is insensitive
to her feelings, and that she resents it. She sees a couple with a baby and
vaguely describes a dread of emptiness and yet a fear of having a child.
There is some image of threat and pursuit, but it is not defined in terms of
specific unconscious contents. There is a passing reference to a boyfriend
with a temper, and therefore a vague suggestion of fears of violence, but
there is no sense of coalescence and little sense of specificity or depth.
Elsewhere (Langs 1978b) I have termed this linear, nonneurotic communication, and have found that it is consistently developed around a
manifest (direct) adaptive context outside of the therapeutic relationship,
and that while it touches upon aspects of the patient's psychopathology, it
does not communicate or illuminate the underlying pathological factors.

In contrast, if we recognize that the manifest day residues of the
experiences with the boyfriend contain in latent form the patient's
experiences with the therapist in the previous session or two, and that the
external day residue serves as a disguised and derivative expression for a
more latent (indirect) day residue related to the therapeutic relationship,
we discover that the material, including the manifest dream, organizes in a
meaningful, convoluted, derivative way around specific unconscious perceptions and fantasies that relate to the therapist's and patient's psychopathology. If we proceed to organize this material in terms of the
therapist's premature intervention regarding the patient's sexual feelings
towards himself, the third session reveals a series of Type Two derivatives
related largely to the patient's unconscious perceptions of the therapist,
though it also includes some quality of her own pathological sexual
fantasies and wishes—although the latter will be difficult to identify so
long as the therapist has intruded his own pathological needs into the
situation.

As a response to the therapist's interventions, the patient's material
indicates that she found herself in trouble again and that she felt under
pressure from the therapist, who was treating her like a girlfriend, and
toward whom she had feelings similar to those felt toward a boyfriend.
Further, she experienced the therapist as confusing himself with her, and
as attributing to her fantasies and anxieties that actually resided with
him—an unconscious allusion not only to a blurring of self-object boundaries by the therapist, but also to a projective identification.

In some way, the patient had experienced this thrust by the therapist as an unconscious effort to impregnate her, and as a reflection of his incapacity to love and his hatred for himself (Type Two derivatives organized along the "not-me" part of the interface). It is in this sequence of associations that she then recalls her dream, which can, at this level, be seen as a special communication of the patient's adaptive responses—unconscious perceptions and fantasies—to the premature intervention. In it, the patient conveys her sense of being pursued, her feeling unprotected (in addition, a possible allusion to a theme that had come up previously in regard to the fact that the therapist shares his waiting room with two other therapists), and her need to protect herself by shutting herself off to the therapist's communications and projective identifications—an extension of the patient's initial response to the intervention in the prior hour, and an indirect form of validation of the hypotheses generated here in evaluating that initial reaction.

Next, the patient comments upon this having been a repetitive dream, touching upon a relatively neglected topic. There is a relationship here between such dreams and countertransference. This patient is indicating unconsciously that she has been previously exposed to assaults and threats of this kind from the therapist—and others. The repetition may be connected to recurrent and similar day residues (adaptive contexts), and to fixity in the patient's unconscious perceptions and fantasies. The repetitive dream may imply a stalemated situation involving both the therapist's countertransferences and the patient's responses to them.

The repetitive dream also demonstrates that the same manifest content may carry different unconscious fantasies and perceptions, depending on the prevailing adaptive stimulus. Elsewhere (Langs 1978b) I have termed this the "functional capacity" of a manifest sequence, meaning the presence of distinctly different latent contents within virtually identical manifest material.

It was at this point in the session that the therapist intervened. He identified the latent adaptive context, but without the bridges from the patient that would have linked experiences with the boyfriend to the therapeutic interaction; so he again spoke prematurely (see Langs 1978a). He was attempting to interpret a transference resistance, but the patient's communications should have been described as interactional resistances derived from both therapist and patient, and containing important unconscious perceptions. Many therapists in their work with dreams treat the material largely as a reflection of the patient's fantasies and resistances, and valid unconscious perceptions and introjections are excluded.

The patient's responsive feeling that she was drowning in oneness, reflected her specific elaboration of the therapist's efforts to overwhelm her with expressions of his own countertransference fantasies. There is little evidence of validation, and the therapist asks the patient to associate to the couple and the children. She expresses uncertainty as to what is reality and what illusion, and wonders how this couple manages. Monitored around the adaptive context of the therapist's new intervention, these associations reflect an introjection of the therapist's confusion and difficulties in managing the patient's material. The therapist now relates the material to the patient's parents, largely, I believe, as a barrier against meanings that pertain to the patient's relationship to the therapist and the turmoil that it is generating in him—and the patient. The patient accepts this common psychoanalytic cliché—the defensive use of a genetic link—as a momentary barrier to her own inner turmoil, but ends the hour feeling quite depressed and with a further unconscious commentary on the therapist's interventions: they reflect his own incapacities to love (as a therapist) and destroy her hope to develop such a capacity in herself.

If we formulate this material with the dream as the focal point, we would begin with the manifest themes of being chased, the absence of her mother, and having to lock out her pursuers. One might derive Type One derivatives pertaining to the therapeutic relationship simply as a monitoring exercise, and wonder whether the patient was experiencing transference rape fantasies or, on some level, felt that she was actually being endangered and pursued by the therapist (nontransference). As a transversal communication, we might conclude that the therapist had been pursuing the patient, and that the patient unconsciously believed that the basis was a sexual countertransference. These unconscious perceptions and introjects could be evoking unresolved pathological sexual fantasies within the patient.

With the dream as the focal point, the prior associations would suggest latent sexual anxieties and fears of impregnation. The subsequent associations are of emptiness and a lover with a temper. Latent themes are hinted at but the entire formulation remains at the level of Type One derivatives without a specific day residue (adaptive context). Once the context is established in terms of the therapist's intervention in the prior session, the material takes on the specific Type Two derivative meaning already outlined.

Personal preference and style may determine whether the therapist begins with the dream, develops the associational network, and then seeks out the day residue, or begins instead with the day residue, and traces out the dream-associational network. Both approaches, if applied sensitively, would ultimately lead to the same formulations. I have found (Langs 1978b) it more effective to begin with the day residue. In contrast, in those situations in which the adaptive context is lacking, there develops a search for the primary adaptive task that would best fit the dream-associational matrix.

In terms of the communicative styles outlined above, it would appear that this patient is attempting to express herself in a Type A mode, and to utilize the day residue–dream associational matrix to generate Type Two derivatives which convey interpretable unconscious perceptions and fantasies. For his part, the therapist's interventions have qualities of the Type B and Type C communicative modes. The former is evident in his use of interventions to place into the patient his own sexual anxieties and defenses, and several of his own conscious, defensive fantasies (e.g., his effort to connect the material to the patient's parents). The Type C style is evident in his use of questions and is another quality of his intervention about the patient's parents; these appear to be designed as Type C barriers to the underlying sexual fantasies and anxieties existing both within himself and the patient, regarding each other.

In the following session, the patient felt extremely depressed and hopeless. She talked of terminating treatment, and felt sorry for a therapist who had a patient like herself; she was so miserable and so often gave him the business. She didn't want to talk, but she denied that her evil came from therapy. She described how she couldn't handle and old boyfriend who had so often lost his temper and how angry she was at her present boyfriend who had become such a burden.

At this point in supervision, the therapist suddenly remembered that for the past two weeks he had been taking brief notes in the sessions. He had stopped this practice sometime earlier, but he had resumed it in response to the sexual material which he found so confusing. With this awareness, he now suggested that the dream of the gang of boys in pursuit of the patient must have been a response to the notetaking.

This modification in the framework had a significant impact upon the patient. The third session described earlier, including the dream, was clearly a response to several interrelated adaptive contexts, especially the notetaking and the therapist's premature intervention. The day residue that had been repressed by the therapist becomes a significant organizer of the dream-associational network, and serves as a selected fact (a new truth that provides integrated meaning to previously disorganized material; Bion 1962) which provides the material in the third session with clarifying, specific implications in the form of Type Two derivatives organized around that particular adaptive context.

Now we could suggest that the boyfriend who did not tell the patient of his plans and brought her together with his friends is a derivative allusion to the therapist who unexpectedly began to take notes that he may well be presenting to others. The patient wished to assert herself and to protest, but was unable to do so directly toward the therapist.

The patient sees the therapist as frightened and uncertain. Notetaking is a pursuit and means the loss of the therapist as a protective mother figure (both his holding and containing capacities are impaired). The patient wishes to shut herself off from the therapist since his notetaking reflects his pathological fantasies and endangers the confidentiality of the treatment situation.

The notetaking is also seen as a loss of control and an attack upon the patient. It is an attempt to repair the therapist's sense of emptiness and to manage his own dread of losing control—it is a way of locking the door. The patient's reference to oneness conveys the extent to which the notetaking is validly perceived as an effort to merge with the patient, as a kind of exciting form of merger and defense, but ultimately, as a means of destroying the therapeutic and openly communicative qualities of the bipersonal field, and with it, all sense of therapeutic love and hope.

The preceding formulation demonstrates the extent to which the day residue–dream associational network indirectly alludes to the therapeutic relationship, and how it constitutes an intense working over of the unconscious meanings of an alteration of the basic framework of the bipersonal field.

The patient's efforts to bar the door against the pursuing boys is a model of the necessary rectification of the frame in this situation: the therapist should desist from notetaking and exclude the outside observers for whom these notes may have been written. He should no longer pursue, threaten, and attack the patient. The rectification of the frame and the interpretations of the patient's unconscious perceptions and fantasies as evoked by that alteration could be based on this dream-associational network.

The notetaking is also a projective identification in the sense that the therapist is putting into the patient his own sense of confusion, his difficulties in managing, his inability to deal with his own and her conscious and unconscious sexual fantasies and anxieties, his need to introjectively incorporate the patient, and his need for inappropriate barriers. It is also a form of Type C barrier in which the material from the patient is recorded, rendered nonhuman, and extruded from within the therapist, which warns the patient that she should not communicate too meaningfully lest it be exposed publicly.

The patient, however, responded in a Type A mode to these threats from the therapist, incorporating and metabolizing his projective identifications only up to a point, and returning them undetoxified and filled with anxiety. The dream serves as a projective identification on this level, though the associational network suggests less of an effort at discharge than an endeavor to communicate symbolically to a therapist who is expressing himself nonsymbolically—in terms of efforts at direct and inappropriate gratification and defense.

This is a potentially curative dream-associational network, and the depression in the final session may be seen as the patient's sense of hopelessness in response to the therapist's failure to rectify the frame and to appreciate her curative efforts on his behalf. The therapist did soon stop his notetaking, and had a later opportunity to interpret the patient's unconscious perceptions and fantasies, which restored some therapeutic qualities to the treatment.

Miss B

Another patient, Miss B, was in twice-weekly psychotherapy at a clinic with a male therapist. She was a gym teacher in her early thirties and homosexual. She had been in therapy for about a year for episodes of depression. At times, she had been suicidal, especially after breaking up with a recent homosexual lover.

I will present two sessions that followed a two-week vacation by the therapist. These hours occurred four months prior to the expected termination of therapy, and although the patient had been told vaguely of the duration of therapy, termination and disposition had not been specifically introduced by the therapist.

The patient began the first session by describing several telephone calls with a former woman lover who had moved to the West Coast. The girlfriend would write daily letters for a week or so, and then not communicate for days on end. Miss B felt that the girlfriend had found a new lover, and no longer cared for her; the patient was angry but forgiving. She was tired of pursuing the friend, who seldom returned her calls. The girlfriend said that the patient seemed to treat her as a weak, sick asshole who could come in and out of the patient's life whenever the latter wished. It was a battle, but it was no longer important who won.

Throughout this session, the therapist asked a number of detailed questions about the incidents that the patient was describing. He attempted to establish who was rejecting whom, and to clarify the patient's feeling about this former girlfriend. Toward the end of the hour, he said the patient felt out of touch with this girlfriend, and seemed angry. He linked the resentment to his vacation and suggested she had missed the session prior to the vacation because of this anger. He also connected her disillusionment with the girlfriend to feelings revealed prior to that vacation, that therapy was an unfulfilled promise; the therapist added that the patient seemed to feel he was not doing enough for her. He concluded that there was still much unresolved feeling in her about him. The patient denied these connections. Instead, she described her resentment over the therapist's silence in the session before his vacation.

In the next session, Miss B said that she was angry with a female teacher who had cancelled a dinner date. She thought of visiting this friend at her apartment and described an unexpected visit from another woman from California who was probably living with the patient's former girlfriend. The patient had had a strange dream: her mother was standing in front of her and she squirted her mother with water from a plant sprayer until her mother's hair was all wet. The patient didn't know why she did it.

The therapist asked for associations and Miss B recalled that she had this dream while the therapist was on vacation. She had had another dream during the current week: her father (actually dead for several years) was alive, and her mother was dead. Father didn't know that mother was dead, and the patient told him. The patient felt a strangeness over not having been home for so long, but not over having to tell him that her mother had suddenly died.

Miss B reported conscious fantasies of killing her mother because of arguments over her father's will. She was thinking much about her father. The night before the session, she had dreamt about the therapist. She was seeing him and another therapist, a woman, and didn't remember him talking. The woman psychiatrist had said much more than the therapist.

The patient said she feared expecting much from the therapist for fear of being disappointed. She felt that the dream of the therapist connected with his remarks in the previous hour. The therapist said the dreams were important and the patient said that the first dream was silly, but she wasn't hurting her mother. The therapist suggested that the patient wanted proof of love from mother, but it seemed like a hopeless struggle, leaving her hurt, angry, and wanting revenge. Still, the patient didn't hurt her mother because she also really loved and cared about her. He tied this conflict of feelings to the patient's relationship to her homosexual girlfriend and to her feelings toward himself, saying that in general the patient wanted people to care for her and yet felt hurt, angry, and in need of revenge when they did not do so. This was in conflict with her wish to feel close to others, and created considerable confusion.

The patient felt that the therapist had identified why she mistreated herself: she's too concerned with getting back at others and with wishes to scream her mother's guts out. So she hurts herself and overeats. The therapist linked this to her feeling that she needed someone to care about her, and said that if he offered her advice, he fostered that search. He felt that the patient experienced such efforts as encouraging her search to be taken care of, and not caring for herself. He said the patient did not know why she hurt herself, and wanted him to solve that riddle, but realized that this would not work.

The patient then talked about her defensiveness, feeling one way but trying to feel another way. She often feels jealous and takes on the feelings of others toward herself, and then feels guilty and goes against herself. The therapist agreed with this and suggested that the greatest problem was that when she got good feelings toward others, they were mixed up with bad feelings, and she felt confused. He then linked this to a number of confusing incidents in her childhood.

In this clinical situation, we have a series of dreams and several day residues. On the most superficial level, there is the patient's struggle with her former lover, while on the level of the therapeutic relationship, there is the therapist's vacation, his silence in an hour prior to that vacation, his interventions in the session prior to the dream report, and the much-neglected anticipation of a forced termination in mid-year—an expectation that would undoubtedly be aroused by the therapist's vacation.

In the session prior to the dream, the patient described in some detail, with the therapist's encouragement, her conflicted feelings toward her former lover. The therapist, without adequate bridges in the patient's material, linked this to the patient's reaction to his vacation and to dissatisfaction with the treatment. The patient's response was flat; she denied feelings about the vacation, but stated that she felt deprived when the therapist was silent. Without the details of the session in question, it is impossible to evaluate the latent content of that particular complaint.

The following session begins with the patient's talk of pursuing a woman who had cancelled a dinner appointment. Next, there is the dream of spraying her mother's hair and the therapist's query as to the patient's thoughts about it. Technically, when a patient reports a dream, it is best to allow him or her to continue to free associate. Commonly, inexperienced therapists ask patients their thoughts about a dream or what they think a dream means. It is also generally accepted practice to ask the patient for day residues (What do you think prompted the dream?) or for associations to particular dream elements.

VALUE OF SILENCE FOLLOWING DREAM REPORT

A series of interconnected technical principles (Langs 1976a,b,d) begins with entering each session without desire, memory, or understanding (Bion 1970), and extends to allowing the patient to create the meaning of each session and to put the necessary interpretations and rectifications of the framework into the therapist (de Racker 1961, Langs 1978b). The preferred technique in response to a dream report is to allow the patient his own unfolding. Most questions interfere with the therapist's neutrality and often serve defensive purposes (Langs 1978a,b), so it is best to work with the material as expressed by the patient. Thus, the therapist can observe whether the patient permits dream reports to be part of meaningful communication, and whether dreams are used to generate meaningful resistance, or confusion and nonmeaning. The latter is extremely common when patients present more than one dream, or a single lengthy dream (Langs 1978b, chapter 10). A therapist's search for meaning is often accentuated when a patient communicates a dream. However, the patient may use dreams to place confusion into the therapist and to destroy meaning, often as a response to comparable projective identifications by the therapist. This particular dream-associational network has some such qualities, as I will discuss below.

By allowing the patient to associate to the dream, his communicative mode can be discerned. If there is no allusion to an adaptive context, the Type B or Type C communicative mode is probably in use. But if a day residue is in the material, the therapist probably will be able to generate

Type Two derivatives and is probably dealing with Type A communication. By being silent, the therapist may observe the links between the patient's prior and subsequent associations, and the manifest dream, and the extent to which there are or are not evident connections. Thus, he can determine whether the patient is using splitting and fragmentation, or in contrast, generating derivatives that tend to coalesce around meaningful, unconscious nodal points.

The therapist's silence also permits an appreciation of whether the day residue–dream associational network is serving resistance, or is unconsciously designed to reveal latent meaning. The patient's style of working with dreams is, as a rule, a representation of the patient's basic associative style and communicative mode. Premature interventions by the therapist tend to generate pressures toward the utilization of Type B and Type C communicative modes, and greatly interfere with the expression of the patient's own communicative preferences, defenses, and inner contents—fantasies and perceptions. So, a dream report requires no modification in the therapist's approach to the patient's communications. Allowing the patient to lead the way, an attitude of neutrality, and efforts to understand in order to generate interpretive interventions remain essential (for further details, see Langs 1978a).

The practice of asking the patient her impression of a dream, her thoughts about it, or what she believes it to mean, creates a significant thrust toward a Type C field. It asks the patient to intellectualize and speculate about her own dreams, an effort that is bound to be defensive and have qualities of a Type C barrier. It contrasts with the patient's spontaneous associations which may or may not be imbued with direct and indirect meaning. Many of the questions asked of the dreamer are based on an erroneous conception of the nature of neurotic communication, and on a failure to appreciate the importance of indirectly communicated derivatives (see Langs 1978a,b).

Miss B (continued)

Returning to this material, the patient says that she had the dream of her mother while the therapist was away. She then reports the dream in which she is to tell her father that her mother is dead. Thoughts follow about killing her mother and the dream about the therapist and a second therapist. In part, this last dream connects with the patient having been seen by a previous therapist in the clinic. Also, she had been suicidal from time to time and the therapist gave her his home telephone number, which she had called on several recent occasions.

However, the patient spoke of her fears of wanting too much from the therapist and her associations then became ruminative. The therapist then intervened making almost no use of the manifest dream as a bridge to their possible latent meanings. His comments lacked a specific adaptive context, and the dream–associational network was shorn of its specific derivatives, and utilized in a vague and nonspecific way. The patient accepted the Type C barriers offered by the therapist in his intervention, and unconsciously conveyed her perception and introjection of the therapist's extended intervention as a kind of screaming his guts out. The therapist intervened again with his own impressions and associations, and the patient responded by ruminating about defensiveness. The therapist concluded the hour with another general intervention.

VALID INTERVENTIONS IN THE BIPERSONAL FIELD

First, a comment upon the therapist's interventions. The basic principles of intervening apply to all sessions, including those in which the patient has reported a dream. I have discussed the therapist's interventions in a separate communication (Langs 1978a). Many therapists intervene when the patient reports a dream, and I will comment here in regard to some common errors.

The listening process is the key to proper interventions. We need some reconceptualization about the therapist's interventions and their implications and consequences. It will not be possible here to develop these principles in detail, but they are inherent to this entire presentation.

Identifying the formal nature of the therapist's interventions (e.g., silences, questions, clarifications, confrontations, interpretations, and reconstructions) is only an initial step in evaluating an intervention. Most important to the therapist's interventions are their unconscious functions and nature, implications unconsciously perceived and introjected by the patient. I have concluded, from my studies, that there are six essentially valid interventions by the therapist (Langs 1978a): silences, managements of the framework, interpretations-reconstructions, the playing back of derivatives in the absence of an acknowledged adaptive context (usually one that pertains to the therapeutic relationship), the metabolism of projective identifications, and the identification of metaphors of the Type C communicative mode. In a Type A field, when the frame is secure, interpretations-reconstructions, and sometimes the playing back of derivatives, are the essential tools. It is to be stressed, however, that such interventions should be as specific as possible and should include all possible instinctual drive representations as well as unconscious fantasies and perceptions, as reflected in the dream-associational network.

In the presence of meaningful communication, therapists may neglect the specific derivatives in a manifest dream and the associations, and not interpret them as Type Two derivatives around a specific adaptive context. Even when the dream-associational network is devoid of an adaptive context, and the therapist elects to play back selected derivatives in search of that context, it is important to be as specific as possible. Dreams are often the special vehicle of derivatives of unconscious fantasies and perceptions, and if the therapist drains away the definitive contents reflected in a dream, it causes a Type C barrier which obliterates underlying instinctual drive fantasies and conflicts. Such interventions are a misuse of the concept of interpreting upward (Loewenstein 1957) and reflect a defensive need on the part of the therapist. They constitute the offer of a sector of misalliance (Langs 1975a) and of interactional obsessive defenses (Langs 1976a,b)—which this patient momentarily accepted—and efforts to destroy the meaning of the patient's material for both herself and the therapist, a directive toward a Type C field (Langs 1978c).

Miss B (continued)

Returning to this material, if we take first the adaptive context of the patient's conflicts with her homosexual lover, the dream about the mother suggests that unconsciously the homosexuality expresses sexual fantasies about the mother, and possibly has some meaningful relationship to earlier actual sexual experiences with her. In actuality, the patient had reported incestuous contact with her father, of which her mother was ignorant for some years, but which she later discovered so that the sexual involvement was stopped.

The second dream serves as a further response to that particular day residue. On one level, as a further association to the first dream, it reflects the patient's destructiveness toward her mother, a constellation readily termed ambivalent. The third dream, of the therapist and a woman therapist, quickly brings the therapeutic relationship into the picture, and at this level suggests that the presence of the woman lover was designed as a protection against underlying sexual feelings toward the therapist—here, I make use of the associational network to generate a formulation in need of validation. However, if we continue to organize the material around the adaptive context of the patient's relationship with her girlfriend, her fantasies about the therapist and her fears of expecting too much of him have to be seen as displaced from the girlfriend—the central object who is related genetically to both her mother and father.

It is difficult to further formulate this line of thought because of the therapist's interventions and the subsequent ruminative qualities of the session. However, once again, this particular formulation of the day residue–manifest dream associational matrix has a rather linear quality. It relates to the patient's psychopathology, but offers no insights. Alternatively, we could organize this material around a series of adaptive contexts related to the therapeutic relationship.

In this regard, the day residues are the therapist's vacation, his intrusive interventions, his alternating periods of silence (when interventions may be needed) and overactivity, and his silence regarding the pending forced termination. In light of these several adaptive contexts, the material about the lover who writes often and then disappears, immediately takes on indirect meaning in terms of an unconscious perception of the therapist. Here, too, the contents related to mutual sexual involvement must be formulated as alluding to unconscious perceptions of the therapist and to needs of the patient—a transversal communication—and the two could not be adequately sorted out until the therapist's countertransference-based contributions are rectified.

Then, in this first session, indirect representations of the patient's anger at the therapist appear, along with the patient's feeling that she is weak and being manipulated, which may allude to her unconscious perception of the therapist's weakness as well (applying the me/not-me interface). The intervention in that hour attempts to relate the material, which is quite general and superficial, and all too evident for a neurotic communication, to the therapist's recent vacation and to some general discontent with treatment. As such, it is inadequate, and the patient responds with denial and a complaint about the therapist's silences, which relates to what is being left out and missed currently, including the pending forced termination.

In the next hour, there are initial derivatives related to the theme of sudden cancellation and the undoing of separation. The dream of the mother is difficult to decipher within this adaptive context, though it suggests an unconscious perception of the poverty and sexuality of the therapist's interventions, which cover his destructive impulses. The therapist's question interfered with spontaneous associations, leaving a sense of an unfinished associational network. The patient did, however, indicate that the dream was somehow related to the therapist's absence, and the material suggests a genetic link to the patient's relationship with her mother. It is impossible to determine whether this is a transference-based distortion or primarily a nontransference communication related to the therapist's repeating a trauma that the patient experienced at the hands of her mother.

The next dream involves the father coming to life and the mother being dead. This relates to the pending forced termination, and the fragmentation and vagueness may relate to the therapist's complete avoidance of this subject, despite its importance to the patient. This is a fragmented dream-associative network based on defensive needs in both the patient and the therapist.

Next are the patient's thoughts of killing her mother, which relate to the struggle over the inheritance left by the father—again, the final separation theme. The dream of being with two therapists is the wish to be protected against loss, though more specific associative links are lacking. Still, once a meaningful adaptive context is established, the manifest dream itself will often reflect meaningful Type Two derivatives—which may then be enriched by other associations. The patient goes on to express her fear of wishing for too much from the therapist and later comments about feeling better because she doesn't hurt her mother in the dream.

This last association may be the key: the patient is attempting to fragment her associations and to generate some degree of nonmeaning, a narrative form of Type C barrier, in an effort to spare the therapist her rage and murderous feelings toward him over the pending forced termination and his erroneous interventions. This is a tentative hypothesis that I will be unable to validate from this material, although I can state that subsequent sessions offered strong support for this thesis.

Here, the therapist began the series of interventions that distanced the patient from the dream-associational network and deprived the material of its specific unconscious meanings. I would view this as a reflection of defensive needs within the therapist, and, in part, as an unconscious response to the relative absence of meaning in the patient's material. The patient's associations are an effort to reproject back into the therapist the confusion, sexual anxieties, concern about the therapeutic relationship, and the like, which the patient had introjected from the therapist himself. These dreams here serve as projective identification in addition to their function, for the moment, as a kind of Type C barrier. As a result, any effort to interpret the contents of these dreams, either in the adaptive context of the relationship with the girlfriend (which would be highly defensive) or in an adaptive context related to the therapeutic relationship, would be met with nonconfirmation.

The essential intervention would entail the processing of the patient's projective identifications. I would not have intervened in this session but would have allowed the material to settle and then blossom, so to speak. Such silence might well have permitted a far more meaningful intervention; if not, I would have waited for subsequent sessions and for more definitive material.

Still, in an effort to offer a model intervention related to dealing with the Type B and Type C communicative qualities of a particular series of dreams, I would propose the following hypothetical (silent) intervention (Langs 1978a,b): "You seem quite confused about the therapeutic situation: the nature of our transactions as reflected in the way in which you spray your mother's hair with water; the conditions of the treatment as seen in the presence of a woman therapist in the session; and the nature of what's actually happening, as expressed by the uncertainty about whether your father is dead or alive." (Since I am attempting to build my intervention on the material placed into the therapist by the patient, I could not as yet allude to the pending forced termination.) "It's not clear what is specifically evoking this confusion, though it may well have something to do with separation and death—since you refer to a cancelled dinner engagement and undo the death of your father." (This is an attempt to indicate to the patient an awareness of a crucial adaptive context that had been omitted; here, I am playing back selected derivatives in search of the pertinent adaptive context.) "As a result, you present a series of dreams that seem rather unrelated and fragmented, and designed, it seems, as an effort to generate some degree of confusion, some of which you may have been experiencing from me." (I would only impart this to the patient if she herself brought up the theme of confusion, and would add the part related to the therapist when the patient has referred to his silences or to concerns about his being able to help her.) "In a way, then, all of this seems designed to place your sense of confusion into me and to make it impossible to decipher its underlying basis." (This is the metabolism of her projective identification, and the interpretation of the metaphor for the Type C barrier.)

I have reluctantly offered this model intervention in order to illustrate some of the techniques that I have described on a more abstract level. The intervention itself is extremely unsatisfactory because the patient was not permitted sufficient time to freely associate in order to build the necessary elements, and because I have had to introduce some of my own impressions without sufficient basis in the material from the patient. However, in the course of listening, therapists will make silent hypotheses (Langs 1978b) of this kind again and again, though they should not be expressed to the patient unless they have been silently validated by the patient's ongoing associations, which in addition provide adequate bridges to the therapeutic relationship and adequate derivatives of the essential components needed for the intervention.

THE THERAPIST IN THE MANIFEST CONTENT
OF A DREAM

The manifest dream of the therapist permits a few comments about that class of dreams. I will not here enter the debate concerning manifest dreams of the analyst reported in first sessions, except to note that such dreams in particular, as I have now attempted to demonstrate for all dreams, call for careful examination for contributions from the therapist as well as the patient. The conditions under which this dream was reported suggest that it may well pertain to important countertransference-based inputs from the therapist, and from the uncertainty regarding the pending forced termination. Such circumstances, in which the therapist's inappropriate needs are being directly gratified are often, in my experience, evocative of dreams in which the therapist appears directly. Similarly, such dreams often occur when the patient is experiencing needs for direct and inappropriate gratification from the therapist, satisfactions that extend beyond those afforded to him through valid interpretations and management of the framework. These latter situations are often characterized in terms of the presence of an erotized misalliance and interactional syndrome (see Langs 1976a).

The manifest appearance of the therapist in a dream of the patient, then, calls for a detailed examination of the unconscious therapeutic interaction, and often signals the presence of pathological inputs from both patient and therapist. In addition, it is important to recognize that such a communication is a manifest element, and that in terms of the patient's neurosis, it is the latent, derivative contents and functions that are crucial. Often, therapists will intervene on a manifest level in the presence of such dreams, suggesting, for example, in terms of the material here, that the patient wishes to have someone else present in the treatment situation, or that the patient feels that the therapist is not being sufficiently helpful, and bring in a second therapist to assist. Such interventions are based on direct readings of the manifest content and have a minimal Type One derivative quality—they constitute very evident inferences from the manifest material. As such, they do not meet the criteria of valid interpretations (Langs 1978a), and will tend to be countertransference-based and overly defensive, generating Type C barriers. The meaning of such dream elements can be ascertained only through a full assessment of the day residue–manifest dream associational matrix, and must include the derivation of Type Two derivatives around a specific adaptive context related to the therapeutic interaction, through which the manifest dream elements take on specific unconscious meaning—fantasy and perception.

DREAMS IN TYPE B AND TYPE C FIELDS

I will not attempt a further description of various types of dreams in other communicative fields. The reader will undoubtedly be familiar with massive dream reports that unconsciously are designed as assaultive projective identifications on the therapist, although he must be certain to examine his own interventions as a possible means of evoking such dream communications. Type C patients who rarely report dreams, or quite realistic ones, or primitive dreams to which they provide virtually no meaningful associations, are easily recognized and fairly common (for an illustration, see Langs 1978c). The variations are infinite and it is my hope that the basic discussion and the two illustrations offered here will enable the reader to develop some general principles of listening and intervening that will serve in all situations.

CONCLUSION

Dreams reported in psychotherapy are part of a rich and interpretable associational matrix, and they can be understood in the therapeutic situation. Dreams can serve resistance and be used for pathological projective identifications and for the establishment of Type C barriers. I would stress that the psychotherapist should strive toward a maximal understanding and interpretation of the day residue–manifest dream associational network. Dreams should not be treated in isolation, but entirely as part of the day residue–associational complex. We need no new principles of technique in responding to dreams, but should apply the basics of the listening process and of intervening in their presence.

I have offered as a basic thesis, and tentatively documented, the concept that every day residue–dream associational network has a significant bearing on the therapeutic relationship, and is best understood and interpreted in that context. Possessing both special and ordinary qualities, dream communication should evoke special and ordinary reactions within the therapist. As signals of particular needs to communicate, either in terms of resistance or meaning, the report of a dream can heighten the therapist's listening capacity and sharpen his interpretive and framework management endeavors. Dreams offer an elegant opportunity to comprehend the therapeutic process and interaction, and to provide the patient in psychotherapy with adaptive insight and inherently positive introjective identifications. The mastery of the technique of dream interpretation, as it is called, is tantamount to the mastery of the psychotherapeutic situation. It is an ideal well worth seeking.

References

Bion, W. (1962). *Learning from Experience.* In W. Bion, *Seven Servants.* New York: Jason Aronson, 1977.

——— (1970). *Attention and Interpretation.* In W. Bion, *Seven Servants.* New York: Jason Aronson, 1977.

——— (1977). *Seven Servants.* New York: Jason Aronson.

Blum, H. (1968). Notes on the written dream. *Journal of the Hillside Hospital* 17:67–78.

Freud, S. (1900). The interpretation of dreams. *Standard Edition* 4:1–338 and 5:339–627.

——— (1905). A fragment of an analysis of a case of hysteria. *Standard Edition* 7:1–122.

Grinberg, L. (1962). On a specific aspect of counter-transference due to the patient's projective identification. *International Journal of Psycho-Analysis* 43:436–440.

Langs, R. (1971). Day residues, recall residues, and dreams: reality and the psyche. *Journal of the American Psychoanalytic Association* 19:499–523.

——— (1972). A psychoanalytic study of material from patients in psychotherapy. *International Journal of Psychoanalytic Psychotherapy* 1(1):4–45.

——— (1973). *The Technique of Psychoanalytic Psychotherapy,* vol. 1. New York: Jason Aronson.

——— (1974). *The Technique of Psychoanalytic Psychotherapy,* vol. 2. New York: Jason Aronson.

—— (1975a). Therapeutic misalliances. *International Journal of Psychoanalytic Psychotherapy* 4:77–105.

—— (1975b). The therapeutic relationship and deviations in technique. *International Journal of Psychoanalytic Psychotherapy* 4:106–141.

—— (1976a). *The Bipersonal Field.* New York: Jason Aronson.

—— (1976b). *The Therapeutic Interaction,* vols. 1 and 2. New York: Jason Aronson.

—— (1978a). Interventions in the bipersonal field. In R. Langs, *Technique in Transition.* New York: Jason Aronson.

—— (1978b). *The Listening Process.* New York: Jason Aronson.

—— (1978c). Some communicative properties of the bipersonal field. *International Journal of Psychoanalytic Psychotherapy* 7:87–135.

—— (1978d). Validation and the framework of the therapeutic situation. *Contemporary Psychoanalysis* 14:98–124.

Little, M. (1951). Countertransference and the patient's response to it. *International Journal of Psycho-Analysis* 32:32–40.

Loewenstein, R. (1957). Some thoughts on interpretation in the theory and practice of psychoanalysis. *Psychoanalytic Study of the Child* 12:127–150.

de Racker, G. (1961). On the formulation of the interpretation. *International Journal of Psycho-Analysis* 42:49–54.

Searles, H. (1965). *Collected Papers on Schizophrenia and Related Subjects.* New York: International Universities Press.

—— (1975). The patient as therapist to his analyst. In *Tactics and Techniques in Psychoanalytic Therapy, Vol. II: Countertransference,* ed. P. Giovacchini. New York: Jason Aronson.

Segal, H. (1977). The function of dreams. In *The Work of Hanna Segal.* New York: Jason Aronson, in press.

Wangh, M. (1962). The "evocation of a proxy": a psychological maneuver, its use as a defense, its purposes and genesis. *Psychoanalytic Study of the Child* 17:451–469.

CHAPTER 22

THE DREAM IN JUNGIAN ANALYSIS

Joseph L. Henderson, M.D.

The contributions to this volume are concerned primarily with the dream in clinical practice, so I shall try to avoid theorizing about dreams as much as possible until the actual evidence for correct interpretations is full enough to be substantiated. One cannot omit theory entirely, however, since in a certain sense it is intimately bound up with the methods we use. It is impossible to hear a dream told by a patient without taking mental note as to whether it is a wish fulfillment in the old Freudian sense or a compensatory image in a Jungian sense. Nonetheless, it is at least possible to reserve judgment until the dream has been sufficiently empathized with and processed by both therapist and patient.

FOUR KINDS OF APPROACHES TO DREAMS

In Jungian analysis, as in Freudian analysis, the first thing we ask the patient is what he associates to his dream. I consider it highly important to take *the very first thing* he associates spontaneously as authentic rather than associations that have been subsequently qualified and thereby falsified. This follows Freud's original methods as far as personal associations are concerned; we take care not to read into the dream what we or the patient may have previously learned about dream interpretation. The continuing use of free associations is not encouraged by the Jungian analyst, however, because elaboration forms a series of associations that leads away from the dream content. It is preferable to encourage direct associations that lead toward the dream content and to provide necessary amplifications derived from previous knowledge of these contents. To this may be added the analyst's own amplifications insofar as they enlarge the dreamer's further awareness of the dream's meaning and as long as they do not go off into directionless speculations. Thus, we have four kinds of approaches to the dream: free association, direct association, amplification by the patient, and amplification by the analyst.

DIAGNOSTIC AND PROGNOSTIC IMPORTANCE OF THE INITIAL DREAM

Let us take an actual dream to illustrate these points. At the end of the second world war, a fighter pilot who had distinguished himself in action by completing sixty-five missions, appeared to be suffering, upon discharge, from post-war depression. He was sent to me by a former patient. Following our first interview he had a dream that may be classified as an "initial" dream, by which is meant a dream that provides diagnostic and prognostic material. (This is not always the first dream a patient brings, and in some cases the initial dream has preceded the first interview.) I quote from a previous account (Henderson 1967) of this dream:

Dream 1: I had to get somewhere by a certain time. On a diagram I saw how to get there. First I was to go along a narrow street called 65½ Street, which cut obliquely into a broad boulevard paved with many-colored, bright, glazed bricks. I was to go to a house numbered 654, a sort of roadside residence or restaurant. I was there received by a fat, semi-Oriental maid of no particular age, in a black silk dress, named Todida. She handed me a glass of orange juice. She was big and jolly, and there was a sense of rightness about her. I saw I had arrived ahead of time, 9:00 A.M. I was not due till 1:00 P.M. I asked her to have ham and eggs with me. Instead of answering, she put her face in her hands and went into a trance.

Associations: The narrow roadway numbered 65½ suggests the period of training in England immediately preceding the active period of service and the break-through of my feeling when I found I could overcome fear and enjoy my role as fighter pilot. This was the first time in my life I had the full enjoyment of my powers. In school and college I was popular but found no enjoyment in it. Sixty-five is the number of missions over Germany in which I flew successfully. One-half refers to the flight leader who "flunked out" through fear, who said he couldn't pick up the target and flew back. This was an object lesson to me. The boulevard suggests Reims Cathedral and the chateau where I stayed in Belgium, enjoying the favor of the general and his friends. I stayed there four months, and this may account for the number 4 following 65 on the number of the house—654. The maid is like no one I have ever seen or imagined. Her name, Todida, suggests three other words: *Tod,* the German word for death; the English verb *to die;* and Dido, the Carthaginian princess in Virgil's *Aeneid,* who voluntarily died upon her funeral pyre when Aeneas, whom she loved, went off and left her. The glass of orange juice suggests the hopeful feeling I had when I saw the orange groves of California on my trip west to seek help from a psychiatrist at the advice of a friend. I had been miserable and depressed for weeks before making up my mind to undertake this trip [p. 2].

The only "free" association to this dream is the spontaneous recognition that the glass of orange juice stands for the feeling of hopefulness he had upon entering therapy. The main account is composed of direct associations, filling out an autobiographical picture of his wartime experience in which a successful adaptation to the army, with its officer father-figures, repeats previous achievements in school and college. This man had always had a positive relation to his own father, but a very ambivalent, if not actually hostile, relation to his mother. His mother had deserted him as a small child for long periods of time when she went home to her own mother, leaving him in the care of his father; and he had never really forgiven her, although later she had cared for him adequately. These facts concerning the early life situation provided me with a clue to that ambiguous statement in the associations, that he "found no enjoyment" in his popularity at school and college. I thought the relation to his father, who had made it possible for him to be popular, was no longer adequate to sustain him without some equivalent sense of love and trust from his mother.

I was able to understand the manifest part of the dream and part of the latent content by conjecturing that the "big jolly woman with a sense of rightness about her" might be the missing mother-figure so much needed to supply a sense of joy to match his achievement and without which he would easily fall into periodic states of depression. But she is associated with death. Here he provides a good example of amplification, taking the name *Todida* apart to reveal his experience of death as a literal death he had barely escaped in Germany and then a more subtle form of death as rejection of the feminine (Dido) by a hero-figure (Aeneas). The fear of actual death is suggested by the fraction in the number 65½, while the symbolic restoration of a sense of wholeness is suggested by the 4 in the number 654.

At this point, as the analyst, I was able to supply a further amplification to the figure of Todida by recognizing that she is, as a "semi-Oriental" in a Jungian context, not just a mother but also, because of her exotic quality, an anima-figure. This is an archetypal image suggesting a universal symbolism of the feminine in a man's psychology, like Goethe's "eternal feminine." Here she is an anima-of-death, but her natural attributes suggest she could become an anima-of-new life. Paradoxically, however, she merely provides a promise of something hopeful, but does not stay to enjoy a healthy meal with the dreamer. Instead, she goes into a trance. Jung's definition of the anima (in men) or animus (in women) is that the contrasexual component of the psyche is a kind of guide to the mysteries of the unconscious, providing a *function of relatedness between the conscious and the unconscious*. I took it as a good sign that this man's anima-figure was ready to abdicate her power and her euphoria and seemed to tell him that he should be encouraged to follow her example and to let himself sink into an introverted mood (the trance) from which to learn more about the nature of the missing elements he might retrieve from the unconscious through dreams, in analysis. But, at the same time, I was mindful of the danger of the patient's giving in too easily to the influence of the unconscious. Occasionally, where patients have entered therapy too passively, a first encounter with the unconscious may lead to a delusory invasion of hallucinatory imagery, with a corresponding clouding of consciousness (cf. Janet's [1909] term, *abaissement du niveau mentale,* lowering the mental threshold).

This dream helped me diagnostically, and its prognosis was correct in suggesting that this man needed a deep analysis, not merely a brief period of psychotherapy for readjustment to peacetime behavior patterns. Accordingly, I advised him to undertake a trial analysis for several months. Just as one might have expected from the dream, arriving early for his appointment he thought he was more than ready to begin; but no sooner did he actually begin than he was assailed by all manner of self-doubt. Dreams of men shooting at each other, or escaping from other dangers of equal violence (suggestive of the Jungian shadow-personality), made me realize that he was still far from being ready to receive the healing balm offered by the anima in his first dream. All this pointed to a hitherto unresolved resistance to his father's early authority over him, and this was projected to some extent by his seeming to give me a similar authority over him. But the positive transference and countertransference feelings were stronger between us than the resistances, and this was represented in a later dream which I will recount presently.

ARCHETYPAL THEMES AND REINTEGRATION

It should be clearly stated from the outset that the Jungian analyst has no preconceived idea about the ultimate success of such a case, nor can he even allow himself to assume anything at first about the analytical process. Only then can dreams reveal their true nature. But how is it possible for the analyst not to have a secret agenda for what he hopes to accomplish? If it were only a question of resolving a personal problem, it would, of course, be humanly allowable to have some such agenda, but a dream like the one I have related hints at a mystery that Jungians have learned to recognize as the role of the *archetypes* as they appear in therapy, and the main thing about an archetype is that it remains concealed from rational consciousness and appears only in symbolic form as a procession of images that suggest mythological themes. Jung, in association with the religious historian, Karl Kerenyi, referred to these themes as "mythologems" (Jung 1940, p. 151; 1941, p. 182) because of their repetitive character in the religious history of mankind. One of the most universal of these themes is death-and-rebirth, and we find it appearing in just such cases as this, where a man in a life-crisis undergoes some fundamental change. In his dream this young man is presented with the paradox that his anima-of-death is also, or may become, the anima of new life, and so this mythologem of death-and-rebirth is likely to become active in ways that are unpredictable but will fill out the promise of his initial dream.

During the two years of our work together this patient came to terms with his problem concerning his father and mother. The first unexpected insight emerged when, as he dug deeper into his negative mother-complex, he found that the real problem lay in his rejecting her, not her rejecting him. He had fallen into his father's habit of putting her down, and I suspected that her absences from home were mainly in response to this treatment and not merely a rejection of him. Certainly during this period of his analysis he became as negative toward his father as he had been positive in early life, and a new feeling for his mother began to emerge. But he was still afraid of finding in me an overexpectant, loving father-figure. A still more alarming prospect, I suspected, was that his love, newly awakened in response to the anima-image, might be transferred to me in a homosexual way if he allowed himself to submit to my full therapeutic influence over him.

At last there came a dream, with its attendant insight, which allowed him to carry the necessary transference of feeling to an archetypal level and, because of this, to go a long way in resolving it. Soon after this he was able to get back into life and make a mature choice of vocation and marriage. This was the dream: "Some teeth were loose in my lower jaw. When I examined them more closely, I found that all the teeth, together with the whole jaw on one side, seemed to be giving way. I panicked. I came to you as a therapist to help me. You were dressed in a white coat like a medical doctor. When you examined me you were firm but compassionate, and I felt I could trust myself to you. With a syringe you injected some life-giving fluid into my umbilical scar. This made me feel revived, but it was the recovery of a spiritual, not a physical strength."

A direct association was the patient's sense that, following this dream, he felt relieved for the first time of any restraint or defensiveness in relation to me. He felt a new sense of self-confidence.

My amplification of the dream led me to suggest that loss of teeth—in this case, a loss also of the jaw holding them—pointed to a still deeper disturbance to his ego structure than was apparent on the surface of his life. I thought I could recognize this as typical of the symbolic death of a boy in preparation for renewal as may be found in the initiation rites of tribal societies. The patient himself recognized this as spiritual rather than physical. The loss of the teeth or the hair, or the foreskin, or whatever part of the body is sacrificed, signifies total dismemberment of the novice in tribal initiation rites. The primal ancestor of an Australian tribe, Duramulun, is described in a myth as being a master of initiation during which "he killed the boys, cut them to pieces, and then restored them to life, 'new beings, but each with a tooth missing'" (Henderson 1967, p. 97).

This amplification led to the following interpretation: The patient's acceptance of his therapist as both trustworthy and humane restores his basic trust in the nurturant mothering he had so missed and had also repressed. In the transference of feeling from mother to father (and then to a sense of new self-confidence), he accepts the role of the doctor as a transitional figure, a master of initiation, who is both mother and father, firm and skillful in his use of instruments, but also compassionate. The treatment emphasizes this androgynous role of the doctor, who performs his operation by an act suggestive of phallic aggression, yet who actually produces, as it were, the maternally nurturant effect of feeding some revivifying substance, injected precisely at the place from which the embryo was fed by its mother through the umbilical cord. The homosexual fear is apparently allayed, since the transference is not erotically binding but is spiritually liberating.

On the evidence of these two dreams we can now make a theoretical deduction. In the first dream the archetype of death-and-rebirth is embodied in an ambiguous anima-figure combining a sense of death and new life that is not really available except as an erotic wish that something pleasantly sweet (the glass of orange juice) should be given to him without his making any effort. His wish to partake of a more substantial meal, one that he would give her and share (a breakfast of ham and eggs), is frustrated. This need can only be made good by submitting to the analytical process in the spirit of an initiation which allows him to experience the archetype of death-and-rebirth himself without having to project it into others or live it vicariously as he had done during his wartime experience. His response to therapy awakened a cultural memory of initiation in a spiritual, inner sense to balance his experience of initiation in a worldly outer sense, as in his heroic achievement as a fighter pilot. C. A. Meier (1967) has written a monograph on this parallel between a modern experience in analysis and ancient practices of incubation in classical Greece. He says: "The general attitude of mind toward dreams prevalent in the ancient world requires some explanation. Incubation's effectiveness is very closely bound up with the importance accorded to dreams. Only when dreams are very highly valued can they exert great influence" (pp. xii–xiv).

COMPENSATORY ROLE OF DREAMS

This attitude is characteristic of Jungian analysts who have learned from their own experience how to value the autonomous nature of psychic experience mirrored in dreams. There is a certain danger, however, in taking the dream statement to represent a development that has already taken place. Jung was careful to emphasize that dreams are compensatory to conscious attitudes and can only be reintegrated with consciousness afterwards, sometimes long after the dream has been reported. In the above case, it might be assumed that the patient was totally cured of his neurosis after the last dream. But this was only a beginning of incorporating what he had learned in analysis in preparation for the life he was yet to lead. He recognized that his psyche was still on shaky ground, especially where his relation to women was concerned, and following his treatment by me he entered into further analysis with a woman analyst for another year or two.

It must also be recognized that some patients do not remember their dreams clearly, reporting fragments rather than whole dreams, and the main course of treatment may then follow the more direct method in which the interpersonal relationship between patient and analyst is predominant. But even here dreams may be of great importance, by setting off a train of fantasy which can be directed partly by consciousness but which honors the inner reality of the unconscious. The role of consciousness should not be undervalued, as some of the early analysts tended to do, for if too much value is accorded the unconscious and it is treated as superior, Jung (1966, para. 491) says "we should then be degraded to the level of fortune-tellers and would be obliged to respect the incoherence of superstition, or else, in accord with crass opinion, to deny any value at all to dreams." Mary Ann Mattoon (1978), in her valuable and comprehensive work, *Applied Dream Analysis: A Jungian Approach,* has given me permission to quote the following passages:

> The compensatory action of dreams can be lost also when the conscious mind is overemphasizing the importance of the unconscious. . . .
> Thus the values of the conscious personality must remain intact if unconscious compensation is to be effective. "Assimiliation is never a question of this *or* that, but always of this *and* that," wrote Jung. The conscious values must be maintained, especially when dream compensation is considered in making decisions. If the conscious mind does not "fulfill its tasks to the very limit," the unconscious will be overrated and the power of the conscious decision impaired [Mattoon 1978, pp. 135–136].

A review of the Jungian theory of compensation together with a modification is found in a previous paper of mine, *The Psychic Activity of Dreaming* (Henderson 1972).

> Jung, after his break with Freud, pushed his explorations of the dream world for the first time into real depth and saw that, for all their superstitious willfulness, the true occultists had seen something that was really there, a world of symbolism which evoked emotions that were universally experienced by all people of whatever cultural conditioning, and he called it the collective unconscious. But he, too, following Freud's initial observations, mistrusted any interpretations of a dream that did not relate it personally, as well as impersonally, to the dreamer. On the basis of this viewpoint which he shared with Freud he found that dreams only have the appearance of expressing wishes; what they really do is to present images or actions which effectively compensate "the conscious attitude" of the dreamer.
> At first it may seem that this renders dream interpretation rather easy;

all you have to do is find the conscious mental content of the dreamer's reactions the day before the dream, look for its compensation in the dream and, lo, you have the meaning of the dream [p. 102].

It is true that some dreams can be interpreted as easily as this. More often they cannot, and this is due to the fact that

the dream compensates not only a conscious attitude by a psychological complex of thoughts, of observations and emotions that are unconscious to the dreamer as well as conscious. In fact, if he were not unconscious of the psychic activity of the dream he would not need the message the dream conveys but would have corrected the situation consciously by himself. It is therefore a good rule in interpreting a dream to ask oneself what the dream is saying that one does not know. If one thinks one has the whole meaning of it straight away it is almost certain that the real meaning remains concealed. The interpretation of a dream then involves a search for those areas of unconscious activity in which the psyche may reveal more of its secret workings than is ordinarily perceived in waking consciousness [p. 104].

NONCOMPENSATORY OR COMPLEMENTARY DREAMS

Even with this comprehensive view of dreaming there appears to be a class of dreams that are not compensatory but complementary. Many of these dreams are immediately understandable when we find in them memory traces pointing to cryptamnesic phenomena. These "forgotten" elements do not appear to have been repressed so much as mislaid, and they turn up occasionally in dreams. They could just as well have appeared in consciousness as in the dream, so far as we can tell. More often their appearance gives them a symbolic rather than a literal meaning in which case they are not really complementary but compensatory after all.

Perhaps the commonest type of noncompensatory dream is the one that tells us that the normal compensatory function of the dream, as a defense against traumatic experiences, has broken down. Mattoon (1978) tells us:

Military psychiatrists in World War I had, according to Jung, an intuitive awareness of the non-compensatory nature of dreams of war scenes. They noted that, ordinarily, "Soldiers in the field dreamt far less of the war than of their homes. Military psychiatrists considered it a basic

principle that a man should be pulled out of the front lines when he started
dreaming too much of war scenes, for that meant he no longer possessed any
psychic defenses against impressions from the outside" [p. 142].

Mattoon lists four categories of noncompensatory dreams: prospective, traumatic, extrasensory, and prophetic (p. 139). She says: "A prospective interpretation is appropriate when the conscious attitude is highly
unsatisfactory and the unconscious produces a dream that is more than
compensatory." The initial dream, such as I have already demonstrated,
has a prospective character which suggests a positive prognosis. Another
kind may give a negative prognosis. Mattoon writes:

> A prospective dream can be likened to a preliminary exercise, sketch or
> plan which is roughed out in advance. It may outline the solution of an
> unusually difficult conflict or it may prepare the dreamer for a future
> attitude that may not be recognized as needed until weeks or even months
> after the dream" [p. 140].

As in the dreams of the war hero I described, who had to be made
aware of the spiritual consequences of his experience of the archetype of
death-and-rebirth, Jung states:

> The unconscious manifests an intelligence and purposiveness superior
> to the actual conscious insight. . . . This is a basic religious phenomenon
> observed sometimes even in a person whose conscious mental attitude
> seems most unlikely to produce religious phenomena [quoted in Mattoon
> 1978, p. 141].

As such, dreams are not literally prospective but symbolic. Prophetic
dreams, however, refer to something that literally does occur, though one
can never know this until afterwards. What possible function, therefore,
can they perform? Premonitions of dangerous possibilities may render a
dreamer more cautious and tend to prevent serious mistakes, such as
accidents, infectious illness, and the like. Certain precognitive dreams may
be useful for the therapist when he can grasp their meaning, even
retrospectively. I had a dream one night about a patient I was currently
treating in analysis. In the dream, as I sat in my chair opposite him, I
noticed he was turning black. I reached over anxiously and, taking his
hand, said, "Please don't turn black. You must write!" The next day I
received a call from this man's wife asking me to treat him carefully that
day. He was in a deep depression, she told me, because the day before his

father had shot himself, and he, in reaction to this, was convinced he would some day do likewise. I did not remember my dream when this man came to my office, and I bent all my effort in trying to think of a reason why he need not follow his father's example. He was a writer and in recent months had been writing nothing. I said that I did not see a sufficient likeness between him and his father that would cause him to imitate his self-destructive action. I reminded him that, unlike his father, he was a creative individual, and then I heard myself saying, just as I had in the dream, "You must write," meaning that this is how he would rescue himself from his black mood. Then I remembered my dream which then seemed like a dress rehearsal for what I had to say at this critical moment in his life. His depression did lift.

Traumatic dreams are retrospective and repetitive, as if some painful experience had to be enacted over and over again until the pain is completely withdrawn, as if it were like having to extract a kind of psychic poison. Extrasensory dreams may be telepathic as well as precognitive. What both telepathic and precognitive dreams have in common is that they are found only "in the manifest content, that is disregarding context. ... Jung saw telepathic dreams not as supernatural but based on something inaccessible to our present level of knowledge (Mattoon 1978, p. 143). Also, "the rather common experience of *déjà vu* may be based on an earlier dream image, perhaps with a telepathic source" (p. 143). Thus, "Jung approached all such dreams with empiricism rather than the mysticism of which he was accused. . . . (p. 145).

FAIRY TALE ARCHETYPES IN CHILDREN'S DREAMS

Let us now return to explore somewhat further the use of dream interpretation in Jung's analytical psychotherapy. Jung's own statements, and those of numerous of his followers, emphasize the importance of understanding dreams in the light of the age and development of the patient. The case I reported earlier was a man in his middle twenties, still emotionally immature and uprooted. The dream interpretation I gave was predicated upon the knowledge that he needed to find his way back into life in a totally new way after his war experience. His analysis would provide him, and indeed the initial dream outlined it, with a *rite de sortie,* as described by van Gennep in his *Rites de Passages* (1960), where a young warrior in a tribal society is kept quiet and systematically discouraged from acting like a warrior until his inflation is reduced to normal limits, and until he is ready to adjust once more to peacetime society. In my patient's initial dream, 65½ Street corresponded to a similar tribal rite, the *rite d' entrée.*

The dreams of patients in other age groups require a different attitude for their interpretation, and this is especially true of the analyst's attitude toward any archetypal material that may appear in them. Children's dreams usually contain archetypal elements in fairy-story form. These "are the last vestiges of a dwindling collective psyche," according to Jung. What is creative for the child is to exchange this fantasy world for reality, and the fairy-story dream either helps him or hinders him in doing this. In some cases a "big dream" does more than this by providing the child with a kind of myth to effect a meaningful transition from mother to father, and thence into life. Fordham (1970) reports some interesting children's dreams in this respect, in his section on "The 'Transitus' From Mother to Father," one of which I shall quote along with his interpretation.

[Christopher] was a lively sensitive boy aged five, referred because he wet the bed, suffered from 'gastric attacks' and offended his parents by expressing uncomplimentary opinions about others in their presence. [He dreamed:]
    'My Dad smelt a smell of burning and we went in and there was a small flame that came from a match Dad had dropped. The flame danced like the fairies. My Mummy was very worried because the house might get burned, and you don't get anything back if the house is burned down.'
    The central event in this dream is the fire seen by Christopher as a fairy flame. Fire as an object into which fantasy is projected is common amongst small children; not realising its objective properties, they may put their fingers into it, conceiving it as something to play with. Even when they do know its dangerous properties they continue to play with it, and they may become excited by its heat and vitality, dancing or shouting when it flares up; Christopher sees it as dancing and so rhythmic. Rhythm can form the basis for a wide field of transformative changes. . . .
    The fairy world is related to nature in that fairies live in the earth, streams or woods, and represent a highly organised magical community of kings, queens, courtiers and so on. There are good and bad fairies who perform white and black magic. It is minor magic; they are neither as good or as bad in their own right as are the major gods and devils. Of them an aetiological myth says: 'The popular belief in Ireland also is, that the fairies are a portion of the fallen angels, who, being less guilty than the rest, were not driven to hell, but were suffered to dwell on the earth. They are

considered to be very uneasy respecting their condition after the final judgment'. . . .

The collective significance of fire is further recorded in common speech, its universality as a symbol is revealed in the world-wide distribution of myths concerning its origin, and in innumerable others in which fire is a central feature. Fire can be understood to stand for the passion which this boy expresses in his behaviour and enuresis—there being a common association between dreams of fire and bed-wetting. That the fire is started by Christopher's father is of interest because he, like his son, is lively but erratic, thus the dream suggests an identification between the son and his father. By contrast Christopher's mother shows anxiety about a real possibility. As in the dream it is she in reality who keeps the rather unstable pair 'down to earth', thus providing a necessary compensation.

This dream portrays the individual responses of the child and his parents to what may figuratively be called the flame of life. That knowledge of the real parents can be easily used to further understanding suggests that Christopher has acquired a good appreciation of essential parts of their natures mainly through introjection.

Fordham's work as a Jungian child analyst thus reflects, in the comments expressed here, an interesting mutation that has taken place in the understanding of child psychology in recent years in Jungian circles. Originally Jung tended to regard the child's psychic identity to depend almost exclusively upon that of the parents because he felt that ego identity had not been formed until well along in later childhood. He modified this viewpoint in his seminars on "Psychological Interpretation of Children's Dreams"[1] where he noted that certain dreams, especially those of adults who remembered their childhood dreams, were conditioned by unrecognized problems in the parents, while others had a diagnostic and prospective character. "Still others, unlike adult dreams, may reveal 'retrospective intuitions' in respect to the lives of the child's ancestors," say Mattoon (1978, p. 166). Fordham, in his practical work with children, tested these observations, revealing the fact, illustrated in Christopher's dream, that a child may put his lively awareness of the archetypal images together with his need for appropriate separation from the parents, at the same time correcting, with the therapist's help, what was wrong for him in their psychological makeup. For this reason, children need not be regarded as lacking ego identity even at an early age, and within the limits of the parent-child relationship may function as real invididuals.

1. Unpublished manuscript in private circulation by the C. G. Jung Institute, Zurich.

MYTHOLOGICAL ARCHETYPES
IN ADULT DREAMS

There is, however, a basic difference between children and adults which may be seen from dreams. Whereas the child should move away from the archetypes because their fascinating power may inhibit ego development, a patient over thirty at the onset of the second half of life may need to respond again to that fascination and be drawn once more into the world of the fairy story and mythology. This may accordingly promote a healthy increase in consciousness, by correcting the hubris of having been identified too strongly with a will-to-power in the Adlerian sense, or in the Jungian sense where the youthful ego has been strongly identified with the hero-myth. I have reported some dreams of this sort in *Ancient Myths and Modern Man* (Henderson 1964). Several dreams of women, one at an earlier, another at a later, period of development, both produced dreams which acquainted them with a need to honor their feminine nature in the reworking of a well-known mythologem, *Beauty and the Beast*.

Marie-Louise von Franz (1964) has described in detail certain dreams of mid-life that mirror the unconscious need for an overdeveloped ego to submit to the greater power of the Self, as a superior value, sometimes represented in human form, as a superior man or woman. A dream of this type may instigate a process of individuation symbolized by a "wounding of the personality and the suffering that accompanies it." von Franz continues as follows:

This initial shock amounts to a sort of "call," although it is not often recognized as such. On the contrary, the ego feels hampered in its will or its desire and usually projects the obstruction onto something external. That is, the ego accuses God or the economic situation or the boss or the marriage partner of being responsible for whatever is obstructing it.

Or perhaps everything seems outwardly all right, but beneath the surface a person is suffering from a deadly boredom that makes everything seem meaningless and empty. Many myths and fairy tales symbolically describe this initial stage in the process of individuation by telling of a king who has fallen ill or grown old. Other familiar story patterns are that a royal couple is barren; or that a monster steals all the women, children, horses, and wealth of the kingdom; or that a demon keeps the king's army or his ship from proceeding on its course; or that darkness hangs over the lands, wells dry up, and flood, drought, and frost afflict the country. Thus it seems as if the initial encounter with the Self casts a dark shadow ahead of time, or as if the "inner friend" comes at first like a trapper to catch the helplessly struggling ego in his snare [pp. 66–67].

At a still later stage this Self-image may appear in dreams as a supraordinate being with numinous, religious power or as a precious object, a stone or crystal, sometimes as a flower, like the lotus whose symbolism in the Buddhist iconography denotes an awakening conscious-ness of Self, appropriately represented as growth. Hence, the tree as an archetypal image may be the most convincing Self-symbol of all. By the law of compensation, a young person may dream of the Self as a wise old man, whereas an old man may dream of it as a divine child. The best known symbol for the Self, and one that has become associated with Jung as its Western "discoverer," is the Tibetan mandala or magic circle. This is a kind of yantra for meditation and healing in Mahayana Buddhism. But it should be remembered that Jung did not borrow the mandala from Tibet and advise his patients to use it in this imported form to heal their psychic wounds. He found it in the actual dreams of his patients, or his own, with-out oriental trappings, not in a theological frame of reference. Because the mandala-type design is symmetrical and ordered combining circle, square and center in four major parts with a suggestion of rhythmic movement in a clockwise direction, it may appear in dreams by way of therapeutic compensation to a state of conscious dissociation or disorientation.

The process of individuation may be studied profitably in a series of dreams and directed fantasies of a man patient in Jung's *Psychology and Religion* (1938), and in Gerhard Adler's *The Living Symbol* (1961) there is an excellent series of a woman's dreams, showing the value of regarding such material as part of a series and not as some kind of instant revelation. Above all, it is thought to be desirable to free the dream images of any exotic decoration that might obscure their basic archetypal (i.e., original) meaning. This type of dreaming is regarded as distinct from dreaming of things that are culturally known and have been transmitted by education, whether we know it or not.

DREAMS AND THE CULTURAL UNCONSCIOUS

However, dreams reflecting culturally known patterns abound in dreams, and in recent years I have come to speak of a *cultural unconscious,* as well as a *personal* or an *archetypal unconscious.* In this way, we may avoid calling a cultural symbol an archetypal image unless we know that the cultural symbol does have archetypal content. Many cultural images have lost their symbolic value, as Jung used to point out, becoming mere signs that can only be understood allegorically. A true symbol may repeat a known cultural image, but there is always something strange about it, something that does not fit the mind's expectation. That strange element is precisely the thing that brings the old image to life. My patient's dream of the woman called *Todida* is an example of such meaningful strangeness. Numerous culturally recognizable elements may be derived from her paradoxical name, but the true meaning lies in her embodiment of the death-and-rebirth archetype, which she both reveals and conceals in a paradoxical manner. Great storytellers, like dreamers, may tell the same story many times and, like Homer or Shakespeare, plagiarize shamelessly; but they never tell it the same way and there is an arresting, surprising twist of meaning that once more awakens the original, imaginative response that brought the story into being in the first place.

There is no evidence from dreams that cultural patterns are transmitted in the genes. Only the archetypes are inherited, and the word *inherit* in this sense must be qualified to mean something innate or latent, not something that can be passed on directly from parents to children. Cultural attitudes pregnant with significant imagery are passed on, not from parents to children, but from the whole environmental situation. The dreaming mind picks up this imagery from anywhere in its cultural milieu. Amplification reveals the source and interconnection between the different parts of this cultural complex of ideas and feelings. To this end the Jungian analyst usually advises his patient to record his dreams in a dream book or diary where he writes down not only the dream but also the associations and amplifications that come to him, as they so readily do, while writing. He is also encouraged to draw rough sketches of significant places or objects seen in the dream to provide further amplification.

MATTOON'S PARADIGM FOR CORRECT DREAM INTERPRETATION

How do we know that we have interpreted a dream correctly? Mattoon observes that an affirmative answer to any one or more of the following questions verifies the interpretation.

1. Does the interpretation "click" with the dreamer?
2. Does the interpretation "act" for the dreamer?

3. Is the interpretation confirmed (or disconfirmed) by subsequent dreams?

4. Do the events anticipated by the interpretation occur in the dreamer's waking life? [1978, p. 178].

The first question cannot be objectively tested since it is purely subjective, but when an interpretation "clicks" there is no doubt at the time that it has "struck home." It is patently an affective reaction experienced affirmatively. However, some affective affirmations of an interpretation may meet subsequent resistances and be repressed, so their verification may be in doubt.

The second question provides a more reliable test. Mattoon says:

A dream interpretation can be verified by "setting the dreamer's life in motion again" (Jung) whether or not it is accepted cognitively by the dreamer. The new vitality may become apparent in the stimulation given to the therapeutic process and the flow of positive feelings between therapist and patient. The obverse occurs also, Jung found: Errors in dream interpretation are reflected in "bleakness, sterility, and pointlessness" of the sessions [1978, p. 178].

The third question is the most important from a clinical point of view. Is the interpretation confirmed or disconfirmed by subsequent dreams? Mattoon reports:

When a dream has been interpreted incompletely or incorrectly, the dreamer sometimes brings in a subsequent dream in which the major motif of the first dream is repeated more clearly or given a negative twist through "ironic paraphrase", or the interpretation of the first dream is clearly opposed [pp. 179–180].

In my experience, it is a valuable sign of positive transference when subsequent dreams reject or make fun of a previous wrong interpretation. Where there is resistance the corrective dream may be repressed, leading to stronger resistances.

The fourth question is answered very clearly by Mattoon as follows:

Jung's fourth test for verification of dream interpretations consists of facts from the dreamer's waking life: events that are anticipated by dreams, including the occurrence or avoidance of difficulties; the persistence or disappearance of symptoms; and other physical events, such as accidents, organic illness or death. . . .

A dream interpretation providing a differential diagnosis between organic and hysterical symptoms may be verified by the subsequent course of the illness . . . [p. 181].

THE FLEXIBILITY OF JUNGIAN DREAM INTERPRETATION

When we sum up the varieties of interpretation that Jung envisaged in his long career as a dream interpreter, we might suppose that his flexibility rules out any theory of dream interpretation. Possibly because of his flexible approach, as Mattoon says (1978, ch. 16), "his theory remains remarkably stable over the years." In my own words, this theory states that, regardless of whether the dream content is personal, cultural, or archetypal, or whether it is referred to past, present, or future, and in spite of its few exceptions, the unconscious core of the dream is compensatory to the life situation and normally provides a therapeutic corrective to any one-sidedness it may show. Dreams sometimes may also be pure products of the imagination, like poems or plays existing in their own right, providing meaningful aesthetic or philosophic or religious allusions, at the same time as they perform their compensatory function.

References

Adler, G. (1961). *The Living Symbol.* Bollingen Series, LXIII. Princeton, N.J.: Princeton University Press.
Fordham, M. (1970). *Children As Individuals.* New York: Putnam.
Franz, M. von, (1964). The process of individuation. In *Man and His Symbols,* ed. C. G. Jung, and M. von Franz. New York: Doubleday.
Gennep, A. van (1960). *Rites of Passage,* trans. M. B. Vizedom and G. L. Caffee. London: Routledge and Kegan Paul.
Henderson, J. L. (1964). Ancient myths and modern man. In *Man and His Symbols,* ed. C. G. Jung. New York: Doubleday.
——— (1967). *Thresholds of Initiation.* Middletown, Conn: Wesleyan University Press.
——— (1972). The psychic activity of dreaming. *Psychological Perspectives* 3.
Janet, P. (1909). *Les Névroses.* Paris: Flammarion.
Jung, C. G. (1921). Psychological types. *Collected Works,* vol. 6. Princeton, N.J.: Bollingen Series, Princeton University Press.
——— (1934/1954). Archetypes and the collective unconscious. *Collected Works,* vol. 9, op cit.

————— (1938). Psychology and religion. *Collected Works,* vol. 11. Princeton, N.J.: Bollingen Series, Princeton University Press.

————— (1940). The psychology of the child archetype. *Collected Works,* vol. 9. Princeton, N.J.: Bollingen Series, Princeton University Press.

————— (1941). The psychological aspects of the Kore. *Collected Works,* vol. 9, op cit.

————— (1966). Two essays on analytical psychology. *Collected Works,* vol. 7. Princeton, N.J.: Bollingen Series, Princeton University Press.

Mattoon, M. A. (1978). *Applied Dream Analysis: A Jungian Approach.* Washington, D.C.: V. H. Winston and Sons.

Meier, C. A. (1967). *Ancient Incubation and Modern Psychotherapy.* Evanston: Northwestern University Press.

CHAPTER 23

THE DREAM IN ANALYSIS OF EXISTENCE

Werner M. Mendel, M.D.

ANALYSIS OF EXISTENCE AS DIFFERENT FROM PSYCHOANALYSIS

Analysis of existence can best be described by its differences from psychoanalysis. Unlike the variety of analytic approaches of modern schools of psychotherapy, analysis of existence (ontoanalysis, *Daseins-analyse,* existential analysis) does not derive from the theories of Freud. Historically, analysis of existence developed parallel to psychoanalysis, and its theoretical foundation is entirely different. I emphasize this difference between analysis of existence and psychoanalysis only by way of elucidation. No conflict or opposition between these points of view is implied or exists.

Analysis of existence focuses on aspects of human experience that are not stressed in psychoanalysis; it therefore allows a different approach to therapeutic intervention. The difference between psychoanalysis and analysis of existence can best be understood from the difference of development. Psychoanalysis is essentially based on a medical model. Freud dealt with the psychological superstructure, but he had basic faith in the biological substrate. He viewed aberrant behavior as illness and intervention as treatment. The analysis of existence developed from a philosophical foundation. The work of the German philosopher Franz Brentano (who was also a teacher of Freud's) was the basis of German phenomenology. In France, Eugene Minkowski developed categories for phenomenological observation as a basis for understanding human beings—their behavior, thinking, and feeling. In Switzerland during the 1930s, 1940s, and 1950s, Ludwig Binswanger, V. E. von Gebsattel, and Medard Boss refined the techniques of observation and intervention in this unique approach to understanding human behavior. In 1958, some of the major European work was translated into English and published in the United States as *Existence: A New Dimension in Psychology and Psychiatry* (May, Angel, and Ellenberger).

As is frequently the case in our country, a suggested approach to the understanding of human lives became a movement. The book title became a slogan: existentialism, existential psychiatry, existential analysis, and existential therapy swept the nation. Professional associations were formed and journals published; institutes for the training of existential therapists opened in New York and Chicago. Only a few members of these new schools understood the philosophical background and the theoretical assumptions. In the 1960s, existential therapy and existential analysis seemed to include the Gestalt therapies, psychodrama techniques, reality therapy, Sartre's confused mixture of philosophy and education, and therapies derived from Zen philosophies. The fad lasted for fifteen years.

DEFINITION OF THE TERM "ANALYSIS OF EXISTENCE"

Now that "existential therapy" and "existential analysis" are no longer fads, I would like to find a term which means what we are trying to say. Any term we use to describe analysis of existence as a theory of human behavior, technique of research, or approach to treatment, must designate what about it is different from the analysis of the psyche or psychoanalysis. It must describe what is unique about the theory and methodology. The German-speaking Swiss group has found and used a perfect term for this approach. It is *Daseinsanalyse,* which, literally translated, means "the analysis of being there." This term focuses on the analysis of psychological function of the central nervous system and also emphasizes the analysis of being and, even more important, of being there. Analysis of the being can be understood only in the context of, and imbedded in, the arena in which the being is. The term which has been used in English, *ontoanalysis,* is not adequate. Ontoanalysis is the analysis of being, and it leaves out *being there.* Ontoanalysis implies that the being is independent of, and can be studied separately from, *where the being is*. Analysis of existence *(Daseinsanalyse)* means that being can be understood only in terms of where the being is. Therefore, the best literal translation of *Daseinsanalyse* is "the analysis of being there." Unfortunately, this term is clumsy and uncomfortable.

In the American literature, the term "existential analysis" is applied to such a variety of theories of human behavior and therapeutic approaches that I propose it be dropped. Most therapies which are action-oriented and which focus on the here-and-now claim to be existential. Philosophies of human behavior and of psychological treatment derived from the French school of existential philosophy and the work of Sartre have also been called existential psychotherapy. The term is now devoid of any clear meaning.

I propose the term *analysis of existence* for what is called *Daseins-analyse*. "Analysis" is derived from Greek, meaning the resolution of the whole into its parts, so as to discover their nature, proportion, function, and relationships. "Existence" is derived from the Latin "existere," meaning to come forth, emerge. "Existence" implies development and differentiation in the context of the whole, coming into focus from the background.

THE METAPSYCHOLOGY OF ANALYSIS OF EXISTENCE

The metapsychology of *analysis of existence* can be described. Here are six major issues:

1. *The psyche.* In psychoanalysis the psyche is a reified structure, somewhat related to the brain and the soul, and seen as the source of observable verbal and nonverbal behavior. In analysis of existence many of the functions attributed to the psyche by the psychoanalyst are seen as part of the environment in which the existence is there. The biological structure (the central nervous system with its anatomy, physiology, and chemistry) is part of the biological world of the existence. The psychological structure of the psyche (memories, habits, and intellectual capacities) is part of the personal world in which the existence lives. The language patterns, cultural and societal influences, and the life style possibilities and limitations are seen as part of the surrounding world. What psychoanalysts term the psyche becomes part of the world of biology, history, and culture in which the existence is and can be understood.

2. *History*. In analysis of existence, as in psychoanalysis, a great emphasis is placed on the personal lived history of each individual. We each carry with us our history and it is part of us. This personal lived history, which is the basis for making judgments and decisions in the present moment of action, is a process which is constantly changing in human existence. History is always being rewritten. If you ask me how my childhood was on a day when I am happy, I would tell you about all the good things that happened to me. If you ask me about my childhood when I am sad, I will tell you about all the deprivations and unhappiness. Both are true, both are aspects of my childhood; but what I choose to tell you now is dependent on how I feel about myself, about you, and what my agenda is with you in telling you my history. For this reason personal lived history is constantly rewritten and is seen as active behavior in the present.

3. *Time, space, and causality*. Psychoanalysis views time as a straight line stretching from the past through the present and into the future, moving relentlessly forward in Aristotelian fashion. Analysis of existence sees time as a circle. The past and the future (the anticipatory aspect of time) impinge equally on the present, which is observed in the moment of action. Such an understanding of time takes more seriously the anticipatory affect of the pull of the future. The future is more than the projection of the past. The pull of the future is easily demonstrated. How I experience the moment is as much influenced by what I anticipate happening three hours from now as what happened three hours ago. Optimistic or pessimistic expectancy influence human behavior. Expectation is altered in certain states of psychopathology such as depression and mania, paranoia and obsessive-compulsiveness. French categorical phenomenologists have described various states of psychopathology in terms of differences in the experience of passage of time. In depression, time drags on endlessly; in euphoria, it passes quickly.

How space is structured, lived in, and used is another dimension of phenomenological observations which become part of the analysis of existence. The child living in the physical world of adults seeing the undersides of tables and chairs lives in a different world from those seeing the top.

Causality can be used to describe differences in states of psychopathology. The world of the paranoid is dominated by determinism, while the world of the manic is ruled by chance and caprice. When we look at dreams from the analysis of existence point of view, we pay particular attention to how time, space, and causality are portrayed.

4. *Reality and fantasy.* The context in which an existence lives is, in part, the space and dimension of consensually validated reality, including the world of things, other people, geography, climate, and structure. However, part of that world is the internal environment. This environment consists of the available personal, lived history (historicity), of the fantasy for which existence writes the script, of biological processes, of the capacities and limitations determined by genetics, and biological states. Reality and fantasy are both aspects of the environment in which existence must be understood. The influence of fantasy on feeling, thinking, and behavior is as important as the influence of consensually validated reality. Human existence is in a matrix of physical, personal, biological, psychological, and interpersonal dimensions.

5. *Behavior.* In analysis of existence, we take behavior very seriously. Behavior, both verbal and nonverbal, is the only data available. All else is conjecture and inference. I can never know what anybody else thinks or feels unless he tells me about it or conveys it to me by his behavior. I cannot read thoughts, I cannot measure feelings. Behavior is the final common path of existence in action in the world of its own making. Behavior is the data from which we draw inferences. We must always clearly differentiate observed data from inferences. Each of us thinks, feels, and acts in the world in which we live, a world which is partially of our own creation.

6. *Conscious, unconscious.* Even though much behavior is motivated by factors which are out of awareness at the moment of behavior and these factors can be brought to awareness by attention and by training and concern, we do not use the concept of the conscious and the unconscious in analysis of existence. Analysis of existence avoids reification of the conscious and unconscious as structures or geographical locations. In analysis of existence we take conscious production and acts and thoughts more literally than those who subscribe to the psychoanalytic point of view. An implication in psychoanalytic theory and technique is that the really important motivational factors are unconscious and stand behind the conscious ones. In analysis of existence, reality and fantasy, conscious factors and those factors which are at the moment out of awareness, personal lived history and the anticipation of the future, are all equally valued and seen as aspects of the world in which the existence lives.

DREAMS IN ANALYSIS OF EXISTENCE

Dreams are important in the work of Freudians, Jungians, and neo-

Freudians; they are also taken very seriously in the analysis of existence. Dreams have a primary position as they are a special part of the world of existence. They are especially useful in the analysis of existence because it is in the dreaming existence that the individual is totally in charge. The dreamer alone writes the script and produces the dream itself. Dreams are the best example of the world construction of the individual existence while it is relatively uninfluenced and unmodified by the world of reality, or by input from others.

In the analysis of existence, we are concerned only with the dream itself. We do not postulate "latent" content behind the "manifest" content. No "dream-work" which translates latent content to manifest content, nor "analysis of dreams" which undoes the dream-work, is part of this approach to dream analysis. Associations to the dream itself are not used to "get back" to the supposed latent thought or conflict which "gave rise" to the dream. Only the dream itself counts.

The technique of dream analysis in analysis of existence is quite similar to standard psychoanalytic techniques—except for the emphasis on the details of the dream itself. I ask my patients to keep paper, pencil, and a light available at the bedside and to write down the dream before getting up or having any conversation, to minimize forgetting and secondary elaboration.

During the session, the content of the dream itself is read by the patient and discussed item by item. The inquiry is conducted by the analyst while the patient tells the dream. For example, the analyst may ask who this or that person is, whether the setting reminds the patient of anything in real life, and so on. Next, the patient is asked to analyze the dream in terms of seven categories of phenomena. The analyst will use his knowledge of the patient and of other dreams the patient has produced to extend the understanding of these categories.

SEVEN CATEGORIES OF PHENOMENA
IN DREAM ANALYSIS

The questions we explore with the patient by asking for associations to the dream itself and the questions we ask of the analysis are the following.

1. *Role of the dreamer.* What roles does the dreamer play in this dream? How does he populate the dream? Who are the other actors in the dream? All of the roles are entirely creations of the dreaming existence and therefore give us important clues.

2. *Transactions in the dream.* What is the feeling tone in the dream? Are the individuals in the dream fighting or loving? Are they afraid or courageous? Do they overcome crises or are they overwhelmed?

3. *Relationships.* What are the relationships between people in the dream? Are there big people with little people? Are there dragons and slayers of dragons? beautiful and ugly people? Are they doing things together or against each other? Are they helping or hindering, are they creating or using?

4. *Temporality.* What is the experience of the passage of time? Is there a dominance of the past or the future? Does the dream represent a moment or an eternity? Does time move slowly or rapidly? The under-standing of the temporality of the dreaming existence gives us important clues to the psychiatric diagnosis, the major themes of existence, and the openness of the future. In depression, both in the dreaming and waking existence, time moves incredibly slowly, while in states of elation, time flies.

5. *Spatiality.* We analyze the dream itself for the space in which it occurs and the spatial relationships. Is this a dream of holes and caves and constraint? Does the dream occur in wide-open spaces with infinite panoramas and outstretched horizons? Does the action occur in closed dark places, or is the sun shining warmly over wide expanses? Since the dreaming existence creates not only the figures and story line, but also the setting in which this all takes place, an analysis of spatiality of the dream gives us important clues about the world design of the existence. During the dream the existence is most free and most creative and most like itself.

6. *Causality.* We analyze the causal relationships in the dream. There is an attempt at understanding the logic and the causal relationships which the dreaming existence creates in the dream itself. There is no differentiation between primary process and secondary process as there is in psychoanalytic metapsychology. Does the dreaming existence create a world of determinism, as we see in its ultimate form in the paranoid world? Does the dream present a world full of chance and accident, of free-floating attention and scatter, as is typical of the world of the manic existence? Is causality rigidified and codified, as in the world of the obsessive-compulsive, or are there lapses in the chain of causality such as we see in the world of the hysteric? Since the dreaming existence does not have to consider external reality, the causality in the dream itself is an excellent diagnostic tool for understanding the world view and response style of an individual.

7. *Emotional means.* One of the most useful and important contribu-

tions of the analysis of existence technique of dream analysis is using the dream itself for assessment of the emotional means of the person at a particular time in life. The assessment of emotional means is important in the conduct of psychotherapy. For example, if the dreaming existence creates a dream in which it is overwhelmed by the consequences of expressing an assertive attitude, such a patient is certainly not ready to express his assertiveness in the real world. Clearly, the expression of assertive and aggressive feelings is beyond the emotional means of that patient at that time in his dreaming world. The therapist would use this information obtained from dream analysis and recognize that in the strategy of treatment, the patient should not be encouraged to engage in behavior in the world of reality which is beyond the emotional means. The analyst fosters extension of understanding by asking questions as well as reminding the patient of other material which has come up previously. Finally, the analyst will remind the patient that the patient alone is the author of the dream. The analyst will request the patient to relate any new and extended understanding which can be obtained from the dream itself by the author.

EXAMPLES OF DREAM ANALYSIS

The Dream Itself

"I was in a large, one-story house with several wings. Many people lived there. There was a narrow winding stair that led to a special bedroom. I had something to do with arranging things so that people would be comfortable. There were hundreds of books there. Some were very old that had come with the house, others were my books. The owner was away. He was a very wealthy, titled, elderly aristocrat. I spend much time stacking the books but they are always in the way. It was crowded. I asked someone to stack them and that person piled them on the stairs that led to the bedroom. Judy lived in the special bedroom. Whenever anyone used the stairs or walked in the space just below, they stepped on the books and began breaking them and tearing them. I was very upset because no one seemed to care. There were some old editions in lovely leather bindings that were broken in this way. After I tried to go up the stairs and fell and slid on them, I got some people together and we took them all down. I went into different wings looking for a place to put them. In one wing, which was very elegant, my mother was lying on a lounge, resting.

She wanted to know what I wanted. I told her about the books. We found an alcove that had room for shelves. A man said that he would build some and guessed at the cost. As he walked out he said, *'pas plus de cinq livres,'* in a language so that others would not understand. I thought it was rather affected. There were lots of children and crying babies trying to nap but being awakened. They lived in different crowded areas around the stair that led upstairs. I kept picking them up, comforting them, and putting them down. They kept waking up and fussing. The phone rang. It was John Brown. The phone had a long cord and I walked around climbing over books and babies trying to find a quiet spot. Finally I asked him what he wanted. He said something about 'this life'— and again I couldn't hear him."

Discussion of Dream With Patient

"The house has no resemblance to any I know—large and expansive.

"Taking care of people is what I mostly do—my children, parents, clients, etc.

"Books and money are somehow connected. My father paid for my professional education and I still owe him $8,000; I can't really afford therapy if I am going to pay him back. But without therapy right now, I can't work and also can't pay him back.

"Judy is now twenty-seven. She is in Europe and out of touch with the family; all of her creditors are after her. She left them my address; I don't think I want to pay her bills this time. But that will ruin her credit rating.

"Mother and father have become very feeble. They were upset by the stroke a friend had recently. I need to look after them more and more.

"John Brown is a patient—doing very well since we worked on his communication difficulty."

History of Patient

This fifty-four-year-old woman was a member of the helping professions, whose three children were grown up and on their own, and who had been divorced from her husband for many years. She came into treatment for symptoms of depression, approximately three months prior to this dream. Her depressive symptoms had lifted with the use of medication (tricyclics), and she was now in psychotherapy two times per week. The goal of therapy was to identify the issues and problems in her life so that she could feel in charge of her existence rather than feel overwhelmed by it. She hoped to prevent future depressive episodes. The major problems which were identified during the three months of psychotherapy related to her dependency wishes. She had handled most of her life by taking care of others; now she was middle-aged, busy and effective in her career, and finished with the mothering of her own children. She was facing a changing relationship with her parents who suddenly were becoming old and feeble and who had previously been strong, powerful, and frequently rejecting.

Analysis of the Dream

Role. The patient plays the role in the dream, as in life, as the caretaker. However, the other roles portrayed include the crying babies who cannot be stilled by her care, the absent daughter in the bedroom above, the worker who demands payment for building bookshelves, the resting mother, the patient who calls from far away and cannot be heard, and the absent, titled, aristocrat owner.

Transactions. Her responsibility and concern is to make everyone comfortable. She has to look after the babies and the adults, she feels responsible for the books, and she is responsible for order. The other transactions she has created in her dream are babies who cry and are crowded and fussy, a resting mother who has advice and answers, a workman who offers to be helpful but expects to be paid and is rather affected. Other transactions include the absent aristocrat who owns the setting in which the dream itself occurs and a client who calls on the phone but with whom not much contact can be made because difficulties in communication occur. The interactions are all concerned with taking care of and being taken care of.

Relationships. The relationships are those of helpless babies and a concerned adult. They also include a grown daughter who seeks help with problems and gets advice from the resting mother. There are men who are offering to help structure but expect to be paid (not more than five British pounds—the patient had lived in England most of her life), and a man asks for help by phone but cannot be heard. There is also the influence of the wealthy aristocrat and the aloof, absent, grown daughter. All of these relationships are part of the dreaming existence's repertoire of responses to the demand for relationships made by her life situation.

Attempts are made to communicate with men but are difficult. One man speaks French (the patient is fluent in French as well as in English) in order not to be understood by some. Another (a male client of the dreamer) attempted communication, but this is interfered with because of a disturbed telephone connection.

Temporality. The time in the dream is portrayed as *ongoingness.* There is no specific event, there is no beginning and end, simply a continuum. No one is in a hurry, there are no deadlines. There is no crisis in the drama, simply a process which does not begin or end or go on to resolution.

Spatiality. The setting in which this dream occurs is a large one-story house with several wings. There is much room. In spite of this largeness it is crowded, so many people live there, including many babies. Even though the house is one-story and all on one level, there is a narrow stairway that leads to a bedroom in which Judy, the patient's daughter, lives above all this. Access to her is impeded by the crying babies, the stacks of books, and the narrowness of the winding staircase. There are hundreds of books, some of which are beautiful and leatherbound, some of which belong to the old, absent aristocrat, and some of which belong to the patient. These books are important, respected, and beautiful but in disarray and eventually are damaged. There is room for reconstruction and a chance for order, but this must be paid for and involves a man. Throughout the setting there is a feeling of largeness, expansiveness, and yet crowding. It is hard to find a quiet spot in all this crowding and with all the crying babies. However, mother has found such a spot.

Causality. It is the patient's responsibility to make order out of chaos, to satisfy the needs of all the crying infants, and to take care of the books. Cause and effect are represented in terms of responsibilities, duties, obligations, all to be carried out within the caretaker role the dreamer has assigned to herself in her dreaming existence.

Assessment of emotional means. It is clear that the dreamer cannot meet all of the dependency needs in the dream itself. She cannot quiet all of the babies; she cannot do it all alone. She needs help even from the resting mother. She cannot take care of all of the books for the absentee aristocrat. Some are ruined. She even needs to buy help to build shelves to put the books in order. Looking at this dream for the assessment of emotional means we would not encourage the patient to terminate therapy at this time. She needs help with meeting her dependency and in modifying her major transaction of taking care of others.

The Dream Itself

"I was landscaping the entrance and back of a large house. There were people whom I was trying to please and others whom I didn't care about. I showed a woman the arbor I had made. She made some suggestions which I liked. There was a terrible girl in the house. She was ugly, loud, rude, and was embarrassing everyone. Someone asked me to get rid of her because the guests had come and they would be annoyed and upset. I tried to keep her quiet and to get her coat on. She kept getting away and coming in through various doors and windows."

Discussion of Dream With Patient

"The girl is loud and rude, an embarrassment and uncontrollable. Someone asked me to get rid of her, to put her coat on, to get her out of the way. She kept oozing back in.

"I think these are aspects of myself. I feel I have to hide and be explained away to people so guests wouldn't want to leave. That is how I felt about myself until several years ago.

"I think people can still see this in me once in a while, and then they break off relationships. I hide part of me so other people won't want to go away.

"I have never allowed people to know every part of me or let every part of me be seen. Only you and my daughter Judy. You two are the only uncensoring people I know.

"This was an early California hacienda type, like in Pasadena. I knew some people like that once, the Johnson family. She was a college friend, Joan. She went to Redlands University. Her brother became a Lutheran minister. Both eventually became UCLA business graduates. They had large grounds, the parents were very formal, they were a socially prominent wealthy family. I didn't feel part of the family but I could be part of it all, just as I can be part of many things. It was sort of success in the social sense.

"The girl was deformed. She was a woman who was like a woman at work, who walks on a crutch. She has a lot of social skills I don't have. She has the personality of someone who is handicapped.

"I make an effort not to make waves, to be careful and to be pleasant and not to be apart from the group. Yet, in fact, I am really an isolate because I get very sick and tired of trying to get along with everybody."

History of Patient

This is the same patient as in the previous dream, only this is approximately two months later in her treatment.

Analysis of the Dream

Role. In this dream, too, the patient plays the role as the caretaker who is arranging things. However, in this dream she is a designer, an architect. It is her job to put everything together and come out with a pleasing design. She tries to please some people but she recognizes other people whom she doesn't want to or need to please. She is also attempting to control an uncontrollable, deformed child.

Transactions. Her task is to come up with a design that is pleasing. She accepts the fact that there are some people she does not need to please. Her attempt at control is unsuccessful and the outcome is frustration and failure; yet she is eager for praise. She wants someone to praise the arbor which she has made.

Relationships. The relationships represent her in the adult role of someone who designs life space, who controls or attempts to control the uncontrollable, who wants to please some people, and who doesn't care about pleasing others. There is some concern in these relationships of hiding certain things.

Temporality. This dream has a crisis. Something has to be done by a certain time (when the visitors come). It does not get accomplished. People are visiting who must not see certain things. Pushing it under the rug does not work.

Spatiality. Once again the dream is set in a large, expansive, aristocratic house, a type of California hacienda belonging to rich people. There is much space, and there is a front and back which requires landscaping. There is a feeling of largeness, expansiveness, yet the house does not work well to keep out the unwanted. The girl oozes back through windows and doors.

Causality. It is the patient's responsibility to provide order and design, to cover over the unwanted and the unpleasant.

Assessment of emotional means. It is clear in this dream that the patient fails and is frustrated in her attempt to deal with the unwanted. She is not successful in putting on the coat and hiding that part which needs to be hidden.

SUMMARY

Analysis of existence is a view of human behavior which has its roots in a philosophy derived from German phenomenology. The therapist who functions within the framework of the metapsychology developed from this point of view tends to work with observed phenomena and avoids high levels of inference. This emphasis on observed phenomena has a profound influence on the material we use and the techniques we employ in the treatment of patients.

In analysis of existence as a technique of treatment, we pay special attention to dream analysis. The technique of dream analysis in analysis of existence is somewhat different from psychoanalysis. We emphasize the analysis of the dream itself. We are not interested in symbolism, dream-work, or latent content. There is only the dream itself which we understand as the world created by the dreaming existence. We search the dream itself for clues about the dreamer, the world view, and life style, the problems, abilities, and emotional means.

References

Boss, M. (1958). *The Analysis of Dreams,* trans. A. J. Pomerans. New York: Philosophical Library.

——— (1963). *Psychoanalysis and Daseinsanalysis,* trans. L. B. Lefebre. New York: Basic Books.

Brenneis, C. B. (1975). Developmental aspects of aging in women. A comparative study of dreams. *Archives of General Psychiatry* 32(4):429–435.

Caligor, L., and May, R. (1968). *Dreams and Symbols: Man's Unconscious Language.* New York: Basic Books.

Freud, S. (1900). The interpretation of dreams. *Standard Edition* 4:1–338 and 5:339–627.

Frosch, J. (1976). Psychoanalytic contributions to the relationship between dreams and psychosis—a critical review. *International Journal of Psychoanalytic Psychotherapy* 5:39–63.

King, P. (1975–1976). The dream as dream stimulus. *Psychoanalytic Review* 62:659–661.

Kramer, M., Hlasny, R., Jacobs, G., and Roth, T. (1976). Do dreams have meaning? An empirical inquiry. *American Journal of Psychiatry* 133(7):778–781.

May, R., Angel, E., and Ellenberger, H., eds. (1958). *Existence: A New Dimension in Psychiatry and Psychology.* New York: Basic Books.

Mendel, W. M. (1963). Existential emphasis in psychiatry. *American Journal of Psychoanalysis* 23:1–4.

———(1964). Introduction to existential psychiatry. *Psychiatry Digest* 25:23–34.

Merrill, S., and Cary, G. (1975). Dream analysis in brief psychotherapy. *American Journal of Psychotherapy* 29:185–193.

Rotthaus, E. (1974). Meaning and effect of dreams in psychotherapy. *Krankenpflege* 28(11):462–464.

Schnetzler, J., and Carbonnel, B. (1976). Thematic study of the narration of dreams of normal, and of schizophrenic and other psychotic subjects. *Annals of Medical Psychology* (Paris) 1(3):367–380.

CHAPTER 24

THE DREAM IN BRIEF
PSYCHOTHERAPY

Marquis Earl Wallace, Ph.D. and Howard J. Parad, D.S.W.

ISSUES, DEFINITIONS, AND DEVELOPMENT

Brief psychotherapy is neither a single approach to treatment nor a specific technique. Employed with a variety of patient populations, symptoms, and problems, its historical roots are multiple and its applications multidisciplinary. Particularly effective in the hands of the most experienced practitioners, beginning therapists find it useful as well. It can be successful as a treatment of choice, or expediency, with patients who need only short-term treatment, or those who want only short-term help. While some believe it is a deviation from accepted approaches to treatment, others regard it as an application of accepted principles in a special context.

Although brief therapy is more than half a century old and is offered in community clinics as a matter of public policy, many practitioners regard it as new and unproven, and it is scorned by some of the best-trained and highly skilled clinicians.

This chapter serves as an introduction to brief psychotherapy and describes an experimental method in which dreams are used as a central focus. As there is no consensus as to the length of brief psychotherapy, even among those who employ it (six, twelve, twenty or forty sessions are commonly accepted), the authors define brief psychotherapy by the common denominator: any approach to treatment where a limit of time, or number of sessions, is a consideration at the outset of treatment.

Contrasting Principles of Brief Psychotherapy and Psychoanalysis

Many therapists oppose brief therapy. The opposition stems from a commitment to well-established principles of intensive psychotherapy taken from psychoanalysis. These principles were determined by Freud and have become so much a part of psychotherapy today that often the origins have been forgotten and, in the case of some younger therapists, not even learned.

The following will orient the reader to some of the contrasts between the principles of brief psychotherapy and those of psychoanalysis. Four principles of brief psychotherapy are presented in this way, while two others follow later.

Principle 1. As defined above, brief treatment is based on time limits. The therapist, unilaterally or with the patient, sets either a time period or a number of sessions that he and the patient will work together. This limitation may be precise, or more imprecise, such as, "We will work together for a few months."

While Freud reported setting a time limit on the remainder of a patient's analysis (Freud 1937)—itself a fact often used to justify brief psychotherapy within a psychoanalytic framework—he would not have posed a time limit at the beginning of an analysis. His reason was that unconscious change takes time, and the amount of time cannot be known in advance.

Principle 2. Due to the time limitation and other considerations, brief treatment focuses on specific symptoms, problems, and stresses, or combinations of these. This focus organizes the content of the treatment and the therapist's and patient's attention.

While Freud (1913) acknowledged that patients often desire to focus on a particular symptom, this is neither the goal nor a part of the method of psychoanalysis. Freud felt it was an exaggeration of the "selective capacity" of the analysis to do this, the purpose of analysis being broader.

Principle 3. Brief psychotherapy uses a variety of different techniques. Rather than fitting the patient and his problem into a specific technical or methodological approach, the therapist will pragmatically tend to use what he thinks will be effective to solve the problem given the time limitations. The range of techniques includes the traditional ones of silence, questions, clarification, confrontations, and interpretations (Langs 1973), but more proactive ones as well, such as suggestion, persuasion, mobilization of personal and social resources, and environmental manipulation, to name a few. In sharp contrast, the major interventions of psychoanalysis are silence and interpretation of the transference.

Principle 4. Successful resolution of a chosen problem or symptom in therapy will generate an effect which can carry over after the therapy (Heinicke and Goldman 1960, p. 489). The hope is that the patient will be able to solve other problems and symptoms on his own after the therapy, based on the success in the treatment and its aftereffects.

Freud (1912) believed that one had to cure the neurosis, not the symptom. Otherwise, he feared, another symptom would arise to take its place.[1]

Historical Development

Within psychoanalysis, brief therapy can be considered an outgrowth of interest in the ego. While emphasis on the ego does not necessitate modification in technique, and in fact many people oppose such modifications, some innovators have modified the method itself but retain psychodynamic conceptualizations of the patient's problems. A major turning point came with the publication of *Psychoanalytic Therapy* by Alexander and French in 1946, just seven years after Freud's death. Building on the earlier thinking of Ferenczi and Rank, they believed what was most helpful about psychoanalysis was the patient's emotional experience in the treatment rather than the genetic reconstruction of the patient's past (Barten 1971, p. 6), and that a wide variety of techniques could be employed using psychodynamic principles.

Modifications in technique are still a matter of debate, and at the time Alexander and French presented their ideas, there was vigorous opposition. Malan (1976, p. 19) believes they brought a "storm of hostility" on themselves and brief treatment in general in the way they presented their ideas, that is, as a modification of the technique of orthodox psychoanalysis rather than as a method of brief psychotherapy based on psychoanalytic principles.

Outside of psychoanalysis there were other events contributing to the development of brief psychotherapy. While Malan (1976, p. 8) traces the origins of brief treatment back to the establishment in 1934 of the Psychiatric Emergency Service at Massachusetts General Hospital, Boston, in fact Reynolds (1932) had earlier experimented with short-contact interviewing in social work and had concluded it was neither "a truncated nor a

---

1. For diametrically opposed views regarding symptom substitution, see Sloane et al. (1975, p. 100) and Schwartz and Goldiamond (1975, pp. 281–283).

telescoped experience, but is of the same essential quality as the so-called intensive casework."

The psychiatric emergency service was founded by Stanley Cobb as a part of the first psychiatric department established in a general hospital in the United States. Patients in emotional crisis could be seen in the emergency ward or the medical or surgical wards. Erich Lindemann, a member of Cobb's staff, developed his ideas about crisis intervention in the 1940s during the events following the Coconut Grove fire, in which many people died and which produced many emotional casualties. Lindemann then included preventive intervention crisis services as a part of the Wellesley Human Relations Service, a community mental health program he founded. Later, when he took over Cobb's position at Massachusetts General in the 1950s, he created the Acute Psychiatric Service as a part of the psychiatric department.

Several similar services were established in other cities, such as the Los Angeles Psychiatric Service, and the Trouble Shooting Clinic in Elmhurst, New York, founded by Bellak and Small (1965). The availability of emergency and brief treatment was expanded nationwide through community mental health centers during the 1960s, following passage of the Federal Community Mental Health Centers Act in 1963.

DREAMS IN BRIEF PSYCHOTHERAPY

In contrast to Freud, who feared evoking a resistance to remembering dreams if the analyst showed a special interest in them, the brief therapist, keeping time in mind, may well show an interest in eliciting dreams during the first session. This is part of a total effort to obtain as much information as quickly as possible.

Principle 5. In brief psychotherapy, one expeditiously seeks missing information and general patterns. Bellak and Small (1965) write:

> Certain forms of historical data are seldom volunteered by the patient during the initial history-taking hour, but an inquiry into their nature should be pursued by the psychotherapist. Early memories and dreams particularly yield psychodynamic information of value in establishing the meaning of the present symptomatology. Dream information may be investigated by beginning with recollected childhood dreams: dreams persisting in the memory over the years are usually pregnant with dynamic content. Repetitive dreams provide a unique opportunity for establishing patterns which have persisted. Recent dreams, of course, often shed considerable light upon

the patient's unconscious reactions to the dynamics of the precipitating situation [p. 44].

Elicitation of dreams is another device for eliciting communication, not only from those who find verbal communication difficult from others who speak more freely . . . the search is for the theme, the repeated common denominator, the latent content. . . . In brief psychotherapy, it is wise to choose for interpretation only those parts of the dreams which contain manifestly-discernible recurrent patterns [p. 47].

The active solicitation of dreams is also advocated by Merrill and Cary (1975, p. 186). They found that dreams can be used to help break down denial, so that the patient is able to recognize his conflicts and his own contribution to his problems. Used with selected cases which had been resistant to change, the solicitation of the dreams created a new stage in the treatment characterized by more active participation on the patient's part. "Through layer-appropriate interpretation of dreams, the therapist has a powerful tool in recognizing the conflict and showing the patient even in brief psychotherapy that, if such an impulse is being considered during sleep, it must have remained unresolved during the day" (p. 190).

Dreams as the Central Focus in Crisis Intervention Short-Term Therapy

The approach presented here views brief psychotherapy from a crisis intervention perspective. It is possible to differentiate between brief and crisis therapies (e.g., see Parad et al. 1976, pp. 308–311). It is also possible to view brief psychotherapy as crisis psychotherapy. Phenomenologically, a patient seeking psychotherapy is in a crisis whether he is responding to a stimulus that most people would consider an overwhelming stress or reacting to a stimulus dynamically determined to be overwhelmingly stressful by that individual.

Crises, then, are a normal part of life, a common way of responding to significant life stresses. In crisis, the stressful event creates a strain beyond the individual's (or family's) capacity to adapt. Often, previously unresolved but analogous problems and conflicts are reawakened and become part of the crisis. With or without professional help, solutions arrived at during the crisis will effect the resolution of the earlier issues as well as the immediate situation. Therefore, a short-term approach based on crisis intervention thinking may make a significant contribution to the patient's overall psychosocial functioning as well as to his current adjustment.

Principle 6. The psychotherapist using a crisis approach to short-term therapy will use the patient-therapist relationship for specific ends related to the patients' needs. Some of the more common uses are to (1) help the patient develop an awareness of his problems, (2) break down excessive denial but discourage pathological regression, (3) meet specific needs such as reduction of guilt or relief of anxiety in the process of creating the relationship, (4) communicate confidence in the patient's capacity to deal with the problem, (5) steer the patient toward ego-adaptive behavior and away from maladaptive behavior, and (6) offer concrete social and environmental services as needed (Parad 1965, pp. 291–293).

The following is a specific approach to brief treatment. The therapist introduces the idea of time-limited therapy in the first session. After hearing sufficient information to decide that brief psychotherapy should be used (some therapists use it for every case just as some therapists use long-term therapy for every case), the therapist may tell the patient that it is his preference to work intensively for a short period of time and ask the patient if he is willing to do so as well. If reluctant, the therapist may motivate the patient to accept this approach by pointing out some of the obvious advantages, such as saving of time and money. The therapist may set a specific time limit or number of sessions, such as twelve or twenty, or the therapist may be somewhat more informal by proposing that the process last a "few" months.

If the patient agrees, dreams may become a central part of the therapy. In the first session, the therapist asks the patient about his dreams and obtains whatever dream reports he can. The patient is told that dreams can be an invaluable aid in facilitating the treatment, that they are a rich, creative source of material and often furnish answers to current problems, and that the progress in therapy can be greatly enhanced by remembering them.[2]

For those patients who do not remember dreams, or who feel that they do not dream, additional help can be offered in this way. They can be reassured that they do have dreams every night and can learn to recall them. A suggestion to keep a pad and pencil next to the bed to remember whatever they can about their dreams is helpful.

Being expectant and hopeful that the patient can and will remember dreams, and that they will be a helpful part of the therapy, is usually sufficient to start the flow of dream material by the second session. When

2. It is interesting to note that Hollis (1972, pp. 195–196), among others, argues against the active solicitation of dreams in a clinical social work context.

dream material is not forthcoming, a careful confrontation of this lack of material and a reminder about the need for it is usually advisable. If only minimal dream material is presented, the therapist may strongly reinforce whatever is remembered either by his verbal reaction or by making special notes about the dream.

Miss A, in her second session, said she did not remember any dreams. The therapist said, "Remembering dreams will help." She said she did remember just one thing from a dream, a "worm squiggling." The therapist asked what that brought to mind. She said, "Like a snake in the grass. That must be that s.o.b. boyfriend of mine" (who had just abandoned her). The therapist asked if she were angry at him, a fact she had denied up to this point. She responded by reporting some of the history of her relationship with him, and as she did, she became angry. She spoke about what a snake in the grass he had been, and how she felt as insignificant as a worm herself after losing him. Excited at first, and then appropriately upset by her own revelations, Miss A was able to make use of her dream material and was later able to learn more about her true feelings through her dreams.

Dreams are as valuable to brief treatment as this method's emphasis implies. The dream material gives the therapist immediate access to information it would take longer to obtain in other ways, such as by reports of other behavior or by waiting for the issues to become aspects of the treatment situation itself. The genetic origins, major conflicts, and missed affects may easily be perceived and related to the current psychosocial situation. The focus on dreams facilitates the patient's interest in his own intrapsychic processes, which improves the quality of other reporting as well. Solutions to problems first conceived in dreams can be recognized by the therapist and supported. Even when dream reports reveal serious defects in problem-solving capacities, the awareness of the defects gives the therapist a better understanding of how to deal with the total situation and a better appreciation of the patient's true struggle.

CLINICAL VIGNETTES

The following cases illustrate how dreams can be used as a tool in brief treatment.

Case I: Jane

In this case, the patient was unable to find anyone to listen to her dreams, neither her husband nor even her previous therapist. The current therapist cooperated with the patient's desire to find meaning in her dreams. After a period of improvement, the patient produced new dream material, but this time she became alarmed. The therapist then helped her with the reinternalized fear of her own intrapsychic contents in a way that enhanced her self-esteem. This case also demonstrates the eclectic nature of many brief therapy approaches. The husband was invited for a few conjoint sessions so that the patient's interpersonal environment could be more accepting, thus illustrating the use of an interactional approach in brief psychosocial therapy.

Jane was an attractive, well-groomed, thirty-one-year-old woman, married to Sid, a "rigid, inflexible" engineer, aged forty-one. She had a lively, twenty-three-month-old daughter, Sandra. Jane asked for brief therapy to deal with "my anxiety, my depression, my relationship with my husband, my relationship with my mother-in-law, my mother and my baby." She cried throughout the intake interview. While she had been occasionally sad during the last few days she had been crying more than usual; in fact, she couldn't stop crying at times.

The precipitating event that triggered her request for therapy was a quarrel with her husband in which he pointed out that he thought she needed to straighten herself out because she was "exceptionally emotional." She would get very angry with him when he overconcentrated on what he was doing, whether reading the paper or watching a TV show. She felt cut off. Her dilemma was, if she told him how she felt, he seemed to get angrier, which would only make her angrier, as well. She complained of "feeling caught in a vicious circle—the trouble is I get hurt, not he." Therefore, she was keeping everything inside. She had considered taking diazepam but thought it would be better to talk with a therapist. She had a brief period of counseling three years earlier and it seemed to help to have someone to talk to.

An only child, her husband had a very strong attachment to his mother, aged seventy-two. Jane's problem with her mother-in-law was that "we are totally different." The mother-in-law was a religious person, and Jane was not a churchgoer. Jane felt very distant from her own mother as well. She was, however, very close to her father, who died three years ago. His death had precipitated her request for the previous period of counseling.

Her parents were divorced when she was ten. Since that time her mother had had a succession of boyfriends and two unsuccessful marriages. Jane also complained of feeling alienated from her brother, who she said was jealous of her close relationship with her father. She described her mother as cold and indifferent and mentioned how hard it was to talk with her. "I feel all mixed up and afraid to let out my anger. I don't want to lose Sid because he really is good to me and gives me and our daughter a lot of security." She said the only happy time she can remember in her whole life was a brief period during adolescence when she was a class officer in high school, had a boyfriend, and seemed less dependent on her mother, brother, and father for support.

After hearing all of this, I commented that she was obviously in a very unpleasant and painful place, and that I would like to help her. I asked what bothered her the most. She said it was her feeling that her husband's distance was "like my mother," and she wondered whether she "married her mother." Yet her husband was also supportive, gave her a lot of freedom, and maybe she shouldn't complain so much. I asked what she was experiencing while she was crying, and she said "a kind of terrible emptiness and a vague dread that some harm" would come to her daughter Sandra. She said she was a prolific dreamer, but her previous therapist, while otherwise sensitive, did not pay any attention to her dreams and was interested only in "problem solving." I told her I was very interested in her dreams, that they were a rich source of self-awareness, and often creativity, and when properly understood, a source of strength in helping people get a better feeling about themselves.

She seemed visibly relieved, dried her tears, and recalled a dream that she had the night before in which she felt utterly helpless. She was angry in the dream and seemed overwhelmed with the feeling that "nobody takes me seriously." She went on to say, "I was upset that I allowed myself to be so helpless." She reported the following dream sequence.

"A mason was building a fence out of bricks; however, instead of using mortar, he was using diapers, rags, and other items of clothing. I looked closely at these items of clothing and realized that they were Sandra's clothes. I was trying to control my anger. I first began to talk calmly and rationally to the mason whose identity seemed vague and inscrutable. The mason looked back at me in an equally vague way. I began to raise my voice louder and louder, but no matter how much I shouted, it made no difference. Other people began to watch. No one was upset; no one flinched. It felt the way it usually does—me against the world."

She began sobbing, saying she was feeling totally miserable. I asked what she was experiencing, and she said "misery and helplessness, and a kind of vague anger." I asked what the dream meant to her—"let yourself go and see what comes to mind." She said that it was as if she just couldn't get through to other people. I asked who the mason was, and she said she didn't know; she became anxious. I suggested the mason might be her mother, and she immediately responded to my suggestion and said, "Yes! Now I remember what I thought when the dream awakened me; it was my mother and she wasn't listening to me; it was the way she is when she calls and feels cold and distant. No matter what I try, I don't get through, as I keep saying." I asked what the meaning of using her daughter's clothes as a substitute for mortar was, and she said: "Well, I hate to say it, but my mother is not someone I trust alone with my daughter. She smokes and drinks a lot, and I'm always afraid she's going to harm my daughter the way she harmed me. My mother knows my feelings and gets even angrier when she picks them up. I also have the feeling that my mother is jealous of me because she has never had a relationship as good as the one I have with Sid, despite the problems we have. She said I was being patronizing toward her because I had a husband and she didn't, and that I was more happily married than she had ever been, and compared me also with my brother who was recently divorced." I asked her what her feeling was now, and she said "a feeling of powerless rage against my mother." She recalled that the dream was probably precipitated by a phone call in which her mother asked for her husband and paid no attention to her. Drying her tears, she decided immediately that the next time this happened, which would be soon, she would confront her mother directly.

The following week she reported that her mother had indeed called, abruptly asking for Sid. But before Jane turned the phone over to her husband, she confronted her mother with her feelings, and her mother became apologetic. Jane said she began to feel some strength within herself, and instead of crying as she usually does, she expressed her feelings toward her mother who then seemed to be on the defensive. The look on Jane's face as she reported this led me to believe she felt more self-assured.

She asked if it would be all right to tell me about a sequence of repetitive dreams she had been having off and on for the last several months before she came for help. She said these dreams were very disturbing to her, although her husband made light of them, saying, "They are only dreams so stop fussing, they have nothing to do with reality." This made her feel furious at him and freaky. The recurrent dreams consisted of variations on a chasing scene.

"Someone is always after me; I am a fugitive; I am running and running. The chaser has a kind of cloudy quality to me. Whenever I seem to be getting away from the chaser, the chaser gets close to me. If I run into a room and close a strong door against the chaser, the chaser in the dream would turn into a liquid and slip under the door and envelop me that way. It was terrible; I would keep waking up. Funny, since coming to see you, my dream has suddenly gone away, but when I think of the brick and the mason dream with the rags, I am reminded again about the chaser."

Jane paused, seemed thoughtful, and I inquired what she thought the dream sequence meant. "Well," she said, "for one thing, I'm glad it's over, but knowing me, I'll start a whole new sequence before our work is done." I repeated that dreams were important to the work that we were doing, and that by understanding them, she would be better able to deal with her helplessness, her anger, and, we would hope, improve her communication with her husband, her mother, and her mother-in-law; and she would also worry less about her daughter. She said one of the dreams that was so scary involved her husband's getting killed in a hospital. It was because her husband Sid was trying to help her get away from the chaser.

I asked what all of this meant to her. She said it was hard to figure out. She had tried to talk with her husband, but again he belittled the dream and said it was just a dumb nightmare, that "I was too emotional."

I wondered whether the chaser was her mother and if the chaser and the mason were one and the same person. The brick wall was made out of rags instead of solid mortar, symbolizing that the wall was not going to be strong enough to keep mother away from her. The positive meaning is her desire for separateness, her wish to lead her own life. She seemed startled and said she just remembered that her mother, in one of their angry encounters, had accused her of putting a wall between them since she married and had the baby. I said perhaps the mason partly represented herself as well as her mother. She said her mother was jealous of her relationship with Sid and she was fearful that "mother would take away anyone who was good for me since I never had anything that was good. The things that are good to me are my husband and my daughter. So I guess I put up a wall against her, too."

After a period of anguished crying, she became silent, wiped her tears, and then heaved a sigh of relief, saying she felt better. She realized that she had emphasized to her mother how confident she felt in taking care of Sandra, how great she felt as a homemaker and wife, and she thought that this was probably to her mother "like rubbing it in." Then she said, "I guess mother got back at me in the dream, chasing me down and telling me that I couldn't do that to her." Brother and mother had both said to her, "You're so damn perfect, you're disgusting."

After the first two sessions with Jane alone, I arranged with her to see her husband, who reluctantly participated in three conjoint sessions. Jane was surprised that Sid, with encouragement from me, was able to listen to her; he indicated that perhaps dreams did have meanings, though he wished she would be more rational and realize how harmless they were. He said, "I do not dream, or if I did, I would not bother to remember." He indicated there was nothing about himself he wanted to change, but he did love his wife. He was sorry she was hurting so much and was willing to come for a few times to help her.

In our second and third conjoint sessions, tension between Jane and Sid was markedly reduced after their intensive discussions about some of the sources of disagreement between Jane and Sid's mother. They worked out a number of practical solutions to their disagreements which they said, and I believed, brought them closer together.

However, during the sixth session of a planned series of sixteen interviews, Jane reported that, as feared, a whole new series of dream sequences have "come upon me." In the new dream sequence, she kept dreaming of high school.

"I don't know anyone; I am a misfit; here I am thirty-one, and everybody in the dream is sixteen; I have trouble finding my classes; I can't find my locker; I can't find my key; I'm back working as a waitress doing things I did before, but I don't remember anyone. I go up to people and they don't recognize me. I want them to see how much more confident I am than when I was a class officer and it's as if no one recognizes me."

I suggested that the dream was actually a very positive one; although it seemed to her like a put-down, there was some important, perhaps hidden meaning in it. This time she was reflective rather than tearful, and asked what that might be, commenting that I had earlier stated that dreams could be creative. I reminded her that, as she said, she wanted people to see how much more confident she now was than the insecure girl who had been a class officer, even though as a class officer she felt better than she had before she entered high school. Could it be that it was not they (former fellow students) who could not recognize her, but Jane, as it were, looking in the mirror was surprised by her own image of increased self-confidence and couldn't recognize her own accomplishments? After all, during the last two weeks she had not been having prolonged crying episodes, had been able to communicate more effectively with Sid without feeling distant from him, was less intimidated by her mother and mother-in-law, and was no longer panicky or having feelings of dread about Sandra's well-being. She nodded vigorously, said she was very relieved, that maybe she could stop having all these dreams now that she understood they were positive. She said, "Thanks to you, I'm not having anymore chasing dreams." I replied, "You had the courage to remember and record your dreams; you were able to work hard with me to master feelings of insecurity. You risked asserting your feelings to your husband, mother, and mother-in-law; *you* did it!"

In follow-up sessions, Jane indicated that she did not have the heavy, depressed feeling or the emptiness she experienced before, was sleeping better, and was thinking of devoting more time to volunteer and club activities. She reported that she had a babysitter for Sandra so that she would have more time for herself, and was generally less worried. She promised herself she would keep track of her dreams in her diary. "It's a wonderful feeling to be glad about your dreams instead of scared to death by them the way I used to be."

Impression: Jane, an intelligent, introspective young woman, found herself reacting to her husband as if he were her mother, thus reexperiencing fears of abandonment and powerless rage. Recalling her strong feelings of attachment to her father who had died a few years ago, she became aware of the fact that she thought that her mother and brother would be revengeful toward her because she and father were close, while mother and brother were close to each other. It was as if there were two coalitions in the family—Jane and Dad versus Mother and Brother.

Deep within herself Jane was struggling not only with fears of anger, but desires for independence from the negatively-perceived mother and fears of success, symbolized in the chasing and high school dreams. Jane's active dream life was, of course, her way of expressing her positive growth strivings as well as finding outlets for these tensions; and yet when she wished to share her dreams, her husband seemed critical and again reminded her of her mother. Three conjoint husband/wife interviews—in which I reenforced Sid's willingness to listen to Jane, letting her ventilate her dreams without being judgmental—seemed to produce a marked reduction in tension, along with problem-solving discussions about areas of disagreement where Sid and Jane could talk more directly with each other about their relationships with relatives. Jane's drive toward healthy individuation found expression in a markedly improved self-image.

The nature of the transference is also worthy of note. The therapist deliberately played an implicitly benevolent parental role, supportive of

Jane's impressive growth efforts but confrontive when necessary. For example, when Jane hesitated to ventilate suppressed feelings of anger against her husband and relatives, the therapist was firm in insisting that Jane become aware of how she depressively turned her hostile feelings against herself.

Case II: Hilda

In this case, the tragic trauma of a rape victim was treated by using a crisis intervention approach. Although relatives were not brought to the session in person, the therapist, influenced by Bowen's (1978) theory, encouraged the patient to work toward a rapprochement in her relationships with her family as a significant part of the treatment. This demonstrates one of the hopes of the crisis therapist, that the crisis victim's post-therapy level of psychosocial functioning will be *above,* not just up to, the level before the onset of the crisis.

Hilda was a twenty-five-year-old student nurse who came for help after being raped two weeks previously. She had reported the rape to the police, began to feel better, and then all of a sudden couldn't stop crying; she began to feel scared and had difficulty in keeping up with her nursing responsibilities. She had gone to her boyfriend's for a week after the rape. He seemed very protective, but then she said, "He accused me of trying to get my hooks into him, and we parted, and I guess that's what got me started crying again." Hilda had an older brother whom she described as "spaced out." She had little or nothing to do with her parents who lived a rather isolated life in a community only about one hundred miles away. She felt they always disapproved of her.

One of the nursing supervisors at her hospital urged her to seek therapy to talk out the rape trauma. Hilda said she was a terrific dreamer, but didn't know what to do with her dreams. I expressed interest and encouraged her to save them.

We agreed on the following goals: (1) to help Hilda work through her feelings of terror, depression, and violation relating to the rape trauma; (2) to sort out her ambivalent feelings of dependence as compared with her desires for independence from parents; (3) above all, to get a better feeling about herself. She said, "Sometimes my self-esteem is about one on a scale of ten, ten being high."

Very tearfully, she reported a dream that she said went back to early childhood, probably beginning when she was six or seven. She kept having it. In the dream she is, she said sobbingly, "invisible." She is in a desert area. "I am there, but not there." She went on to say, "I see my grave. I wonder what it would feel like not to exist. I am afraid of being by myself. I wake up." "Do you feel invisible?" I queried. "Yes," she replied, "that's the way it was when I was a kid. My mother was always sewing and cooking, and my father drinking or telling crazy stories about the Korean War, and my brother would be doped out, and I felt no one even saw me."

She immediately reported another dream:

"I am on a country road, I see a beautiful wheat field. My mother and brother and myself are there. We stop at the top of a hill. It seems that my mother and brother—and father who suddenly shows up—don't even know that I'm here. I wake up with my mouth open. I am lonely. I have the strange feeling it is so easy for them to leave."

I asked, "What do you feel now?" She said, "Sad." I nodded, "Feeling lonely?" She responded, "Yes. Missing my boyfriend, angry at him."

In the second of about twenty planned sessions, Hilda reported a very disturbing dream in which she saw her father, but suddenly her father became her boyfriend, and then her boyfriend became her father again. The dream woke her, and she was sobbing.

Crying profusely in an agonizing manner, Hilda said, "I've heard a lot about this Oedipus stuff; I can't believe it! I can't believe it! I always felt so close to my father when I was little, but then when I was about seven or eight, he wouldn't get close to me or hug me. He seemed to prefer to be nice to other kids in the neighborhood."

I said it was natural to want a close relationship with her father, and it hurt when he became distant. She seemed appreciative of my concern.

Hilda reported another dream sequence:

"I am in a house in the country with my family. Again I see my father and he looks like my old boyfriend, the one who rejected me. There's a whole bunch of kids, maybe nine or ten. They all live in a farm house. They are poor. They seem to have an idiot child. Should they put her away? God, could I be that child? The father keeps going in and out of the bathroom, and I find myself left out. All of a sudden, the father grabs two infants and throws them into the river. I see him do this, and I want to kill him. He seems like a King Kong macabre monster, but says I'm attractive. Suddenly another father emerges who says he can smash the monster, but has no effect on him. Finally, the good father goes off and finds a way to kill the bad monster father. I remove myself from the struggle."

I asked, "How do you feel?" She replied, "Not as upset as I would think. You know what, this time I can see that one of the fathers, the one who was unable to slay the monster, is like my boyfriend, ineffectual." She added she was relieved to be able to talk about her dreams; she was feeling less depressed.

In two subsequent sessions, we reviewed the details of the rape trauma. There were several dreams in which there were terrifying themes of violence and dismemberment. I commented that these were normal reactions to the rape trauma, that it was good that she could remember her dreams and talk to me about them, and it was good that she was able to discuss the rape episode with her roommate and some of her friends, all of whom were supportive. She was back at work now, after having had a brief leave, and beginning to be able to concentrate again and work more productively.

She reported another dream in which she and her mother and brother were in the country (a frequent idyllic theme in her dreams).

"We are in the middle of nowhere. There are rolling hills; the wheat is blowing in the wind [another familiar scene]. It is beautiful, endless, like a landscape version of outer space. Nobody else is there for a hundred miles. Suddenly my mother has done something wrong. Looks like a minor traffic violation. The sirens are blaring, two policemen come up, they take my mother and brother away; my mother protests; I wait for the police to see me. Mother says, 'There's no use, you won't be able to do anything.' I feel tiny. I shrug my shoulders; I feel upset. I try to yell, but nothing comes out of my mouth. I feel powerless and helpless. Mother, brother, and police all drive off. I ask myself why they left me. I feel doomed to die. I'm just a little kid and they ignore me. I go into total shock; again I am invisible [accompanied by agonized weeping]!"

I encourage her to go on, and she said that she felt like a little ghost.

"I ask myself if I'm really here. I can see my body, but it's as if everybody, especially my mother, looks past me, again as if I don't exist at all. Wow, God, what a feeling! She should know where I am. I guess I am angry at my brother for not telling mother that I am there. I wake up while trying to scream, but again, nothing comes out of my mouth."

I commented, "Sounds like a very disturbing dream!" Hilda replied, "Yes, that dream or something like it always seems inside of me. It's like a monster dream. I remember when I was a girl fearing that I would be chased by monsters." I asked, "When do you think of your monster-type of dream?" She answered: "Mostly when I feel mad at my parents. I used to get upset at my parents and then dream. The dreams would just sort of pop into my mind while I was sleeping and I would sometimes feel guilty—I should have been dead. I feel my existence means nothing." I said, "You wanted your parents to notice you more—to care about you."

She replied, "Yes, it's as if they didn't know I was there sometimes. I used to ask myself if I'd done something wrong? I wasn't worthwhile. I asked my mother if my birth was planned. It was a mistake; so was my brother's."

I connected part of her fear in the dream with her need to go to court to give testimony against the rapist, who had been found by the police. Hilda stated she felt very scared in court and wanted to be invisible; she was afraid of retaliation from the rapist, who was like the monster in the dreams.

She had to give testimony for the district attorney's office at the preliminary hearing. We role-played what she would say in subsequent discussions with the district attorney, and she seemed to become empowered to feel more confident about continuing to press charges against the rapist. She pointed out that she felt a lot of support from me, looked forward to our interviews.

In another dream, she saw me standing by while she was screaming. She reexperienced the rape and this time she said she was able to run, suggesting my help empowered her to escape.

She brought out more feelings of fury against the boyfriend who failed to be nurturing to her after a "lousy one week of taking care of me." She called him a "chickenshit person like her brother." She continued, "Men are cowards; even the rapist was a scared man when he put the knife to my throat. You can't count on men; my father was never there for me, nor my brother, nor my boyfriend. When men try to support you, they are half-assed." I asked, "Are you having such feelings toward me?" She hesitated, "Well, yes, or not really; I don't know. I guess I would like to come in more frequently for sessions." We talked about meeting on the average of once a week, but we could meet twice a week for the next couple of weeks if she wished. She was relieved, but confirmed her regular appointment for the following week.

She brought out other dreams in which she fantasized that she was being nursed and complimented by the mother figure who was nursing her, "You are so beautiful!"

We discussed her desire to be cared for, which was understandable in view of the desolate feeling she had about her childhood.

I pointed out that along with her fears of weakness, she obviously had considerable strength. I reminded her of her excellent school record, her ability to tune in on feelings. I expressed the hope that she would continue to keep in consciousness her feelings about the rape episode so she could continue to work them through and "get to the other side." Soon we would talk more about her mixed-up feelings toward her parents.

The rapist finally confessed and was put in jail.

During our fifteenth session, Hilda reported another dream:

"A ferocious bear was trying to get me. It attacked. I tried to counter-attack, but was helpless. I am close to getting eaten, and someone is trying to help me. The bear claws at me all night, over and over again. It reminds me of frog and spider dreams I used to have."

Her interpretation: "All my angry feelings are coming out. The bear is, I guess, my fear of my father's anger. It also reminds me of that goddamn rapist." I commented, "You seem to be running, too, from your own anger against the rapist, always making excuses for him, saying he's mixed up."

Hilda responded with a torrent of anger directly expressed at the rapist, saying, "I wish he would die! I wish he would hang himself. I could claw him." I suggested, "Perhaps you are also the bear who wants to claw the rapist." She responded, "It seems to go back and forth. First maybe I'm the bear, and then father is the bear, or the rapist is the bear."

We talked more about the theme of anger. Hilda became thoughtful and said: "There is a staff member at our clinic who is really inept. I get angry at him, but then I say, 'Poor boy, he has problems, and if I love him, he'll get along better.' This is what I always do. I feel angry and pissed at someone when they don't do what they're supposed to do, like my father or mother—then I make excuses, then I hate them, or myself, or some-times I just detach myself the way I have from my parents. Then I feel that terrible emptiness or invisibility."

I inquired, "Of the many dreams we have discussed, which one seems to be the most important to you? Hilda responded tearfully, "The most important was the dream when I realized I pick men as if I was going to get back the father I once had when I was a kid, and that's unreal."

In a later session, she reported her parents had called her: "My conversation with them was just phony, strictly on the surface. My roommate commented on that and asked when I was going to level with them. It's as if you [the therapist] and roommate are in league with each other."

I laughed, and we talked about her desire to make peace with her parents. I actively encouraged her to visit them. They still didn't know about the rape and she would have liked to tell them. Using the techniques of anticipatory guidance, we role-played what she might say to her parents.

She said she was feeling better about herself now, had a new boyfriend. She didn't know how long it would last, but somehow there was a different quality about her. She was not glued to him the way she was to her other boyfriend.

Treatment reached a culmination when, after the sixteenth session, Hilda visited her parents for a weekend, told them about the rape, felt much relieved when they were supportive instead of being critical. She hoped she had established a basis for a much more open relationship with both parents. Her father, contrary to her expectation, did not drink too much, was not explosive. She realized that when she felt strong inside, her parents attended to her more. Her father told her that actually her brother was not as freaky as she thought, just different from her (he had a stable job, was married, had two children). Her parents also expressed interest in her future career plans, were much more supportive than she thought they would be.

Commenting on her fear of growing up, Hilda said, "I guess I'm trying to be a perpetual adolescent." I laughingly said, "Sometimes you act as if you will be dragged screaming into adulthood." Smiling, she said, "Funny thing that when I visited my parents over the weekend, my father asked when I was going to stop being a teenager."

The day after visiting her parents she wore a dress instead of her usual jeans. Feeling uncomfortable, she said, "Symbolically, I guess I am ready to start growing up."

Impression: This was an hysterical young woman who came for therapy at a time of extreme emotional crisis. Not only was she reacting to the terrifying trauma of the rape episode which threatened her with death, but the rape reactivated previously suppressed and repressed memories of her own vulnerability and invisibility as a child. Oedipal feelings of longing for her father (and accompanying guilt about her wish to be loved and stroked) as well as oral-dependent strivings toward her mother (to be nurtured and succored) rose to consciousness, causing her anxiety and tension. These were dealt with selectively and derivatively. Suppressed, angry feelings toward her former boyfriend resulted in depression, along with her inhibited anger and longing toward her parents. Bringing out her anger, as well as her natural desire for dependence, as well as independence, brought her much relief. Insight into her fear of growing up was a dramatic step forward in the therapy.

Dreams were used as an important tool. Hilda became much less depressed, and her self-esteem improved. Though she still had painful memories about the rape, she became increasingly involved in professional and social activities. Moreover, reopening communication with her parents released a growth spurt toward age-appropriate individuation. The transference relationship was positive, with the therapist playing an alternating nurturant parental role (during periods of extreme anxiety and depression) and challenging role (during periods where opportunities for growth and independence were presented). By therapeutic design the transference relationship was kept on an implicit nonregressive level.

SUMMARY AND CONCLUSIONS

While a dream is an individual psychological event, reporting a dream is an interpersonal one. When the report is made to an interpreter of dreams, the way he understands dreams will influence the meaning of the dream in the relationship and to the dreamer. For example, a fortune teller may recognize the wish aspects of a dream to predict the future, while an analyst will use it for a different purpose, to recall the past, excavate repressed material, or detect transference phenomena.

Brief psychotherapy is a special context as well, and time is the crucial variable. A therapist who undertakes brief psychotherapy will likely modify his approach, keeping this limitation in mind. Typical consequences include focus on specific problems, greater variability of technique, and more active solicitation of material, including dreams. In dream interpretation, there is greater tendency to focus on what the dream reveals about the here and now—the specific person-situation configuration being confronted in the treatment—than about the genetic material. However, even genetic content can become important, again in a different derivative context, more limited and specific than generalized.

The authors believe that brief psychotherapy is particularly comprehensive within the context of psychoanalytic ego psychology, for the ego "knows" time while the id does not. A variety of ego functions are involved. Examination of the effects of the brief treatment approach in relation to each function (Bellak, Hurvich, and Gediman 1973) is beyond the scope of this paper. Yet the importance of structuring the therapeutic relationship, using time boundaries and other principles of crisis-oriented brief psychotherapy, influences ego functioning in general, with implications for self-esteem, management and control of affects and impulses, superego functioning, and object relatedness.

In order not to be misunderstood as proposing yet another fad in the gimmick-ridden field of therapy, we close with four caveats. (1) While the patient's dreams have been emphasized, other communications are equally relevant, whether facts, fantasies, or silences. (2) Although dream solicitation and interpretation are the central focus of the approach described, the therapist obviously utilizes other techniques such as exploratory clarifications, interpretation of other material, persuasion, mobilization of outside resources, and environmental manipulation. (3) True, the dream can be a promising tool in brief therapy, yet solicitation of dreams is neither a necessary nor sufficient condition for effective psychotherapy to occur, for in the final analysis the therapist can only create an environment which the client will use to change himself. (4) Obviously the observations presented here have been at the practice wisdom and theoretical level; more systematic research (using random assignment of subjects to therapy in which dreams will be solicited versus a control group) would scientifically test the efficacy of the dream as a central focus in brief psychotherapy.

References

Alexander, F., and French, T. (1946). *Psychoanalytic Therapy.* New York: Ronald Press.

Barten, H., ed. (1971). *Brief Therapies.* Morningside Heights, N.Y.: Behavioral Publications.

Bellak, L., Hurvich, M., and Gediman, H. (1973). *Ego Functions in Schizophrenics, Neurotics, and Normals.* New York: John Wiley and Sons.

Bellak, L., and Small, L. (1965). *Emergency Psychotherapy and Brief Psychotherapy.* New York: Grune and Stratton.

Bowen, M. (1978). *Family Therapy in Clinical Practice.* New York: Jason Aronson.

Freud, S. (1912). Recommendations for physicians practising psycho-analysis. *Standard Edition* 12:109–120.

——— (1913). On beginning the treatment. (Further recommendations on the technique of psycho-analysis I). *Standard Edition* 12:121–144.

——— (1937). Analysis terminable and interminable. *Standard Edition* 23:209–253.

Heinicke, C., and Goldman, A. (1960). Research on psychotherapy with children: a review and suggestions for further study. *American Journal of Orthopsychiatry* 30:483–494.

Hollis, F. (1972). *Casework: A Psychosocial Therapy,* 2nd ed. New York: Random House.

Langs, R. (1973). *The Technique of Psychoanalytic Psychotherapy.* Volume 1. New York: Jason Aronson.

Malan, D. (1976). *The Frontier of Brief Psychotherapy.* New York: Plenum.

Merrill, S., and Cary, G. (1975). Dream analysis in brief psychotherapy. *American Journal of Psychotherapy* 29:185–193.

Parad, H. (1965). Preventive casework: problems and implications. In *Crisis Intervention: Selected Readings.* New York: Family Service Association of America.

Parad, H., Selby, L., and Quinlan, J. (1976). Crisis intervention with families and groups. In *Theories of Social Work with Groups,* eds. R. Roberts and H. Northern. New York: Columbia University Press.

Reynolds, B. (1932). An experiment in short contact interviewing. *Smith College Studies in Social Work* 3:3–107.

Schwartz, A., and Goldiamond, I. (1975). *Social Casework: A Behavioral Approach.* New York: Columbia University Press.

Sloane, R. B., Staples, F., Cristol, A.H., Yorkston, N. J., and Whipple, K. (1975). *Psychotherapy Versus Behavior Therapy.* Cambridge, Mass.: Harvard University Press.

CHAPTER 25

THE DREAM IN ANALYTIC GROUP THERAPY

Martin Grotjahn, M.D.

CHANGING USE OF DREAMS IN PSYCHOTHERAPY

The Twenty-eighth International Psychoanalytic Congress, held in London, July 1975, was devoted to "Changes in Psychoanalysis." A special debate dealt with "The Changing Use of Dreams in Psychoanalytic Practice." The first and most valuable contribution was made by Harold Blum (1976). He pointed out that dreams have been subject to extensive investigation in experimental studies of sleep. This remarkable and important laboratory research added little to the understanding of dreaming as a psychological phenomenon or to the clinical significance of the dream in the psychoanalytic procedure. Freud's theory about dreams remains valid.

The situation changes when dreams are considered in relationship to contemporary analytic technique, especially in regard to modern ego psychology. Freud (1900) considered the interpretation of dreams as the royal road to the unconscious. Originally, the technique of psychoanalysis was almost synonymous with the technique of dream interpretation. This has certainly changed. Very early, Freud made it clear that dream interpretation should never become an art for its own sake; it should always be subordinated to the treatment by free association.

It was soon realized that there was no "royal road" to the unconscious without resistance. The roots of this resistance, as expressed in the transference, became the central focus of psychoanalysis as a treatment. The dream was seen as a form of communication, similar to other forms. The dream became a link in the chain of associations with special relevance for the understanding of transference resistance. The process of dreaming is similar to the process of free association. At all times the patient, not his dream, is analyzed.

No dream can be analyzed completely. Even to attempt such complete dream analysis would disrupt free associations. Dreams can be used in the service of resistance and may obstruct free associations. The dream may serve as a guide to the understanding of the transference, and that is the way dream analysis is now used in everyday analytic technique. Remembering, forgetting, and reporting dreams are all details of communication and must be understood in the framework of transference.

In the discussion of Harold Blum's presentation (Curtis and Sachs 1976), several speakers stated that the theory of dreams has changed the least in the development of psychoanalysis. Also mentioned, in the discussion of the analytic group process, was that according to Freud, the dream does not seek to be interpreted by the dreamer; this has to be done by the analyst (or, as may be added, by the group).

Nowhere in the discussion were dreams in analytic group therapy mentioned.

DREAMS AND GROUP REACTIONS

As an illustration, "an hour of dreams" in a group of eight members, four male and four female, will be presented here. Such emphasis on dreams is rare. It happened in this group at that time because of the competitive peer relationship within that group and the relatively high number of analytic therapists who were group members. The preoccupation of this group with dreaming was limited to this session and was not repeated.

James started the hour by telling a dream which he could not understand: "My divorced wife was sitting in the back seat of a car. She held a very tiny baby. I hoped she would take care of it. All the next day I felt grown up, strong and sure of myself."

James was startled by the dream and did not know how to deal with it. The group had no difficulty coming up with an interpretation. A female group member expressed it thus: "You return the baby in you to your mother or to your divorced wife. You must have realized the meaning of your dream because you behaved as if you had grown up overnight and became a man. You felt as if you had said farewell to the infant in you."

Stimulated by the dream and its interpretation, Marsha told one of her dreams: "I looked down on me and I had a growth from my vagina like a salami, or something like it. I woke up and felt empty. I was hungry and I went to the kitchen and had to eat until I vomited." This patient, too, was totally naive about the dream.

The group reacted seriously to the dream, offering to Marsha the interpretation that she was working on her wish to be a man and a woman at the same time. She did not wish to be just a man—she wished to remain a woman and become a man in addition.

At this point I decided to intervene in the group process since I did not want the entire session to become bogged down in dream interpretation and result in the neglect of more urgent problems. However, a third member of this group, Hans, was faster than I was and presented a dream he had a week before and which he had been ashamed to report in last week's session; now he felt he could risk it:

"I had a disgusting dream which I did not want to tell the last time. I had defecated into a tin cup and then tried to hide it. I put it into the garbage disposal. My wife asked me what I was doing and I said, 'Oh, nothing.' Then she prepared dinner and I felt awful. I felt guilty—as if I had poisoned the whole family."

For a while the group did not respond and listened to Hans's associations, until suddenly a member of the group said: "You do think you are full of shit—you are afraid that you are responsible for the depression of your wife and the difficulties with the children."

Irving, another member of the group and a therapist by profession, offered a transference interpretation and said to Hans, as if testing something he had read in an essay about "the group dream": "You want to poison this group." Hans rejected this interpretation firmly by saying: "The group is my good mother, especially at dinner, after the session, and away from this office."

Then the same man who had offered the transference interpretation started to tell his own dream which involved several members of the group. By now, however, one of the members of the group had enough of dreams and said: "Don't tell us what you dream about us! Tell us what you feel about us!" This man had the habit of telling dreams about the group at every session, and the group rightfully suspected this to be a resistance and refused to listen to his dreams any longer.

DREAMS AND SPONTANEOUS GROUP
INTERACTION

The dream about the feces in the kitchen, told by Hans, has many more and deeper meanings and could lead to an interpretation of Hans's immense hostility, his guilt, and his fear that he may destroy people, including his family and the group. Such deeper interpretation would not have been appropriate at the time. The group therapist's ambition should be to stay ahead of his patients just a couple of inches, not a couple of miles.

In psychoanalysis, the dream should be subordinate to the primary principle of free association; in analytic group therapy the free, honest, spontaneous response and interaction of the group is more important than the detailed analysis of the dream. The group relates to the dream like an invading army to the hostile territory to be conquered. There may be strongholds of individual resistance which the army bypasses and which have to be cleared up later. The group may be satisfied with a general interpretation of a dream, leaving deeper and individualized understanding to a later time when the increased sophistication of the group allows it, or when the individual is capable of continuing self-analysis within the group.

When I look at this group as a whole and at the dreams as one message, I would say: After an interruption and after getting acquainted again in the last session, the group now announced its intention to proceed immediately to analytic work, as they understood it. Each dreamer stated more or less his central conflict as disguised in a dream. James dreamed about separation anxiety and the hope for individuation; Marsha dreamed about the wish to be both man and woman; Hans has to deal with his fear of being dangerously hostile; and finally, Irving announced his wish to become the therapist of the group.

DREAMS AND TRANSFERENCE DIMINISHED IN
GROUPS

The group may disregard transference interpretations to a certain extent even though they stand in the focus of standard analysis. Transference in the group does not become an intensive, regressive neurosis which may exceed the intensity of the infantile neurosis which it is supposed to replace. The group does not develop such intensive transference neurosis, even though transference feelings and transference situations occur constantly and have to be interpreted. The difference between the transference neurosis of individual standard analysis and the transference situations in analytic group therapy allows a difference in the focus of interpretations, be it a dream or any other communication. There is little resistance against insight into the unconscious of any individual of a group by the other group members. The individual protects himself against his unconscious, but the group does not need such protection and understands individual defenses in its members.

The transference situation in an analytic group is quite different from the transference neurosis as it develops in standard analysis. This leads to a diminished use of dreams in analytic group therapy.

The transference in groups is divided and includes transference feelings toward the therapist, the peer members, and the group as a whole, symbolizing the preoedipal mother. Since the peers tend to correct instantly and consistently most transference distortions, this is a factor in diminishing the intensity of transference. The division of the transference among therapist, peers, and the group as a whole interferes with the development of a regressive, intensive transference neurosis, as in standard analysis.

GROUP DREAMS IN THE AGED

Raymond Battegay (1977) pointed out in his remarkable essay on "The Group Dream" that this kind of dream in which the disguised group appears in the manifest dream content allows the study of the individual's real and transference relationship to the members of the group.

The following cluster of dreams was dreamed by an elderly man who lived in stormy, joyless, and tearless isolation; he had joined the group in the past month, since I considered group therapy as the treatment of choice for this kind of character neurosis.

Here are the dreams about the group that he reported shortly after he had started in the group:

"I took a test which was easy, but still I tried to see what the other people in the group of students had done. I tried to read their test papers without turning my head."

"I watched a group of people killing sharks in a tank—or were they being thrown into the tank to be eaten by the sharks?"

"All this could be one dream in three parts; anyhow, I watched scuba divers walk into the ocean with their equipment in their hands. They had not put it on. Then there came a fisherman in a boat, trying to steer between the divers."

All three dreams refer to the dreamer's feeling about the group situation which was so new to him. He watched other people to see how they behaved, and he was afraid that he would be thrown to the group of young sharks and they would tear him to pieces. They were all fishermen who dived into the deep sea and got into deep water, and they all could be killed. These dreams show the dreamer's deep fear of being exposed, of getting involved, and perhaps of having his defenses shattered. His solution: living at a safe distance from all feelings in a state of isolation and alienation seemed to him better than becoming exposed to the existential sufferings of being human.

BEAUTIFUL DREAMS OF DEATH

In groups of the aged it is startling when members speak about dreams of indescribable beauty and exquisite colorfulness. Therapists are not always prepared to accept the fact that beautiful dreams are dreams of death. Only when the weight of associative evidence becomes overwhelming does the tragic truth become evident. Here is one example representing many, some of which were reported previously (Grotjahn 1972, 1977):

One of the old men of the group, aged seventy-three, reported the following dream: "I was walking with my wife and son, who was perhaps six years of age, through a medieval city, with houses leaning against each other, as seen in old engravings or in the background of Flemish paintings. We, or perhaps only I, visited an old physician, who showed me around his primitive but clean and efficient office. He opened a door which I had not seen, and we entered a most beautiful Gothic cathedral, like Chartres. Sunshine was filtering through the stained glass windows. It was most beautiful and peaceful."

The whole scene reminded the dreamer of the bedroom of Philip II of Spain, in El Escorial, with his own private entrance to the Royal Chapel. The old country represented the dreamer's father, separation from his family, death, and joining his ancestors in the hereafter.

This was one of the dreams which was not immediately understood by the members of the group, who had not worked together for a long enough time and had not achieved analytic sophistication. As time went on, the man continued talking about the dream and associating to it. His father had died many years before, and the patient expected to follow him soon. The medieval city represented the place of the family where all the dead members would come together and meet again. The church, the mother church, expects her children to return to her and so symbolizes the grave, peace, and the final answer to all problems of living—and, as such, it looked good, right, and beautiful.

Beauty in dreams symbolizes death, regardless of whether the dreamer is a church-going member of some religion or has been a free-thinking individual all his life, without any special expectations about the hereafter, as was the case with the dreamer here mentioned. Such dreams do not fulfill a regressive, infantile wish for eternal life or paradisic happiness; they symbolize in living color a time of peace, beauty, and truth.

The following dream was reported by a man who had lost his best friend two months previously. On the morning before his death, the dying friend had told him about a dream of a blue wheelchair; now he was at peace with himself and the world and was ready to die. He wished the physicians would keep him comfortable and would stop any further attempt to sustain his life—a decision with which everybody silently agreed. Two months after the death, my surviving friend dreamed the following dream:

"I was walking through a beautiful landscape and recognized it as reminiscent of the grounds of the cemetery where my friend had been buried. There came a tall man dressed in a dark black suit who joined me silently. We admired the blue sky, the green grass and the flower beds. We came to a blooming bush which I now recognized as Mountain Lilac. I held my arm underneath it and tapped one branch so that blue blossoms rained on my arm. This was supposed to show my friend that I will join him soon—we all will at the end."

UGLY DREAMS OF DEATH

It seems almost obvious that ugliness, disorder, and any reference to fecal matters may also symbolize death, as in the following dream by a man in a group of terminally ill people:

"I found myself in an office where I had started my career fifty years before. I had been gone for a long time and had not done my duty during this time. Of this I was painfully aware. My former colleagues were very old, sitting silently everywhere, and signing forms. There was dirt and disorder all around. On the papers were standing dirty trays, coffee cups and spoons, and it was disgusting. I discovered that I was barefoot, and I was fearing that I was stepping into filth."

The symbols of death are ugliness and beauty. Perhaps the secret of all beauty is to show that truth is ugly and sad—but the symbol can make it beautiful. Similar dynamics may explain the emotions felt in the musical experience.

References

Battegay, R. (1977). The group dream. In *Group Therapy,* eds. L. Wolberg and M. Aronson, pp. 27–41. New York: Stratton International Medical Books.

Blum, H. (1976). Changing use of dreams in psychoanalytic practice: dreams and free associations. *International Journal of Psycho-Analysis* 57:315–324.

Curtis, H. C., and Sachs, D. M. (1976). Dialogue on 'The changing use of dreams in psychoanalytic practice.' *International Journal of Psycho-Analysis* 57:343–354.

Freud, S. (1900). The interpretation of dreams. *Standard Edition* 4:1–338 and 5:329–627.

Grotjahn, M. (1972). *The Voice of the Symbol.* Los Angeles: Mara Books.

——— (1977). *The Art and Technique of Analytic Group Therapy.* New York: Jason Aronson.

CHAPTER 26

THE DREAM IN GROUP PSYCHOTHERAPY

Joseph M. Natterson, M.D.

In an early session of an analytically oriented group, a middle-aged man reported the following dream. He is living in a beach house when suddenly he becomes aware of an enormous tidal wave moving toward his home. He flees in terror. He witnesses the wave engulf his house. But then with relief he observes that after the wave has passed the house is still intact, and he returns to his home.

This dream occurred at a time when the dreamer had been experiencing a merciless and excessive attack from virtually all other members of the group for his cruelty toward a vulnerable group member and for other annoying character traits. He felt as though he had been engulfed by the tidal wave of criticism, and he recognized that the attack from the outside had brought him into closer contact with his inner aggression and that this growing realization was the basic source of the dread which he experienced in the dream.

ABUNDANCE OR PAUCITY OF DREAMS IN GROUPS

It is fairly common for a dream or two to serve as the central axis around which a group session develops or crystallizes. Group psychotherapists know that the frequency of dreams in therapy groups depends upon a number of factors. Yalom (1970) believes that both the number and type of dreams a patient brings into the group are functions of the therapist's response to the initial dream brought into the therapy. The therapist's receptivity to that primary presentation of dreams indicates to the patient and the group the therapist's depth of interest in dreams. Additionally, I would say that the number of dreams is influenced by the characteristics of the group patients and their individual and collective interest and sophistication in working with dreams. It is also true that the total dynamic circumstance of the group at a particular moment or phase will influence the numbers of dreams reported and worked on or neglected. For instance, dreams are more likely to be offered when the group is in a reflective period than during intense, interactional impingement among the members.

LESSENED DISGUISE IN DREAMS IN GROUPS

Dreams in groups tend to be less disguised than in individual therapy or analysis. The available explanations are interesting. Klein-Lipschutz (1953) attributes this to the fact that in group therapy transference provokes less anxiety and, therefore, a lessened need for repression. In his dream example, each member is asked to associate to the manifest content as though it were his own dream. Active group interpretation proceeds less hampered by the censorship and inhibitions of the dreamer, who in turn may feel encouraged by the group process to offer subsequent dreams quickly and often. Kadis et al. (1963) emphasize the utilization of other group members' associations to overcome the dreamer's resistance to dream material. As in children's dreams, the separation between manifest and latent content tends to be diminished. Klein-Lipschutz (1953) believes that the understanding of symbols is greatly facilitated by the group process. He states, "Psychoanalytic group psychotherapy with its particular medium and procedure provides for a less distorted and more abundant dream material."

If an individual's dream is blatantly revealing and evokes excessive anxiety, the group is available to share responsibility and to protect the individual. The group may also obfuscate the meaning of a dream in the service of the group resistance.

VARIABLE MEANING OF DREAMS IN GROUP THERAPY

An individual's dream obviously derives from the individual's deep, unconscious psychological core. But when the dream occurs in the context of a group therapy experience, the group becomes a powerful influence in the evocation of the dream and the shaping of its manifest as well as its submerged form and structure. A dream occurring in the group will be different from a dream occurring in individual therapy which involves only the dreamer and the therapist. The importance, then, of any theme in a dream during group therapy is an inconstant, shifting one, and only imprecise statements can be made. A group member may be powerfully absorbed in matters of consummate personal significance. A dream in such a circumstance, even if brought to the group and even if manifestly about the group, may not be significantly relevant to the group dynamics and transferences. So, with each dream a judgment is made about whether to emphasize its group or individual importance. Yalom (1970) corroborates this idea that selectivity must be exercised by the therapist in attending to dreams brought to the group. Does the dream point to the group process? Does it reflect the dreamer's feelings toward one or more group members? Does it comment on the dreamer's relation to the therapist? Does the dream express conflicts and personal preoccupations mainly unrelated to the group?

DREAM INTERPRETATION IN GROUPS

In psychoanalysis the well-known approach to dream interpretation is as follows: the dreamer reports the dream and associates to the entire dream and its various elements. Not so with dream interpretation in a group. The difference is characterized by a diminished tendency to free association by the dreamer, the other group members, and the group therapist. Instead, opinions and interpretations are offered readily, even hastily, by the standards of individual therapy. These interpretations may be about the dreamer or the group, but they come easily and without the careful support provided by extensive free association. Group dynamics are characteristically intense and interactional, as opposed to the more reflective, intrapsychic tendencies of individual therapy. These dramatic interactional phenomena reduce the opportunity and inclination toward free association in groups. Individual members are more likely to be silently mobilizing for the next maneuver by one or more group members. This is a kind of conservation of psychological energy which might be dissipated by free association. The therapist also participates. He or she has less occasion for leisurely reflection focused on the dreamer—there are six or seven other hungry psychological mouths waiting for the food of insight and change. So, in evaluating the dream, the therapist will be guided by the reactions—and "reflex" interpretations—of the other group members. Wolf and Schwartz (1962) also emphasize the art and skill demanded of the group therapists in using dream material. Not only must the therapist make judgments about the relevance of the dream to the group process, as mentioned before, but he or she must also decide when to interpret and when to bypass intervention and interpretation.

THE GROUP DREAM: MEANINGS AND EXAMPLES

Group therapists and researchers have extensively studied the "group dream," a type of dream often reported in groups that evinces similar characteristics: a reference to the group overtly or in thinly veiled disguise, the appearance of the therapist by name or in the form of a leader type, and the presence of an emotional climate derived from the group situation. Breger, Hunter, and Lane (1971) observed experimental subjects in a structured group setting prior to dreaming and noted the frequency with which pre-sleep group events and the subject's symbolic constructs of the events were incorporated into all of the dream content. They attribute their findings to the intense emotional involvement fostered by the subjects' participation in the group sessions.

Kaplan (1973) provides several examples of the group dream. One of his examples was reported by a male in a private group.

I'm in a concentration camp sitting around a table with a group of people. Across from me a young woman with blond hair is seated. It seems strange that it's a concentration camp because everyone is well-nourished and healthy looking and there is food on the table. Two Nazi guards are standing there [the patient points to where the two cotherapists are located in relationship to the group]. I become very angered and I stand up with a gun and yell out, "I'll take you bastards with me," but instead of shooting at the Nazi guards, I seem to shoot at another person or object [p. 422].

This dream is a thinly disguised representation of the patient's therapy group as indicated by the use of the group situation and the allusion to a blond patient. Another group member is a blond-haired woman in whom the dreamer had expressed interest for some time, and she had been seated opposite him in the last group meeting. The dreamer was experiencing distress at the loss of a girlfriend, and a few sessions prior to the dream he had likened the distress to his grandmother's grief when she learned that members of the family had been killed in concentration camps (the patient was eleven at the time).

Group themes in dreams are manifestations of the influence of the group on its members and may express prevailing concerns of the group members. Also, it is not uncommon that new group members will report group dreams, which indicate the intensity of early fascination with the group. Here is a second example from Kaplan (1973) of a group dream, reported by a female in a clinic group.

> I'm with the group and we're sitting in straight chairs. Dr. Kaplan has a clipboard and he is arranging for the group members to take their turn in gymnastic exercises. I was not included. As he was talking, his pants fell down and he said, "They were supposed to be hiphuggers but they aren't hugging anymore." He picks up his pants and continues unflustered.
>
> The room seemed to be able to absorb increasing numbers of members even though each chair was filled. There were only men in the room and they were looking at me. Dr. Kaplan suddenly came up behind me and said, "Trust me. It will be all right." Then women came into the room with other men and I felt relieved [p. 422].

The therapy group is directly referred to, including the therapist, by name. The dreamer had been selected by her employer to attend a training course leading to career advancement. In the past she had avoided such opportunities. The dreamer's sensitivity to the group's developments is documented by the circumstance that several months later the dreamer does, in fact, become the only woman in the group who remains committed to continuing membership.

Dreams of group members convey the juxtaposition of the inner world of the individual and his social world. To French and Fromm (1964), almost all the problems their patients brought to them arose "out of difficulties or failures in their attempts to find satisfying ways of fitting into some group. In other words, individual psychology is only one indissoluble part of the psychology of groups" (p. 6). Whitman (1973) identifies three aspects of the group as illustrated in dreams: the representation of the group as a group; the representation of distinct object relations in the group; and the representation of the narcissistic elements in the group. Yalom (1970) finds dream interpretation most valuable inasmuch as until dreamed the dreamer's and other members' concerns are not fully conscious. He writes about a woman who dreams that she is in a large, strange room with the rest of the therapy group who were all expected to undress. The other group members disrobed, but the dreamer became frightened: "Everyone else took off their clothes. I was afraid and ran out of the room." This dreamer had been the silent member of the group prior to this dream. The dream exposed fears of self-disclosure. She felt that if she began to participate, she would be humiliated "by being forced to disrobe completely." Yalom comments that this dream allowed the patient to forewarn the therapy group of her vulnerability and sensitivity to criticism. The dreamer did not discriminate among the group members; each member was seen as approximately equal, which demonstrates her anxiety about the group as a collection of individuals. In other circumstances, members of a group may take on different valences, and different object relationships are recognized. The dream offers an opportunity to see the various levels of memory schemata that are activated by the group situation.

Manifest and latent content of a group dream are both significant as mirrors of transference and the affective state of the group toward the therapist. Since the group exists as a unity or dynamic entity in the inner perception of the participants, the dream which is brought to light by a single participant also expresses the current affective state of the whole group, thus making an understanding of the dream important for the grasping of the group situation. Zimmerman (1967) cites a clinical example of a female medical student who suffered from depression and reported the following dream (paraphrased here) in a group therapy session.

The dreamer observes several persons sitting around a sometimes hilarious and sometimes serious leader, a noted pathologist and follower of a famous German anatomist. Suddenly the dreamer guesses what the pathologist's first action with the scalpel will be and takes the instrument to show the others that she can teach as well. She feels ashamed for having taken the scalpel in her left hand, exposing ineptness.

The scene changes. The students, together in a morgue or anatomy room, begin dissecting a corpse named Zé. They inject into the corpse, an epileptic when alive, a substance able to induce epileptic contractions after death. The whole group begins to dissect different parts of the body, and the dreamer works on the shoulder. Not hilarious now, everyone becomes deeply engrossed and anxiously awaits the convulsions. The dreamer is impressed and frightened. Suddenly, the corpse stands up, deeply emotional and confused, and talks about past fears and sufferings. "Why do you hurt me?" he asks. Someone had stuck a knife through his leg. His despair provoked anxiety, and everyone wanted to escape from the room; but his continuous movements and naked expression prevented them. Abandoning him in this situation would make the dreamer feel guilty. A blond girl appears, and the corpse treats her gently and kindly. He then pushes her with care in the dreamer's direction, as if offering something valuable.

The group members understood the first part of the dream and recognized the role distinctions as being the same as in their group sessions. The group therapist is the pathologist in the dream, a dissector of the unconscious and follower of Freud. The emotional climate paralleled the group sessions, which were sometimes hilarious and sometimes marked by complaints that the analyst was not understandable. The individual dream revealed a group feeling that they, the group members, wanted to demonstrate that they also knew how to analyze and interpret (dissection in the dream) without the analyst's help.

In the second part of the dream, after pursuing a false notion that the corpse represented a part of themselves coming to life again with the therapist's assistance, the group recognized their latent aggressive feelings toward the analyst. He is the corpse, whom they have killed, but cannot leave because of guilt—he treats them well, "gently and kindly." Dissection expresses aggressive and restorative activities, referring to the meaning of analysis and the interpretative skills that make resurrection possible. The dream recount changed the group's mood, and all members participated in a lively discussion to ascertain manifest and latent meanings. They found a collective group fantasy, articulated in the individual participant's dream, concerning their unconscious impulse to destroy the leader with the consequent opposite need to restore him.

Zimmerman (1967), following Bion, emphasizes the existence of a group structure which constitutes a dynamic entity. Zimmerman speculatively asserts that dreams in groups verify the existence of this group structure. Through these dreams the progress of treatment can be followed, regressive and progressive trends discerned, and defenses and attendant anxieties defined.

TRANSFERENCE ASPECTS OF DREAMS IN GROUPS

The issue of transference and the affective state of the group toward the therapist merits further comment. The manifest and latent content in a dream may reveal whether patients feel part of a "familylike" group, according to Klein-Lipschutz (1953). This, in turn, can help determine whether an optimal climate exists for the individual to accomplish the necessary therapeutic work. Dreams may show the omnipotent image members have of the therapist and are useful in discovering latent aggressive impulses toward a leader. The transference in groups is divided, and many transferences are obviously present in any group situation. These include transference to the various individuals, especially the therapist, and to various combinations of individuals, depending upon the emotional conflicts that exist. Wolf and Schwartz (1962) believe that "everything in the dream of a group patient can be viewed as a manifestation of action in the transference relationship to the analyst—the same as with individual therapy" (Gold 1973). This statement is true if it is amended to include transference to others in the group in addition to the therapist.

SIGNIFICANCE OF DREAMS IN GROUP THERAPY

The analysis and interpretation of dreams in group therapy offer many significant uses. Dreams accelerate effective group therapeutic work by involving the group as an entity (Yalom 1970). They play a role in understanding group dynamics and the relationship of the individual to the group as a whole (Gold 1973). They elucidate a dreamer's and the other group members' concerns which are not yet fully conscious, especially shared, unconscious emotions. They facilitate exploration of the "here-and-now" interpersonal relationships of the group members.

References

Breger, L., Hunter, I., and Lane, R. (1971). *The Effects of Stress on Dreams.* Psychological Issues, Monograph 27. New York: International Universities Press.

French, T., and Fromm, E. (1964). *Dream Interpretation: A New Approach.* New York: Basic Books.

Gold, V. (1973). Dreams in group therapy: A review of the literature. *International Journal of Group Psychotherapy* 23:394–407.

Kadis, A., Krasner, J., Winick, C., and Foulkes, S. (1963). *A Practicum of Group Psychotherapy.* New York: Harper and Row.

Kaplan, S. R. (1973). The group dream. *International Journal of Group Psychotherapy* 23:421–431.

Klein-Lipschutz, E. (1953). Comparison of dreams in individual and group psychotherapy. *International Journal of Group Psychotherapy* 3:143–149.

Whitman, R. (1973). Dreams about the group: An approach to the problem of group psychotherapy. *International Journal of Group Psychotherapy* 23:408–420.

Wolf, A., and Schwartz, E. (1962). *Psychoanalysis in Groups*. New York: Grune and Stratton.

Yalom, I. D. (1970). *The Theory and Practice of Group Psychotherapy*. New York: Basic Books.

Zimmerman, D. (1967). Some characteristics of dreams in group-analytic psychotherapy. *International Journal of Group Psychotherapy* 17:524–535.

CHAPTER 27

THE DREAM IN SOCIAL WORK PRACTICE

Marquis Earl Wallace, Ph.D.

LITERATURE REVIEW

While many social workers use dream interpretation in practice and many more are interested in doing so, the knowledge needed to understand dreams and the skill required to use dream material in practice have not been central concerns of social work education or practice. This is reflected in the dearth of dream material in social work literature. For example, neither of Kasius's volumes (1950, 1962), which assembled some of the most important articles of the 1940s and 1950s, indexed dream material. More recently, a review of the tables of contents and indexes of new texts on social work practice (Siporin 1975, Meyer 1976, Turner 1976, Strean 1978, Golan 1978, and Reid 1978) also does not refer to dream material.

The reason for social work's inattention to dream material seems to reside in the traditional professional division between social work and psychoanalysis. Social work has focused more on reality, the environment, the ego, and the real relationship between worker and client whereas psychoanalysis has focused more on fantasy, the internal, the id, and the transference relationship. Dreams have traditionally been associated with the latter.

Since casework does not deal with . . . "buried" material directly, but only as it is expressed via ego-derivatives, dream analysis has not been a technique appropriate for social casework. This does not mean that on occasion a caseworker may not discuss some dream material with a client if this has been disturbing to the client . . . and the worker may indeed ask the client what is his perception of and reaction to the dream experience. The difference lies in the distinctive ways the psychoanalyst and the caseworker would handle the material: the caseworker's focus is on relating the dream content to a reality and ego-accessible focus, rather than emphasis on the interpretation of the unconscious content itself [Wood 1971, p. 91].

Hollis (1972, pp. 195–196) makes a similar point. She believes the worker should limit interpretations to conscious and preconscious material, bypassing the unconscious significance even when it is known to the worker.

Recently, however, several articles about dreams have been published in social work professional journals. These articles reflect ongoing and, perhaps, increased social work interest in dream material. They focus on both diagnostic and treatment aspects of dreams and work with individuals, groups, and families. Looney (1972) reported how dreams of heroin addicts can be used diagnostically to reveal personality attributes which do not show in waking life—such as feelings of inadequacy, unhappiness, and difficulties in obtaining gratification. Both Sackheim (1974) and Edwards (1978) focused on the use of dreams in individual treatment. Sackheim described how dreams can be used to clarify resistances, sharpen the focus of therapy, reinforce interpretations, and reveal previously denied material; while Edward has described how dreams can be used to recall early experiences and master painful stimuli. Maduro and Martinez (1974) reported on the use of dream analysis in groups to reveal hidden stress, sources of support, and to enhance communication, self-expression, and self-awareness. Beck (1977) described how dreams can be used in family treatment to enable family members to communicate thoughts and feelings which otherwise would not be expressed. Family members are able to help understand the dream, and the process leads to symptom resolution and problem solving. In addition to these, there are articles in journals adjunctive to social work (e.g., Foulkes 1969, Gold 1973) as well as those in this volume which provide additional diagnostic and treatment considerations relevant to contemporary social work practice.

COMPREHENSIVE REASSESSMENT
IN EACH INTERVIEW

This paper focuses on the use of the dream as a tool in assessment of the client's person-situation configuration (Hollis 1972, p. 136) in each session. Reassessment is necessary each time the worker and client meet if (1) worker activity should be focused (Perlman 1957, p. 145) on the person-situation configuration at the time of the interview; (2) the client's real problems, his reactions and conflicts, as well as his motivations and needs can change between sessions; and (3) any of these changes would require modification in the social worker's activity.

Five different levels of assessment seem important in each interview (Wallace 1979). One needs to know what *reality* is most disturbing the client. The reason for this is that the client will likely be most reacting to and motivated to solve this problem. Second, an evaluation of the client's *responses* to this reality should be made to see if professional help is needed. Third, if there is dysfunction present in the client's responses, the *reason* for this dysfunction should be identified so the social worker can focus his attention on the sources of the dysfunction. Fourth, the implication of this explanation for the social worker's *role* in the interview must be determined so that the social worker can decide what to do. And finally, an evaluation of the influence of the worker's activity on the client, the *results,* should be made to validate or invalidate the diagnostic and treatment services delivered.

FOCAL CONFLICT APPROACH TO DREAM INTERPRETATION AND ASSESSMENT

French and Fromm's (1964) focal conflict model, because of its person-environment emphasis, is an approach to dream interpretation particularly relevant to social work practice and is used in this paper. The elements of this approach are as follows. A dream can be understood as a series of attempts by the sleeping ego to solve a "focal conflict" which has been elicited by something in the client's waking life. This disturbing reality elicits a wish or impulse (such as sex, aggression, independence, or dependence) called a "disturbing motive," which in turn evokes a fear or anxiety (such as guilt, feelings of inferiority, fear of being punished, fear of being abandoned, shame, fear of being destructive or being destroyed, or inconsistency with reality) called a "reactive motive." The combination of the disturbing motive and reactive motive constitutes the "focal conflict." Clinically the focal conflict is determined by listening to the dream, what was on the client's mind the day before, and other associations to the dream material. Keeping in mind the stimulus for the dream and using unconscious perception, empathy, and intuition, one speculates what impulses and fears might constitute the focal conflict, checking these speculations against the content of the dream. This process is continued until a conflict is found which best explains all of the material present in the dream. A complete understanding of a dream will include a recognition of (1) what reality elicited it, (2) the disturbing and reactive motives, and (3) the various ways the ego tried to solve the conflict in the dream.

Focal conflict theory can be used to understand the client's overall ego activity in the session as well. The sum total of the client's communications in an interview may primarily reflect a single focal conflict stimulated by the disturbing *reality*. The client's dysfunctional *responses* may be considered attempts to solve this conflict. The focal conflict, then, is the *reason* for the dysfunction. The way the client tries to make use of the worker, including his perception or misperception of the worker (i.e., the client's view of the worker's *role*— see below), may be a new attempt to solve the focal conflict in the session with the worker.

CLINICAL EXAMPLES

In each of the cases below, the report of a dream solved a critical assessment problem. The level of the problem differed for each case. For Mr. and Mrs. A, the "reality" was what was missing; for Miss B, the "response"; for Mr. and Mrs. C, the "reason," and so forth. In addition to highlighting the role the dream played in the assessment, a complete assessment at all five levels using focal conflict theory is presented following the description of the interview.

A Dream Reveals the Most Disturbing Reality

The reality which most disturbs a client in a given session may be something outside the helping process or something within it (Langs 1973–1974, vol. 1, pp. 311–334). In the example which follows, an event outside the treatment elicited responses in the client which threw the session into jeopardy. The report of the dream exposed what the client was responding to which facilitated appropriate development of a session.

Background. The "client" in this case was a marital couple. Mr. and Mrs. A had previous marriages, raised families, and were divorced. Shortly after their marriage to each other, Mrs. A began seeing a social worker at a family service agency. A few months later, Mr. A suddenly left town, traveling to a distant state. A few weeks later he called, and Mrs. A invited him to return home. Mrs. A's worker felt that marital treatment rather than individual therapy would be most helpful to Mr. and Mrs. A upon Mr. A's return. She referred them to a worker who could see both of them together.

The marital treatment went "well." There was increased marital happiness. Mr. A began to find more work in his trade. He began to feel better and became more aggressive. Mrs. A felt more secure in the marriage. Finally, she led efforts to begin socializing with friends and family. In the sessions the relationship of Mr. and Mrs. A to each other and to the worker was predominantly positive, although negative feelings were expressed from time to time and relatively superficial blocks to progress were overcome. In the session to be described, all this changed dramatically.

Session. Mr. A began, saying he felt tired. He complained that the treatment was making him feel restricted. If it were not for these sessions he could move out of town whenever he felt like it. He now felt a demand to do well financially, something he had never wanted before. Mrs. A complained that she too felt tired. This was now the beginning of the busy season at work, and she could look forward to no relief for a long time.

As the session continued, no new material came out. The worker could find no clues as to why Mr. and Mrs. A felt so down, came across so helpless, or why this session had such a different, resistive quality. Finally the worker asked, "Have either of you had a dream?"

Mr. A responded, "I had a dream that was sort of vague. I was protecting a little girl—I later realized it was my wife—from a woman who I think was my mother-in-law."

The worker waited for any associations. Mr. and Mrs. A began to discuss her mother. She was doing "better now," they said. The worker had the distinct impression that he was supposed to know something about the mother that he did not know. Finally it came out that Mrs. A's mother was in the hospital and had been for a week. They thought the worker knew this. Then they realized that the mother had gone into the hospital the night after their last session rather than the night before.

The issue of mother now to the surface, Mrs. A began to describe her feelings about a visit she had with her mother a few days earlier. She felt her mother was telling her to give up her life to take care of her. Mr. and Mrs. A left feeling depressed, frustrated, and tired. Mr. A felt a need to protect his wife from her mother because of stories she had told him about physical and mental abuse at mother's hands. He also felt Mrs. A was avoiding facing the impending death of her mother. As he had had more therapy (several years elsewhere) than she, he knew how hard it was to face these feelings. He himself was in Korea when his mother died. By the time he got back from overseas, she was buried. He never grieved her death. He does not even remember much about her except that she and he fought a lot when he was a teenager.

The worker commented that the hospitalization of Mrs. A's mother seemed to be getting both of them down. For Mrs. A it meant a potential loss of a relationship that was not as gratifying as she would have liked, and for Mr. A it reminded him of a loss of his own, which despite all of his therapy, he had never grieved.

Analysis of the session. The reality most disturbing Mr. and Mrs. A was the hospitalization of her mother, a fact brought into the session through the report of a dream about a "mother." They were responding to this hospitalization by avoiding talking about important material, and they were clearly depressed and helpless. The reason for this avoidance and helplessness was anger (disturbing motive) at the imposition the mother's illness made upon them and guilt (reactive motive) for being angry at a sick relative. The role they had in mind for the worker was that he would join with them in avoiding what was really disturbing them. The worker's actual role was to elicit dream material which exposed what was on their minds. The result was the impasse was overcome, and the underlying concern exposed.

A Dream Reveals the Client's Responses

Because a client has an interview with a social worker does not necessarily mean the client needs professional help in that session. An evaluation of how he is responding to the realities facing him is necessary to see if there is evidence of psychological symptoms, personality problems, or serious obstacles (resistances) to his obtaining help (Langs 1973–1974, vol. 1, pp. 324–326). Typically, the worker relies on his own observations of the client as well as the client's self-reports to decide. Reports of dreams as a part of the client's self-report can reveal aspects of the client's responses not readily apparent in other ways. In extreme cases, such as the one which follows, the dream may be the primary way to get to know the client.

Background. Miss B was a twenty-two-year-old Catholic, a college dropout working as a cocktail waitress. She recently moved to this state with her boyfriend of four years. She sought treatment for anxiety she felt in crowds and because of fears that she might go crazy. A rather shy, inhibited person, she was unable to talk about herself in the initial interviews except in very limited ways. In a sense, it was almost as if there was nothing to discuss. She lived with her boyfriend, and they got along well. And she did well in her work.

She reported dreams freely, and these became the major vehicle for understanding her. At the end of the session prior to the one to be described, she expressed fears she was a lesbian. She said this anxiously as if an immediate response was called for. As the time was up, the worker offered her a defensive displacement. He said this fear might be a part of a larger problem they had already discussed. Much like her fears she was going crazy or was manic-depressive, her fear that she was a lesbian followed from her not knowing exactly what she was, and she feared the worst.

Session. She came in asking what the worker does between interviews. She felt much relieved last time when she left. The worker's response to her fears made her feel much better. She had two sides to her personality, she said. One part was very secure, and that was the side she likes. The other was afraid and insecure.

"I had a dream," she continued. "I was driving back to my house in Virginia with a guy I once knew. His house was haunted. There are spirits that move things around. I am afraid. We stop at his house before going to mine. We park at a curb. There is an accident involving nuns and black people. There is a truck full of people there. Loud speakers are blaring that the seventies are bringing in a new era of sexuality and freedom. I stay in the car and lock up the windows, almost drowning out the loudspeakers. I felt many fears. My mother and sister were with me.

"I had the dream the night after my last session. Virginia is where I lived from when I was one to eleven. My two big 'neuroses' are in the dream—the 'spirits and the devil' thing and 'homosexuality.' I used to be afraid of the devil. The speakers were telling me to experiment sexually. I think the dream means my fearful side originated in Maryland."

The worker asked for further associations to the dream. Guy—"He was a guy who once told me a lie." Black people—"There were many in Washington, D.C. They could not afford to go to the school I went to. Homosexuality is more accepted among the blacks." Sex—"I did not have sex until I was eighteen. Something was wrong with my first boyfriend. He was impotent. In college I did not do anything sexually. Second semester I met R (current boyfriend)." Mother—"Was old fashioned and is old. My friend did not say very much." Car—"There was a lot of fear, something was going to come in and make me lose control. My sister was outside the car. Someone else was inside. Reminds me of a feeling I get, and I get more anxious. I want to get another job so I can have more sessions, but I do not want to deal with people that much."

After these associations she looked to the worker to give her an interpretation. He replied that he did have some thoughts in mind, yet he felt in a way she did not want him to comment.

She said that was true. She was afraid of what he would say, that she was homosexual or schizoid or schizophrenic.

The worker commented that she seemed quite worried about what she might find out about herself in treatment because she thought that knowledge could somehow be harmful.

Analysis of the session. Miss B was reacting to the beginning of treatment itself, the most disturbing reality. Her responses involved considerable anxiety; she feared being overwhelmed by sexual and aggressive impulses, being manipulated and lied to, and she felt inadequate to defend herself, all of which are communicated in the dream material. The underlying conflict was one of dependency wishes toward the worker (disturbing motive) versus fears of being destroyed (reactive motive). The client's fantasized view of the worker's role was one of being an overwhelming stimulus (loudspeakers blaring). The worker's actual role was a low-key comment about her not really wanting him to interpret her dream, and acceptance of her fears about what she would find out about herself. The results were inconclusive as the client did not have immediate opportunity to respond to the interpretation with confirmation (see the case of Miss E). Yet her revelation of important material in the following sessions indicated confirmation of the overall process.

A Dream Reveals the Reason for the Client's Dysfunctional Responses

When it is clear that a client is responding dysfunctionally, it is helpful to determine what conflict is being resolved in the dysfunction. Identification of the disturbing impulses and reactive fears makes other aspects of the client's behavior more comprehensible and gives clues as to how to intervene.

While focal conflict theory originally was developed as a way to understand the ego functioning of individuals, Whitaker and Lieberman (1964) extended the focal conflict model to formed groups. Their point of view is that the behavior of groups can be seen as directed toward the solution of shared group conflict which can be expressed in focal conflict terms.

In the case below (as well as with Mr. and Mrs. A, above) this concept of shared conflict is extended to work with a family. Theoretically it is conceivable that the various symptoms, character disturbances, interpersonal difficulties, and resistances of a family can be seen as different ways of managing a shared family conflict. In the work with the C family, the worker was aware that the family had difficulty allowing the normal late adolescent separation process. However, it was not until the report of a dream by a family member that the underlying conflict behind this problem was revealed. At the same time, other family difficulties became identified and understood as other ways of dealing with the same conflict.

Background. Mr. and Mrs. C, a couple in their mid-fifties, were referred for short-term treatment by a social worker who was working with their seventeen-year-old daughter, Martha. The referring worker felt the parents were being too passive in their management of Martha.

In the first few sessions with the parents, it became clear that they were incapable of dealing with Martha. Instead they retreated to the bedroom, giving her full run of the house. Other problems surfaced as well. Mother was depressed. There was considerable unresolved marital tension. Father was passive, quiet, and had a tendency toward psychosomatic problems. An older son, Peter, and older daughter, Olivia, had left the home and appeared academically successful, yet were personally isolated. Another daughter, Nancy, nineteen, lived at home, did not communicate with her parents, and always drank before going on a date, usually with a married man on whom she was "throwing away her money." In light of these many problems, the short-term relationship was extended to an open one. However, the parents were seen only every other week at their choice.

Over the next few months, Martha improved in her treatment sufficiently to go off to college. Within a few months she dropped out and returned home. She got a job and got back into treatment with her worker. Mrs. C's sister died, and Mrs. C's grief over this shock was worked through in treatment. Soon Olivia dropped out of her graduate program and returned to the family neighborhood, spending a good deal of time at home. Then she got engaged. Martha moved out to an apartment with a friend, but shortly thereafter, her roommate moved back to her family, leaving an opening in the apartment for sister Nancy still living at home. Nancy had had one interview with Mr. and Mrs. C's worker a year earlier.

Treatment for her on an individual basis had been recommended, but she had not followed through.

At this point the parents became worried about Nancy. Parents and worker agreed it would ease the transition for everyone if Nancy would attend the parents' sessions temporarily. The parents hoped it would improve "communication." In the first four-way session (Mr. and Mrs. C, daughter Nancy, and the worker) the reasons to get together were clarified, as was what each expected to "get" from the sessions.

In the second four-way session, communication was stifled. The source of this block could not be determined by the worker. The difficulties they had in communicating at home had now been moved to the worker's office, but it seemed the worker could do no more about them than the family could. The worker confronted the difficulty, but that led to no change. He then took the point of view that not communicating must be serving some purpose, perhaps to protect one another. The session still going nowhere, the worker made a logical but incorrect guess that family members were afraid of hurting one another by what they might say. Still no response. In desperation the worker asked Nancy, "How do you handle disagreements with your boyfriend?"

Responding with laughter, Nancy said, "Oh, I had a dream about that last night. I asked him to go with me to a party at an old girlfriend's house. He said he did not want to go—he wanted to go off riding. I said 'okay' and slammed the door on him to make him feel guilty."

As the report of the dream came at the end of the session, nothing could be done with it then. Between sessions the worker reflected that the dream probably indicated Nancy's desire not to attend the family session projected into the boyfriend. But more importantly the dream could be revealing a family conflict about independence, that it would lead to rejection and guilt.

Session. The next session started again with little communication. Finally the worker said, "From your dream last time I got the idea that this family may have trouble with 'letting people go their own way.' By that I mean there may be a fear that if you do go your own way—like off to school, or to live someplace else, or even to go your own way in terms of having your own opinions about things and expressing them at home or even here in the sessions—you fear you will be rejected by the others and made to feel guilty."

This was followed by a stunned silence. The worker said, "So what do you think about that?" An avalance of communication followed. Mother said she was afraid to tell Nancy what she thought of her boyfriend, because she was afraid Nancy would never speak to her again. Nancy said she was afraid to talk to her sister Martha, and Martha had mentioned that just that day. The worker remembered how Mr. and Mrs. C had been afraid to go off for a weekend by themselves without telling her mother, who lived 3000 miles away. At this point Mr. C began to pull at his socks; he did this twice in one minute. Attention to his socks revealed that he had sciatica. He got it just a few months before when he went to visit his sick mother, just as he was leaving. Ever since then, he could not take walks, but instead he drove everywhere with his wife. Mrs. C wondered if this explained her fear of asking her boss to take time off so she could pick her daughter up at the airport.

Analysis of the session. The reality most disturbing the C family was the new four-way sessions with the worker. Their response was an inability to communicate, a family pattern which acted as a resistance in the treatment situation. The reason for this was finally presented in the dream, which was interpreted as a shared conflict to speak one's own mind (independence wish, disturbing motive) and a fear of being punished for doing so (reactive motive). The family's major expectation of the worker's role was that he would enable them to communicate safely without risking themselves. Instead he exposed the central conflict which provided insight instead. As a result the inability to communicate was overcome, and in addition, new symptoms and concerns were revealed which elaborated the meaning of this conflict beyond the session into other aspects of family and individual functioning.

Finally, it is interesting to note that there are shared family solutions to the independence-versus-fear of punishment conflict as well as individual ones. The family-group solutions are that no one ever really gets away and forms another relationship with someone else, yet when together they cannot enjoy each other for fear of saying something that will lead to rejection and guilt. Additional individual solutions are sciatica (Mr. C), poor choice of boyfriend (Nancy), academic failure (Martha, Nancy and Olivia), excessive dependence on mother (Mrs. C), and not getting married (Martha, Nancy, Olivia, Peter).

A Dream Reveals the Client's View of the Worker's Role

The worker's role, what he actually says and does in a session, is determined by a variety of forces. Yet the use the client makes of the worker is determined by the client and how he internalizes the relationship with the worker. This internalization depends upon what aspects of himself he attributes to the worker, and how the worker responds.[1] The client can attribute earlier relationships (transference) or make more simple externalizations of aspects of his ego, superego, or id (Hollis 1972, p. 234). If the worker is to influence the course of treatment consciously, it is incumbent upon him to determine how the client is perceiving him. In a session, what the client externalizes and perceives in the worker often is related to the focal conflict of that session, and this externalization may be an attempt to solve the conflict in the interview. Thus, the disturbing motive, reactive motive, defenses, or personality traits related to the focal conflict are often perceived in the worker. When the worker is able to diagnose this misperception and understand the function it serves in conflict resolution, he is able to decide whether to allow the misperception or attempt to interfere with it in some way. Interpretation and process comments are but two of many ways to interfere with a client's misperception of the worker.

A dream can be helpful in determining how the client is perceiving the worker. This might be said to be the client's view of the worker's role. This is true of Mr. D's dream below. He sees the worker as "arrogant." Deciding that such a perception would not be helpful to Mr. D's treatment, the worker acts nonarrogantly while helping the client to express this misperception. As a result the client is partially able to accept this as a projection of an aspect of himself of which he was previously unaware.

Background. Mr. D was a professional person in his early thirties who had been in once-weekly treatment for six months. His two chief complaints were excessive anxiety when speaking to a group, a normal demand in his work, and a tendency toward being too ingratiating, a trait his wife abhorred.

In the session prior to the one to be described, he had reported a dream which was interpreted as a fear that he would be abandoned if he got angry. Also in that session he mentioned that he was anxious about a talk he was going to give that day. The worker responded by reminding the client that his reports about the last talk he had given sounded quite good; both he and the audience had enjoyed it. This was intended as a confrontation; the client was to consider his anxiety in the light of his prior

1. In a private consultation, Dr. Peter L. Giovacchini first made me aware that the client always makes a place for the worker in his mind. His comment was something like this: "When a patient enters your office, his ego fills the room. Your task is to find out where he is putting you in the process." The reader is referred to his collected papers (Giovacchini 1975).

performance. As is clear in the following session, he felt the worker was attempting to do something else.

Session. Mr. D began with a dream. "I am walking into a motion picture theater, part of the 'Mann' theater chain, with no clothes on. I am with a friend from high school who is also naked. Seeing that the theater is filled with people with their clothes on, I decided to find a seat as quickly as possible. My friend and I sat in the first row. Then I realized it was not a movie theater at all, but a playhouse. The lead actress walked on stage, then right over to my friend, and told him he was 'arrogant.' My friend seemed not to be upset. But I was nervous that she would attack me too."

Mr. D went on to associate to the dream. The friend was not a good friend in high school. He was a self-confident, attractive, guy. But he was not very nice to his girlfriend. "When I woke up, I told the dream to my wife. She gave a 'quick' interpretation. [His wife is in therapy.] I got mad at her because her interpretation was so instantaneous. I cannot stand people who do not take the time to understand me but instead make quick and easy comments not intended to be helpful to me at all. They just use the situation for their own benefit. I want interest from her, but she is only interested in showing how smart she is. People use a person's question to talk about themselves. This is also true of Q [same first name as friend in the dream; someone in authority position to Mr. D]. He asks questions but is really self-absorbed. My father was also this way; he just gave off opinions without ever thinking through them.

"In relationships with people I always get the short end of things," he continued. "The other person gets all the credit. I don't get my share. I make weak attempts to get some credit, but it does not work. This is what I like about women: they do give me credit. But men do not. I want to be good at something without having to try. I want to come by it naturally, not because I work hard to get it."

The worker noticed a distinct shift in how the client was relating in this interview. He was talking more freely and asking fewer questions.

The worker said, "You said something about not feeling understood, that someone was making wild interpretations." The client hesitated, smiled and then said, "Yes, like you. You do that all the time. Take last session for example. You told me that I was doing better with groups. But on what did you base that? It made me feel good at the time. But after I left, a few days later, I began to wonder what you had up your sleeve in saying such a thing."

"If I follow your line of thought," the worker replied, "I guess you feel that I said that more to toot my own horn or make myself important than to help you."

"Yes," Mr. D replied, "and I do the same thing. With people at work [in his position as authority] I will say things just to make them feel better to make myself important."

Analysis of the session. The most disturbing reality for this session was the worker's confrontation in the last session. The response of Mr. D was an outburst of negative feelings following a misperception that the worker was trying to tell him he was doing better. The reason for this was the client's need for recognition (dependency wish, disturbing motive) which provoked a sense of shame (reactive motive) which he covered with overcompensatory arrogance. What the dream revealed about the worker's role was that the client perceives this arrogance projected into the worker whom he then experiences as an arrogant and shameless social worker who makes quick interpretations without any foundation. The worker's role in reality was to avoid acting arrogant while accepting the negative feelings. As a result the client was able to accept the arrogance as an aspect of his own functioning, thus diminishing the excessive negative feelings toward the worker.

A Dream Reveals Results

Many ways can be used to evaluate the effects of the social worker's activity. Typically the process is validated over time as the client's total life situation improves. Dreams can play a part in this longer term evaluation, as dreams may over time reflect lessened disturbance in ego functioning.

More relevant to session by session reassessment is the role dreams can play in confirming the worker's interventions within the session. Langs (1973–1974, vol. 2, p. 34) describes several forms of immediate confirmation. Confirmation of an intervention is found in the client's response to it: the client responds with material that significantly adds to the process of the session. Among the types of confirmation is the recall of repressed material, and spontaneous recall of a dream is one subtype.

In Miss E's session which follows, the worker seemed excessively confrontative. The worker justified the use of excessive confrontation on the basis that Miss E had a tendency to act out, and confrontative technique had been helpful to her in the past. In this session, the spontaneous recall of a dream was further confirmation of this approach.

Background. Miss E, a welfare mother in training at a local college to become a hairdresser, had been in treatment for about a year. Presenting symptoms included overeating, promiscuity, chronic failure, and excessive dependence in relationships, both on parents and boyfriends. She missed the session prior to the one described below because her car was in the repair shop and was not completed in time. She called at the last moment to inform the worker she could not make it.

Session. She began by saying she felt the worker was suspicious about her reason for missing the last session. She felt that he did not believe her. So she decided to hell with them (the worker) if they did not believe her. The worker asked what he had done to make her feel that way. She said she was not sure, just something in his voice. Anyway, she continued, there is no use getting into "fault finding" because that does not get her anywhere.

Then she changed the subject. "Something has come up that I am afraid to talk about. A hairdresser is interested in taking me on as an apprentice. This would mean I would not have to go to school full time. Although it would take me twice as long to get a license, I could be making money the whole time." She then asked the worker if he thought she should go talk to him about it.

As the worker had been consistently refusing to give Miss E advice or permission to do anything, and in this atmosphere she had given up overeating, promiscuity, and some of her excessive dependence in relationships, he responded by asking her why she wanted him to give her advice.

"Well," she replied, "whenever I get things, people complain. For example, when my relationship was going good with my boyfriend last time, look what happened [he left her for another woman]." The worker: "So you feel if you get something good, someone will take it away from you."

"Yes, I lost him before. And my house, just as I was getting used to it, my landlord raised the rent. Now if I take the job, how do I know someone else might not come along and take it away from me?"

The worker then confronted her envy. "You seem to feel that people will be envious of what you get, and try to take it from you? But isn't this something that is true of you, as you have said before, you want what other women have: a home, a husband, a family?"

She replied, "I just remembered a dream. My mother comes in acting like a witch. She says my boyfriend is no good. It led to a big fight between me and my mother." The worker replied, "So in the dream your mother depreciates something valuable to you and in doing so attempts to take it from you. But was there something you wanted from her?"

"Yes, her power. She could do anything she wanted. She had the car and made all of the decisions. She told me if my dad and I were drowning, and she could save only one of us, she would save my father. I would never do that. I put my son ahead of my boyfriend.

"Anyway I have decided to go for the interview. I will have time to try it before the fall when school starts, and then I can make up my mind after having tried it."

Analysis of the session. The client is most disturbed by the job offer. She reacts with excessive anxiety and a wish to be told what to do. The reason she is so frightened is the job offers independence to her, a wish (disturbing motive) that she fears will end with her ultimately losing all (reactive motive, fear of abandonment). The client wants the worker to tell her what to do so she will feel protected from doing anything independently. The worker instead confronts her projected envy. As a result she recalls a dream which confirms the worker's activity, and she ultimately makes up her own mind.

DREAMS: A MISSING LINK IN ASSESSMENT IN SOCIAL WORK PRACTICE

In each of the five interviews summarized above, complete assessment at all five levels—reality, response, reason, role, and result—would have been difficult, if not impossible, without the report of the dream. The dream in Mr. and Mrs. A's session helped the worker identify what they were truly upset about (reality) which had otherwise not been mentioned. For Miss B dreams were the only way to reveal herself, particularly her reactions (responses) to the treatment, in a safe way. The dream in the C family session identified the central conflict (reason) responsible for other family problems as well. Mr. D's dream revealed the content of a negative treatment response (his intrapsychic view of the worker's role) which he was able to accept as a projection when the worker acted to not confirm it with his behavior. And Miss E's spontaneous recall of a dream validated the worker's confrontative approach. In each of these cases the information provided by the dream led to more comprehensive understanding and productive sessions than would have been expected otherwise. This may imply that the worker who is able to use dream material may be in a better position to assess his client's situation and therby to offer better service.

References

Beck, D. H. (1977). Dream analysis in family therapy. *Clinical Social Work Journal* 5:53–57.

Edward, J. (1978). The use of dreams in the promotion of ego development, *Clinical Social Work Journal* 6:261-273.

Foulkes, D., Larson, J., Swanson, E., and Rardin, M. (1969). Two studies of childhood dreaming. *American Journal of Orthopsychiatry* 39:627-643.

French, T., and Fromm, E. (1964). *Dream Interpretation: A New Approach.* New York: Basic Books.

Giovacchini, P. (1975). *Psychoanalysis of Character Disorders.* New York: Jason Aronson.

Golan, N. (1978). *Treatment in Crisis Situations.* New York: Free Press.

Gold, V. (1973). Dreams in group therapy: a review of the literature. *International Journal of Group Psychotherapy* 23:394-407.

Hollis, F. (1972). *Casework: A Psychosocial Therapy.* New York: Random House.

Kasius, C., ed. (1950). *Principles and Techniques in Social Casework.* New York: Family Service Association of America.

——— ed. (1962). *Social Casework in the Fifties.* New York: Family Service Association of America.

Langs, R. (1973-1974). *The Technique of Psychoanalytic Psychotherapy.* Volumes I and II. New York: Jason Aronson.

Looney, M. (1972). The dreams of heroin addicts. *Social Work* 17(6):23-28.

Maduro, R. J., and Martinez, C. F. (1974). Latino dream analysis: opportunity for confrontation. *Social Casework* 55(8):461-469.

Meyer, C. (1976). *Social Work Practice,* 2nd ed. New York: Free Press.

Perlman, H. H. (1957). *Social Casework: A Problem Solving Process.* Chicago: University of Chicago Press.

Reid, W. (1978). *The Task-Centered System.* New York: Columbia University Press.

Sackheim, G. (1974). Dream analysis and casework technique. *Clinical Social Work Journal* 2:29-35.

Siporin, M. (1975). *Introduction to Social Work Practice.* New York: Macmillan.

Strean, H. S. (1978). *Clinical Social Work Theory and Practice.* New York: Free Press.

Turner, F. J. (1976). *Differential Diagnosis and Treatment in Social Work,* 2nd ed. New York: Free Press.

Wallace, M. (1979). A Framework for Self-Supervision in Social Work Practice. Unpublished manuscript.

Whitaker, D. S., and Lieberman, A. (1964). *Psychotherapy Through the Group Process.* New York: Atherton Press.

Wood, K. M. (1971). The contribution of psychoanalysis to social casework. In *Social Casework: Theories in Action,* ed. H. Strean, pp. 45-122. Metuchen, N. J.: The Scarecrow Press.

CHAPTER 28

THE DREAM IN SEXUAL
DYSFUNCTION THERAPY

Roy M. Whitman, M.D.

Dreams have been used in an increasingly wider variety of ways by psychologists, psychiatrists, and psychoanalysts (Kramer et al. 1969). They have been used for purposes of communication and clarification in therapeutic (French and Whitman 1969) as well as in nontherapeutic situations (Whitman et al. 1967). They have been used to guide and modulate therapeutic intervention (Whitman 1963). They have been used to study the psychology of thinking (Jones 1970, Whitman 1973). We have found them most useful as a form of illumination of what is going on responsively in the intrapsychic apparatus. Using dreams this way we have investigated diagnosis (Kramer et al. 1967), dynamics (Whitman et al. 1970), genetics (Kramer et al. 1967), transference (Whitman 1963), countertransference (Whitman, Kramer, and Baldridge 1969), therapeutic possibilities (Whitman 1974b), and, indeed, many of the processes that go on in psychiatric organizations such as research (Whitman et al. 1962), supervision or presentation of material at conferences (Whitman, Kramer, and Baldridge 1963).

One of the current concerns of present-day psychiatry is the polarity that has arisen between psychoanalytic therapy and psychoanalysis as contrasted with behavior therapy. Masters and Johnson sex therapy (1966, 1970) has usually been considered as a form of behavior therapy; the proponents and authors of this therapy have insisted that essentially they are utilizing a scientific behavioral approach. This paper will use illustrative dreams during the course of Masters and Johnson sex therapy to demonstrate the internal reverberations and ramifications of certain manifestly behavioral recommendations such as sensate focus exercises. In addition, dreams will be used to demonstrate some of the resistances and pitfalls of this form of therapy. We will use dreams as a way of insight into the nuances and subtle aspects of such catchall terms as "performance anxiety," which is central to all sex therapy. Finally, dreams will be used as a determinant of termination of therapy.

METHOD OF DREAM COLLECTION

The method used in collecting dreams from patients in this form of therapy was to ask the couple to pay attention to their dreams between sessions and for both the man and woman to try to bring at least one dream to the ensuing session. In order to understand what processes are being illuminated by these dreams, a brief review of Masters and Johnson therapy is in order. While the broad outlines of this method of "brief treatment" are well known, the particular modifications used by the author are somewhat unique.

Generally, I see the couple together, have individual interviews with each member of the couple, come together for a round table discussion, and then launch into increasingly intense sensate focus exercises. Some variations to the original descriptions of Masters and Johnson are employed, in keeping with the work of Helen Singer Kaplan (1974) as well as a number of other authors (Whitman 1976). We have found it satisfactory to see the couple once a week for an hour. I have seen couples by myself and with the aid of a female co-therapist when I think it is indicated. She may be present initially, continue during the intermediate phase of therapy, and terminate with us.

Sex therapy is initiated essentially with an intensive psychosocial history which emphasizes the sensual erotic aspects of personality, but not omitting other aspects of the developmental cycle (GAP Report 1973). The material gleaned from this intensive history of the marital or sexual relationship as well as from the developmental history of the individual, both autoerotically and with other individuals, leads to a uniquely constructed framework and set of "tasks" within which they may realize their sexual potential. Some of the issues stressed by Masters and Johnson are to treat the "marital unit" rather than the individual, to deemphasize the transferential aspects of the treatment, and to emphasize behavioral rather than intrapsychic processes.

In the course of collecting these dreams, some patients (just as all patients do with dreams) have shown an inclination and curiosity to examine them minutely, whereas other patients have tended to gloss over them and get back to the main work at hand, this is, the sexual interaction. The author has not sought to derail that particular approach and asks only for associations to the extent that he feels sufficiently comfortable to understand the meaning of the dream. However, increasingly, I have utilized dreams for insight, and patients have been quite willing to use the dream as take-off points for their feelings in sexual and interpersonal relationships. No analyst would be surprised by this observation.

INITIAL DREAMS REVEAL SEXUAL PROBLEMS

I will not spend a good deal of time on these dreams since they are well known to all psychoanalytically oriented therapists. However, it is fascinating that the initial dream almost invariably contains an allusion to or statement of the problem with which the person is dealing.

Case 1. An attractive twenty-seven-year-old graduate student in philosophy came to treatment complaining of orgasmic dysfunction: she was unable to reach orgasm via intercourse. The initial dream that she presented in the diagnostic interviews was that there was a dilapidated house and on the front porch was a fairly deep accumulation of snow and frost.

It is here that we come to our first statements about the usefulness of dreams in formulating patients' problems. It is not enough to recognize immediately that the house symbolically stands for herself and that the frost is a clear statement of that dread and negative word, frigidity. Just as important is how she sees that particular house. Its dilapidated state represents her feeling that she has never been fulfilled, that she is deteriorating in her self-feelings and marital relationship, that rehabilitation is desirable but perhaps questionable since the house, as she commented on it, did not seem worthy of repair. We thus see reluctance to enter into treatment and questioning whether she is worth the money, energy, and time that needs to be devoted to her rehabilitation. The inanimate aspect of the symbolism suggests a certain deadness in this woman which yielded only to prolonged sexual therapy followed by individual therapy.

Case 2. A young twenty-three-year-old French teacher from a local high school presented as her first dream one in which a large horse reared up in front of her and frightened her. The diagnosis in this instance was a case of uncomplicated vaginismus.

Historical material revealed dire warnings by her mother about what men would want from her. She had a complete inability to consummate a marriage of four years' duration and even had a long history of difficulty inserting tampons. Her local gynecologist had suggested vaginal dilators and she had used them faithfully, but they had not been successful in allowing penile penetration. In the course of sexual therapy with this couple, not only was the exaggerated unconscious size of the penis (the large horse) important; but, in terms of the dream, its sudden approach, uncontrollability, and great strength were equally frightening.

Case 3. The patient, a twenty-eight-year-old lawyer, presented in the diagnostic interview a dream in which he was sleeping in bed and there was an involuntary accident and release of urine. The diagnosis in this instance was premature ejaculation. What emerged in the course of the sex therapy was a profound unconscious hostility towards the woman (and women), and the equation of semen and urine was deeply embedded in his unconscious.

Case 4. A lower middle class couple presented for mutual sexual dissatisfaction. She had orgasmic dysfunction and he had premature ejaculation. The male presented a dream after the diagnostic interview in which he and his wife were sitting in the back of the bus going to St. Louis.

Both patients recognized that going to St. Louis had to do with their undertaking Masters and Johnson sex therapy with the therapist. When I pressed them for associations about traveling in a bus, they both had the same associations: traveling in a bus is an inferior form of transportation utilized by people who do not have sufficient money to own or drive a car.

To me this expressed both the wish to go to St. Louis and see "the master" and also some disappointment that they were getting an inferior product via the therapist. My own interpretation to them was that they were embarking on a journey with me which they had some doubts about, and they readily agreed that this was so. Since at that time I was under the sway of the injunction of Masters and Johnson that transference manifestations should not be interpreted, I did not elaborate on the extreme negative orientation towards, and the devaluation of the therapy, which both of them shared. I might say, incidentally, that in working with dreams with couples in sex therapy, I have become increasingly impressed by the ability of one or the other member to add pertinent details and, indeed, to make comments about the other's dream that even an experienced therapist familiar with dream interpretation is unable to contribute.

Since I will not have a chance to follow up on all of these beginning vignettes with the ongoing treatment, but have used dreams to sample the problems posed during the therapy and particularly at the beginning, I might add that this particular therapy floundered. The specific issue was that the wife, during the mid-course of therapy, was unable to accept the fact that she had discovered that her husband was masturbating. She insisted that the therapist state a negative position about male masturbation or, indeed, masturbation of any type. Despite my therapeutic stance of wanting to understand what it meant to her, she said, "You men are all alike and think of dirty things like masturbation." At this point she insisted that unless he stop this practice completely, she would withdraw both of them from therapy. At this point my female co-therapist had just left town and I was unfortunately working alone. No remonstrations on my part, no protestations on his part would avail, and this session was the last time I saw the couple. It was one of my two failures out of some twenty cases of sex therapy. Could it have been predicted by the bus to St. Louis dream?

DREAMS OCCURRING DURING SEX THERAPY

Case 5. During the course of early sensate focus exercises with a young couple in their late twenties, one of the exercises prescribed for them was that each give the other a bath. In this particular therapy I was working with my wife as a co-therapist. At the following session the woman came in with the following dream.

"I was visiting the house of a pediatrician and his wife with my husband (we often play bridge with them). Suddenly the house began to fill up with water. Nobody seemed very perturbed and so I was not frightened either. Suddenly from out of the water a snake began to rear up and came almost upright towards me. As it got closer and closer to me I became more and more frightened. I started to yell for help from the couple or my husband, but nobody seemed to pay any attention to me. I woke up sweating."

This was a woman who had come in "bringing her husband" who, she said, had difficulty with premature ejaculation and occasional impotence. She herself insisted that she had no problems at all. As is my wont in such a situation, I asked either for associations. The wife had none to offer but the husband said to his wife, "Wasn't that the night that you took the turn of giving me a bath?" She responded, "Yes, it was." We were then able to work out with the couple that during the course of her giving him a bath he had had an erection. She proclaimed that consciously she had only been pleased by this response. But the dream belied her attitude. The snake rising up from the water was clearly her husband's erection as he emerged from the bath and was very threatening to her. She also associated to her dislike of snakes and said that she had read a D. H. Lawrence story, "The Snake," which unmistakably pointed to phallic symbolism. In doing sex therapy in particular, but psychoanalysis in general, what the symbol itself means is not as important as what it reveals about attitudes and behavior. During the later course of therapy we were able to relate this anxiety to the fact that she had taken baths once with an older brother, something which had been touched upon only in the diagnostic historical formulation.

Case 6. Another couple following the round table were given the typical Masters and Johnson recommendations. Most prominent of these is that they not engage in intercourse as they begin the graduated sensate focus exercises. The next session the woman came in with the following dream: "I started to say something and realized I had no voice at all. Nothing came out of my mouth at all. I started at first to speak and then to scream. But no sound came from my voice. I felt anxious and paralyzed."

This was a couple in which both partners recognized that sex, and particularly intercourse, was especially important to the woman. She had just finished reading *The Pleasure Bond* by Masters and Johnson, in which they point out that sex is primarily a means of communication. She had unconsciously perceived the interdiction that they not engage in intercourse as being not permitted to speak, and this had been very frightening to her.

DREAMS ILLUSTRATING THERAPEUTIC IMPASSE

Case 7. A couple—he had come in for treatment of impotence and she, orgasmic dysfunction—were moving along quite well in the sensate focus exercises and in discussions of their relationship. After several months of therapy they were engaging in nondemand penetration. The husband was fully able to have an erection. The woman seemed manifestly extremely pleased with this advance in the treatment, but on the other hand reported an inner reluctance to continue the treatment and was at a loss to explain why. Indeed she recognized that she had scheduled a social activity which would have precluded their coming to treatment and only his intervention and insistence made her cancel it. She reported the following dream after a "successful" sexual encounter:

"A little colored delivery boy went up into a dilapidated tenement house to deliver something. The house was very shabby on the outside but sparkling and remarkably clean and well painted on the inside. He delivered whatever it was he was supposed to and emerged from the house and tripped on the front stairs. As he was lying there with blood coming from his forehead, a woman ran towards him and cradled his head in her arms. Another woman who was watching this going on said very contemptuously, 'Don't pay any attention to him. He responds to anybody who pays him attention like that!'"

This dream was extremely important not only for understanding what was going on in the woman's attitude towards the sex therapy, but also in resolving her inexplicable resistance which had emerged for the first time in therapy. The little boy was the penis. The house was herself and we can see her negative feelings towards her own external genitalia (the shabby exterior of the tenement house) as well as her positive feelings about her own inner self and genital area (the clean inside). But most important to understanding the dream was the contemptuous statement by the onlooker that the little boy should not be paid attention because he would respond similarly to anybody who cradled his head in such a way. This female patient was afraid that now that her husband had regained his potency he would respond to any woman who stimulated him. A most moving session occurred in which both of them were able to share some of their early feelings about marrying each other, particularly the woman's knowledge that the man was impotent when she married him. She felt that this was a bond that could not be broken and now was afraid that since he had regained his potency he would turn to other women. The man was able to share with the therapist and his wife some of his fantasies that he was in fact anxious to try out his new found potency with other women, with all of whom he had been previously a failure. But he also was able to underline that this was a fantasy, and he had a deep emotional commitment to his wife which he was unwilling to threaten. Once we had gotten by this hurdle the woman's resistance disappeared, and the couple were able to carry through the rest of the therapy to the point where the man was fully potent in the sexual relationship and she eventually became orgasmic in response. This was a case of primary impotence, which usually has a poor prognosis. This particular case was extremely successful once the couple had gotten to their deepest feelings of commitment and fear of losing the other within and without the marriage.

DREAMS AND PERFORMANCE ANXIETY

Case 8. A widower in his early forties came for treatment complaining of impotence. His wife had died a year or so before, and he had remained isolated and depressed until recently when he had begun a relationship with a recently divorced woman who was willing to participate in sexual therapy with him. Everything was right, they felt, about this relationship, but he had been unable to perform sexually because of impotency.

He had read a great deal in the area of sexuality and mentioned the various factors that he thought might be related: (1) He was taking antilipid drugs for his mild hypertension; (2) he had some extramarital guilt even though his wife was dead; (3) he had some general sexual guilt about having intercourse in a nonmarital relationship; (4) there was competition with her ex-husband; (5) he was afraid of the great amount of her responsiveness; and (6) most of all, he felt there was some indefinable standard he could not live up to. He was able to put all these into terms of extreme performance anxiety and spectator anxiety in which he was always watching himself to see how well he would do. He knew this was counterproductive sexually, but he could find no way of stopping it.

He reported that he had the following dream the night before the third session: "My father was recuperating [he actually is] and I had transformed him into a weak and sickly being. I still knew he was my father but he was also me. I peeked through a hole near his bed. He was crawling through this hole and would hit his head on the concrete. I guided what now had become a baby to the ground. He was going to fall but I let him hit his head a little bit to teach him a lesson."

He associated to his father's recent illness and coronary surgery. His father had always been a powerful and overwhelming man and, indeed, was a senior executive of the corporation in which the patient was a junior executive. I asked him if he had any thoughts about why the father was also himself. He answered, "We are both patients, but also you know my name is William Black, Jr., and we often become confused for each other in the organization. Sometimes I get his mail and sometimes he gets my mail."

I then commented on guiding the baby to the ground after it had gone through the hole; while I did not wish to impose any sexual meaning on it, it sounded very sexual to me. He answered with excitement, "Well, you know, I am called Junior and have been all my life. Now I suddenly recall that my wife and I used to refer to my penis as 'Junior.'"

Over the next several weeks, with the full cooperation of his girlfriend, he was able to recognize that he was totally identified with his father, that he felt inferior to his father, and that he was also totally identified with his penis. When his penis failed, he felt he was a failure. The initiation of the sensate focus exercises with the deemphasis on the penis enabled him to become more identified with his total body and self and less with his penis.

This was a clear narcissistic identification of himself with his penis, and indeed the patient could be diagnosed as a narcissistic character disorder (Kohut 1971). Of all the issues he had mentioned as influencing his performance anxiety, most crucial was his constant, lifelong feeling of failing to measure up to his father. This emerged clearly in the dream.

When the woman could assure him that she was interested in him as a person, albeit also a physical person and not just his penis, his anxiety began to abate. He was able to restate in a different way that all the people that he felt he had to perform for, measure up to, and, indeed, compete with, lurked in the room during his sexual encounters with Rita, his girlfriend. Her former husband was there, his former wife was there, his fantasy image of himself was there, her image as a highly orgasmic sexual being was there, and most of all the overwhelming image of his powerful father was there. All of these represented standards that he had to live up to. Recognizing the powerful burden he had placed on himself caused a rapid remission of the sexual dysfunction (which was secondary impotence since he had performed almost without any difficulty with his wife during the previous fifteen years) and in eight sessions he was completely potent.

I emphasize this particular case because it illustrates how the dream rapidly pointed up to his narcissistic identification with his penis and his identification and competition with his father. But also the issue of performance anxiety was broken down into the component parts of all the people he felt were watching him and whose standards he had to live up to.

Finally, I was able to make an important contrast between sexual therapy and psychoanalytic psychotherapy or psychoanalysis. I remember that when I was a student at the Chicago Institute for Psychoanalysis, Therese Benedek succinctly defined psychoanalysis as that process in which the observer teaches the observed to become the observer. A previous period of psychotherapy that this patient had undergone before he came to me had taught him just that. But now we come to the crucial point. Though it is important to have a self-observing ego for insight, such an observing ego nevertheless often functions as an antisexual ego. Could this be the reason that in Masters and Johnson's initial report some 25 percent of their sample came from people who had previous psychotherapy or psychoanalysis and felt that they had not resolved their sexual problems?

TERMINATION DREAMS

Dreams may often signal the end of treatment (Cavenar and Nash 1976). In sexual therapy one has the additional objective criterion of actual sexual performance, not often given so clearly in a prolonged therapeutic endeavor. Nevertheless, we are interested not only in symptomatic relief (although it is primary) but also in some inner feeling of confidence that the treatment is at an end.

Case 9. A young graduate student with problems of premature ejaculation surprised himself in the course of treatment with the following dream: "I was rowing along in a boat and it seemed I entered a tunnel which was very black and long. I was frightened until I could see far off in the distance a very dim light."

This patient immediately associated to the metaphor that there was a light at the end of the tunnel. Sexual symbolism and anxiety were also involved in this dream inasmuch as the tunnel stood for some of his deep anxieties about the female vagina.

Toward the end of the treatment of a patient mentioned earlier with primary impotence (Case 8), he reported the following dream: "My wife and I were at a motel and a woman stuck her head in the room to clean up. We were on a new mattress. I invited her in for coffee. I was in bed without clothes but I have three pairs of underwear on [his wife immediately said that he was protecting himself, protecting it again, and he agreed]. A guy came in and said, 'You don't need all those old shorts. I have a new pair for you.' I accepted them." His associations mostly dealt with the fact that he was in the process of decreasing his extreme feeling of protectiveness, of his penis and of himself, against the close relationship with his wife in bed. He felt that the guy who gave him a new pair of shorts was the therapist and, indeed, he pointed out it was only one pair of shorts. He also commented that the woman who was taking care of the place looked like his mother and now he was aware more than ever that she had contributed greatly to his problem by making him ashamed of his penis and his erectile responses.

Termination dreams may also be a signal to the therapist that the couple is not ready for termination. A couple who had made remarkable strides from sexual relations once every six months to three times a week with an orgasmic response by the wife came to what was going to be their final session. The woman expressed a great deal of understandable anxiety about ending the treatment, particularly fearing that her husband would lapse back into his previous, noninitiating stance which had actually brought them to therapy. She presented the following dream:

Case 10. "I was on top of a school building and a group of school kids were trying to push me off the roof."

She associated that the kids were rich kids that had tormented those in her class who were crippled or deformed. Her only treatment association was that the office of the therapist was on the top floor of the medical school building. When we considered what this might have to do with this being the last session, she anxiously verbalized her fear of being pushed out before she was ready. The extreme anxiety in the dream plus the ensuing discussion guided the decision to see them again in one month rather than terminate, and she was vastly relieved.

USEFULNESS OF DREAMS DURING SEX THERAPY

As indicated by these many vignettes and examples, dreams are extremely useful at various times of the therapeutic contact. Particularly in this form of therapy it is often very difficult to help patients get at their subtler and deeper feelings. One way to deal with this reluctance is to examine the behavioral effects of the treatment and the feelings which they evoke by examining the reporting of the couple's various sensate exercises and interactions in great detail. Certainly this is essential to this form of treatment. But what turned out to be an original search for reverberations of sexual behavior and interactions within the individual and his or her intrapsychic apparatus, led to further insight into the individuals and their transactions. It would seem, despite the claim of behavioral therapists for various forms of external treatment of therapeutic disorders, that there is an internal affective and cognitive response to all events of significance (Whitman 1974b). All the prescriptions for behavior, such as encouraging certain sensate focus exercises and forbidding actual genital intercourse, are seen by the person in the context of the relationship with the therapist, the other member of the couple, and most of all as a meaningful event of his own life history.

Dreams often became, in the course of the treatment of these subjects, an extremely important avenue of insight. As I have described in a previous study on dreams (Whitman et al. 1967), the ability of each member of the couple to offer insights into the other person's dream often is equal to or exceeds the ability of a skilled dream interpreter because of the intimate knowledge of the other person and a particularly sensitive reaction to the same precipitating stimuli. Thus, I have evolved the technique, after asking the dreamer for his associations, of asking the spouse for her or his associations, and often the two of them can collaboratively come up with important insights into the dream, to which the therapist can add or which he can refine in a way that makes a very satisfying final product.

Dreams are therefore not only useful diagnostically in formulating the initial problem and how it is seen unconsciously, but they are also able to track the course of the therapeutic endeavor. Dreams also sensitively pick up resistances to the ongoing course of the therapy (as in the dream of the little delivery boy in the apartment house, Case 7) which might have led to a stalemate blocking further progress. Dreams can enlarge the meaning of such terms as performance anxiety and trace them to narcissistic and compulsive sources. And finally the dream can tell us, with other indices, when we are through or approaching the end.

Some ten years ago, when the Committee on Medical Education for the Group for the Advancement of Psychiatry first began work on their report, the "Assessment of Sexual Function "(GAP Report 1973), both William Masters and Virginia Johnson were naturally asked to be consultants to the committee. I had the idea then, and suggested to Mrs. Johnson, that dreams might be a useful additional avenue of understanding of both the problem, the interaction of the couple, and the nature of the sexual problem. I wondered if she and Dr. Masters might consider this. She said that she had reported my suggestion to him but felt that he did not want to deal with the area of dreams. Though she did not explicitly say so, I had the feeling that in his strong efforts to make sexuality and sexual therapy a truly scientific endeavor, the "unscientific" subject of dreams was seen as a dilution rather than addition to the process. This current research, although still in a beginning phase, suggests otherwise.

One final statement might be made about the use of dreams in the course of such a sensitive undertaking as sexual therapy. For the first time I have seen couples share inner feelings of wishes, misgivings, fears, and other fantasies which they would not otherwise have brought into the treatment. We know that a dream is a highly private matter, especially when one cracks the shell of the manifest content and goes to some of the issues of the latent content. Just as a couple is amazed, for example, to find out that each of them has been masturbating during the course of their ten-year marriage, so some of the fantasies contained in dreams have import of equal power. Though it sometimes has potentially dangerous implications, such affect-laden material by and large functions in the direction of facilitating communication, closeness and intimacy, and sharing, which can make good marriages better and better marriages exhilarating.

CONCLUSION

Dreams seem to be a useful way of formulating psychosexual problems, evaluating the course of the treatment of psychosexual problems, looking at the reaction of the couple to some of the guided interactions suggested by the therapists, and can be a means of private yet public communication between two involved partners.

The dream has an important place in the armamentarium of sex therapists. Though sex therapists emphasize behavior rather than feelings, the two cannot be artificially split. Indeed, Freud in one of his important statements in the dream book said that above all men should be judged by their actions. Thus in his most perceptive study of the mental apparatus, via dreams, he still strove for a linkage between behavior and action. Dreams provide an avenue to the underlying motivations and in a strikingly high-powered way focus the microscope of our examination on those seemingly small but immensely important issues which occur between people. Dreams are not dreamt about trivial things, and sexuality and the relationship between a couple is never trivial.

References

Cavenar, J. O., Jr., and Nash, J. L. (1976). The dream as a signal for termination. *Journal of the American Psychoanalytic Association* 24:425–436.
French, T. M., and Whitman, R. M. (1969). *Focal Conflict and the Physiology of Dreaming.* Springfield, Ill.: Charles C Thomas.
GAP [Group for the Advancement of Psychiatry] Report No. 88. (1973). Assessment of sexual function: a guide to interviewing. Volume 8, pp. 756–850.
Jones, R. (1970). *The New Psychology of Dreaming.* New York: Grune and Stratton.
Kaplan, H. S. (1974). *The New Sex Therapy.* New York: Brunner/Mazel.
Kohut, H. (1971). *The Analysis of the Self.* New York: International Universities Press.

Kramer, M., Ornstein, P. H., Whitman, R. M., and Baldridge, B. J., (1967). The contribution of early memories and dreams to the diagnostic process. *Comprehensive Psychiatry* 8:344–374.

Kramer, M., Whitman, R. M., Ornstein, P. H., and Baldridge, B. J., eds. (1969). *Dream Psychology and the New Biology of Dreaming.* Springfield, Ill.: Charles C Thomas.

Masters, W. H. and Johnson, V. E. (1966). *Human Sexual Response.* Boston: Little, Brown.

——— (1970). *Human Sexual Inadequacy.* Boston: Little, Brown.

Whitman, R. M. (1963). Remembering and forgetting dreams in psychoanalysis. *Journal of the American Psychoanalytic Association* 11:752–774.

——— (1966). An overview of current dream research. *Journal of the Ohio State Medical Association* 82:1271–1273.

——— (1973). Dreams about the group: an approach to the problem of group psychology. *International Journal of Group Psychotherapy* 23:408–420.

——— (1974a). A decade of dreams. *International Journal of Psychoanalytic Psychotherapy* 3:217–245.

——— (1974b). Psychoanalysis and behavior therapy. Presented to the Symposium of the Medical College of Pennsylvania, April.

——— (1976). The approach to the patient. In *Clinical Management of Sexual Disorders,* ed. J. K. Meyer. Baltimore: Williams and Wilkins.

Whitman, R. M., Kramer, M. and Baldridge, B. J. (1963). An experimental study of the supervision of psychotherapy. *Archives of General Psychiatry* 9 (6):529–535.

——— (1969). Dreams about the patient: an approach to the problem of countertransference. *Journal of the American Psychoanalytic Association* 17:702–727.

Whitman, R. M., Kramer, M., Ornstein, P. H. and Baldridge, B. J. (1967). The physiology, psychology and utilization of dreams. *American Journal of Psychiatry* 124(3):287–302.

——— (1970). The varying uses of the dream in clinical psychiatry. In *The Psychodynamic Implications of the Physiological Studies on Dreams,* ed. L. Madow and L. Snow. Springfield, Ill.: Charles C Thomas.

Whitman, R. M., Pierce, C. M., Maas, J. W., and Baldridge, B. J. (1962). The dreams of the experimental subject. *Journal of Nervous and Mental Disease* 134(5):431–439.

CONTRIBUTORS

Florence Bonime is an editor, novelist, short story writer, and ten-year member of the writing faculty at The New School for Social Research. She has worked with Walter Bonime on his writings for twenty-five years. Her article "On Psychoanalyzing Literary Characters," written in collaboration with Marianne Horney Eckardt, M.D., appeared in the Spring 1977 issue of the *Journal of the American Academy of Psychoanalysis*. "Psychoanalytic Writing: An Essay on Communication" appeared in the July 1978 issue of the same journal.

Walter Bonime, M.D. received his medical degree from the Columbia University College of Physicians and Surgeons in 1938. He is presently clinical professor, Division of Psychoanalytic Education, Department of Psychiatry, New York Medical College, where he has been a faculty member since 1947, as supervising and training analyst in the psychoanalytic program and teacher and supervisor in the residency program. He was a member of the first class of the American Institute of Psychoanalysis and was certified in psychoanalysis at New York Medical College. He is a charter fellow of the American Academy of Psychoanalysis, a life fellow of the American Psychiatric Association, a founding member of the Society of Medical Psychoanalysts (president 1963–1964), and a member of the Association for the Psychophysiological Study of Sleep (APSS). With Florence Bonime he is the author of *The Clinical Use of Dreams* and a section of *Dream Interpretation: A Comparative Study*.

Louis Breger, Ph. D. did graduate work in clinical psychology at Ohio State University and received a doctorate in 1961. He has taught at the University of Oregon, the Langley Porter Neuropsychiatric Institute, the University of California (Berkeley), and is presently associate professor of psychology at the California Institute of Technology. He is currently associated with the research program of the Southern California Psychoanalytic Institute.

Samuel Eisenstein, M.D. is associate clinical professor of psychiatry at the University of Southern California; training and supervising analyst, Southern California Psychoanalytic Institute; and attending physician and instructor, Cedars-Sinai Medical Center, Los Angeles. He served as dean of the Southern California Psychoanalytic Training School from 1969 to 1977. Coeditor of the book *Psychoanalytic Pioneers* and author of the article "Otto Rank, The Myth of the Birth of the Hero," he has also contributed a chapter on Rank to the *International Encyclopedia of Neurology, Psychiatry, Psychoanalysis and Psychology*.

Claude T. H. Friedmann, M.D. is assistant professor of psychiatry at the University of California (Irvine) School of Medicine, where he is Director of Psychiatric Education. A graduate of the Johns Hopkins School of Medicine, Dr. Friedmann had a successful career in medicine and public health before entering psychiatric training at UCLA and USC.

John E. Gedo, M.D. has practiced psychoanalysis in Chicago for the past twenty years. A native of Czechoslovakia, he had his undergraduate and medical education at New York University, and his psychiatric and psychoanalytic training in Chicago. Currently he is a training and supervising analyst at the Chicago Psychoanalytic Institute. He has served on the editorial boards of numerous publications, including a term as assistant editor for the book section of the *Journal of the American Psychoanalytic Association*. He has written extensively on the intellectual history of psychoanalysis and on its theory. He is senior author of *Models of the Mind* (1973) and principal editor of *Freud: The Fusion of Science and Humanism* (1976). His most recent book is *Beyond Interpretation: Toward a New Theory for Psychoanalysis* (1979).

Robert D. Gillman, M.D. is a training and supervising analyst with the Baltimore–District of Columbia Institute for Psychoanalysis, and is past president of the Baltimore–District of Columbia Society for Psychoanalysis. Certified in both adult and child psychoanalysis by the American Psychoanalytic Association, he is a fellow of the American Psychiatric Association and is a diplomate of the American Board of Psychiatry and Neurology. He is a consultant to the Arlington County Mental Health Center, where he is a former director; an adjunct associate professor at the School of Social Service, Catholic University; and a consultant both to the psychology department, Catholic University, and to the Counseling Center, University of Maryland.

Ramon Greenberg, M.D. approaches the subject of dreams from two directions. One is from his psychoanalytic training and work with psychoanalytic patients; the other is from about fifteen years of research on the psychophysiology of REM sleep. Dr. Greenberg's background includes training in neurology, psychiatry, and psychoanalysis. He is currently director of clinical Psychiatry at University Hospital, professor of psychiatry at Boston University Medical School, and chairman of the faculty at the Boston Psychoanalytic Institute, where he teaches a course on dream research and its relation to psychoanalysis.

Martin Grotjahn, M.D. received his medical, psychiatric, and psychoanalytic training in Berlin, emigrating to the United States in 1936. He was the first dean of the Training School of the Southern California Psychoanalytic Institute, a position he held for many years. He is now professor emeritus of psychiatry at the University of Southern California and training analyst emeritus at the Southern California Psychoanalytic Institute. He is a life fellow of the American Psychiatric Association, life member of both the American and the International Psychoanalytic Association, and diplomate of the American Board of Neurology and Psychiatry. He has produced over three hundred publications, including six books, on such subjects as dreaming and awakening, and on clinical and theoretical issues in psychotherapy, psychoanalysis, and group psychotherapy.

Joseph L. Henderson, M.D. is a founding member and training analyst of the C. G. Jung Institute in San Francisco. He is a graduate of St. Bartholomew's Hospital Medical School in London, with the degrees of M.R.C.S. and L.R.C.P. He is a special lecturer emeritus for Stanford University Hospital Neuropsychiatric Department and has taught analytical psychology in San Francisco, New York, Zurich and London. His publications include a contribution to *Man and His Symols,* edited by C. G.

Jung; *The Wisdom of the Serpent,* coauthored with Manuel Oakes; and *Thresholds of Initiation.*

John S. Kafka, M.D. was born in Linz, Austria. He received his secondary education in France and emigrated to this country in 1940. After serving in the army in World War II, he trained in clinical psychology. He obtained his medical degree in 1953, did his psychiatric residency at Yale University, and trained at the Washington Psychoanalytic Institute, where he is now a training and supervising analyst. He is clinical professor of psychiatry, George Washington University, and has been closely associated with Chestnut Lodge. He is also a consultant, to the National Institute of Mental Health.

Frank M. Kline, M.D. is professor and vice chairman, Department of Psychiatry and Human Behavior at the University of California (Irvine) and chief of the psychiatry service at the Veterans Administration Medical Center, Long Beach, California. He is on the faculty at the Southern California Psychoanalytic Institute. He has a particular interest in the education and supervision of psychiatric residents, and spent fifteen years training psychiatric residents in outpatient psychotherapy at Los Angeles County/University of Southern California Medical Center.

Robert Langs, M.D. is editor-in-chief of the *International Journal of Psychoanalytic Psychotherapy* and author of several books on psychotherapeutic and psychoanalytic technique. These include *The Technique of Psychoanalytic Psychotherapy,* Volumes 1 and 2, *The Bipersonal Field, The Therapeutic Interaction* (two volumes), *The Listening Process, Technique in Transition, The Supervisory Experience,* and *The Therapeutic Environment.* He has written several papers on dreams and has carried out psychoanalytically oriented research into their manifest content and functions within the therapeutic situation. He is a graduate of the Chicago Medical School and of the Downstate Psychoanalytic Institute. He is program director of the Lenox Hill Hospital Psychotherapy Program and is engaged in the private practice of psychoanalysis and psychoanalytic psychotherapy.

Doryann Lebe, M.D. is a member of the Southern California Psychoanalytic Institute and associate clinical professor of psychiatry at UCLA Medical School. She is in full-time private analytic practice in Los Angeles and teaches courses and seminars on technique and dynamics and on character disorders. She is particularly interested in patients who reveal their dynamics in behavior, affects, and actions rather than in strictly verbal processes, and in the preverbal mother-child interactions and how they can be clarified and elucidated when working with adult patients.

Harold Levitan, M.D. obtained his medical degree from McGill University. He did his residency training in psychiatry at the Boston Veterans Administration Hospital and at the Albert Einstein College of Medicine, where he taught for many years. At present he is associate professor in the Department of Psychiatry at McGill University. Since the beginning of his career he has been dedicated to the task of elucidating the role played by dreams in the construction of the particular symptoms which characterize the various psychiatric and psychosomatic syndromes. His numerous articles on this subject have appeared in *Psychoanalytic Quarterly, International Journal of Psychoanalytic Psychotherapy, International Review of Psycho-Analysis,* and *Psychotherapy and Psychosomatics.*

Robert E. Litman, M.D., Ph.D. is a graduate of the University of Minnesota Medical School. He is professor of psychiatry, UCLA School of Medicine; training and supervising analyst, Southern California Psychoanalytic Institute; co-director, institute for Studies of Destructive Behaviors; co-director and chief psychiatrist, Suicide Prevention Center, Los Angeles; chief psychiatric consultant and deputy coroner, Los Angeles County Medical Examiner–Coroner's Office.

Stephen S. Marmer, M.D. received his medical degree at the University of Southern California School of Medicine, his psychiatric training at the Neuropsychiatric Institute of the University of California at Los Angeles, where he was also chief resident. He received his psychoanalytic training and his Ph.D. in psychoanalysis at the Southern California Psychoanalytic Institute. He was the recipient of the 1978 Clinical Essay Prize of the British Psychoanalytic Society. He has given scientific programs on dissociation and multiple personality at UCLA, the Southern California Psychiatric Society, and the Southern California Psychoanalytic Society. He is currently in private practice in Los Angeles and is assistant clinical professor of psychiatry, UCLA School of Medicine. He is on the faculty of the Southern California Psychoanalytic Institute.

Werner M. Mendel, M.D. is professor of psychiatry at the University of Southern California School of Medicine and director of the Division of

Professional and Staff Development. He received his medical degree at Stanford University and his psychiatric training at St. Elizabeths Hospital, Washington, D.C., and the Menninger Foundation, Topeka, Kansas. He received his psychoanalytic training at the Southern California Psychoanalytic Institute in Los Angeles, where he currently is an instructor.

Arnold Namrow, M.D. studied at Washington University in St. Louis, where he received his medical degree in 1947. He took his psychiatric and psychoanalytic training in Washington, D.C., he is clinical associate professor at Georgetown University Medical School. He is on the faculty of the Washington Psychoanalytic Institute and is in the private practice of psychiatry and psychoanalysis.

Joseph M. Natterson, M.D. attended West Virginia School of Medicine and received his medical degree from Washington University in St. Louis. He took his psychoanalytic training at the Southern California Psychoanalytic Institute, where he serves as a training analyst. He is in addition clinical professor, Department of Psychiatry, University of Southern California School of Medicine, and coauthor, with Bernard Gordon, of *The Sexual Dream* (1977).

Ping-nie Pao, M.D., a graduate of the National Medical College of Shanghai, received his psychiatric and psychoanalytic training in Baltimore and in Washington, D.C. In 1957 he joined the staff of Chestnut Lodge and since 1967 has been director of psychotherapy there. A teaching analyst at the Washington Psychoanalytic Institute, he has been interested in psychoanalytic psychotherapy with severely emotionally disturbed patients. He has written on manic-depressives, schizophrenics, and severe borderlines.

Howard J. Parad, D. S. W., formerly dean of the Smith College School for Social Work, is professor of social work at the University of Southern California and consultant in emergency mental health to the California Department of Health. A graduate of Harvard University, Dr. Parad earned his master's degree at Boston University and his doctorate at Columbia. His publications include *Crisis Intervention: Selected Readings, Ego Psychology and Dynamic Casework,* and *Emergency and Disaster Management: A Mental Health Sourcebook.*

Chester Pearlman, M.D. is assistant chief of psychiatry at the Veterans Administration Medical Center in Boston and associate clinical professor at Tufts University School of Medicine. In collaboration with Dr. Ramon Greenberg, he has been investigating the function of dreaming or REM sleep since 1965.

Sydney L. Pomer, M.D. is associate clinical professor of psychiatry at the University of Southern California and training and supervising analyst, Southern California Psychoanalytic Institute. He is an attending psychiatrist at the Los Angeles County–USC Medical Center and at the Cedars-Sinai Medical Center, teaching in their psychiatric residency programs. He is editor of the *Bulletin of the Southern California Psychoanalytic Institute and Society,* and has served for several years on the Board on Professional Standards of the American Psychoanalytic Association. He has also served on the executive council of that body.

Robert A. Shain, M.D. received his medical degree from the University of California (San Francisco) in 1965. After interning at the Los Angeles County–USC Medical Center, he took a psychiatric residency at the Neuropsychiatric Institute, UCLA School of Medicine, where he is now an assistant clinical professor of psychiatry involved in teaching psychiatry to senior medical students. He is currently a senior clinical associate at the Southern California Psychoanalytic Institute and a staff member of both Cedars-Sinai Medical Center and St. John's Hospital.

Charles W. Socarides, M.D. is clinical professor of psychiatry, Albert Einstein College of Medicine, New York City and attending psychiatrist, Bronx Municipal Hospital Center, New York City. A graduate of the Columbia University Psychoanalytic Clinic for Training and Research, College of Physicians and Surgeons, he is a fellow of the American Psychiatric Association and a member of the American Psychoanalytic Association. He is the author of *Beyond Sexual Freedom, The Overt Homosexual,* and *Homosexuality,* and the editor of *The World of the Emotions: Clinical Studies of Affects and Their Expression.*

Marquis Earl Wallace, Ph.D. is assistant professor, School of Social Work, University of Southern California. He also practices privately in west Los Angeles and is a consultant to various agencies and clinics. He was awarded his M.A. in casework from the University of Chicago in 1968, and in 1977 received his doctorate in social treatment from the School of Social Service Administration. His article "A Focal Conflict Model of Marital Disorders" appeared in *Social Casework* in July, 1979.

Roy M. Whitman, M.D. is professor of psychiatry at the University of Cincinnati College of Medicine, department of psychiatry. He is a training and supervising analyst at the Cincinnati Psychoanalytic Institute. He has been working in the area of dreams and dream research for over twenty years. His previous training included Indiana University School of Medicine and residencies at Duke University and the University of Chicago. Formerly assistant professor at the University of Chicago and associate professor at Northwestern University, he moved to the University of Cincinnati upon his graduation from the Chicago Psychoanalytic Institute.

INDEX

Abraham, K., 125
abstractness, versus concrete-
    ness in schizophrenic
    dreams, 107-108
acting out disturbances, dream
    in, 209-23
  acting out by therapist, 220-22
  action following 209-10
  altered consciousness in, 210-
    11
  behavioral change in contrast
    to, 213
  case examples, 216-20
  dreams of convenience, 211-
    12
  necessity of analyzing actions
    following, 222-23
  as prelude to remembering,
    213-14
  as resistance, 214-16
  two types of behavior follow-
    ing, 216

various behaviors following,
    211
Adler, G., 383
affect
  existence of formed un-
    conscious, 227
  projection of intense, onto
    dream character, 226-227
aged, group dreams in, 431-32
agoraphobia, dream in case of,
    187-88
Alexander, F., 50, 200, 225, 320,
    407
Altman, L.L., 180, 259, 319, 320,
    321
Alvarez, A., 295
analysis of existence, dream in,
    389-402
  definition of, 390-91
  as different from psycho-
    analysis, 389-90
  examples of, 396-401